Rereading Chaucer and Spenser

Manchester University Press

The Manchester Spenser

The Manchester Spenser is a monograph and text series devoted to historical and textual approaches to Edmund Spenser – to his life, times, places, works and contemporaries.

A growing body of work in Spenser and Renaissance studies, fresh with confidence and curiosity and based on solid historical research, is being written in response to a general sense that our ability to interpret texts is becoming limited without the excavation of further knowledge. So the importance of research in nearby disciplines is quickly being recognised, and interest renewed: history, archaeology, religious or theological history, book history, translation, lexicography, commentary and glossary – these require treatment for and by students of Spenser.

The Manchester Spenser, to feed, foster and build on these refreshed attitudes, aims to publish reference tools, critical, historical, biographical and archaeological monographs on or related to Spenser, from several disciplines, and to publish editions of primary sources and classroom texts of a more wide-ranging scope.

The Manchester Spenser consists of work with stamina, high standards of scholarship and research, adroit handling of evidence, rigour of argument, exposition and documentation.

The series will encourage and assist research into, and develop the readership of, one of the richest and most complex writers of the early modern period.

General Editors Joshua Reid, Kathryn Walls and Tamsin Badcoe
Editorial Board Sukanta Chaudhuri, Helen Cooper, Thomas Herron, J. B. Lethbridge, James Nohrnberg and Brian Vickers

Also available

Literary and visual Ralegh   Christopher M. Armitage (ed.)
The art of The Faerie Queene   Richard Danson Brown
A Concordance to the Rhymes of The Faerie Queene   Richard Danson Brown & J.B. Lethbridge
A Supplement of the Faery Queene: By Ralph Knevet   Christopher Burlinson
& Andrew Zurcher (eds)
A Companion to Pastoral Poetry of the English Renaissance   Sukanta Chaudhuri
Pastoral poetry of the English Renaissance: An anthology   Sukanta Chaudhuri (ed.)
Spenserian allegory and Elizabethan biblical exegesis: A context for   The Faerie Queene
Margaret Christian
Monsters and the poetic imagination in The Faerie Queene: 'Most ugly shapes and horrible aspects'   Maik Goth
Celebrating Mutabilitie: Essays on Edmund Spenser's Mutabilitie Cantos   Jane Grogan (ed.)
Spenserian satire: A tradition of indirection   Rachel E. Hile
Castles and Colonists: An archaeology of Elizabethan Ireland   Eric Klingelhofer
Shakespeare and Spenser: Attractive opposites   J.B. Lethbridge (ed.)
Dublin: Renaissance city of literature   Kathleen Miller and Crawford Gribben (eds)
A Fig for Fortune: By Anthony Copley   Susannah Brietz Monta
Spenser and Virgil: The pastoral poems   Syrithe Pugh
The Burley manuscript   Peter Redford (ed.)
Renaissance psychologies: Spenser and Shakespeare   Robert Lanier Reid
European erotic romance: Philhellene Protestantism, renaissance translation and English literary politics   Victor Skretkowicz
God's only daughter: Spenser's Una as the invisible Church   Kathryn Walls
William Shakespeare and John Donne: Stages of the soul in early modern English poetry   Angelika Zirker

Rereading Chaucer and Spenser

Dan Geffrey with the New Poete

EDITED BY RACHEL STENNER,
TAMSIN BADCOE AND GARETH GRIFFITH

Manchester University Press

Copyright © Manchester University Press 2019

While copyright in the volume as a whole is vested in Manchester University Press, copyright in individual chapters belongs to their respective authors, and no chapter may be reproduced wholly or in part without the express permission in writing of both author and publisher.

Published by Manchester University Press
Oxford Road, Manchester M13 9PL
www.manchesteruniversitypress.co.uk

British Library Cataloguing-in-Publication Data
A catalogue record for this book is available from the British Library

ISBN 978 1 5261 3691 6 hardback
ISBN 978 1 5261 7904 3 paperback

First published 2019

The publisher has no responsibility for the persistence or accuracy of URLs for any external or third-party internet websites referred to in this book, and does not guarantee that any content on such websites is, or will remain, accurate or appropriate.

Typeset by Newgen Publishing UK

Contents

List of figures	*page* vii
List of contributors	viii
Acknowledgements	xi
Introduction *Rachel Stenner, Tamsin Badcoe and Gareth Griffith*	1
1 Chaucer's *Troilus and Criseyde* in Spenser's *Amoretti* and *The Faerie Queene*: reading historically and intertextually *Judith H. Anderson*	19
2 'Litle herd gromes piping in the wind': *The Shepheardes Calender*, *The House of Fame* and 'La Compleynt' *Helen Barr*	37
3 Diverse pageants: normative arrays of sexuality *Helen Cooper*	60
4 The source of poetry: Pernaso, Paradise and Spenser's Chaucerian craft *Claire J.C. Eager*	75
5 Chaucer in Ireland: archaism, etymology and the idea of development *William Rhodes*	98
6 Wise wights in privy places: rhyme and stanza form in Spenser and Chaucer *Richard Danson Brown*	113
7 Romancing Geoffrey: Chaucer and romance in the manuscript tradition *Gareth Griffith*	137
8 Cultivating Chaucerian antiquity in *The Shepheardes Calender* *Megan L. Cook*	150
9 Worthy friends: Speght's Chaucer and Speght's Spenser *Elisabeth Chaghafi*	168

10 Chaucer's 'beast group' and 'Mother Hubberds Tale' 189
   Brendan O'Connell

11 Propagating authority: poetic tradition in *The Parliament of Fowls*
   and the Mutabilitie Cantos 212
   Craig A. Berry

12 'New matter framed upon the old': Chaucer, Spenser and Luke
   Shepherd's 'New Poet' 224
   Harriet Archer

   Select bibliography of books and essays on Chaucer and Spenser 243
   Index 249

Figures

4.1 The woodcut at the opening of 'June' in the 1579 edition of *The Shepheardes Calender* (F2v) (by permission of the Folger Shakespeare Library)	*page* 78
6.1 Page spread from 1590 *Faerie Queene* showing Proem to Book II (Huntingdon Library copy from EEBO)	118
6.2 *Troilus and Criseyde* IV.1604–31 in Thynne's edition, showing minimal punctuation between stanzas	122
9.1 Title page of Speght's 1598 edition of Chaucer's works (by permission of the Folger Shakespeare Library)	172
9.2 'The progenie of Geffrey Chaucer' (1602) (by permission of the Folger Shakespeare Library)	176

Contributors

Judith H. Anderson is Chancellor's Professor Emeritus at Indiana University and author of six single-author books: most recently, *Translating Investments: Metaphor and the Dynamic of Cultural Change in Tudor-Stuart England*, *Reading the Allegorical Intertext: Chaucer, Spenser, Shakespeare, Milton* and *Light and Death: Figuration in Spenser, Kepler, Donne, Milton*. She is also co-editor of five volumes, including *Will's Vision of Piers Plowman*, *Spenser's Life and the Subject of Biography* and *Go Figure: Energies, Forms, and Institutions in the Early Modern World*.

Harriet Archer is a lecturer in Early Modern English Literature at the University of St Andrews. She previously taught at the University of Oxford, the University of Colorado, Boulder, and Newcastle University, where she also held a Leverhulme Early Career Fellowship. Her first monograph, *Unperfect Histories: The Mirror for Magistrates, 1559–1610*, was published by Oxford University Press in 2017. She is currently co-editing Thomas Norton and Thomas Sackville's *Gorboduc* with Paul Frazer for the Manchester Revels Plays Series, and the Tudor English translations of Erasmus's *Colloquies* for *Erasmus in English 1523–1584* (MHRA), with Alex Davis, Gordon Kendal and Neil Rhodes.

Tamsin Badcoe is a lecturer in English at the University of Bristol. Her first book project, *Edmund Spenser and the Romance of Space* (Manchester University Press, forthcoming), is interested in the relationship between literary genre and geography, and the role that subjectivity and the imagination play in spatial practices. She also has research interests in the early modern book trade, the work of Thomas Nashe, and the literature of travel and navigation.

Helen Barr is Professor of English Literature at the University of Oxford and Fellow and Tutor in English at Lady Margaret Hall. She is the author of *Socioliterary Practice in Late Medieval England*, and has edited *The Poems in The Piers Plowman Tradition* and *The Digby Lyrics*. Her most recent monograph is *Transporting Chaucer*, a study of finding Chaucer where we might not expect him to be between the late medieval and early modern periods.

Craig A. Berry is an independent scholar who makes his living as a software project manager. He holds a PhD in English from Northwestern University and is the author of essays on Chaucer, Spenser and the *Roman de Silence*. He currently serves as Digital Projects Editor at *The Spenser Review*.

Richard Danson Brown is Professor of English Literature at The Open University. He is the author of several books including *The New Poet: Novelty and Tradition in Spenser's 'Complaints'* (1999) and *A Concordance to the Rhymes of the Faerie Queene* (with J.B. Lethbridge, 2013). Since 2014, he has been the book reviews editor for *The Spenser Review*. His latest book – on the poetic forms of Spenser's epic – is *The art of The Faerie Queene* (2019).

Elisabeth Chaghafi's research focuses on book history and the works of Edmund Spenser and Gabriel Harvey. She has written on Spenser's 'Astrophel', the quarto reprints of *The Shepheardes Calender*, the so-called Spenser–Harvey letters, and imagined friendships between early modern poets in the biographical works of Izaak Walton and John Aubrey. Articles on Harvey's sonnets, and the structure of John Derricke's *Image of Irelande*, are forthcoming. She is currently working on papers about the function of anecdotes in seventeenth-century lives of Spenser, and Harvey's stylistic revisions in his 'letter-book'. She teaches at Tübingen University.

Megan Cook teaches medieval literature and book history at Colby College in Waterville, Maine. She is the author of *The Poet and the Antiquaries: Chaucerian Scholarship and the Rise of Literary History, 1532–1635* (Penn, 2019). With Elizaveta Strakhov, she is also the co-editor of *John Lydgate's Dance of Death and Related Works* (Medieval Institute Publications, 2019). Her work on the fate of Middle English texts and books in the early modern period has appeared in *Spenser Studies, Chaucer Review, Manuscript Studies, Studies in Philology* and elsewhere.

Helen Cooper is Professor Emerita of Medieval and Renaissance English at the University of Cambridge, and a Life Fellow of Magdalene College, Cambridge. She has written extensively both on Chaucer and on topics that cross the medieval–early modern divide, including *Pastoral: Mediaeval into Renaissance, Oxford Guides to Chaucer: 'The Canterbury Tales', The English Romance in Time* and *Shakespeare and the Medieval World*.

Claire J.C. Eager is Visiting Assistant Professor of Medieval Literature and Shakespeare at Colorado College. Her research and teaching focus on Renaissance literature, visual and material culture, poetic forms, book history to 1800, and the ecology of space and place. In her book project, *Vertuall Paradise: Vaulting Ambitions Brought to Earth in Tudor and Stuart England*, she analyses how poets from Spenser to Milton construct paradisal spaces, and how they put them to use as poetic, political or ethical statements, alongside material practices of printing and horticulture. Her work on John Donne and the garden at Twickenham belonging to Lucy, Countess of Bedford, will appear in *Studies in Philology*. Her next project will investigate the aesthetics and ethics of war landscapes in sixteenth- and seventeenth-century Britain.

Gareth Griffith is Senior Teaching Associate and Director of Part-Time Programmes in the Department of English at the University of Bristol. His research interests include medieval romance, manuscript culture and biblical translation and adaptation, and he has published essays on Merlin, Layamon and Chaucer.

Brendan O'Connell is a lecturer in Medieval Literature at the School of English, Trinity College Dublin. His research focuses on the poetry of the fourteenth century, with particular emphasis on Chaucer and the *Gawain*-poet. His publications include studies of violence and resistance in the *Man of Law's Tale*, the ethics of literary representation in Chaucer's poetry, and the themes of fraud and falsification in the *Canterbury Tales*.

William Rhodes is a postdoctoral fellow in the Dietrich School of Arts and Sciences Humanities Center at the University of Pittsburgh. He has published articles on late medieval and early modern literature, including Langland, Chaucer and Spenser, in the *Yearbook of Langland Studies*, *ELH* and *The Open Access Companion to The Canterbury Tales*. His book, *The Ecology of Reform*, considers the intersection of agrarian discourse and vernacular reformist poetry in the long English Reformation.

Rachel Stenner is a lecturer in English Literature 1350–1660 at the University of Sussex. She works on late medieval and early modern literature and her publications include studies of William Baldwin, Spenser, Robert Copland and Renaissance dialogue. Her first monograph, *The Typographic Imaginary in Early Modern English Literature*, came out with Routledge in 2018. In it she discusses the representation of the printing press by authors from William Caxton to Alexander Pope. Her work is closely engaged with the history of the book and the history of the print trade. With Kaley Kramer and Adam Smith she is currently working on a study of the ways that regional printers helped to shape regional identities in the British Isles.

Acknowledgements

This project evolved through conversations at the University of Bristol with friends and colleagues, leading first to the conference, in July 2014, *Dan Geffrey with the New Poete: Reading and Rereading Chaucer and Spenser*, and then to this book. Our early interlocutors, to whom we are grateful for their insight and counsel and for the gentle nudges they provided in the right direction, were Simone Fryer-Bovair, Pam King, Ad Putter, Jane Griffiths and Cathy Hume. We would like to thank the fellow scholars who were involved in the conference, but whose writing does not appear here: Anne Baden-Daintree, Rachel Eisendrath, John Lee, Tom Mason, John McTague, Joseph D. Parry and Mark Sherman. We were helped by Emily Derbyshire, Jimmy Packham and Camilla Temple. The conference took place under the auspices of Bristol's Centre for Medieval Studies and the Bristol Institute for Research in the Humanities and Arts. We would like to thank the Modern Humanities Research Association, for their generous funding, and the Society for Renaissance Studies, who supported the attendance of our postgraduate delegates and speakers. Two readers of the introduction, Laurence Publicover and Charlotte Steenbrugge, offered good advice at a timely moment, and for that we are grateful. Our editors at The Manchester Spenser, first Julian Lethbridge and then Joshua Reid, have been supportive and wise throughout. And our heartfelt thanks go to the colleagues, friends and loved ones without whose patience and encouragement we could not do what we do.

Introduction

Rachel Stenner, Tamsin Badcoe and Gareth Griffith

[...] let this duncified worlde esteeme of Spencer and Chaucer, Ile worshipp sweet Mr Shakspeare, and to honoure him will lay his *Venus and Adonis* vnder my pillowe, as wee reade of one (I do not well remember his name, but I am sure he was a kinge) slept with Homer vnder his beds heade.
The First Part of the Return from Parnassus (1600)[1]

In the above lines, from a play written and performed by students at the University of Cambridge at the turn of the sixteenth century, Spenser and Chaucer are paired in an image that suggests their complex reception by early modern readers. The words are spoken by a character called Gullio who, as his name suggests, is a foolish young man; yet, his reasons for pairing the poets, and his understanding of literary relations, are provocative for this collection. Gullio employs his quick-witted associate, Ingenioso, to compose poetry in order to help him woo a mistress. Initially, Ingenioso offers three very uneven stanzas of rhyme royal, which do a fair job of aping Chaucer's *Troilus and Criseyde* but are dismissed by Gullio as 'dull, harshe, and spiritless' (IV.i.1167), and then only gets as far as a ribald burlesque of the opening line of *The Faerie Queene* before being cut off by his exasperated patron. Whilst Ingenioso's laboured imitations may not amount to much (although he does eventually earn a financial reward after turning his hand to Shakespeare), his efforts teach us that the pairing of the Old and New Poet had accrued a recognisable cultural currency by the end of the sixteenth century.[2] The student audience was expected to recognise that Chaucer and Spenser, in spite of Ingenioso's travesties and Gullio's appreciation of the latest literary fashions, were far more than the darlings of a 'duncified worlde': their coupled reputations were sufficient to withstand the use and misuse occasioned by irreverent student dramatists.[3]

---

1 *The First Part of the Return from Parnassus*, in *The Three Parnassus Plays (1598-1601)*, ed. J.B. Leishman (London: Nicholson and Watson, 1949), IV.i.1200–5.
2 See Patrick Cheney, 'The Voice of the Author in "The Pheonix and Turtle": Chaucer, Shakespeare, Spenser', in *Shakespeare and the Middle Ages*, ed. Curtis Perry and John Watkins (Oxford: Oxford University Press, 2009), 103–25.
3 For a discussion of Chaucer's reputation amongst Spenser and his contemporaries, see Glenn A. Steinberg, 'Spenser's *Shepheardes Calender* and the Elizabethan Reception of Chaucer', *English Literary Renaissance*, 35.1 (2005), 31–51.

By imagining the act of appropriating a book for a pillow, Gullio not only insinuates that *Venus and Adonis* will inspire erotic dreams, but also places himself in the venerable company of Alexander the Great, who was purported to have slept with Homer's *Iliad* under his head.[4] The resulting motif haphazardly combines an image of inspiration and utility with the anticipation of textual pleasure. In Gullio's indirect evocation of private reading and study, the authority of the classical poet Homer is juxtaposed with the names of the two poets that came for many to define the poetic accomplishments of the Middle Ages and the Renaissance respectively. Francis Meres, for one, observes in *Palladis Tamia* (1598) that 'as *Homer* is reputed the Prince of Greek Poets; [...] so *Chaucer* is accounted the God of English Poets' and as '*Homer* and *Virgil* among the Greeks and Latines are the chiefe Heroick Poets: so *Spencer* and *Warner* be our chiefe heroicall Makers'.[5] Meres connects the literary authorities of Greece and Rome with those of England, past and present; his Chaucer is of divine stature and his Spenser is of foremost skill, working on the craft and handling the materials of his poetic inheritance. Creative inspiration and readerly connection may be enacted across different times and spaces but, to revisit the motif of the book placed under the head, they also build on material artefacts. In *The First Part of the Return from Parnassus*, Gullio's proposed action offers an intensely material image for the eliciting and creation of his personal response. In addition, the moment offers a brief insight into how the play as a whole richly demonstrates the polyvocality and ambivalence of a literary culture that was highly attuned to mimicry and imitation. Following in the footsteps of a literary forerunner and extending the echo of a predecessor's voice were not just markers of taste but also undertakings that characterised, as Judith H. Anderson writes, 'a profound habit of mind'.[6]

Spenser, then, is of his time when he engages with the work of his predecessor Chaucer; the inventions formed by his poetic consciousness are intrinsically relational. If the pairing between the poets is thought to be in any way exceptional it is owing to the sustained nature of Spenser's engagement with Chaucer's influence and his claim to a greater degree of explicit kinship than was shown by any other early modern writer for any other medieval poet. The chapters that have been brought together in this collection respond to the concern that we have not fully understood what Chaucer meant to Spenser – neither the values he represented nor, more literally, the meanings that were made available to Spenser by Chaucer's works via the forms in which Spenser encountered them. *Rereading Chaucer and Spenser* firstly contends that the relationship between these two poets does not only illuminate their respective canons, but can also teach us about how early modern England perceived, and constructed, both its use of the vernacular and its claims on a classical, literary past. Yet, the connections between Chaucer

---

4 See Plutarch, *The Lives of the Noble Grecians and Romanes*, trans. Thomas North (London: Thomas Vautroullier, 1579), STC 20065, sig. PPP3^r.
5 Francis Meres, *Palladis Tamia* (London: P. Short for Cuthbert Burbie, 1598), STC 17834, 279^r; 282^v.
6 Judith H. Anderson, *Reading the Allegorical Intertext: Chaucer, Spenser, Shakespeare, Milton* (New York: Fordham University Press, 2008), 4.

and Spenser frequently become legible as sites where literary temporality is out of joint. These figures are neither reducible to individual synecdoches of the Middle Ages and Renaissance, nor to a revisionist agenda that seeks to erase any sense of clear-cut division between traditionally perceived periods of history. As the chapters in this collection demonstrate, the relationship between Chaucer and Spenser can be calibrated to indicate both continuity and rupture. Secondly, the essays' combined insights suggest that Spenser's response to Chaucer is best understood as interventionary. Spenser's reworking is always more than imitation; he intervenes in the modes, forms and genres that Chaucer offers him, so that the conversation between poets can also be regarded as a conversation framed by acts of making. Spenser inscribes himself into literary tradition by advancing the technicalities of his craft; his engagement of Chaucer participates in that project, so that his labours imprint themselves over and between those of the earlier poet. The volume's final contention is that Spenser's reading of Chaucer, and our reading of them both, is affected by the conceptual frameworks that can be inferred from the material forms in which the authors' writings have been arranged. When read together, the chapters here characterise the relationships between Chaucer and Spenser as involving intervention rather than imitation, as temporally disruptive, and both playfully and materially bound to the conceptual and physical spaces of the text as object.

The emblematic motif of a book placed beneath a dreamer's head offers a useful entry point for thinking about the nature of poetic intervention; as an image of readerly contemplation, it is an especially helpful way of figuring a kind of poetic usage and borrowing that is not always wholly conscious or deliberate, but which retains a sense of the artifice of literary allusion and making. In Chaucer's *Book of the Duchess*, for example, the action of falling asleep upon a book prompts a complex meditation on the relationship between reading, consolation and poetic vision:

> That sodeynly, I nyste how,
> Such a lust anoon me took
> To slepe that ryght upon my book
> Y fil aslepe, and therwith even
> Me mette so ynly swete a sweven,
> So wonderful that never yit
> Y trowe no man hadde the wyt
> To konne wel my sweven rede; [...][7]

The dreamer understands that his 'sweven' will both invite and frustrate the desire to 'rede', that is, to read and to interpret, its contents. This imagined future act of reading implicitly inspires another moment of dreaming which is a prompt

---

7 Geoffrey Chaucer, *Book of the Duchess*, in *The Riverside Chaucer*, ed. Larry D. Benson (Boston: Houghton Mifflin, 1987), 272–9. All quotations from Chaucer's works are taken from this edition.

for yet further interpretive engagement. Chaucer offers here an image for what Anderson, who opens our collection, describes in *Reading the Allegorical Intertext* as 'a condition of potentiality and relationship' which 'comes into being in the act of reading a text'.[8] There are many ways of gauging the historical results of 'potentiality', of course, and the chapters collected here reflect a range of methodologies rather than privileging a single critical or interpretive strategy. The collection is led by a desire for an encounter with the relationship between two canonical authors that is refreshed by multiplicity and variety; yet, our sojourn with these poets is made all the richer for the moments of concord that emerge from the interpretive gallimaufry. Anderson's opening chapter, for example, thinks through the metaphors that are most often used to describe the energies of intertextual relations, coming to rest on the term 'resonance', which is in turn productively employed by several of our contributors to grasp 'an experience that is affective, subtle, suggestive and, probably for some readers, at times too elusive to accept' (23).[9] Her chapter finds a partner and a counterpoint in Helen Barr's playful close reading of *The House of Fame* and *The Shepheardes Calender*, where Spenser's pastoral songs are shown to be vulnerable to the 'bursts of rude wind' (59) trumpeted from Chaucer's dream vision.

Readers must also reckon with the historical potentialities that have been created by the medieval and early modern material contexts of Chaucer's works. One particular strand of discussion in this volume is dedicated to understanding better what Chaucer, his language, and the interplay between his literary and material forms meant to Spenser and his contemporaries. Paying attention to the mediated versions of Chaucer available during the early modern period and the discursive patina surrounding them, to which Spenser's authorial voice also contributes, results in carefully and rewardingly historicised accounts. Richard Danson Brown dramatises the 'culture of formal assumptions' (114) in which *The Faerie Queene* operated, for example, and chapters by Gareth Griffith, Megan L. Cook and Elisabeth Chaghafi all adopt the techniques of book history to extrapolate Chaucer's sixteenth-century valences. As William Rhodes reveals, a Chaucerian vocabulary was one of the tools used by Spenser to gain a measure of the task he perceived the New English to be facing in Ireland, and he identifies moments in *A View of the Present State of Ireland* that only come into focus when read alongside the earlier poet's work. These chapters illuminate the formal, lexical and bibliographic character of Chaucer as presented to a sixteenth-century reader.

The act of reading is thus characterised as a contingent act shaped by circumstance. Seen in this light, to return to our example above, Chaucer's *Book of the Duchess* operates as merely one of the many books kept beneath Spenser's pillow. As previous critics have noticed, echoes of this particular elegy appear in several places in Spenser's works, from Archimago's procurement of a false dream from the House of Morpheus in the first book of *The Faerie Queene* to

---

8 Anderson, 2. See also Rosemarie P. McGerr, *Chaucer's Open Books: Resistance to Closure in Medieval Discourse* (Gainesville: University Press of Florida, 1998), 45.
9 See Wai Chee Dimock, 'A Theory of Resonance', *PMLA*, 112.5 (1997), 1060–71.

Spenser's own elegy, *Daphnaïda*, which is his most explicit homage to Chaucer.[10] For Glenn Steinberg, writing in 1998, *Daphnaïda* demonstrates a shift in habits of thought that emphasises the differences between the poets, rather than their likeness; by 'juxtaposing the two works, we may see [...] differences between the artistic decorum of the late Middle Ages and the passionate Protestant iconoclasm of Elizabethan England'.[11] More recently, a closer degree of sympathy between the two pieces has been identified. Jamie C. Fumo states that the poem 'is best viewed as an alternative Chaucerian reality: it reveals what [the *Book of the Duchess*] might look like were it to unfold differently'.[12] In the same poetic site, then, critics have historically found both likeness and difference. Such doubleness and contradiction, even paradox, is characteristic of the poets' connection across the centuries. Scholars discern both closeness and distance in Spenser's self-positioning as Chaucer's follower, albeit as one eight generations removed. Chaucer's professional early modern readers, such as the compilers and editors of his works, also locate him dually, emphasising by turns his cultural relevance to their audience and that audience's anticipated estrangement from his texts and his language. As Kathryn Walls writes in a brilliant recent essay that calls for greater nuance in our understanding of Spenser's histories, his 'indebtedness to and alienation from medieval culture turn out to be two sides of the same coin'.[13]

There are clearly aesthetic choices in the works of both poets that are predicated upon a sense of rupture with the historical past. Spenser's famous archaism, most prominently displayed in *The Shepheardes Calender* and *The Faerie Queene*, puts his work, as Lucy Munro states, in a disruptive relation to time and historiography: 'archaising writers demonstrate their awareness of historical difference, as evidenced in linguistic and stylistic change, but through their desire to imitate and reinvigorate outmoded styles they also challenge the smooth narrative of progression'.[14] Archaists' time is 'queer time – out of joint, askew, at odds with conventional notions of temporality'.[15] In a related dynamic of separation and proximity, Chaucer dispatches *Troilus and Criseyde*, his 'litel bok' (v.1786), to follow in the footsteps of its ancient poetic predecessors: to 'kis the steppes where as thow seest pace / Virgile, Ovide, Omer, Lucan, and Stace' (v.1791–2). Yet soon after this immersive and affective moment, the reader is emphatically distanced from the 'corsed olde rites' (v.1849) of pagans and 'the forme of olde clerkis speche

---

10 For a classic approach that identifies echoes and borrowings see Thomas William Nadal, 'Spenser's *Daphnaïda*, and Chaucer's *Book of the Duchess*', PMLA, 23.4 (1908), 646–61.
11 Glenn Steinberg, 'Idolatrous Idylls: Protestant Iconoclasm, Spenser's *Daphnaïda*, and Chaucer's *Book of the Duchess*', in *Refiguring Chaucer in the Renaissance*, ed. Theresa M. Krier (Gainesville: University Press of Florida, 1998), 128–43 (129).
12 Jamie C. Fumo, *Making Chaucer's 'Book of the Duchess': Textuality and Reception* (Cardiff: University of Wales Press, 2015), 172.
13 Kathryn Walls, 'Spenser and the "Medieval" Past: A Question of Definition', in *Spenser in the Moment*, ed. Paul J. Hecht and J.B. Lethbridge (Madison: Fairleigh Dickinson University Press, 2015), 35–66 (36).
14 Lucy Munro, *Archaic Style in English Literature, 1590–1674* (Cambridge: Cambridge University Press, 2014), 5.
15 Ibid., 5.

/ In poetrie' (v.1855). Rereading the relationship between Chaucer and Spenser shows that these poets are themselves disposed to the gesture of dividing the old from the new, but doing so in ways that do not sever past literary products from contemporary poetic praxis.

Recognising the importance of temporality for our understanding of this relationship takes several shapes in this collection. Helen Cooper's chapter articulates how the poets' shared conception of love and sexuality puts them into a transhistorical dialogue. Cook finds that *The Shepheardes Calender* cultivates 'in readers a proper sense of Chaucer's historical distance' (165), whereas Chaghafi argues that it was Spenser's closeness to Chaucer that sixteenth-century readers valued. A productive frame for our approach is offered by Barr's recent book-length enquiry into Chaucer and periodisation, *Transporting Chaucer*, in which she explores the ways that linear chronology is upset when his characters move 'between texts written at different historical junctures'.[16] Chaucer and Spenser are authors writing two centuries apart and their shared forms and interests are comparable to Barr's transported characters in their capacity to dislodge literary teleology. As the aggregated chapters in this collection demonstrate, the relationship between Chaucer's and Spenser's works – and the individual works themselves – neither supports nor neatly disavows the 'totalizing divisions' between the early modern and the medieval that revisionist accounts of literary history find problematic.[17]

Regardless of how we perceive temporality, Spenser's engagement with the literary past that we now term medieval goes beyond his relationship with Chaucer. When reading Spenser's key evocations of Chaucer, it quickly becomes apparent that Spenser's Middle Ages are made of more than the words of that 'worshipful fader and first foundeur' of English, as William Caxton calls him.[18] In *The Shepheardes Calender*, John Lydgate, in particular, looms large. Spenser's collection

---

16 Helen Barr, *Transporting Chaucer* (Manchester: Manchester University Press, 2014), 4.
17 William Kuskin, *Recursive Origins: Writing at the Transition to Modernity* (Notre Dame: University of Notre Dame Press, 2013), 5. Critical interrogations of periodisation, an enquiry that has gained much recent momentum, form an important critical background to this research. Studies which are of particular significance for this collection include Alice S. Miskimin, *The Renaissance Chaucer* (New Haven: Yale University Press, 1975); Krier, ed.; Andrew King, *The Faerie Queene and Middle English Romance: The Matter of Just Memory* (Oxford: Oxford University Press, 2000). Literary critics, whilst retaining Chaucer as a medieval touchstone, more often turn to Shakespeare than Spenser for the Renaissance half of the equation. The work of Helen Cooper has been instrumental in this respect. See Helen Cooper, *The English Romance in Time: Transforming Motifs from Geoffrey of Monmouth to the Death of Shakespeare* (Oxford: Oxford University Press, 2004); *Shakespeare and the Medieval World* (London: Arden Shakespeare, 2012); Ruth Morse, Helen Cooper and Peter Holland, eds, *Medieval Shakespeare: Pasts and Presents* (Cambridge: Cambridge University Press, 2013); see also Andrew James Johnston, Russell West-Pavlov and Elisabeth Kempf, eds, *Love, History and Emotion in Chaucer and Shakespeare: 'Troilus and Criseyde' and 'Troilus and Cressida'* (Manchester: Manchester University Press, 2016).
18 William Caxton, epilogue to Chaucer's translation of Boethius, *Boecius de Consolacione Philosophie* (Westminster: William Caxton, 1478), STC 3199. A. Kent Hieatt, in *Chaucer, Spenser, Milton: Mythopoeic Continuities and Transformations* (Montreal: McGill-Queen's University Press, 1975), argues that whilst 'Spenser's strongest medieval affiliation is with Chaucer' his 'knowledge and use of other medieval English and French works' (148) was extensive.

of pastorals has a putative editor, 'E.K.', whose precise identity is unknown but whose words frame and gloss the poetry, straddling positions of authority and marginality.[19] E.K. plays an interpretative role that revels in its polyvocality. His citation in the dedicatory epistle of the title that Chaucer's 'scholler Lidgate' gives him – 'the Loadestarre of our Language' (3–4) – immediately presents Chaucer, as William Kuskin points out, as 'an author mediated by his major reader: John Lydgate'.[20] Lydgate resurfaces in E.K.'s notes on 'February', glossing the word 'Gride' as 'perced: an olde word much vsed of Lidgate, but not found (that I know of) in Chaucer' (gloss, 4). This is the very first note given in explanation of one of Spenser's 'aunciene' (epistle, 25) words. E.K.'s subsequent comment that the word 'Heardgromes' is taken from 'Chaucers verse almost whole' (gloss, 35) certainly raises Chaucer's profile within the gloss. Yet, as Barr's chapter in this volume suggestively describes, this reference also evokes an anonymous fifteenth-century complaint that was appended to manuscripts of Lydgate's *Temple of Glas*. The reader is thus being asked to notice a Chaucerian line that also points to Lydgate, whilst further pointing nowhere, to 'anon'. Spenser's Chaucer, we come to see, is a product of both authoritative and apocryphal texts, as discussed further in this collection by Griffith, and by Brendan O'Connell in his illuminating reading of 'Prosopopoia, or Mother Hubberds Tale'. By engaging with the manuscript context of the *Canterbury Tales* – a context that Griffith unpacks in relation to Chaucer's association with romance – O'Connell shows Spenser responding to Chaucer's use of satire and beast fable in a manner that is 'profoundly different' (197) from that of modern readers. Through the inclusion of the apocryphal *Plowman's Tale* in Chaucer's oeuvre, a work now 'expunged' (210) from modern editions, Spenser inherits a satirical Chaucer whose sixteenth-century reputation we can only reconstruct, but not experience first-hand. We close this collection with a chapter that reflects on the paradoxes of inheritance. Harriet Archer's contribution takes to task Spenser's much-vaunted claims to newness, revealing both the 'distinct cultural queasiness around the idea of novelty which pervades early modern writing' (224) and the fact that Spenser does not inaugurate but intervenes in a pre-existing discourse of poetic ingenuity and innovation, whose origins are often obscured.

Instead of looking for a Chaucer and a Spenser that exist independently of the forms in which we encounter them, then, what we can perhaps take from these instances of disrupted temporality is a shared interest in self-conscious making that finds itself situated in recognisable literary environments and habitats: such spaces are taken up in this collection by both Craig Berry and Claire Eager.[21] Arboreal, aqueous, elevated and paradisal locations are rarely places of rest, but are used by both Chaucer and Spenser as sites to address conditions of uncertainty and contingency. To make a final return to *The Book of the Duchess*, Chaucer's poem is highly invested in the green worlds of literary tradition and self-consciously

---

19 See David R. Shore, 'E.K.', in *The Spenser Encyclopedia*, ed. A.C. Hamilton *et al.* (Toronto: University of Toronto Press, 1990; repr. 1997), 231.
20 Kuskin, 59. See his chapter 'The Poet' for the full argument. *The Shepheardes Calender* is quoted from Edmund Spenser, *The Shorter Poems*, ed. Richard A. McCabe (London: Penguin, 1999).
21 See Miskimin, 3.

displays the poet's engagement with the travails of his predecessors.²² The small fawning dog who draws the dreamer away from the hunt and into the verdant place of encounter at the heart of the dream, for example, offers a mirror for the narrator's apparent naivety:

> Hyt com and crepte to me as lowe,
> Ryght as hyt hadde me yknowe, [...]
> I wolde have kaught hyt, and anoon
> Hyt fledde, and was fro me goon;
> And I hym folwed, and hyt forth wente
> Doun by a floury grene wente
> Ful thikke of gras, ful softe and swete. (391–9)

In his role as an 'unassuming and playful guide', the puppy can perhaps be thought of as an ancestor of the hound whose finer senses are credited by Spenser's narrator as having the ability to help a reader navigate *The Faerie Queene*.²³ Although the modification is indicative of the strategies of intervention that Spenser often adopts in response to Chaucer's prompts, the non-human companion in both cases offers a model for different kinds of active reading:

> Of faery lond yet if he more inquyre
> By certein signes here sett in sondrie place
> He may it fynd; ne let him then admyre
> But yield his sence to bee too blunt and bace
> That no'te without an hound fine footing trace.²⁴

As an unlikely attendant, the puppy of Chaucer's dream has matured into the scent hound of Spenser's oneiric fiction-making, whose potential movements can 'fine footing trace'. The defence of fiction made by Spenser's narrator in the opening to the second book of *The Faerie Queene*, as quoted above, looks towards the geographies of the New World, to the many 'great Regions [...] now found trew' (II. proem.2). It is striking that the proem frames its outward-looking introduction to the Knight of Temperance with echoes of the thresholds crossed when entering Chaucer's visionary garden and wooded grove: a moment of intertextual relation that situates the ancient greenwoods of literary invention and the speculative novelty of imaginative westward exploration on the same continuum. In both Chaucer's elegy and Spenser's romance epic, the poets fashion narrators whose voices are used to articulate distinctive conditions of knowingness, naivety, and

---

22 See B.A. Windeatt's discussion of the poem in his preface to *Chaucer's Dream Poetry: Sources and Analogues* (Cambridge: D.S. Brewer, 1982), xii–xiii. See also John Block Friedman, 'The Dreamer, the Whelp, and Consolation in the *Book of the Duchess*', *The Chaucer Review*, 3.3 (1969), 145–62.
23 Michael Foster, *Chaucer's Narrators and the Rhetoric of Self-Representation* (Oxford: Peter Lang, 2008), 65.
24 Edmund Spenser, *The Faerie Queene*, ed. A.C. Hamilton, Hiroshi Yamashita and Toshiyuki Suzuki (Harlow: Longman, 1988; repr. 2001), II.proem.4. All quotations of this poem are from this edition.

recognition.²⁵ And, in anticipation of the famous moment in *The Faerie Queene* when Spenser's narrator announces that he will 'follow here the footing' of Chaucer's 'feete' (IV.ii.34), it is ultimately an image of attended movement that is used to address the nature of literary traditions, conventions and transitions.²⁶

Earlier encounters

As Catherine Bates observes, the movements of Spenser's scent hound are allied to the wider dynamic in Spenser's *Faerie Queene* that is concerned with the provisional nature of what might constitute 'the quarry' in the poem: a question she ultimately relates to the impression given by Spenser's 'oeuvre as a whole', with its 'veritable relay of "footings" being traced through the forest of poetry'.²⁷ The chapters collected here recount interpretive narratives of encounter and intervention, where linear progress is complicated by shifting ideas of naivety and novelty, inheritance and tradition. As critics entering this conversation we find ourselves following in the feet of others and we are, of course, greatly indebted to John A. Burrow, whose detailed entry on Chaucer in *The Spenser Encyclopedia* remains one of the most comprehensive readings of the multiple sites of encounter between the two poets.²⁸ We follow him in his identification of the key moments of connection and in his acknowledgement of the poets' difference, wherein Spenser's admiration for Chaucer also included, as Burrow writes, 'a certain amount of genuine misunderstanding, and an incalculable degree of deliberate, though undeclared, independence'.²⁹ Burrow's comments concerning the various genres handled by both authors, including love complaints, fables, chivalric romances, allegorical tableaux, and the connections that occur at the level of metre and language, remain a landmark for understanding the extent and nature of Spenser's debt to Chaucer, both in specific instances and in his wider linguistic and poetic project (and we outline the key moments below).

The connection between Chaucer and Spenser is an enduring one. The inscription on Spenser's tomb referred to their kinship, and writers such as Thomas Nashe, Francis Thynne, John Dryden and William Hazlitt precede us in pairing them.³⁰ In more recent times, it is a coupling that has been put to a variety of uses. In 1999,

---

25 See Anthony M. Esolen, 'The Disingenuous Poet Laureate: Spenser's Adoption of Chaucer', *Studies in Philology*, 87.3 (1990), 285–311.
26 See Laura L. Howes, *Chaucer's Gardens and the Language of Convention* (Gainesville: University Press of Florida, 1997), 37–40. For a reading of the relationship between another of Chaucer's dream visions, *The Parliament of Fowls*, and the tree catalogue in *The Faerie Queene* (I.i.8–9), see Peter Remien, 'Silvan Matters: Error and Instrumentality in Book I of *The Faerie Queene*', *Spenser Studies*, 28 (2013), 119–43 (130–3).
27 Catherine Bates, *Masculinity and the Hunt: Wyatt to Spenser* (Oxford: Oxford University Press, 2013), 240–1.
28 See John A. Burrow, 'Chaucer, Geoffrey', in *The Spenser Encyclopedia*, 144–8. See also Anne Higgins, 'Spenser Reading Chaucer: Another Look at the "Faerie Queene" Allusions', *Journal of English and Germanic Philology*, 89 (1990), 17–36; Esolen.
29 Burrow, 148.
30 On the tomb, see R.M. Cummings, ed., *Spenser: The Critical Heritage* (London: Routledge and Kegan Paul, 1971), 315. See also Caroline F.E. Spurgeon, *Five Hundred Years of Chaucer Criticism*

Derek Pearsall edited a pair of anthologies which used the two poets as book-ends to an era which was posited as a means of dissolving the traditional distinction between the medieval and the early modern. *Chaucer to Spenser: An Anthology of Writing in English 1375–1575* surveyed texts from the late fourteenth to late sixteenth centuries, while *Chaucer to Spenser: A Critical Reader* brought together extracts from critical work on the authors of that period.[31] In each case, whilst our two poets were featured (very heavily, in Chaucer's case), they functioned as chronological markers, rather than as the literary interlocutors in which this collection invests.

Scholarly interest has been shown, especially in the first half of the twentieth century, in the linguistic and philological aspect of the Chaucer–Spenser relationship, but there has been an even greater interest in placing Chaucer and Spenser as two members of a wider poetic tradition, of various kinds.[32] Monographs taking such an approach have been appearing for over a century, beginning in 1912 with William Henry Schofield's *Chivalry in English Literature: Chaucer, Malory, Spenser, Shakespeare*.[33] More recent studies link the two poets in examinations of particular themes, such as heroic suffering or comedy.[34] In such cases, there has often been a tendency for critics to see the two poets as part of a larger 'great tradition', rather than engaged in specific conversation between themselves. In this regard, it is notable that many such projects have focused on Milton as well as Chaucer and Spenser. An early example is Harrison's 1956 study of bird imagery, but there were also monographs in the 1970s by Thomas E. Maresca (focused on the notion of epic, and taking *Troilus and Criseyde*, *The Faerie Queene* and *Paradise Lost* as examples) and A. Kent Hieatt (focused on mythic structures).[35] Hieatt's work is particularly noteworthy for his appreciation of the use of borrowed language and, as he observes, for 'a reader of Spenser who knows Chaucer and Middle English well, the continually met Chaucerian words, forms, and turns of speech are a constant indication of an imagination saturated with Chaucer's poetry.'[36] The triumvirate of Chaucer, Spenser and Milton was expanded to a quartet by the addition of T.S. Eliot in Clare Kinney's 1992 monograph, *Strategies of Poetic Narrative*. Kinney's study, which uses a narratological approach, focuses on the same three long poems as Maresca, but also incorporates *The Waste Land*.

---

and Allusion, 1357–1900, 3 vols (Cambridge: Cambridge University Press, 1925). For Nashe see 1.135; for Thynne see 1.166; for Dryden see 1.272; and for Hazlitt see 2.98–106.
31 Derek Pearsall, ed., *Chaucer to Spenser: An Anthology of Writing in English 1375–1575* (Oxford: Blackwell, 1998) and *Chaucer to Spenser: A Critical Reader* (Oxford: Blackwell, 1999).
32 B.R. McElderry Jr., 'Archaism and Innovation in Spenser's Poetic Diction', *PMLA*, 27 (1932), 144–70; Veré L. Rubel, *Poetic Diction in the English Renaissance: From Skelton through Spenser* (New York: Modern Language Association of America, 1941).
33 William Henry Schofield, *Chivalry in English Literature: Chaucer, Malory, Spenser, Shakespeare* (Cambridge, MA: Harvard University, 1912).
34 Georgia Ronan Crampton, *The Condition of Creatures: Suffering and Action in Chaucer and Spenser* (New Haven: Yale University Press, 1974); Frances McNeely Leonard, *Laughter in the Courts of Love: Comedy in Allegory from Chaucer to Spenser* (Norman: Pilgrim Books, 1981).
35 Thomas P. Harrison, *They Tell of Birds* (Austin: University of Texas Press, 1956); Thomas E. Maresca, *Three English Epics: Studies in Chaucer, Spenser and Milton* (Lincoln: University of Nebraska Press, 1979); Hieatt.
36 Hieatt, 11.

She elegantly demonstrates how 'narrative moments, narrative sequences even, become palimpsests where [...] layers of implicit reference reverberate against the surface narrative'.³⁷ A different quartet is also the subject of Anderson's *Reading the Allegorical Intertext*, which brings together a series of pieces examining the intertextual relations between Chaucer, Spenser, Shakespeare and (again) Milton: it is the first two who dominate the book.

Valuable as all of these works are, the inclusion of more than two poets means that their readings can come under pressure to subordinate the particular relationship between the works of Chaucer and Spenser to a broader thematic concern, of which our two poets become instances or variants. This is particularly the case with studies that present the relationship as emblematic of periodisation. In her 1975 book, Alice Miskimin explored how Chaucer was perceived in the early modern period, and her study culminates in a chapter on Chaucer and *The Shepheardes Calender*. A more recent and highly significant landmark is the volume of essays edited by Theresa Krier in 1998, *Refiguring Chaucer in the Renaissance*, which examines the reappropriation of Chaucer in the early modern period, Spenser figuring prominently in the collection's analysis and overall design. In the current volume, by contrast, we take the nexus of Chaucer and Spenser as our focus, and allow this to generate multiple concerns in itself.

The models of intertextual relations that emerge here are more generous than those theorised by Harold Bloom in *The Anxiety of Influence* owing to their anchoring in a range of possible kinships: our poets, like Shakespeare, belong, in Bloom's words, 'to the giant age before the flood, before the anxiety of influence became central to poetic consciousness'.³⁸ For Chaucer and Spenser, influence is typically volitional and reviving, and plays out in the detailed complexity of particulars which are open, rather than closed, to the possibility of inventive substitutions.³⁹ The patterns of creativity traced by our contributors are alert to the generative potential of 'auctoritee' and *imitatio*. In pursuing these paths, we are building on and extending a body of criticism that has specifically examined how Chaucer was read and re-used by Spenser. Very early examples of this tradition come from Thomas William Nadal's early twentieth-century articles on the Chaucerian basis for Spenser's *Daphnaïda* and 'Muiopotmos'.⁴⁰ At first, little followed in this line apart from brief notes by F.P. Magoun in 1927 (one of which traces Spenser's 'Blandamour' to an early printed edition of Chaucer's *Tale of Sir Thopas*, whilst the other is once again about Milton) and Thomas Pyles in 1942, on how Spenser may have coined the name 'Dan Chaucer'.⁴¹ From the

---

37 Clare Kinney, *Strategies of Poetic Narrative: Chaucer, Spenser, Milton, Eliot* (Cambridge: Cambridge University Press, 1992), 20.
38 Harold Bloom, *The Anxiety of Influence: A Theory of Poetry*, 2nd edn (Oxford: Oxford University Press, 1973; repr. 1997), 11.
39 Ibid., 8.
40 Nadal, 'Spenser's *Daphnaïda*' and 'Spenser's "Muiopotmos" in Relation to Chaucer's *Sir Thopas* and *The Nun's Priest's Tale*', PMLA, 25 (1910), 640–56.
41 F.P. Magoun, 'The Chaucer of Spenser and Milton', *Modern Philology*, 25 (1927), 129–36; Thomas Pyles, 'Dan Chaucer', *Modern Language Notes*, 57 (1942), 437–9.

mid-1960s, however, there was an increasing flow of writing on Chaucer and Spenser, especially exploring the direct links between specific passages or poems. Nadal's work was superseded by Anderson's 1970 article on 'Muiopotmos', and by three further articles on *Daphnaïda*.[42] Anderson was also amongst those looking for connections elsewhere in the Spenser canon, within works such as *The Shepheardes Calendar* and *The Faerie Queene*.[43] 1990 saw an acceleration of this interest, firstly with the publication of articles by Anne Higgins and Anthony M. Esolen, both arguing for the importance of Chaucer and the references to him for understanding Spenser's poetry, and secondly with the appearance of Burrow's entry in *The Spenser Encyclopedia*, as discussed above. Glenn A. Steinberg's work on the Mutabilitie Cantos and Andrew King's important article on the 'medieval' structure of *The Faerie Queene* are further key contributions to this field that have enabled scholars to focus in increasing detail on particular connections between individual works.[44] This extended readerly conversation has increased our understanding of the nuanced texture of the poets' relationship and *Rereading Chaucer and Spenser* allows these nuances to be appreciated in ever fuller ways.

Sites of encounter

Despite the closeness that has long been read into the relationship between these two poets – Burrow writing that 'no Elizabethan writer [...] displays a closer relationship to Chaucer than does Spenser' – there are only eight direct mentions of Chaucer in Spenser's work.[45] As the chapters in this collection demonstrate, however, Spenser's absorption in Chaucer's writings operates not just through open reference but at the level of metre, structure, resonance, mode and attitude. In order to orient our readers, particularly those new to thinking about the intertextual connections between Chaucer and Spenser, the specific citations described below provide a guide to the familiar centres of the relationship, beginning with *The Shepheardes Calender* and 'Colin Clouts Come Home Againe', then moving to *The Faerie Queene* and *A View of the Present State of Ireland*.

---

42 Judith H. Anderson, '"Nat worth a boterflye": *Muiopotmos* and *The Nun's Priest's Tale*', *Journal of Medieval and Renaissance Studies*, 1 (1970), 89–106. See also John A. Burrow, '*Sir Thopas* in the Sixteenth Century', in *Middle English Studies Presented to Norman Davis*, ed. Douglas Gray and E.G. Stanley (Oxford: Oxford University Press, 1983), 69–91; Normand Berlin, 'Chaucer's *The Book of the Duchess* and Spenser's *Daphnaïda*: A Contrast', *Studia Neophilologica*, 38 (1966), 282–9; Duncan Harris and Nancy L. Steffen, 'The Other Side of the Garden: An Interpretive Comparison of Chaucer's *Book of the Duchess* and Spenser's *Daphnaïda*', *Journal of Medieval and Renaissance Studies*, 8 (1978), 17–36; William A. Oram, '*Daphnaïda* and Spenser's Later Poetry', *Spenser Studies*, 2 (1981), 141–58.
43 Alice E. Lasater, 'The Chaucerian Narrator in Spenser's *Shepheardes Calender*', *Southern Quarterly*, 12 (1974), 189–201; Judith H. Anderson, '"A Gentle Knight was pricking on the plaine": The Chaucerian Connection', *English Literary Renaissance*, 15 (1985), 166–74.
44 Glenn A. Steinberg, 'Chaucer's Mutability in Spenser's "Mutabilitie Cantos"', *Studies in English Literature*, 46 (2006), 27–42; Andrew King '"Well Grounded, Finely Framed, and Strongly Trussed up Together": The "Medieval" Structure of *The Faerie Queene*', *The Review of English Studies*, 52 (2001), 22–58. See also Yuasa Noboyuki's 'The Art of Naming: A Study of Fictional Names as an Element of Style in Chaucer, Spenser and Shakespeare', *Poetica*, 41 (1994), 59–83.
45 Burrow, 'Chaucer, Geoffrey', 144.

In *The Shepheardes Calender*, Chaucer is present both in the framing material and the eclogues themselves. Spenser's opening lines, in the verse addressed 'To His Booke', paraphrase Chaucer's 'Go, litel bok, go, litel myn tragedye' (v.1786) from the ending of *Troilus and Criseyde*. Spenser, in the voice of 'Immeritô', writes,

> Goe little booke: thy selfe present
> As child whose parent is vnkent
> To him that is the president
> Of noblesse and of cheualree [...] (1–4)

The book is imagined presenting itself to its intended patron, 'the noble [...] M. Philip Sidney', as the title page describes him. For Spenser, this moment places the text firmly within a patronage economy, whereas for Chaucer's *Troilus*, the gesture locates the work in a literary tradition and signals the author's affiliation with his classical predecessors. Nonetheless, the allusion to Chaucer is meant to be recognised and Spenser is both suggesting that Chaucer is a key poetic spirit behind the *Calender* and stating that he has read, thoroughly, Chaucer's 'litel book'. This is evident from the first lines of E.K.'s dedicatory epistle, which both quote Chaucer and mention him by name: 'VNCOVTHE VNKISTE, Sayde the olde famous Poete Chaucer: whom for his excellencie and wonderfull skil in making, his scholer Lidgate, a worthy scholer of so excellent a maister, calleth the Loadestarre of our Language' (1–4). Spenser's Chaucer, here, is not only ancient and famous but he is a paragon of 'making', or poetic excellence, and a guiding spirit for the English language.

The February eclogue contains the *Calender*'s seemingly most direct reference to Chaucer. An old shepherd, Thenot, and Cuddie, his young companion, rehearse the idea that 'youthe and elde is often at debaat', as Chaucer's Miller puts it (3230). Thenot seeks to educate Cuddie out of his arrogant empty-headedness using the lessons of poetry; he asks,

> But shall I tel thee a tale of truth,
> Which I cond of *Tityrus* in my youth,
> Keeping his sheepe on the hils of Kent? (91–3)

Ever-ready to interpret and ostensibly clarify, E.K. glosses Thenot's mention of 'tale' and 'Kent' (the county where Canterbury is located): 'I suppose he meane Chaucer, whose prayse for pleasaunt tales cannot dye, so long as the memorie of hys name shal liue, and the name of Poetrie shal endure' (92, gloss). This moment suggestively weaves classical and vernacular poetic identities because Tityrus is also a name for Virgil, and for the shepherd in Virgil's *Eclogues*, Spenser's key formal model for the *Calender* (the chapters here by Barr, Cook, and Chaghafi unpack this topic). 'June' both sustains and adds to the image of Chaucer advanced in 'February' in that he becomes not only a poetic teacher but a source of potential inspiration. In 'June', Chaucer is presented by Colin as the arch-poet of tragic love, the courtly poet of *Troilus and Criseyde* who is said to lead all other amorous poets. Colin wails,

> The God of shepheardes, *Tityrus* is dead,
> Who taught me homely, as I can, to make.
> He, whilst he liued, was the soueraigne head
> Of shepheards all, that bene with loue ytake [...] (81–4)

E.K. glosses this but characteristically complicates Colin's utterance: 'that by Tityrus is meant Chaucer, hath bene already sufficiently sayde, and by this more playne appeareth, that he sayth, he tolde merye tales. Such as be his Canterburie tales. Whom he calleth the God of Poets for his excellencie' (81, gloss). E.K.'s Chaucer is different from Colin's; he is the bawdy and witty poet of the *Canterbury Tales*.

The June eclogue contains Colin's crisis of love but it is 'December' that houses his greatest poetic crisis, the moment when he symbolically abandons poetry by hanging up his pipe because his 'Muse is hoarse and weary' (140). 'December' opens with the unusual presence in the *Calender* of a narrator; this stands out because most of the other speakers are shepherds, frequently shepherd-poets. The narrator names Colin, praises his ability and unambiguously states why he is a good poet: 'the gentle shepheard [...] which wel could pype and singe, / For he of Tityrus his songs did lere' (1–4). E.K. pipes up from the gloss to confirm Tityrus' identity: 'Chaucer: as hath bene oft sayd' (4, gloss). Colin Clout is the named persona that Spenser most often adopts and this figure is described very clearly as a Chaucerian not only in these moments of the *Calender* but in his own poem, 'Colin Clouts Come Home Againe'. In this work, the two are yoked together from the opening lines: 'the shepheardes boy (best knowen by that name) / That after *Tityrus* first sung his lay' (1–2). When Spenser, in the envoy at the end of the *Calender*, relinquishes both Colin's voice and the narrative voice, assuming instead a tone resembling Immeritô, he is initially self-effacing. He tells his 'lyttle Calender' that it should not 'dare [...] to match thy pype with Tityrus hys style / Nor with the Pilgrim that the Ploughman playde a whyle' (7–10). This speaker appears humbled and awed by Chaucer, and by William Langland, author of the lengthy dream vision *Piers Plowman*, yet he goes on to direct his book to 'followe them farre off, and their high steppes adore' (11).[46] The moment reprises and expands on Immeritô's opening citation of *Troilus and Criseyde*. Where Chaucer's 'litel bok' (v.1786) was told to 'kis the steppes where as thow seest pace / Virgile, Ovide, Omer, Lucan, and Stace' (v.1791–2), Spenser's is projected as adoring the 'high steppes' of its medieval models. In the *Calender*, Spenser appears to tell his reader that he cannot possibly aspire to the skill of Chaucer but what ultimately plays out are his endeavours to do exactly that.

In *The Faerie Queene* there are fewer direct citations of Chaucer's writings but it is recognised that both the *Knight's Tale* and the *Tale of Sir Thopas* are important sources. When Spenser does engage directly with Chaucer in his epic poem it is mostly to the *Canterbury Tales* that he turns. The encounter between Prince Arthur and Gloriana is famously modelled on Sir Thopas's dream of an elven queen, whereby Spenser transforms Chaucer's ludic romance into the basis for a visionary

---

46 See O'Connell's chapter for the alternative allusion to the *Plowman's Tale*.

quest. Book IV's 'Legend of Cambel and Telamond, or of Friendship' contains Spenser's continuation of the *Squire's Tale*, which he introduces with three prologue-like stanzas referring to 'that renowmed Poet [...] / Dan *Chaucer*, well of English vndefyled' (IV.ii.32). These stanzas also open with a near-verbatim quotation of the first line of the *Knight's Tale*, except Spenser substitutes 'antique' for Chaucer's 'olde': 'Whylome as antique stories tellen vs' (IV.ii.32). In this inset prologue to the continuation, an idea returns that was important at the close of *The Shepheardes Calender*: that of daring. Spenser asks pardon of Chaucer for stealing the 'meede' of his 'due merit, / That none durst euer whilest thou wast aliue / [...] Ne dare I like' (IV.ii.34). This suggests something of the risk of Spenser's project (and that of other poets) in continuing Chaucer's work. The next reference to Chaucer, which opens canto iii of Book VI, the book of 'Covrtesie', paraphrases the Wife of Bath; Spenser writes, 'True is, that whilome that good Poet sayd, / The gentle minde by gentle deeds is knowne' (VI.iii.1). The 'good Poet' is, of course, Chaucer, but the Wife in fact says 'he is gentil that dooth gentil dedis' (1170). Spenser's shift from 'gentil' actions to a 'gentle' mind emphasises *The Faerie Queene*'s concern with representing the movements of individual psychology alongside its character typologies. In most of these instances there is praise for Chaucer, if not a recollection of his excellence, and a productive tension is established with the Chaucerian text.

The final moment from *The Faerie Queene* is less lionising, in that it explores a perceived failure of Chaucer's own daring. In the fragmentary Mutabilitie Cantos, the goddess 'great dame *Nature*' (VII.vii.5) features prominently but Spenser's narrator finds it impossible to describe her and comments that he is not alone in this. He is consoled by the fact that 'old *Dan Geffrey* (in whose gentle spright / The pure well head of Poesie did dwell) / In his *Foules parley* durst not with it mel' (VII.vii.9). Tracing Spenser's citations of Chaucer chronologically through the poetry finishes with him finding a moment of shared experience, rather than antagonism or awe. In addition to his place in Spenser's poetry, a debt to Chaucer can also be located in Spenser's political prose dialogue *A View of the Present State of Ireland*. This text circulated extensively in manuscript but did not reach print publication until well after Spenser's death in 1633, despite being entered into the Stationers' Register in 1598.[47] Spenser, in this work, not only alludes to the dress of Chaucer's hapless errant knight Sir Thopas but also makes borrowings at the level of individual word-choice: a dynamic that hints at how the mind of the colonial administrator was shaped by his literary pursuits and imaginative predilections.[48]

New encounters

The above instances form the core of the material explored by the chapters in this collection but several contributors move well beyond them. The textual focus of

---

47 Edmund Spenser, *A View of the State of Ireland*, ed. Andrew Hadfield and Willy Maley (Oxford: Blackwell, 1997), xi.
48 See Thomas Herron, *Spenser's Irish Work: Poetry, Plantation and Colonial Reformation* (Aldershot: Ashgate, 2007).

Judith H. Anderson's opening chapter is the clustering of memories of *Troilus and Criseyde* in *The Faerie Queene* and in Spenser's sonnet sequence, *Amoretti*. The chapter serves as an opening theorisation of intertextuality that demonstrates and describes the dynamism of intertextual forms and metaphors. Anderson unpacks the idea of resonance, a term that proves especially useful for many of the critics in this collection, including Helen Barr. Barr's essay uses *The House of Fame*, *The Shepheardes Calendar* and the persona of E.K. to explore resonance as a figure for the relationship between Spenser and Chaucer, or rather between Spenser and many different 'Chaucers' and Chaucerian voices. Hearing and mishearing are not only what the figures in these poems do, she argues, but also what we as readers can fruitfully do to and with them, in order to be sensitive to the rich tonalities sounded when one text echoes or re-speaks another. Helen Cooper's chapter offers a series of frames for thinking about the ways in which generative love and friendship interact as pervasive thematic preoccupations for Chaucer and Spenser. By eschewing previous critical narratives of influence and anxiety and identifying the difficulties that New Historicist approaches have encountered when dealing with the transhistorical, Cooper offers a reading of continuity and variety that moves elegantly amidst the friends and lovers that populate the worlds of both authors' works. When read together, the three opening chapters present a persuasive case for reading intertextually, playfully, and transhistorically.

Claire Eager then takes the common ground of the *Franklin's Tale* and *The Shepheardes Calender* as her point of departure to think about the crafting of paradisal spaces and the agony of being excluded from their pleasures. Her consideration of the relationship between place and affect contributes to current critical debates concerning the writing of literary geography and the relationship between ethics and aesthetics in both poets' works. In a study of a different kind of space, William Rhodes turns the focus away from poetic making and towards Spenser's most extensive prose writing, *A View of the Present State of Ireland*. Rhodes offers a probing reading of how Spenser utilises Chaucerian vocabulary in order to articulate a series of pressing local concerns identified by the New English administration in Ireland. Closely attentive to archaism, Rhodes's chapter models how the representation of discrete times and places is complicated by words and attitudes that retain the memory of previous use and accrued cultural value. When juxtaposed, these chapters illuminate the habits of mind that shaped Spenser's writings as both poet and planter.

Richard Danson Brown offers a detailed examination of rhyme and metrics in *The Faerie Queene*, comparing Spenser's practice here with Chaucer's in *Troilus and Criseyde*. He finds rich evidence not only of the power of rhyme to create meanings in multiple ways within each poem, but also of Spenser's indebtedness to, and creative development of, Chaucer's own inventive ways with rhyme and stanza form. This enables Brown to query Spenser's positioning between the continental Renaissance and English vernacular poetics. The Spenserian stanza not only attempts to overgo Italian *ottavo rima* but reconstructs Chaucer's rhyme royal into a recognisably English form. Chaucer emerges as inspirational for Spenser in matters of structural detail, as well as content.

Introduction 17

Like others in this collection, Gareth Griffith's chapter examines what Chaucer meant to Spenser and his contemporaries, in this case through an examination of manuscripts of Chaucer's poems and the idea of romance that they transmit to a later generation. Focusing on *The Tale of Gamelyn* and *The Tale of Beryn*, the chapter suggests that this transmission makes romance a wider and more centrally Chaucerian mode than might appear from modern editions, and that it is this Chaucer with whom many sixteenth-century readers would have engaged. Retaining the interest in the material text, Megan Cook's chapter is the first of a complementary pair concerning how Spenser's presentation of Chaucer shaped subsequent receptions of him, particularly in Thomas Speght's 1598 and 1602 editions of *The Workes of our Antient and Learned English Poet, Geffrey Chaucer*. Cook identifies the importance of E.K.'s commentary to the reimagining of Chaucer and his works as 'historically antecedent but culturally current' (151). Meanwhile, Elisabeth Chaghafi's reading of the voluminous supplementary materials in Speght's editions firstly reflects on his efforts to promote Chaucer's 'worthinesse' (181) to a sixteenth-century readership, before illuminating the paratextual sleights of hand used to reinforce the perceived affinities between the Old and New Poet. The narrative of friendship that emerges is played out in the spaces of the printed page.

Sustaining the collection's interest in matters of voice and ventriloquism, Brendan O'Connell delineates the influence of Chaucer's beast group of *Canterbury Tales* – the *Nun's Priest's Tale*, the *Manciple's Tale*, the *Parson's Tale* and the *Plowman's Tale* (the latter now recognised as apocryphal) – on Spenser's 'Prosopopoia, or Mother Hubberds Tale'. The particular order and position in which early readers experienced Chaucer's tales is important, he writes, because together they explore the possibilities of the fable as a vehicle for satire. Specifically, O'Connell argues, Spenser reads and responds to the tales as the culmination of Chaucer's thinking about the poet's role as a mimic of other voices. Craig Berry's chapter takes us to *The Parliament of Fowls* and the Mutabilitie Cantos to argue that both Chaucer and Spenser placed themselves within a wider virtual-textual community of readers, writers and authorities that bridges gaps between different times and worlds (this world and that to come). In this reading, every named author becomes multiplied, simultaneously speaking as himself and transmitting other voices, and this allows Berry to explore the overlap between ideas of tradition and witness.

Finally, Harriet Archer's chapter asks the fraught question of what it meant for Spenser to present himself as a 'new Poete' in sixteenth-century England. She situates his claim to newness amidst the multiple, and often problematic, contemporary connotations of novelty, finding that he is only the most vocal exponent of a poetics of novelty that in fact has ancient roots. The reformist satire of Luke Shepherd, *Philogamus* (1548), proves to be a particularly complicating discursive predecessor for Spenser's self-positioning in the vanguard of poetic invention.

In previous writings on this topic, Krier has remarked upon the 'inexhaustible' quality associated with Chaucer's works by writers of the Renaissance, which was coupled with a sense 'that he makes possible one's own inventiveness'.[49] G. Wilson Knight observes a similarly generative capacity in Spenser's longest work, namely that '*The Faerie Queen* is more a storehouse for poets of the future than itself a poem'.[50] Readers from different epochs, then, have thought of Chaucer and Spenser as sharing a generous capaciousness that is responsive to literary inheritance and legacy. In the contributions collected here we cannot claim to be exhaustive or to have addressed all the potential variations on our theme; there are inevitable omissions and silences which we hope other readers and rereaders will take up. We show that Spenser's adoption of Chaucerian paradigms allowed him the scope to vitalise his reading of the past as an intervention in the literature of his present, frequently with a keen eye on the path he was breaking for readers of the future.

---

49 Krier, 'Introduction', in *Refiguring Chaucer*, 1–18 (3).
50 G. Wilson Knight, 'The Spenserian Fluidity', in *Elizabethan Poetry: Modern Essays in Criticism*, ed. Paul J. Alpers (Oxford: Oxford University Press, 1967), 329–44 (334).

1

Chaucer's *Troilus and Criseyde* in Spenser's *Amoretti* and *The Faerie Queene*: reading historically and intertextually

Judith H. Anderson

The presence of Chaucer's *Troilus and Criseyde* in Spenser's *Amoretti*, as well as in *The Faerie Queene*, and the kind of presence it is in both are my major concerns in this chapter, but I will start by summoning what we already know about the relationship of this particular poem by Chaucer to Spenser's poems more generally. The few references in the Spenser canon that indubitably involve *Troilus and Criseyde* include, first, the phrase 'Uncouthe unkiste', in E.K.'s epistle to *The Shepheardes Calender*, which E.K. attributes to Chaucer and which updates Pandarus's proverb 'Unknowe, unkist' and thus preserves in Elizabethan English the phonic consonance of Chaucer's hard 'k'; and second, the *Calender*'s envoy, '*Go lyttle Calender*', which has been anticipated by Immeritô's dedicatory poem, beginning '*Goe little booke*'.[1] Beyond these, Clare Kinney has demonstrated parallels between the Petrarchan posture of Chaucer's Troilus and that of Spenser's Colin Clout in the *Calender*.[2] Humble as the figure of Colin might purport to be,

---

1 I thank Tamara A. Goeglein for her helpful suggestions regarding an earlier version of this chapter.
   With the exception of *The Faerie Queene*, citation of Spenser's poems is from *The Yale Edition of the Shorter Poems*, ed. William A. Oram, Einar Bjorvand, Ronald Bond, Thomas H. Cain, Alexander Dunlop and Richard Schell (New Haven: Yale University Press, 1989), here 12–13, 213. *The Faerie Queene* (*FQ*) is cited from the second edition of A.C. Hamilton, with text by Hiroshi Yamashita and Toshiyuki Suzuki (Harlow: Pearson, 2001). Unless otherwise specified, citations of Chaucer are to *Chaucer's Poetry*, ed. E.T. Donaldson, 2nd edn (New York: Ronald Press, 1975), here *Troilus and Criseide* (*TC*), I.809, V.1786; I have elected the spelling 'Criseyde', however. I have also consulted *The Riverside Chaucer*, ed. Larry D. Benson (Boston: Houghton Mifflin, 1987). The Renaissance text of Chaucer I have used is *Works 1532, with supplementary material from the Editions of 1542, 1561, 1598 and 1602* (London: Scolar, 1969; repr. 1976), here fol. clxxiiii^v, ccxviii^v; there are no differences affecting my argument between my textual citations of Chaucer from Donaldson's edition and this Renaissance facsimile – indeed, no substantive differences at all; I offer folio numbers as a convenience. Although A. Kent Hieatt (*Chaucer, Spenser, Milton: Mythopoeic Continuities and Transformations* [Montreal: McGill-Queen's University Press, 1975], 19–24) speculates regarding the specific edition of Chaucer that Spenser used, his evidence - the word 'checklatoun' - establishes only that this was one of the Thynne family of editions. Craig A. Berry's suggestion that Spenser knew more than one edition of Chaucer – an earlier edition than Thynne's – does not cancel Hieatt's evidence for one or more Thynne editions: '"Sundrie Doubts": Vulnerable Understanding and Dubious Origins in Spenser's Continuation of the Squire's Tale', in *Refiguring Chaucer in the Renaissance*, ed. Theresa M. Krier (Gainesville: University Press of Florida, 1998), 106–27 (112; 124, note 14).
2 Clare R. Kinney, 'Marginal Presence, Lyric Resonance, Epic Absence: *Troilus and Criseyde* and/in *The Shepheardes Calender*', *Spenser Studies*, 18 (2003), 25–39 (especially 29–30).

convincing parallels are there, together with Spenserian aspirations. In *The Faerie Queene*, other readers have suggested memories of Chaucer's *Troilus* in Arthur's enamourment by his Fairy Queen, his complaint to night, Busirane's pageant, the Temple of Venus, and the Mutabilitie Cantos.[3] All these memories are occasional, casual and brief.

The Spenser *Variorum* records additional words, figures and sayings shared by Chaucer's *Troilus* and Spenser's poems, especially the *Calender* and *The Faerie Queene*. These similarities, while suggestive, are inconclusive separately or in the aggregate, however, because they are neither exact nor unique to the *Troilus* and Spenser.[4] But this relative lack of evidence relating the two is actually germane to my purpose. It emphasises from the outset that intertextual relationships are not limited to the so-called 'hard evidence' of source study, which is useful but unimaginative in itself and, when applied restrictively, as alien to the reading of poetry as a Baconian hostility to Homer's winged words.[5] Intertextuality is a dynamic relationship that can range from authorial control to cultural subjection, from deliberate imitation to linguistic free-play, or from intentional allusion to the agency of the signifier. It enriches and reorients the significance and reception of texts.

The *Troilus* is Chaucer's major achievement as a love poet, which is the kind of poet most Elizabethans supposed him to be, and some moderns – memorably C.S. Lewis – have thought *The Faerie Queene* to be focally concerned with earthly love, especially but not exclusively in its two central books, III and IV.[6] In the six years between the publication of these books, Spenser published the *Amoretti*, his sonnet sequence, whose erotic discourse the central books share. Along with the first book, the central books and the sonnets also engage Chaucer's *Troilus*. Simultaneously, they recall the matter of love and the matter of Troy.

Generically, the *Troilus* is a romance, as well as a '*tragedye*', its narrator's term for it, and, like the tragi-comic romance of the *Knight's Tale*, it is presided over by Boethian fortune, a complex attitude towards experience that is recurrent, if

---

3 E.g., see Judith H. Anderson, *Reading the Allegorical Intertext: Chaucer, Spenser, Shakespeare, Milton* (New York: Fordham University Press, 2008): indexical entry for 'Chaucer: *Troilus and Criseyde*'. I treat Arthur's complaint to Night later in the present chapter. C.S. Lewis memorably mentions Troilus in connection with the pageant in the House of Busirane: *The Allegory of Love: A Study in Medieval Tradition* (New York: Oxford University Press, 1936; repr. 1958), 341; Lewis's reference occurs in the generic terms of courtly love rather than more specifically.
4 *The Works of Edmund Spenser: A Variorum Edition*, ed. Edwin Greenlaw et al., 11 vols (Baltimore: Johns Hopkins Press, 1932; repr. 1966): see vol. 8 for the *Amoretti*; each book of *The Faerie Queene* has a correspondingly numbered volume, 1–6, with the Mutabilitie Cantos also included in volume 6.
5 On this hostility, see, for example, Judith H. Anderson, *Words That Matter: Linguistic Perception in Renaissance English* (Stanford: Stanford University Press, 1996), 37, and indexical entry 'Homer, winged words of'; also my *Biographical Truth: The Representation of Historical Persons in Tudor-Stuart Writing* (New Haven: Yale University Press, 1984), 159–69.
6 See John A. Burrow, 'Chaucer, Geoffrey', in *The Spenser Encyclopedia*, ed. A.C. Hamilton et al. (Toronto: University of Toronto Press, 1990), 144–8. In the present volume, Helen Cooper develops the emphasis by Lewis and Burrow on love. Recently, Andrew Hadfield's biography of Spenser further identifies sex and politics as the major concerns of *The Faerie Queene*: *Edmund Spenser: A Life* (Oxford: Oxford University Press, 2012).

underappreciated, in *The Faerie Queene* as well.[7] The *Troilus* features a version of Boethius that is secularised in the main and, until the end of the poem, more compatible with a cyclical, fatalistic emphasis on history than with transcendent idealism.[8] Both Chaucer and Spenser, incidentally, invoke Clio, muse of history, and Calliope, muse of epic song (and more broadly of eloquence for medieval poets), as inspiring sources for their major romances.[9] In addition to an attraction by genre, Spenser's romance epic shares with the *Troilus* not only a pronounced engagement with the story of Troy, Petrarchism and complaint, but more generally with antiquity and memory. Both authors, moreover, deploy the aphoristic mode conspicuously in their major poems, in which the deftness of its sustained use in argument is a shared trademark: recall, for salient examples, Pandarus's effort to persuade Troilus to confide in him or the lovers' last night, in which they debate whether Criseyde should leave Troy, or Troilus take action against their separation; in Spenser's epic, concentrated instances include Una and Arthur's dialogic exchange over the fallen Redcrosse's armour, Redcrosse's temptation by Despair, and Melibee's aphoristic wisdom. So conspicuous a display of simultaneously disparate proverbs in the *Troilus* and *The Faerie Queene* signals an exploratory questioning of received wisdom – the cracking of cultural nuggets, whether comically, in deadly seriousness or with the in-betweenness of irony. Small wonder, given these many similarities, that readers should recall Chaucer's major tragi-comic romance when reading Spenser's romance epic, along with the sonnet sequence Spenser published between its two instalments.

As another, more theoretical frame for discussing this Chaucerian presence in Spenser's epic and sonnets, I want to consider some of the metaphors we use for intertextual relations – intertext (or weaving: > Latin *intertextere*), influence (or flowing: > Latin *influere*) and allusion (or playing: > Latin *alludere*) – these being just three general forms of intertextuality. A more specific variant for the Chaucer/Spenser relationship that I have previously highlighted is Spenser's own figure of the 'euerlasting scryne' that contains the 'antique rolles' out of which *The*

---

7 On Boethian fortune, which receives much emphasis in the first two books of *The Consolation of Philosophy* (trans. V.E. Watts [Baltimore: Penguin, n.d.]), see especially Book II.i (54–6), and note 8 below. Boethian philosophy gets beyond fortune's power as *The Consolation* progresses. Until a leap into faith at the end, the *Troilus* does not.
8 On Boethius in the *Troilus*, see Lee Patterson, *Chaucer and the Subject of History* (Madison: University of Wisconsin Press, 1991), chap. 2 (especially 152–3); and Mary Carruthers, 'On Affliction and Reading, Weeping and Argument: Chaucer's Lachrymose Troilus in Context', *Representations*, 93 (2006), 1–21 (12). See also Eugene Vance, 'Chaucer, Spenser, and the Ideology of Translation', *Canadian Review of Comparative Literature*, 8 (1981), 217–38. On fate in Boethius, see especially Book IV.vi. Boethian fate is, while subject to God, ever-moving, ever-mutable, an 'indissoluble chain of causes' (Boethius, 136–7). Seen from below, rather than from above, it is relentlessly mutable, as in Spenser's Mutabilitie Cantos, and in the *Troilus*, until its very end. On the power of Boethian fortune and fate in Spenser, see my *Allegorical Intertext*, especially 87–90, 116; on the association of Spenser's Arthur with pessimism and a sense of historical loss, see also Andrew Escobedo, 'The Tudor Search for Arthur and the Poetics of Historical Loss', *Exemplaria*, 14 (2002), 127–65 (e.g. 131, 156–7, 165).
9 Benson, ed., 1038, note on *TC* III.45. Donaldson, ed., 814, note on *TC* III.45: 'eloquence'. Thomas Maresca argues that Chaucer's *Troilus* is an epic: *Three English Epics: Studies of Troilus and Criseyde, The Faerie Queene, and Paradise Lost* (Lincoln: University of Nebraska Press, 1979).

Faerie Queene is fashioned (I.Pro.2).[10] The scrine, a treasure chest, represents both written and mnemonic sources, indeed, the whole cultural archive available for imaginative *poiesis*, or 'making'. As a figure, it belongs to the mnemonic tradition, and, not surprisingly, it reappears in Book II within the chamber of Eumnestes, 'remembering well', or Memory. In this chamber of memory within Alma's brain turret, Arthur and Guyon find, respectively, a book of British history and a book of mythic history. If the antique rolls within Eumnestes' scrine suggest the external sources of history, the mnemonic tradition also suggests internal ones.

Recently, Rebeca Helfer, likewise identifying the mnemonic tradition as the source of Spenser's poetics, has highlighted the importance for Chaucer and Spenser of houses as topoi of the past with metaphorical potential for edification (a pun). Such edifices, though ruined, are not to be abandoned but instead to be reconstructed creatively in the present. Helfer founds this tradition in Cicero's *De Oratore* and in Chaucer's *House of Fame*, which includes literary tradition but on its lowest level, consisting of twigs woven, text-like, together, further includes the noisy stuff of life, rumours arising from *conversation*, or social life. For Lee Patterson, these same materials more specifically belong to the historian; they are 'history verbalized'.[11]

Both metaphors, the scrine and the edifice, emphasise not only memory but also writing and location. There is something artefactual and also visual about them – an object, a chamber, a building, a graphic image. Such metaphors bear on the nature of the relationships envisioned through them. Like a phantasm, a memory can derive from any of the senses, but there is nonetheless a notable cultural tendency – needlessly limiting – to ground it mainly in sight and things seen, especially material ones.

Another of my own metaphors for the Chaucer/Spenser relationship has involved reflection and refraction, optical phenomena of pronounced interest both to the Middle Ages and to the early modern period. Poetic self-reflection and self-refraction likewise attach to this two-sided optical metaphor, which originates in the physics of light. Both derive from the throwing back or bending of light: reflection indicates a mirroring effect, refraction a deflected, reoriented or otherwise modified one. I found refraction especially useful in discussing Spenser's Temple of Venus in the fourth book of *The Faerie Queene* in relation to Chaucer's Temple of Venus in the *Parliament of Fowls*, one of three such Chaucerian temples and also one instance of a Court of Love tradition so rich yet so reiterative as to have been the object of book-length study.[12] When many instances in the cultural archive compete for attention or when common texts, such as the Bible, Ovid or Petrarch, mediate intertextuality, this relationship is at once less certain and more

---

10 Anderson, *Allegorical Intertext*, 79–90.
11 Patterson, 100–1: Patterson writes in the heyday of heightened, deconstructive verbalism, but his sense of the importance of history in the *Troilus* remains illuminating; also Rebeca Helfer, *Spenser's Ruins and the Art of Recollection* (Toronto: University of Toronto Press, 2012), 124–7. On the twigs as text (Latin *textus*: 'woven'), Helfer cites Penelope Reed Doob, *The Idea of the Labyrinth from Classical Antiquity through the Middle Ages* (Ithaca, NY: Cornell University Press, 1990), 328–30.
12 E.g. Earle Broaddus Fowler, *Spenser and the Courts of Love* (Menasha: G. Banta, 1921). Chaucer's Temples of Venus are in *The House of Fame* and the *Knight's Tale*.

suggestive than it is precise and more cumulative than it is punctual. With a form as traditional and culturally overdetermined as a Temple of Venus, refraction is a useful conception. A metaphor of refraction enables recognition of the *degrees* to which the original is present, in the instance of Spenser's Temple, especially in a veiled Venus.[13] In contrast to a vegetable metaphor like the rhizome, refraction can be further useful in recognising an element of human control, whether instrumental, teleological or otherwise: refraction is readily manipulated by context or medium. Whereas Spenser's scrine pertains to sources, materials and origins, refraction, while including these, also addresses intertextual relationships more directly and with greater discrimination.

Unlike the mnemonic and optical metaphors I've treated or the more abstract conception of parallelism between textual components, others frequently used for the Chaucer/Spenser relationship are auditory rather than visual. Probably 'echo' is the commonest, invoked so often and so casually that its metaphoricity gets forgotten and incongruously applied to gestures, shapes, landscapes and the like that are primarily visual. The notion of an echo remains useful in its very breadth, however. *The Faerie Queene* is rightly described as a vast echo chamber; this is one of its outstanding and defining characteristics, which its highly, even endlessly, figurative surface enables.

Finally, 'resonance' is another metaphor that some of us have employed, as does Helen Barr in the present volume, and I was especially drawn to it in thinking about the poems for this chapter. *Resonance* is associated by definition with the prolongation of sound and therefore, like *scrine*, with memory and imagination; like *refraction*, moreover, *resonance* suggests degrees of presence. Yet it also implies an experience that is affective, subtle, suggestive and, probably for some readers, at times too elusive to accept. They don't *hear* it for any number of reasons, including the resources familiar within their own textual and cultural archives. This is not the place to do more than mention that medieval and Renaissance pedagogy, mnemonic training, greater orality and other ingrained cultural practices also led to richer and wider capacities for 'hearing' than in our own time. Earlier readers had whole libraries in their heads. It isn't quite the same to read a printed footnote or do a word-search on the web.[14]

The metaphor of resonance, which Wai Chee Dimock has connected with material theories of aurality and background noise in modern physics, is itself widely resonant.[15] Dimock connects it specifically with Plato's hostility to poetry in *The Republic* and with the Longinian sublime, for example, and more generally with what she terms 'diachronic historicism', as opposed to synchronic historicism,

---

13 See Peter S. Hawkins, 'From Mythography to Myth-Making: Spenser and the *Magna Mater Cybele*', *Sixteenth-Century Journal*, 12 (1981), 51–64 (57, 59).
14 An oral aside by William A. Oram (lecture: Bloomington, IN, 2013) inspired the addition of this comment about a footnote.
15 Wai Chee Dimock, 'A Theory of Resonance', *PMLA*, 112 (1997), 1060–71. For a discussion that refuses to oppose the aural to the visual, as, at least for the sake of argument, Dimock does, see Veit Erlmann, *Reason and Resonance: A History of Modern Aurality* (New York: Zone, 2010), 9–27 (12, 14–15).

which situates texts exclusively 'among events in the same slice of time'.[16] Modern revisions of theory can never be identical with past ones, yet Dimock's wonderful characterisation of the 'semantic fabric of the text' as a 'space-time continuum, alive with memory of probabilities, memory of alternatives, and memory of change' is not as 'unfamiliar [a] description' of 'the literary object', as it might seem initially.[17] Her characterisation resonates unmistakably with historical studies of linguistic change in the Renaissance when neologism, linguistic sublation/supersession and linguistic reformation were widespread. It resonates more distantly with the New Critical view of the poem as an object, like the artefact in Wallace Steven's 'Anecdote of the Jar', in which the jar is set in, yet set off from, the surroundings it affects; *tone*, a word Dimock favours, is itself a central concept of New Criticism. More distinctly, Dimock's sense of the word as a temporally shifting object recalls for me Rabelais's episode of the frozen words in the fourth book of *The Histories of Gargantua and Pantagruel*.[18] Dimock's essay mentions Bakhtin's dialogism, too, in connection with her own 'diachronic historicism', although without developing its direct connection with Kristevan intertextuality, which builds on Bakhtin and affords another relevant linguistic approach to historical complexity.[19] In the main, Dimock's article is a theoretical effort that does not assay the analysis of specific literary texts, as will the rest of this chapter, together with other chapters in this volume. Specific instances test both the strengths and the limits of theories.

Memories of *Troilus* in the *Amoretti* and *Faerie Queene*

Turning first to the *Amoretti*, I'll start with three resonant, mnemonic instances and later consider two in *The Faerie Queene*. They all raise questions about the relation of these Spenserian texts to the *Troilus* and reveal something about its nature. In my experience of reading the *Amoretti* as a whole, the opening of the forty-sixth sonnet has persistently triggered a memory of the *Troilus* for me:

> When my abodes prefixed time is spent,
>   My cruell fayre streight bids me wend my way:
> but then from heaven most hideous stormes are sent
> as willing me against her will to stay. (1–4)

For a moment, these lines recall the violent rainstorm that permits Criseyde to stay the night in Pandarus's house, where Troilus has been concealed in expectation of this turn of events. The happy result that night is the consummation of

---

16 Dimock, 1061, 1067.
17 Ibid., 1060.
18 For historical studies of linguistic change, see, for example, my *Words That Matter* and Hannah Crawforth, *Etymology and the Invention of English in Early Modern Literature* (Cambridge: Cambridge University Press, 2013). Relevantly, on the New Critical view, see *Words That Matter*, 4–5, and 9–13, on Rabelais's episode of the frozen words.
19 On the relation of Bakhtin to Kristevan intertextuality, see Mary Orr, *Intertextuality: Debates and Contexts* (Cambridge: Polity, 2003), 6–7, 20–2, 24–7, 31–3, 66–7; also my *Reading the Allegorical Intertext*, 2–4.

Troilus and Criseyde's love. Of course the situation in *Amoretti* 46 differs to begin with, since it is the male speaker whom the rain urges to stay against the lady's wish, and as the sonnet continues, any similarity to the *Troilus* disappears, to be replaced by a humorous complaint hovering between overblown exasperation and self-pity. The lady having declined the speaker's desire to linger until the rain relents, the speaker seeks mercy instead from above:

> But ye high hevens, that all this sorowe see,
>   sith all your tempests cannot hold me backe:
> aswage your stormes, or else both you and she,
>   will both together me too surely wrack.
> Enough it is for one man to sustaine
>   the stormes, which she alone on me doth raine. (9–14)

By the end, the rainstorm outside has been matched and surpassed by the thunderclouds of the lady. For an irreverent moment, a reader with Chaucer already in mind might even be distracted by a ludic memory of the Wife of Bath's Prologue: 'But "Er that thunder stynte, comth a reyn."' The Wife's Prologue refers to the well-known anecdote that the angry Xanthippe, Socrates's wife, emptied a chamber pot over his head.[20]

To set the ludic aside and instead to observe the obvious, the *Amoretti* is a Petrarchan sequence about enamourment and courtship; this basic similarity between it and the *Troilus* is a given. Momentarily, a less generic and more striking resemblance occurs with the rainstorms. Until I had reread the *Troilus* for this chapter, what I remembered of relevance were the rainstorm and the consumation. Whether a largely contrasting memory is triggered in whole or in part by Spenser's rainstorm, however, his sonnet is the beneficiary. The Spenserian poet's disappointment, frustration and sympathetic comedy are magnified by contrast with Troilus's good fortune. The recollection therefore answers to a requirement I assume for an active, intertextual relationship, namely, that it have a meaningful function, which here is to heighten comic contrast, which the ludic memory of Xanthippe reinforces. I note in passing that two comments in the Spenser *Variorum* take the rainstorm as 'an actual incident', that is, an autobiographical one, expressive of 'the other side of Petrarchism', which, I imagine, means 'faithful to reality'.[21] I can only wonder whether the *Variorum* commentators remembered the *Troilus*, and, if they did, what sort of expression they took its rainstorm to be. I hope not 'reality'. Surely, Spenser's rainstorm has a significance more artful and cultural as comedic contrast than as autobiography.

---

20 Benson, ed., 729–32 (32); Geoffrey Chaucer, *Workes of Geffray Chaucer*, ed. William Thynne (London: Thomas Godfray, 1532), fol. xliii^v. For the same popular anecdote, see William Shakespeare, *The Taming of the Shrew*, I.ii.71, in *The Riverside Shakespeare*, ed. G. Blakemore Evans et al. (Boston: Houghton Mifflin, 1997). See also my discussion of 'clusters of recollection' in the following pages, as well as Helen Barr's chapter in this volume, which offers a plethora of irreverent memories of Chaucer in Spenser.
21 Greenlaw et al., eds, VIII, 435.

Close enough to Spenser's rainy forty-sixth sonnet to strengthen its reminiscence of the *Troilus*, his forty-fourth sonnet begins, 'When those renoumed noble Peres of Greece, / thrugh stubborn pride amongst themselves did jar' (1–2). Aware of Spenser's recurrent engagement of Trojan matter, I fully expect to hear next about the siege of Troy, only to discover that the quarrelsome peers are the Argonauts, 'forgetfull of the famous golden fleece' (3). This correction fails to cancel my momentary recollection of the Trojan war, however: simply put, it has happened. Once it has, it contains a strange pertinence to this war and specifically to Chaucer's *Troilus* if a reader is up on her Trojan matter. In Patterson's telling, Benoît's *Roman de Troie* is 'the authoritative version of Trojan history' for the Middle Ages.[22] It opens with the story of the Argonauts' effort to gain the golden fleece, in which lies the origin of the Trojan War. Briefly, the Trojan King Laomedon refuses hospitality to the Argonauts, and in time his refusal leads to the vengeful destruction of Troy by Hercules, Jason's companion. Then Laomedon's son Priam, the father of Troilus, rebuilds Troy and tries to reinstate its honour by getting his abducted sister back from the Greeks and, having failed to recover her, by assenting to the retaliatory abduction of Helen, the background ever-present in Chaucer's *Troilus*.[23] All this is a long preamble to the working of memory when Spenser's forty-sixth sonnet opens soon after his forty-fourth with a rainstorm recalling the one in the *Troilus* and then goes on to the lady's refusal of hospitality, which just happens to be King Laomedon's fatal error, too. But these associations are not incredible either for a memory stocked with antique rolls or for the maze-like overlays of myth in Spenser's writing. For the latter, a handy example might be the mythic genealogy of the Blatant Beast as it bears on events throughout Book V.[24] For the former, the mnemonic scrine, let me invoke the mnemonic commonplace that the use of a word increases the likelihood of its recurrence soon after; this is a phenomenon with authority in editing and psycho-linguistic study, not to mention experience. Here, I would extend the same likelihood of recurrence to contexts and figures – in this instance, the story of Troy in the sonnets beginning first with the Argonauts and then with the rainstorm.

---

22 Patterson, 115–16.
23 See Guido delle Colonne, *Historia destructionis Troiae*, trans. George A. Panton and David Donaldson, EETS 39, 56 (London: Oxford University Press, 1968), opening of Book 2, 12–13; also Patterson, 115–16. An alternative tradition offers as the cause of the first destruction of Troy Hercules' anger at Laomedon's reneging on a promise to award him the magic horses bestowed by Zeus: see Oskar Seyffert, *Dictionary of Classical Antiquities*, rev. and ed. Henry Nettleship and J.E. Sandys (Cleveland: World, 1956; repr. 1963), 343 (Laomedon), 61–3 (Argonauts).
24 E.g. '*Orthrus*', the 'two-headed dogge' associated with Geryoneo in *FQ* V is begot of 'Typhaon', begetter of unfavourable winds and god of evil. Typhon also kills Osiris, god of justice, who is associated with Artegall. Echidna, mother of Orthrus, is also mother both of the beast that Arthur kills in *FQ* V.x and of the Blatant Beast (Natalis Comes, *Mythologiae sive Explicationis Fabularum, Libri decem* [Geneva, 1651], 679 [Bk. vii.i]; Henry Gibbons Lotspeich, *Classical Mythology in the Poetry of Edmund Spenser*, 2nd edn [New York, 1965], 56, 63, 113). Yet Hercules 'them all did overcome in fight' (*FQ* V.x.9–10), and Artegall is a type of Hercules, the Justicer. Artegall does not defeat the Beast, although Calidore does, but only temporarily. The cyclical implication of limitless repetition in the myths is clear and ominous, much as is the Theban matter recurrently recollected in Chaucer's Troy (Patterson, 130, 132–6).

The next sonnet in the *Amoretti* sequence I'll consider is the seventy-eighth, which resonates with Troilus's behaviour when Criseyde has gone from Troy:

> Lackying my love I go from place to place,
>   lyke a young fawne that late hath lost the hynd:
> and seeke each where, where last I sawe her face,
>   whose ymage yet I carry fresh in mynd.
> I seeke the fields with her late footing synd,
>   I seeke her bowre with her last presence deckt,
> yet nor in field nor bowre I her can fynd:
>   yet field and bowre are full of her aspect.
> But when myne eyes I thereunto direct,
>   they idly back returne to me agayne,
>   and when I hope to see theyr trew object,
> I fynd my selfe but fed with fancies vayne [...] (1–12)

More than one passage in the final book of the *Troilus* is memorable in relation to this sonnet, but I'll settle for the one that follows on Troilus's return from Sarpedon's feasts. He goes to the street on which stands Criseyde's empty house and sees 'hir dores spered alle' and 'How shet was every window of the place' (V.531, 534). His face turns deadly pale, and 'frost him thoughte his herte gan to colde' (V.535). Then he addresses the house, now also called a palace:

> O palais desolat,
> O house of houses, whilom best ylight,
> O palais empty and disconsolat,
> O thou lanterne of which queint is the light,
> O palais whilom day, that now art night,
> Wel oughtestou to falle, and I to die,
> Sin she is went that wont was us to gie. (V.540–6)[25]

Troilus's complaint continues in this woeful vein for another stanza. What makes it resonate with Spenser's sense of loss is the sonnet's second quatrain, 'I seeke the fields [...] I seeke her bowre [...] yet nor in field nor bowre I her can fynd', which is certainly not a verbal match, yet in simple ways is also similar. The very fact of a familiar location, now estranged; the specificity of a dwelling and of its environs, the latter for Troilus a town and for Spenser the fields, are crucial to this sense. The intensity of lack and longing, in both instances heightened by highly rhythmic and verbal repetition, might well play the most notable, mnemonic part, notwithstanding Troilus's emotional outpouring and Spenser's reflective, pastoral lyricism: 'I seeke the fields with her late footing synd, / I seeke her bowre with her last presence deckt.'

Commenting on this same sonnet, the *Variorum* typically cites Petrarch, Horace and, predictably, for Spenser's final couplet concerning an interior image,

---

25 In Thynne, ed., fol. ccxi[r], my previous citation is found on the same page.

a neoplatonising source; this couplet reads, 'Ceasse then myne eyes, to seeke her selfe to see, / and let my thoughts behold her selfe in mee' (13–14). Equally relevant for this sonnet, whose octave expresses bodily longing, is what Troilus does long before he has made any headway with Criseyde: 'Thus gan he make a mirour of his minde, / In which he sawgh al hooly hir figure.' Like Spenser's speaker, Troilus goes on to find some comfort in the fact 'that he wel coude in his herte finde [...] To love swich oon' (I.365–9).[26] Spenser's speaker might well be on his way to neoplatonic sublation, but if we have been listening to sonnet 78, his sudden expression of it in the last two lines lacks emotional credibility, a lack the more substantially figured Chaucerian memory heightens, illuminates and resonantly enriches, simultaneously by similarity and by contrast. Logically and structurally, Kristevan intertextuality, 'the reconstitutive synergies of text[s]', expresses the doubleness of metaphorical relationship, being at once quite the same and quite different.[27] Dimock's diachronism observes a similar doubleness, albeit never to the exclusion of other, seemingly limitless possibilities.

Another reason for hearing the *Troilus* in Spenser's sonnet 78 comes in sonnet 79, associatively but ironically with a full dose of neoplatonism. Although resemblance to the *Troilus* is verbal this time, the *Variorum* refers us to Desportes, Tasso, Ariosto, Buoni and a host of cross-referenced others, but not to Chaucer. As elsewhere, my point is not that all such commentary is mistaken but that editorial bias has often depreciated or denied the importance of the English Middle Ages to writers of the English high Renaissance. Sources and analogues like the *Variorum*'s need hardly be abandoned, but they cannot exclude a verbal parallel in English in a medieval poem known to be familiar to Spenser. This time, the evidence is incontrovertible.

The seventy-ninth sonnet devalues the lady's 'fayre' (1) appearance and 'glorious hew' (6), on both of which the lady prides herself. The speaker supersedes these outer qualities with what alone 'is permanent and free / from frayle corruption, that doth flesh ensew' (7–8). But unlike Troilus and his narrator at the end, Spenser's lover gets to keep the living lady even as he raises his eyes to 'true beautie', which is 'divine and borne of heavenly seed' (9–10). He derives the lady's inner qualities, her 'gentle wit, / and vertuous mind' (3–4) from 'that fayre Spirit, from whom al true / and perfect beauty did at first proceed' (11–12), the kind of thing the idealistic Troilus had a go at earlier and might have been willing to try again if Lady Fortune and Criseyde had not betrayed him so mercilessly. Of course the 'fayre Spirit' to whom Spenser's lover refers is God, and his concluding couplet wraps up the matter: 'He onely *fayre*, and what he *fayre* hath made, / all other *fayre* lyke *flowres* untymely fade' (13–14, my emphasis).

Spenser's couplet recalls another that concludes a poignant stanza at the end of Chaucer's *Troilus*, in which the narrator advises 'younge fresshe folkes' to turn their hearts 'fro worldly *vanitee*' to God and to think 'al nis but a *faire*, / This world that passeth soone as *flowres faire*' (V.1835–41, my emphasis).[28] Talbot Donaldson's grasp of the simple, resonant affect of Chaucer's concluding couplet

---

26 Ibid., fol. clxxii^r.
27 See Orr, 31 (citation); Anderson, *Allegorical Intertext*, 2–3.
28 Thynne, ed., fol. ccxviii^v.

is unsurpassed: 'All the illusive loveliness of a world which is man's only reality is expressed in the very lines that reject that loveliness.'[29] The final couplet of this stanza is the one that Spenser recollects again in the final stanzas of the Mutabilitie Cantos, in which he, like Chaucer's narrator, reflects on the *transitoriness* of this *vain* world, recalling earthly pleasure and beauty even as he renounces it:

> Which makes me loath this state of life so tickle
> And loue of things so *vaine* to cast away;
> Whose *flowring* pride, *so fading and so fickle*,
> Short Time shall soon cut down with his consuming sickle
> (VII.viii, my emphasis)[30]

Given the echo in the *Amoretti* of Chaucer's couplet about fading flowers, another of Chaucer's lines in the same stanza gains added resonance. Intertextuality, as distinct from chronological influence, can be mutual, working both ways: Chaucer's earlier line refers to the young lovers in whom 'love up groweth with youre age' (V.1836), and by 'up groweth' means 'increases', but when recalled by a reader of sonnet 79, it also suggests 'matures'. The middle-aged lover of the *Amoretti* and the reflective poet of Mutabilitie are distanced from the youthful Troilus in a way young Colin was not in *The Shepheardes Calender*, but Chaucer's stanza still resounds in the scrine of the older Spenser: the 'antique rolles [...] lye hidden *still*' (I.Pro.2, my emphasis) – motionlessly, silently, yet always awaiting renewed life.

The resonance of the *Troilus* in the *Amoretti* is cumulative, both locally and over its course. Spenser's memories of it can be so assimilative as to be hard to distinguish. This is so in *The Faerie Queene*, as well. Spenser seems to have lived with the *Troilus* to the extent that it became part of himself. What now draws my attention are *clusters of recollection* in *The Faerie Queene* whose very clustering persuasively indicates authorial awareness, significance and allusion. A familiar cluster occurs in Prince Arthur's account of his falling in love with the Fairy Queen. His story alludes openly to Chaucer's *Tale of Sir Thopas* and also includes a proverb from the Wife of Bath's Prologue. Both are startling connections for the idealistic love of the Prince whose virtue '*is the perfection of all the rest, and conteineth in it them all*'.[31] More decorously, Arthur's story further includes strong, pervasive reminiscences of the *Troilus*. Like Chaucer's, Spenser's love-stricken

---

29 E. Talbot Donaldson, *Speaking of Chaucer* (London: Athlone, 1970), 98. See also Carruthers's rejection of 'Troilus's disembodied laughter' as 'too cold, too dispassionate, too pagan and Stoic to be wholly true' and her embrace of the narrator's tearful truth at the end (13–14).
30 To emphasise the ambiguity of these lines, I have omitted the comma after 'tickle'; the result is 'things so vain, love so vain, so vainly to cast'; the word 'loath' is also ambiguous (either 'loath' or 'loathe'), as is the word 'pride' (the natural 'splendour' of trees or flowers in bloom or sinful vanity). The authority of punctuation, as well as spelling, in an early seventeenth-century text is notoriously unreliable and likely to be that of the printing house. The Mutabilitie Cantos were also published posthumously, an additional removal from authorial sanction. The last line cited in my text also carries a memory of Spenser's Garden of Adonis (III.vi.39). For a description of the 1609 edition of *The Faerie Queene*, in which the Mutabilitie Cantos were first printed, see William Proctor Williams, 'bibliography, critical', in *The Spenser Encyclopedia*, 92–3 (92).
31 'Letter to Ralegh', Hamilton, ed., 716 (39).

prince is 'in freshest flowre of youthly yeares, / When corage first does creepe in manly cheste' (I.ix.9). He is not yet the mature king better known to history, whose flaws contribute to the failure of his kingdom. Spenser's prince, like Chaucer's before his enamourment, has 'euer scornd' the 'ydle name of loue, and louers life, / As losse of time, and vertues enimy' and has

> ioyd to stirre vp strife,
> In middest of their mournfull Tragedy,
> Ay wont to laugh, when them [he] heard to cry,
> And blow the fire, which them to ashes brent. (I.ix.10)

In the context of Arthur's mockery, the lovers' 'mournfull Tragedy' recalls Chaucer's generic designation of the *Troilus*, as 'myn tragedye' (V.1786), but this parallel pales next to others. Chaucer's Troilus, assessing the ladies of Troy with critical detachment, eyes his companions for signs of eros and scoffs if he detects any: 'O verray fooles, nice and blinde be ye' (I.202).[32] Once smitten by love of Criseyde, he, like Arthur after him, also decries his earlier jests about 'loves paine' and imagines that others will now 'Laughen in scorn, and sayn, "Lo, ther gooth he / That [...] heeld us loveres leest in reverence!"' (I.508, 514–16).[33]

Cupid exacts his due from Troilus and Arthur in similar language and imagery. Arthur, having declared himself 'mated' by Cupid – that is, 'checkmated', a favourite Chaucerian term from chess meaning 'matched' or 'confounded' – adds that this vengeful love-god 'Did soone *pluck* downe' his pride and '*curbd*' his liberty (I.ix.12, my emphasis). In Chaucer, Troilus is 'as proud a pecok' as Cupid might 'pulle', that is, 'pluck' (I.210, 218–24), and he is also compared to a frisky horse in need of restraint or, in Spenser's equine word, of curbing.[34] We can sometimes miss echoes of Chaucer in Spenser simply because modernising – linguistic translation – has occurred. Naturally, it is also spring when Troilus first sees Criseyde and Arthur first finds his elf Queen.[35] A similarity so conventional is insignificant in itself but adds additional texture to an already resonant cluster.

Elsewhere, treating memories of Chaucer in Arthur's tale of enamourment, I have focused on Sir Thopas, notorious knight prickant. The sense I've made of the Chaucerian echoes in this cluster has brought out the delicate layering of parody that underlies Arthur's ideal vision and deepens its humanity. Instead of just mocking the vision, this parody asks that we see it in relation to human reality. Possibility and failure alike abide in the Spenserian echo chamber. Concentrating now on the *Troilus*, I can add to my earlier argument. The shadow of infidelity, unhappiness and betrayal that the 'tragedye' of Troilus casts over Arthur's

---

32 See I.339–50; Thynne, ed., fol. clxxi[r], clxxii[r].
33 Thynne, ed., fol. clxxiii[r].
34 Ibid., fol. clxxi[r].
35 The word 'spring' does not occur in Arthur's account, but his enamourment takes place 'in freshest flowre of youthly yeares' when 'first that cole of kindly heat appeares' (I.ix.9); it is a time when 'The fields, the floods, the heauens with one consent / Did seeme to laugh on me, and fauour mine intent' (12). Further coding the fateful day as the springtime of life and the year is the conspicuously 'verdant gras' (13). This is the traditional 'reverdie', the time of regreening.

idealised love is a long one. At this stage of the poem, it is only a shadow, whose meaning is limited: mainly, Arthur's enamourment alludes to the beginning, not the end, of Troilus's love. The shadow of this end is nonetheless there, and it comes with questions about fortune and free will, about the oppressive dominance of the historical cycle and the possibilities despite and beyond it, such as they are, all of which are prominent in Chaucer's poem. Arthur's language, even at this early stage of Spenser's epic, recalls these questions when he acknowledges his uncertainty as to the cause of his being in 'Fary land', whether 'th'eternall might, / That rules mens waies' has sent him there 'through fatal deepe foresight [...] / Or' the 'fresh bleeding wound' of eros that rankles in his 'riuen brest' has done so (I.ix.6–7).[36] Ideally, both, I should think, but this is not what Arthur's word 'Or' has indicated. The relation of human eros to eternity – of the rankling heart-wound to 'fatal deepe foresight' – is what, in a real sense, he has been brought to Fairy Land to seek. Focusing too exclusively on the idealism of his figure, we have not really listened to the extent to which he is the patron of fatalistic gloom, which strikes another resonant chord with the 'double sorwe', recurrent woes and apostrophes to furies, fates and fortune in the *Troilus* (I.Pro.1). A mere dozen stanzas before Arthur recounts his enamourment, right after he has redeemed the Redcross Knight from Orgoglio's dungeon, he has endorsed the view 'Deepe written' in his 'heart with yron pen, / That blisse may not abide in state of mortall men' (I.viii.44).

On this note, I'll turn to Arthur's loss of Florimell in the fourth canto of Book III, where the Prince seems to have forgotten his earlier resignation. He wildly hopes, indeed fantasises, that the fleeing Florimell he pursues is his elf Queen, now close enough to hear his unheeded call. Florimell is a figure of desire, whatever else she is, and her disappearance is his invitation to despair. The canto that ends with Arthur's complaint to night when she is gone begins with Britomart's complaint to the sea. His concluding complaint recalls Britomart's by word, image and lovelorn longing. Both Arthur and Britomart are 'lineally extract' (III.ix.38) from distant Trojan forebears: small world.[37] Treating Chaucerian memories in this canto elsewhere, I have focused on the *Franklin's Tale*, and to a lesser extent on *Sir Thopas*.[38] But both the complaints that frame it – Britomart's and Arthur's – allude strongly to the *Troilus* as well, thus participating in another concentrated *cluster* of Chaucerian material.

Britomart's complaint addresses the 'Huge sea of sorrow' (III.iv.8) inside her, which mirrors the tempestuous waves outside and threatens her destruction. She imagines herself as a boat rowed by fortune, steered by her 'lewd Pilott' love, sailing without 'starres, gainst tyde and winde', and nearly shipwrecked on the rocks (III. iv.9). Her complaint derives from Petrarch's sonnet 189, along with Chaucerian

---

36 On Arthur's enamourment and search, in which David Lee Miller perceives a 'tragic dignity', see *The Poem's Two Bodies: The Poetics of the 1590 'Faerie Queene'* (Princeton: Princeton University Press, 1988), 7–8.
37 See also II.x.9, III.iii.27.
38 See Anderson, *Allegorical Intertext*, 69–78, 139–43.

texts and the Bible.³⁹ Petrarch's sonnet is also Englished by Wyatt and by Surrey and widely known before Spenser's time. Images of storm and shipwreck like those in the tradition informing Britomart's complaint are further associated, via the Vulgate's Psalm 101 and the 'profundum marum' of its Psalm 67, with the abyss of despair. Other versions of them recur in *The Faerie Queene*, pertinently later in this same canto, and in *Amoretti* 34. In the *Troilus*, the Prince's love song in Book I, which translates Petrarch's sonnet 132, has related imagery, which is common in the Middle Ages:

> thus possed to and fro,
> Al stereless within a boot am I
> Amidde the see, bitwixen windes two,
> That in contrarye stonden evermo. (I.415–18)⁴⁰

Troilus's complaint comes amid his efforts to reconcile the pangs of love he now experiences for the first time with his earlier scorn for lovers. Reflecting Troilus's sorrow, Chaucer's narrator draws on the same tradition linking sea, boat, and despair at the outset of Book II:

> Out of thise blake wawes for to saile,
> O wind, O wind, the weder ginneth clere,
> For in this see the boot hath swich travaile
> Of my conning that unnethe I it steere:
> This see clepe I the tempestous matere
> Of desespair that Troilus was inne. (II.1–6)⁴¹

Similarly, Arthur, having lost sight of Florimell with nightfall, strays like 'a ship, whose Lodestar suddeinly / Couered with cloudes, her Pilott has dismayd' (III.iv.53). Cursing the darkness, he wishes the while that Florimell might be his Queen or that this Queen 'were such, as shee' (III.iv.54), a wish whose meaning is as elusive as Florimell herself. Rather than sleep, he 'outweare[s]' the 'wearie' hours complaining to Night (III.iv.54, 61). Hamilton observes that Arthur 'inverts the usual complaint on the brevity of night' in an *aubade* and cites, if only as examples, the paired complaints of Criseyde and Troilus, the morning after the consummation of their love.⁴² The relation between Chaucer's and Spenser's texts is stronger and more significant than Hamilton's note indicates.

---

39 Susan Snyder, 'The Left Hand of God: Despair in Medieval and Renaissance Tradition', *Studies in the Renaissance*, 12 (1965), 18–59 (18, 54, 68). Snyder specifies Augustine's commentary on Psalm 101 and Gregory's *Moralia* for the imagery of storm and shipwreck. Augustine, Chrysostom, Gregory, Bernard and Bonaventura are among those referring to despair as a deep abyss (related is the image of despair as a prison). I have combined 'profundum marum' and abyss, perhaps the most common image of despair. In connection with Britomart's sea imagery, Hamilton, ed. (323) cites Psalm 69:15 (the Vulgate's 68:16), which is clearly related as well.
40 Thynne, ed., fol. clxxii^r.
41 Ibid., fol. clxxvi^v.
42 Hamilton, ed., 330, note on 55–60.

Troilus's *aubade* predictably decries the arrival of cruel, envious, '*Despitous* day', wishing on it the 'paine of *helle*' and chiding *Titan* for not having enough sense *to linger in bed with the dawn*, thereby resisting the natural, diurnal cycle (III.1450, 1454, 1458, 1464–7, my emphasis to heighten resonance).[43] In contrast, Arthur wishes for day, yet his rhetoric distantly resonates with Troilus's: he banishes deathly Night to *hell*, there to dwell with 'Black Herebus *thy husband*' (III.iv.55, my emphasis), god of darkness and foe of all the other gods.[44] The penultimate stanza of his complaint envisions the coming day with all that light conveys in sacred writ: this is a biblical day when truth will triumph. His final stanza then subsides to a wish, in contrast, but resonant contrast, with Troilus's, a plea that *Titan* might haste to

> chace away this too long *lingring* night,
> Chace her away, from whence she came, to *hell*,
> She, she it is, that hath me done *despight* (III.iv.60, my emphasis to heighten resonances)

In the murky light before sunrise, Arthur then returns to his quest, never more to see an avatar of its object.

Criseyde's complaint is to darkness and Night, surely an ominous sign for any biblical allegorist. Unlike Arthur's wish but in rhetoric anticipating Troilus's, she asks night to linger ('hove[n]') 'As longe as whan Almena lay by Jove', immediately before launching into her complaint (1428):

> O blacke night, as folk in bookes rede,
> That shapen art by God this world to hide
> At certain times with thy derke weede,
> That under that men mighte in reste abide,
> Wel oughten beestes plaine and folk thee chide,
> That ther as day with labour wolde us breste,
> That thou fleest, and deinest us noghte reste. (III.1429–35)[45]

Accusing night of haste and 'unkinde vice', she wishes that 'God, Makere of Kinde' might bind its darkness so firmly to the hemisphere in which she lives that it would never interrupt her joy by revolving 'under the grounde': her phrasing

---

43 Benson, ed., notes that the confusion of Titan with Tithonus, the husband of Aurora, in Troilus's complaint was not without precedent in the Middle Ages (1043, note on III.1464). Aurora was actually the daughter of Titan; in view of Benson's note, I find the supposition of incest in Chaucer's or Criseyde's error silly. Benson's note might obscure the point evident in both Troilus and Criseyde's *aubades* that their desire to undo the natural order, however understandable, does carry moral hazard. Compare Dorigen's desire to have the black rocks disappear in Chaucer's *Franklin's Tale*. Spenser's Arthur has a similarly unnatural desire, in his case to banish night, as I subsequently argue. (See my *Allegorical Intertext*, 71–3, on Dorigen's desire.) Both the intertextuality and resonance of texts are potentially multiple, not necessarily limited to doubleness, as discussed in the final paragraph of the present chapter.
44 Hamilton, ed., 194, note on II.iv.41.
45 Thynne, ed., fol. clxxxxv^{r-v}, my next citation is on the same page.

inadvertently suggests and defies both burial and a natural cycle (1437–42). Notably in her complaint, the unending night of joy she envisions is ungendered.[46]

Arthur's complaint has more of Criseyde than Troilus in it, but it is a rebuttal of hers. It is conspicuously gendered. His opening apostrophe is to 'Night thou foule Mother of annoyaunce sad, / Sister of heaue death, and nourse of woe', and he demands to know why 'th'eternall Maker' (III.iv.55–6) had need of Night at all, thus questioning the natural order. He consigns her praise to the slothful body and the baser mind, who benightedly call her 'Dame Nature's handmaid, chearing euery kind' (III.iv.56). He continues, in direct contravention of Criseyde, 'In stead of rest thou lendest rayling teares […] And dreadfull visions', and he concludes, 'from the wearie spirit thou doest driue / Desired rest, and men of happiness depriue' (III.iv.57). Picking up on Criseyde's charge that Night is guilty of 'unkinde vice' – unnatural vice – he changes its intent from the curtailment of love to the defacing of beauty. Seemingly chafed by her recognition that men 'in reste abide' under night's 'derke weede', or cloak, Arthur really lets go:

> Vnder thy mantle black there hidden lye,
>   Light-shonning theft, and traiterous intent,
> Abhorred bloodshed, and vile felony,
>   Shamefull deceipt, and daunger imminent […] (III.iv.58)

And more: 'For light ylike is loth'd of them and thee, / And all that lewdnesse loue, doe hate the light to see' (III.iv.58). Eventually, however, Arthur recognises that the loss of Florimell accounts for his railing (III.iv.57). In reflecting another text, his figure is thus also self-reflexive, dyspeptically aware of why he speaks as he does: 'But well I wote, that to an heauy hart', he admits to Night, 'Thou art the […] nourse of bitter cares' (III.iv.57).[47] His emotional complaint against the natural order rises out of frustrated desire. Like Troilus and Criseyde's complaints about the natural order, his complaint is morally hazardous but also sympathetically human.

---

46 As evident in my following citations of Arthur's complaint, Night is female, as is Nature. While the feminine declension in Latin bears on the attribution of gender to common nouns in English during the medieval and Renaissance periods, there is also evidence of an increasing tendency in the Renaissance to attribute social significance (morality, gender, economic status) to stylistics, for example to metrics (e.g. feminine endings) and tropology (e.g. metaphor). On the latter, see Judith H. Anderson, *Translating Investments: Metaphor and the Dynamic of Cultural Change in Tudor-Stuart England* (New York: Fordham University Press, 2005), e.g. 159, 164; on the former, see Maureen Quilligan, 'Feminine Endings: The Sexual Politics of Sidney's Rhyming', in *The Renaissance Englishwoman in Print: Counterbalancing the Canon* (Amherst: University of Massachusetts Press, 1990), 311–26; David Scott Wilson-Okamura opposes arguments for the gendered significance of rhyming: *Spenser's International Style* (Cambridge: Cambridge University Press, 2013), 16, 161–73; Richard Danson Brown's view is more sympathetic: '"Charmed with inchaunted rimes": An Introduction to the *Faerie Queene* Rhymes Concordance', in *A Concordance to the Rhymes of The Faerie Queene*, ed. Richard Danson Brown and J.B. Lethbridge (Manchester: Manchester University Press, 2013), 1–75 (21–3, 48–50, 56–7).

47 See Bruno Snell regarding Homeric similes: a 'man must listen to an echo of himself before he may hear or know himself': *The Discovery of the Mind: The Greek Origins of European Thought*, trans. T.G. Rosenmeyer (New York: Harper and Bros., 1953; repr. 1960), 200–1. Snell has reference to a rock (i.e. hardness) in mind: 'our understanding of the rock is anthropomorphic for the same

The sequel of Arthur's complaint – I would like to say of his rebutting Criseyde – is no further development of his erotic quest after Book III.[48] Spenser seems to lose interest in it, partly displacing it by the lyrics of the *Amoretti*, which intervene chronologically between Books III and IV. Arthur continues to appear in each book after the third, but erotic questing effectually passes to other figures, especially to Britomart in her quest for Artegall, one meaning of whose name is 'equal to Arthur'. Britomart, we know, descends from a Trojan past, a feature of her ancestry that Spenser emphasises in Book III (ix). Artegall, another Briton and a half-brother of Arthur, has a Trojan past, too. Artegall also wears the armour of the Greek Achilles, which '*Arthegall did win*' (III.ii.25), presumably an allusion to Hector's killing the disguised Patroclus, which gave the Trojans possession of Achilles' armour. But within this cryptic allusion lies another, to a contest about Greek bravery that was decided by Trojan prisoners, who awarded Achilles' replacement-armour to Odysseus.[49] Artegall's armor, like half-brother Arthur's, thus comes with another long shadow, with complications of victory and loss and of *virtù* and *fortuna*.[50] Arthur's armor is in Fairy Land, as we were told in Book I, because he has already died.[51]

Additionally, the Grecian associations of Artegall's armour carry a whiff of betrayal and self-betrayal, connecting both him and Britomart with Spenser's character Dolon, named after the Trojan who betrayed his own side to the Greeks. Britomart, en route to rescue her imprisoned lover, Artegall, must confront and foil Dolon's guile and treachery, as she does, eliminating Dolon's sons but, noticeably, not Dolon himself (V.vi).[52] With pointed irony, Dolon had initially mistaken Britomart for Artegall, thus implicating them together in his designs. The matter of Troy, which particularly means *Troilus and Criseyde* for any English poet after Chaucer, is for Spenser still fatally, inextricably intertwined with the matter of love, both in lyric and epic.

Thinking of lyric and epic together, while hardly unprecedented, is unconventional. It indicates that our generic taxonomies, which are historical, useful and variously meaningful, should not be rigid with respect to the Elizabethan period, not to mention the medieval one. When based on the ancient genres, Elizabethan forms of them, like Elizabethan tropes, could be loose, mixed and radically variable. They were still alive and evolving.

The doubleness and potentially the greater multiplicity of intertextual and resonant relationships greatly enrich, extend and modify specific texts. Yet they also

---

    reason that we are able to look at ourselves petromorphically' (201). A literary text can offer the same dynamic.
48 Arthur's quest is briefly mentioned in Book IV.ix.17 (3 lines) and in Book VI.viii.30 (half a line). Neither instance is developed, and the latter (also the last) is downright perfunctory.
49 On the awarding of Achilles' armour, see Seyffert, 21: 'Aias'. Trojan prisoners of the Greeks were asked to decide whether their side has been damaged more by Odysseus' bravery or by that of Ajax. They awarded the armour to Odysseus.
50 On Arthur's armour, see Anderson, *Allegorical Intertext*, 126–34.
51 See *FQ* I.vii.36; for discussion, Anderson, *Allegorical Intertext*, 130–1.
52 On Dolon's name, see Hamilton, ed., 551, note on V.vi.32.1.

raise questions about their bearing on textual context, historical situation, interpretative validity and, ultimately, on reason and rational limits, as the title of Veit Erlmann's book on aurality, *Reason and Resonance*, signals. With respect to intertextuality, whose roots are linguistic, such questions have often focused on the possibilities of, and restraints on, what has come to be known as unlimited semiosis – unfettered, associative wordplay. The word-concept *resonance* – like tone and textuality, a metaphor when applied to a written text – raises questions of difference, as well as of similarity; consider *reverberation* as a more linguistic, if also related, alternative. Erlmann, an enlightened foe of binary opposition, refers 'resonance' to electrical circuits and molecular signals, as well as more familiarly to the sympathetically vibrating strings of musical instruments, but he does so without overlooking significant distinctions among domains of experience and existence.[53] I re-emphasise the word *significant*, which returns the reader of verbal texts to their analysis and interpretation and therefore to specific evidence for the mnemonic web, fabric or network that is heard, seen and holistically experienced in literature.

---

53 Erlmann, 9–12.

2

'Litle herd gromes piping in the wind':
The Shepheardes Calender, *The House of Fame* and 'La Compleynt'

Helen Barr

When seasoned Thenot in the 'February' eclogue of *The Shepheardes Calender* rebukes green Cuddie for his lack of endurance against the blasts of winter he leaves his jejune companion with 'the sound of [an] aunctient Poete [...] ringing in his eares':[1]

> The soveraigne of seas he blames in vaine,
> That once seabeate, will to sea againe.
> So loytring live you little heardgroomes,
> Keeping your beastes in the budded broomes:
> And when the shining sunne laugheth once,
> You deemen, the Spring is come attonce.
> Tho gynne you, fond flyes, the cold to scorne,
> And crowing in pypes made of greene corne,
> You thinken to be Lords of the yeare. ('February', 33–41)

Lest our literary ears prove clothful, E.K. supplies a gloss: 'Chaucers verse almost whole.' No work is named, and the quantity of 'Chaucer's verse' sounded in this section of Spenser's *The Shepheardes Calender* remains unspecified. Critical editions of the *Calender* supply the missing details: 34–5 and 40 reprise these lines from Chaucer's *House of Fame*:

> And pipes made of grene corn,
> As han thise lytel herde-gromes
> That kepen bestis in the bromes. (*The House of Fame*, 1224–6)[2]

To a more capacious literary ear, however, Thenot's chiding also sounds like a Chaucerian complaint poem that Chaucer did not write: 'La Compleynt'.

---

1 *The Shepheardes Calender*, dedicatory epistle, 40. All quotations from *The Shepheardes Calender* are from *The Yale Edition of the Shorter Poems of Edmund Spenser*, ed. William A. Oram *et al.* (New Haven and London: Yale University Press, 1989).
2 The reference in *The Yale Edition* of Spenser is on 49. All quotations from Chaucer are from *The Riverside Chaucer*, ed. Larry D. Benson *et al.*, 3rd rev. edn (Oxford: Oxford University Press, 2008).

Surviving in two fifteenth-century manuscripts, this anonymous poem concludes Lydgate's *The Temple of Glass*.³ 'La Compleynt' includes herdgrooms and brooms in a passage in praise of the daisy:

> Where as it doth so fayre sprede
> A-geyn the sunne in euery mede,
> On bankys hy a-mong the bromys,
> Wher as these lytylle herdegromys
> Floutyn al the longe day,
> Bothe in aprylle & in may,
> In her smale recorderys
> In floutys & in rede sperys,
> About this flour til it be nyght;
> It makyth hem so glad & light. ('La Compleynt', 415–24)⁴

Is Thenot, or Spenser, or E.K. recalling Chaucer, or Lydgate, or recalling an anonymous poet who sounds like Chaucer? 'La Compleynt' has no place for the beasts or green corn and the pipes are embellished into flutes, reeds and recorders. That said, the praise of the daisy collates a knowledge both of *The House of Fame* and of *The Prologue to the Legend of Good Women*; not just one Chaucer verse almost whole, but echoes of two poems spliced. It is by no means certain that E.K.'s gloss refers to Chaucer as readers know him from modern critical editions. For early modern copyists, however, neither the *Temple of Glass* nor 'La Compleynt' was clearly separable from Chaucer's oeuvre. Sixteenth-century consumers of medieval texts, Spenser amongst them, were not always able to tell Lydgate, or poets like him (or Chaucer), apart.⁵

---

3 Cambridge University Library MS Gg. 4. 27, fols. 458a to fol. 476b, see *A Facsimile of Cambridge University Library MS G.G. 4.27*, ed. M.B. Parkes and Richard Beadle (Cambridge: D.S. Brewer, 1980), 491–510. The start of *The Temple of Glass* is indicated by a flourished initial but 'La Compleynt' (copied by Scribe B), has no such rubrication. It is copied as if it were part of Lydgate's poem. The poem also survives in British Library Additional MS 16165, fol. 231b to fol. 241b which was copied by John Shirley. It also follows a version of Lydgate's *Temple of Glass* without interruption. Chaucer's *Anelida* comes after. For textual discussion of Chaucer, Lydgate and Chaucerian additions in these manuscripts, see *Fifteenth-Century English Dream Visions: An Anthology*, ed. Julia Boffey (Oxford: Oxford University Press, 2003), 18–23; Seth Lerer, *Chaucer and his Readers: Imagining the Author in Late-Medieval England* (Princeton: Princeton University Press, 1993), 117–46; Eleanor P. Hammond, 'Omissions from the Editions of Chaucer', *Modern Language Notes*, 19 (1904), 35–8, and Ralph Hanna, 'John Shirley and British Library, MS Additional 16165', *Studies in Bibliography*, 49 (1996), 95–105.
4 The text of 'La Compleynt' is quoted from *Lydgate's Temple of Glass*, ed. J. Schick (EETS ES 60 1891), 59–67.
5 Julia Boffey argues that Lydgate's annexation of Chaucerian vocabulary and style was as much responsible for the Chaucerian flavour of many fifteenth-century lyrics as was direct imbibing from the 'stremes hed' itself, 'The Reputation and Circulation of Chaucer's Lyrics in the Fifteenth Century', *Chaucer Review*, 28 (1993), 23–40. See also Kathleen Forni, *The Chaucerian Apocrypha: A Counterfeit Canon* (Gainesville: University Press of Florida, 2001), 36–67. Spenser's response to the early reception of Chaucer is discussed by John A. Burrow, 'Chaucer', in *The Spenser Encyclopedia*, ed. A.C. Hamilton *et al.* (Toronto: University of Toronto Press, 1990), 144–8. Cautioning that the canon of Chaucer's works that Spenser knew was different from our own, Burrow argues that no Elizabethan writer displays a closer relationship to Chaucer than Spenser. Coming to terms with Chaucer involved a mix of admiration, borrowing, genuine misunderstanding and independence.

What is a twenty-first-century literary critic to do with E.K.'s resonant claims? If we are to read Dan Geffrey along with the '[n]ewe poet', how are we to account for hearing not one, but at least two (or more?) poets simultaneously?[6] That the 'newe poet' tells us he wrote [*The Shepheardes Calender*] with the sound of 'aunciente Poetes still ringing in his ears' (dedicatory epistle, 37), issues a literary invitation to read Chaucer, Edmund and somebody else alongside each other democratically and inter-changeably. The 'new poete' asks us to hear the relationship between his work, and the work of his predecessors, as resonant sound. As Wai Chee Dimock argues, literary resonance permits the play of background noise and interference to recharge the soundscapes of intertextuality.[7] To hear the backing pipes of herdgrooms in poems before the *Calender* sets off a sound wave whose undertow is as important as its outward surge. Back and forth, these re-soundings collapse linear chronologies between medieval and early modern works; a resonance that transforms available readings between texts written nearly two hundred years apart.

Soundwaves lack the borders of words that are scripted and seen. With no visual record, claims to what is proper, whether of name or of inheritance, are harder to lodge. Although glossing is a visual phenomenon, the imprecision of E.K.'s supplementary commentary to these 'February' lines charts the truancy of literary resonance. As I shall argue, to have 'La Compleynt' ringing in your ears when encountering the 'February' eclogue, transmits a Spenserian Chaucer decorously appropriate to the serious endeavours of the *Calender*, and respectful to the Chaucerian 'auctor' that the sixteenth century made of him. The most seemly Chaucer for E.K.'s gloss turns out not to be Chaucer at all. But if we persist in hearing Chaucer's *House of Fame* as a sound source, then the literary ground becomes unruly. 'Chaucers verse almost whole' prompts retrieval of more of *The House of Fame* than *The Shepheardes Calender* expressly delivers. How much more of Chaucer's verse may we hear? Rather more, perhaps, than Spenser might have wanted.

'I suppose he mean Chaucer'

Chaucerian soundings bookend the *Calender*: its first words, '[g]oe little booke' (1), recall Chaucer's farewell to his book in *Troilus and Criseyde* (V.1786).[8] Spenser's

---

See also Kevin Pask, *The Emergence of the English Author: Scripting the Life of the Poet in Early Modern England* (Cambridge: Cambridge University Press, 1996), 29–36 and Anne Lake Prescott, 'Sources', in *A Critical Companion to Spenser Studies*, ed. Bart van Es (London: Palgrave Macmillan, 2006), 98–115. Alice S. Miskimin, *The Renaissance Chaucer* (New Haven and London: Yale University Press, 1975), 230–97 is especially insightful on the relationship between Chaucer and Spenser.

6 Helen Cooper notes that there are several poets in play here. Spenser borrowed these lines from *The House of Fame*, and 'Lydgate developed the musical idea further in his lines on the daisy', *Pastoral: Medieval into Renaissance* (Ipswich: Brewer, 1977), 56. Space prohibits consideration of Cooper's third poet: Gavin Douglas, whose 'silly scheip and thar litil hyrd gromys / Larkis under le of bankis, woddis and bromys' (*Aeneid*, Book VII, *Prologue*, 77–9). The lines form part of fabulously vigorous poetry on the progress of a calendrical year.

7 Wai Chee Dimock, 'A Theory of Resonance', *PMLA*, 112 (1997), 1060–71. My discussion is indebted to this article.

8 Lydgate reprises this envoy in *The Complaint of the Black Knight* '[g]o, litel quayre, go vn-to my lyves quene' (674). Text quoted from *Minor Poems of John Lydgate*, ed. H.N. MacCracken, EETS OS 192 (1934), vol. II.

concluding stanza reprises its Chaucerian opening: '[g]oe lyttle Calender' (7). Chaucer's envoy invokes the 'sixth of sixth poets topos' as he bids his book kiss the steps trodden by 'Virgile, Ovide, Omer, Lucan and Stace' (V.1792). Saluting Dante by omission (*Inferno*, IV.88–96), Chaucer inserts his work into illustrious literary history; a grandiose move that is immediately undercut by worries in the next stanza about the work of dialectically diverse copyists. Will the scribes understand his poem? Might they mess up its metre (5.1793–9)? Spenser appropriates Chaucer's end even before his *Calender* has properly started. The literary resonance of its opening words place Spenser's little book in the company, not only of Chaucer, but of all those other famous poets as well. The Epilogue carves out its own space. Even as the narrator bids the poem not to dare to match its style with Tityrus and the author of *The Ploughman's Tale*, but simply to follow them from afar, and adore their steps (9–11), the 'Book' has become the 'Calender', with 'a free passeporte' (7).⁹ No Chaucerian anxieties about metrical wobbles here: the Epilogue glitters with steely metrical precision. Its twelve lines, each with twelve syllables, ring-fence the poem with metrical counterpoint for each of the twelve months of the *Calender*'s progression. Chaucer, and all his illustrious forebears, are trodden under foot.¹⁰

Such arrogance, however, is not characteristic. The tone of the *Calender*'s relationship to Chaucer is deeply unstable, especially but not only in the extensive scholarly apparatus to the eclogues. Here is the opening of the dedicatory epistle:

> Uncouthe unkiste, Sayde the olde famous Poete Chaucer: whom for his excellencie and wonderfull skil in making, his scholler Lidgate, a worthy scholler of so excellent a maister calleth the Loadestarre of our Language: and whom our Colin clout, in his Æglogue calleth Tityrus, the God of shepheards, comparing hym to the worthines of the Roman Tityrus Virgile. (1–7)

Chaucer, along with Virgil, is co-opted into a pastoral agenda. Their illustrious fame vouchsafes the scholarly credentials of a poet who, as yet, has not launched himself on the literary scene.¹¹ The praise of Chaucer's language, ventriloquised by Lydgate, would not look out of place in the panoply of oleaginous tributes to 'the olde famous Poete' from the early fifteenth century onwards.¹² But while the very first words, 'Uncouthe, unkiste', are attributed to the '[l]oadestarre of our Language',

---

9 Alison A. Chapman argues that in transposing the 'Book' into the 'Calender', Spenser authenticates his work *as* a calendar, grounding the work of the new poet in a Protestant version of the measurement of time, 'The Politics of Time in Edmund Spenser's English Calendar', *Studies in English Literature*, 42 (2002), 1–24.
10 Alice S. Miskimin notes that Spenser did not follow the footing of Chaucer's feet; he sought Chaucer's authority for making his own new way, 242. His two imitations of Chaucer's farewell to *Troilus* unequivocally proclaim his faith in his own art, 283.
11 Patrick Cheney argues that the immediate goal of *The Shepheardes Calender* is to establish Spenser's authority as England's new national poet: see *Spenser's Famous Flight: A Renaissance Idea of a Literary Career* (Toronto: University of Toronto Press, 1993), 77.
12 Arguing for a different kind of intervention into literary history, William Kuskin reasons that Lydgate is constructed as a scholar in the dedicatory epistle to create a role in which he constructs the poetic past in the present moment. Lydgate is both a mentor to Spenser, and a threat; he

E.K. knows that it isn't Chaucer who speaks them. 'Uncouthe, unkist' is a 'proverbe' (8), to suit 'Pandares purpose' (9).[13] E.K. bolsters Spenser's reputation with 'baudy brocage' (10) teased out of a moment in *Troilus and Criseyde* when Pandarus tries to convince Troilus he is man enough to pursue Criseyde. What rings in readers' ears is not an excellently wonderful poet, but a pandering love broker. The new poet is a maudlin love-sot who needs the worldly wisdom of an older man (E.K.?) to help him brave the not-so-virgin territory of public pastoral. Pandarus's 'background interference', to recall Dimock's terms, smirches the sheen of the literary roll-call.[14] Purporting to herald an unknown poet into greatness, the recall of *Troilus and Criseyde* (1.809) fashions E.K. into the new poet's literary pimp.

Such Chaucerian sleights of voice turn up with persistent frequency in E.K.'s apparatus. His gloss to line 4 of 'December' runs 'Tityrus) Chaucer: as hath bene oft sayd'. The identification of Tityrus with Chaucer *has* been often said, and in terms that call attention to its repetition. To lines 91–3 of 'February', E.K. appends the note 'I suppose he mean Chaucer' and to lines 81–8 of 'June', 'that by Tityrus is meant Chaucer hath already been sufficiently said'. Why does E.K. keep harping on Tityrus as Chaucer? The iteration is both superfluous, and, it might be argued, part of a literary 'brocage' that is as comically disfiguring as putting Pandarus's words into the mouth of 'loadstarre' Chaucer. Not only are E.K.'s attributions otiose, but read in full, they both ignore *what* the poems have already said, and/or they direct us to problems of *how* they rehearse Chaucer. This is Colin's lament for the death of Chaucer as Tityrus:

> The God of shepheards *Tityrus* is dead,
> Who taught me, homely, as I can, to make.
> He, whilst he lived, was the soveraign head
> Of shepheards all that bene with love ytake:
> Well couth he wayle his Woes, and lightly slake
> The flames, which love within his heart had bredd,
> And tell us mery tales to keep us wake,
> The while our sheepe about us safely fedde. ('June', 81–8)

E.K.'s commentary strikes completely the wrong note:

> and by this more plain appeareth, that he saith he told merry tales (such as be his Canterbury Tales): whom he calleth the god of poets for his excellency, so as Tully calleth Lentulus, deum vitae suae, scilicet the god of his life.

---

operates as a model and a guide to the construction of literary authority that collapses temporalities and models of poetic precursors. See *Recursive Origins: Writing at the Transition to Modernity* (Indiana: University of Notre Dame Press, 2013), 68–9.

13 Though as Julia Boffey observes, Chaucer was received as a source of wisdom and proverbs were attributed to him, 'Proverbial Chaucer and the Chaucer Canon', in *Reading from the Margins: Textual Studies, Chaucer and Medieval Literature*, ed. Seth Lerer, Huntington Library Quarterly, 58 (1996), 37–47.

14 Lynn Staley Johnson notes that the bawdy Chaucerian allusions undercut the high seriousness of Spenser's claims: see *The Shepheardes Calender: An Introduction* (Pittsburgh: Pennsylvania State University Press, 1990), 27–31.

Merry tales are indeed told on the pilgrimage to Canterbury; why mention them in this doleful context? Would Tully really have enjoyed the *Miller's Tale* or the Wife of Bath's 'queynte' quibbling? And a poet less likely than Chaucer to be keeping shepherds awake with jollity while sheep are nibbling the grass is hard to imagine. Chaucer might write about gardens full of birds (*Parliament of Foules*), or a farmyard of chickens (*Nun's Priest's Tale*), but parsonical metaphors apart, flocks of sheep are conspicuous by their absence.[15]

E.K.'s representation of Chaucer as pastoral poetic progenitor, a poet to be revered amongst the ranks of classical 'auctors' and lamented by lovelorn shepherds, does not match the poetry that the glosses reference.[16] E.K. says as much in his 'February' annotations. To Thenot's claim that his tale of the Oak and the Briar was kenned from Tityrus in Kent:

> But shall I tel thee a tale of truth
> Which I cond of Tityrus in my youth
> Keeping his sheepe on the hils of Kent. ('February', 91–3)

E.K. ripostes:

> I suppose he mean Chaucer whose prayse for pleasant tales cannot dye, so long as the memorie of his name shal liue, and the name of Poetrie shal endure. (Gloss to line 92)

E.K. is right to be cautious, and not just about the sheep; for if the hills of Kent appear anywhere in Chaucer's poetry, they are an unnamed location where the Canterbury pilgrims got lost in their pilgrimage somewhere on the outskirts of Blean Forest. Nor, incidentally, is February a month that we would associate with the Canterbury pilgrims. March, April or May would make literary sense, given the density of references to these months in the *Canterbury Tales*.[17] February is named only once in Chaucer's oeuvre, and only then in the un-terrestial *Astrolabe* (45–50; 50–7). February is a perverse choice of month to pitch a tale attributed to Chaucer; almost as perverse as picking June for his elegy, a month that appears in the *Merchant's Tale* only because critical editions emend the majority manuscript

---

15 The Parson tends his figurative flock in the *General Prologue* (I.496, 503, 508); a sheep is invoked in a philosophical argument in the *Knight's Tale* (I.1308); the Pardoner peddles sheep's relics (VI.351). In the *Clerk's Tale*, Griselda's father keeps a few sheep in the field, which she tends when she is not spinning wool or collecting vegetables for supper (IV.222–7). This is about as pastoral as sheep get in Chaucer unless you count the reference to moths in sheep's fleeces in the *Tale of Melibee* (VII.997–8) or the sheep named Malle that belongs to the widow in the *Nun's Priest's Tale* (VII.2831). The Wife of Bath's reference to Wilkyn the sheep when she is recounting how she got the better of her doddery old husband in bed (III.432) is not a recognised version of pastoral.
16 Miskimin notes that Spenser's allusions to Chaucer are fascinating because they pay homage and seem to define relatedness which a reading of his poems does not confirm, 44.
17 For March, I.2; III.546; 1782; V.47; VII.3188, and 3190. For April, I.1; II.6 and III.546. For May, I.92; 1034; 1037, 1042; 1047; 1062; 1500; 1510; 1511; 1675; 2484; II.6; 851; III.546; V.281; 906, and VIII.1343. Though Chaucerian poems do pick out February for attention, mentioning, for example, its cold and gloom as a contrast to the warmer months of flowers and love. From John Stow, *The woorkes of Geffrey Chaucer, newly printed, with diuers addicions, whiche were neuer in printe before: with the siege and destruccion of the worthy citee of Thebes* (Imprinted at London, by

reading of 'Juyl'.[18] E.K. goes on to demolish Thenot's identification completely: 'this tale of the Oak and the Briar he telleth as lerned of Chaucer, but it is clean in another kind, and rather like to Aesop's fables' ('February', Gloss to line 102). E.K.'s quibble points to a different kind of Chaucer from the Tityrus that the poem represents.[19]

At every point when this 'scholler' provides a reference to Chaucer, whether Tityrean or not, something is awry. The commentary to 'April' paraphrases the opening lines of the *Canterbury Tales* (1–7), but neither Chaucer, nor Tityrus, is named:

> [a]ttempered to the yeare) agreeable to the season of the yeare, that is Aprill, which moneth is most bent to shoures and seasonable rayne: to quench, that is to delaye the drought, caused through drynesse of March wyndes.
>
> ('April', Gloss to line 5)

There is the puzzling gloss of 'spell' ('March', 64) as a kind of magic charm whose authority is buttressed by a misquotation from the *Tale of Sir Thopas*.[20] '[G]ride' ('February', line 4), is glossed as 'perced: an olde word much used of Lidgate, but not found (that I know of) in Chaucer'. The old word is not to be found in the *Middle English Dictionary*.[21] Nor is E.K. any more accurate in his assertion that 'glitterand' ('July', 177), is a '[p]articiple used sometime in Chaucer, but altogether in J.Goore'.[22] E.K.'s explanatory notes match neither the Chaucer of modern literary criticism nor, perhaps more importantly, the polished language of the poet of love and complaint anthologised in sixteenth-century editions, and embellished by poeticised paeans to his posthumous reputation. And yet, if we can detach 'Chaucer' from his mainstream sixteenth-century reputation, as the spillage from Chaucer to Pandarus in the dedicatory epistle invites, then I think we might be excused for smelling 'a little Lollius in the wind' of E.K.'s commentary.[23]

Jhon Kyngston, for Jhon Wight, dwellyng in Poules Churchyarde, 1561), they include 'The Floure of Curtesie made by Iohn lidgate' which begins '[i]n feurier, whan the frostye Moone [...]' (fol. ccxviii), and 'A Ballade' '[i]n the season of feuerer when it was full colde' (fol. cccxliii). Miskimin discusses the relationship between Stow's Chaucer and Spenser, 247–50 as part of her more extended discussion of the Renaissance makeover of Chaucer, 226–61; see also Forni, 67–76.

18 See *Riverside Chaucer*, 1128, note to IV.2133.
19 Staley Johnson argues that 'February' is fundamentally Chaucerian in its social commentary and figuration of social tension; she hears echoes of the rivalry between the Reeve and the Miller, 63–71.
20 'And so sayth Chaucer, Listeneth Lordings to my spell'. The line in *Thopas* does not contain the word 'spell', '[y]et listeth, lordes, to my tale' (VII.833). Given the explanations of charm and the mention of 'Nightspel', was E.K. thinking of poor John's protective 'night-spel' in the *Miller's Tale*, I.3480? Or is it just another knowingly misdirected gloss?
21 Unless E.K. means *MED* 'greden' (v); whose prominent sense means to call, or to cry out, and while there are no references to Chaucer or to Lydgate, sense 5 does list croaking birds, hounds and bleating kids.
22 E.K. might be forgiven for thinking that the *Plowman's Tale* was written by Chaucer and 'glitterand' does appear, see the *Plowman's Tale* in *Six Ecclesiastical Satires*, ed. James M. Dean (Kalamazoo: Medieval Institute Publications, 1991), 134. That said, J.Goore seems a very mischievous rendition of John Gower.
23 'Lollius' is the spurious author to whom the narrator of *Troilus and Criseyde* defers authority, e.g. Book 1.394 and Book 5.1653. In the Epilogue to the *Man of Lawe's Tale* the Parson rebukes the Host

While we have no palpable proof that E.K. was Spenser, and E.K. his sheepish literary stalking horse, Spenser would not have been the first early modern writer to provide a provocative new work with elaborately spurious explanatory matter. As Jane Griffiths has recently shown, William Bullein's *Dialogue against the Fever Pestilence* (1564), and William Baldwin's *Beware the Cat* (1553, first published 1570), are amongst his most ingeniously clever precursors.[24] Lynn Staley Johnson has argued that E.K. is a kind of go-between for the hapless Spenser as 'Immeritô' and the poetic fame to which he aspires.[25] If E.K. is Spenser's projection, then we have 'evidence of a comic talent that, like Sidney's, is too often overlooked'.[26] Overlooked, also, like the comic ingenuity of George Gascoigne, whose *A Hundreth Sundrie Flowres* was published as an anonymous anthology in 1573. Containing almost as many aliases as its 'sundrie flowres', its personae include the Green Knight, a non-existent author of Italian *novelle* called Bartello, the fabulously named Marmaduke Marblestone, and a shadowy figure called 'the Reporter'. George Gascoigne is also a shadowy figure in the *Calender*. He turns up in E.K.'s gloss to 'November' (141). 'Ma. George Gaskin', a 'wittie gentleman, and the very chefe of our late rymers, who, and if some partes of learning wanted not (albee it is well knowen he altogether wanted not learning) no doubt would have attained to the excellencye of those famous Poets'. The 'pretty epanorthosis'[27] that dubs Gascoigne with faint praise gives scant indication that E.K.'s merry glosses already had a precedent in a work published only six years before the *Calender*. Gascoigne's subversive play with learned apparatus and annotation needs a wider audience.[28] He also deserves to be better known for one of the most insightful sixteenth-century readings of Chaucer at play. Amongst Gascoigne's *Flowres* is a satire on the history of Troy. Its irreverent potshots include Troilus and Criseyde as transmitted (in part) by Chaucer:

> Thy brother Troylus eke, that gemme of gentle deedes,
> To thinke how he abused was, alas my heart it bleedes,
> He bet about the bush, whiles other caught the birds
> Whom craftie Cresside mockt to muche, yet fed him still with words.
> And God he knoweth not I, who pluckt hir first sprong rose,
> Since Lollius and Chaucer both, make doubt upon that glose. (*Dan Bartholmew his Triumphs*, 29–34)[29]

---

for swearing blasphemously. Harry Bailey retaliates by declaring 'I smelle a Lollere in the wynd' (II.1173).
24 Jane Griffiths, *Diverting Authorities: Experimental Glossing Practices in Manuscript and Print* (Oxford: Oxford University Press, 2014), 123–48. Thomas More is also one of this distinguished company, see David Norbrook, *Poetry and Politics in the English Renaissance* (Oxford: Oxford University Press, 2002), rev. edn, 67.
25 Staley Johnson, 26.
26 Ibid., 26–9; quotation from 29. She argues that Spenser would have found just such a literary model in the works of Chaucer; a persona or literary alter ego who is at once helpful and misleading, halfway between game and earnest.
27 'A pretty epanorthosis', as E.K. explains in his gloss to 'January' (61), 'June' (90) and 'November' (73), is a correction that involves a play on the order and meanings of words.
28 As demonstrated in Jane Griffiths's discussion of his work, 149–61.
29 George Gascoigne, *A Hundreth Sundrie Flowres*, ed. C.T. Prouty (Columbia: Missouri University Press, 1942), 199.

With their intertextual play between *The Romance of the Rose*, *Troilus and Criseyde*, *The Book of the Duchess*, Lollius and Chaucer, Gascoigne's lines provide hard evidence that there existed a learnedly comic alternative to the serious well-streams that flowed from Chaucer's supposedly sugared lips.

If Gascoigne could play the scholar with Chaucer, so could E.K. If we allow E.K. to be Spenser's edgy counterpoint to Lollius, then the *Calender*'s relationship to Tityrean Chaucer turns out to be more comedic than the bulk of its critical reception has always granted. E.K.'s apparatus forms not so much an earnest navigational guide to what Chaucer meant to Spenser, but a series of wily truths intermixed with misdirected authorities. In splendid Chaucerian fashion, E.K. gives us both 'cokkel and corn'.[30] His slipshod pedantry preserves a serious indebtedness to Chaucer that is learnedly ludic. Fully to realise the comic edge to E.K.'s scholarly gravitas helps to make much more sense of those lines in 'February' that E.K. glosses as 'Chaucers verse almost whole'. The recall of Chaucer's herdgrooms piping in the broom bushes is the closest verbatim reference to Chaucer's verse in the eclogues themselves. Why is 'February' singled out for such special treatment, and why *The House of Fame*?

From green corn to ripe pastoral?

One answer is that the recall is entirely appropriate: decorous both to the argument of 'February', and decorous also to how the whole *Calender* charts the poetic endeavours of a new poet's literary *bildungsroman*.[31] Lines 33–41, as Helen Cooper observes, are an example of 'bergerie'. They are recalled from the only instance of 'bergerie' in Chaucer's entire oeuvre, a fleeting moment in his *House of Fame*: little herdgrooms keeping their beasts in budded brooms.[32] 'Bergerie' is a version of pastoral that is characterised by optimism, jollity and fulfilment in love. As such, Thenot's assumption of a 'bergerie' voice with which to chide Cuddie is apposite. Cuddie's youthful piping is callow. Thenot claims that he is petulantly oblivious to the passing of time and irresponsibly ignorant of the harshness of the seasonal world. In his refuge from the cold in the just-budding brooms, Cuddie's piping is as green as the reed of his own pipe, and those pipes of his fellow loiterers. Cuddie and his fellow 'fond flyes' may cocoon themselves in the bushes to rejoice in the first glimmers of the shining sun, but the sound that they produce is not music, but crowing.

These lines from *The House of Fame* seem more fitting to Spenser's verse than the reference to the *Canterbury Tales* in 'June', or to Pandarus in the dedicatory epistle, and indeed to the 'February' fathering of the Tale of the Oak and the Briar

---

30 The Host accuses the Parson of attempting to sprinkle 'cokkel in clene corn' in the Epilogue to the *Man of Lawe's Tale*, II. 1183. In this context, the Host refers to mingling heresy and true doctrine.
31 While Louis A. Montrose observes the ambivalences and contradictions about poetic endeavour in 'February', he argues that the eclogue frames an exemplary fable about ambition within a pastoral debate between youth and age. The argument resembles the relationship between the sage and serious 'Immeritô' and the persona of his younger poet, 'Interpreting Spenser's "February" Eclogue: Some Contexts and Implications', *Spenser Studies*, 2 (1981), 67–74 (70–1). Montrose concludes that the *Calender* is a rite of passage for the new poet (72–3).
32 Cooper, 56. My discussion of 'bergerie' is indebted to Cooper's learned account, 54–6 and 105.

onto sheep-tending Chaucer. Thenot's lines from *The House of Fame* can be seen to be part of an earnest argument about the responsibilities of poetic piping, not just in 'February', but in the *Calender*'s whole trajectory.[33] We should take Chaucer, and E.K., and by extension, the new poet, seriously. Cuddie, the herdgroom of 'February', matures as the *Calender* progresses. While in 'August', he is called a herdgroom on three occasions (45–6, 129–30 and 135–6), he is singled out to judge the singing competition, and with the sagest of judgements, Cuddie awards prizes to both participants: Willy gets to keep the lamb, and Perigot wins the mazer; a judgement regarded as blameless ('August', 125–36). The herdgroom of 'February' has grown up, and appropriately, he crowns the contest with a doleful lay. Composed by Colin, and sung by Cuddie, the exquisite sestina is a song of loss, of sadness and of grief (151–89). Perigot praises 'ech turning of thy verse' (191). There is no crowing in green corn here. Glimmers of spring are become wastefull woods, and budded brooms are ghastful groves. Jolly 'bergerie' is a distant memory as Cuddie turns his 'proper song' to the tune of 'ruthful' pipes ('August', 149–50) with a masterly display of poetic form.

Cuddie returns in the 'October' eclogue for a debate with Piers on the public role of poetry. Piers observes that Cuddie has abandoned the life of 'shepheards laddes' which is characterised by 'rymes', 'ridles' and lowly singing matches ('October', 4–6). His rural singing now makes him fit to be compared to Orpheus ('October', 25–30). Cuddie explicitly repudiates his youthful pipe, a pipe good only to feed the fantasy of youth. He laments that he has piped so long with pain that all his oaten reeds are spent ('October', 13–18). Piers encourages him to leave the lowly dust and pastoral pursuits to sing of stronger notes: of knights and warfare ('October', 37–54). Cuddie recalls the poetic journey of Romish Tityrus, Virgil, who under the patronage of Maecenas moved from pastoral to epic (55–60). But now, Cuddie laments, such patrons are not to be found; only rhyming ribalds such as Tom Piper find favour (61–78). Cuddie does not succumb to Piers's enticements. Instead he counsels Piers to be content in

> [...] thys humble shade:
> Where no such troublous tydes han us assayed,
> Here we our slender pipes may safely charme. ('October', 117–18)

Despite the lure to epic, Cuddie chooses pastoral quiet: shade rather than acclaim, safety rather than perilous patronage. He has, arguably, acquired a deeper wisdom and worldliness than in his appearance in 'August'. He is barely recognisable as his February namesake, chided in the lines from Chaucer's *House of Fame*.[34]

---

33 John Moore discusses Cuddie's role in foregrounding the tensions in assuming pastoral responsibility of national proportions, 'Pastoral Motivation in *The Shepheardes Calender*', in *Edmund Spenser: New and Renewed Directions*, ed. J.B. Lethbridge (Cranbury: Fairleigh Dickinson University Press, 2006), 58–79.

34 Ronald B. Bond argues that while the dialectic between the humble 'Immerito' and the vaunting 'new poet' remains unresolved, the 'true paterne of a Poet' succeeds Cuddie, the lazy lout, the craven cowherd, just as Colin exchanges his oaten reeds for stern trumpets: see 'Supplantation in

Cuddie's education in the proper use of a pipe is, as is well known, part of a much larger argument in the *Calender*. The prefatory argument to 'October' states that '[i]n Cuddie is set out the perfecte paterne of a Poete' (line 1). E.K. provides the first critical response to this assertion:

> 1] Cuddie) I doubte whether by Cuddie be specified the authour self or some other. For in the eyght Æglogue the same person was brought in, singing a Cantion of Colins making, as he sayth. So that some doubt, that the persons be different. (Gloss to line 1)

With characteristic encryption, E.K. teases us to conjecture that Cuddie is a figure under which not only Colin is shadowed, but Spenser himself. Whether the identifications between Cuddie, Colin and 'the authour self' are made with scepticism, or with confidence, the scholarly apparatus invites us to consider them in relationship to each other. Cuddie may, or he may not be, the same person as in the previous eclogues. He does, however, sing Colin's 'August' sestina that showcases the technical bravura of the author's making. Cuddie's final preference in 'October' for the safety of the shade echoes Colin's self-imposed poetic exile from public poetry in 'June':

> I never lyst presume to *Parnasse* hyll,
> But pyping lowe in shade of lowly grove,
> I play to please my selfe, all be it ill. [...]
> With shepheard sittes not, followe flying fame:
> But feede his flocke in fields, where falls hem best. ('June', 70–2, 75–6)

Colin and Cuddie play overlapping roles in a progression of poetic argument that charts the calendrical journey of the emergent poet that is Spenser himself. Although Colin breaks his pipe in 'January', his exquisite skill is showcased, and praised. Hobbinol's performance of Colin's lay for Elisa in 'April' matches the ventriloquised set piece of Cuddie's 'August' sestina. In his own voice, Colin sings the lament for Chaucer in 'June' and for Dido in 'November'. Spenser's education in the proper use of a pipe, staged through Cuddie and through Colin, debates the role of poetry in the public world.[35] All that prevents the poem from moving from pastoral to epic is the lamentable state of contemporary patronage. So, when

---

the Elizabethan Court: The Theme of Spenser's "February" Eclogue', *Spenser Studies*, 2 (1981), 55–65 (62). John D. Bernard argues that Cuddie is an ironic counterpoint to Colin, and Spenser doubly distances himself from them both in order to utilise these pastoral complexities and ambivalences to state his claim to public recognition, *Ceremonies of Innocence: Pastoralism in the Poetry of Edmund Spenser* (Cambridge: Cambridge University Press, 1989), 73–6.

35 Ted Brown charts Colin's progression through the poem, arguing that when Colin hangs up his pipe, it is an acknowledgement of death. Though unfulfilled, Colin does not abandon his poetry. The pipe on the tree is an enduring symbol of Colin's achievement. See 'Pride and Pastoral in *The Shepheardes Calender*', in *Subjects on the World's Stage: Essays on British Literature of the Middle Ages and the Renaissance*, ed. David G. Allen and Robert A. White (Newark: University of Delaware Press, 1995), 100–15. Lin Kelsey and Richard S. Peterson argue that Colin's gesture reveals Spenser's precocious grasp of what comes with the territory of being a poet', 'Re-reading

we return to those lines about the little herdgrooms in 'February' in light of the trajectory of the *Calender* as a whole, their Chaucerian resonance appears entirely apposite. Their place in the whole argument is deserved, and E.K. absolutely right to direct us back to Chaucer in case we miss their 'bergerie' significance. To have cherry-picked Chaucer's only example of 'bergerie' looks like an inspired poetic pluck to furnish forth an argument about the maturity of pastoral. That is, until we recall E.K.'s wayward gloss: 'Chaucers verse almost whole'. If it were so important that the quotation from *The House of Fame* be recognised, why didn't E.K. supply the name of the work? The progression from Chaucerian greenness to Spenserian ripe pastoral would have been signposted much more clearly. With the title of Chaucer's 'verse' withheld, the reader is left unmoored. Is 'verse' to be understood as the allusion to those specific 'bergerie' lines in *The House of Fame*, or to *The House of Fame* as a whole? In either case the distinction (or the lack of it) matters. E.K.'s coy direction to incompleteness prompts a desire to find out what is missing. What happens when we follow that instinct and admit rather more of Chaucer's *House of Fame* into Spenser's new work than E.K. explicitly invites?

Re-sounding *The Calender* in *The House of Fame*

In *The House of Fame* the herdgrooms form a tiny group of musicians in a very long description of the sounds of minstrels and 'gestiours' who stand like statues in the niches and pinnacles of the House of Fame itself. First off are the harpists. Orpheus is followed by Orion, Chiron the centaur and a Welsh bard called Glascurion (1201–8). Below them sit 'smale harpers with her glees' (1209). Gaping up at their more illustrious counterparts, these unnamed harpers, with their more rudimentary instruments, copy their name-sakes like apes (1211–12). Behind them, stands a horde of wind-players:

> That maden lowde mynstralcies
> In cornemuse and shalemyes
> And many other maner pipe,
> That craftily begunne to pipe,
> Bothe in doucet and in rede,
> That ben at festes with the brede;
> And many flowte and lilting horn,
> And pipes made of grene corn,
> As han thise lytel herde-gromes

Colin's Broken Pipe: Spenser and the Problem of Patronage', *Spenser Studies*, 14 (2000), 233–72. M.L. Stapleton describes the *Calender* as Spenser's 'twelve part paean to his own poetic abilities' in *Spenser's Ovidian Poetics* (Newark: University of Delaware Press, 2009), 63, further noting the relationship between emulation and piping, 27–9. '[A]emuling' and 'aemuled' are collocations of 'pipe' in *Colin Clouts Come Home Again*, 72–3 and 77–8. Paul Alpers also describes the *Calender* as an emulative work, one that shows that English pastoral could match that of the continental vernaculars; see *What is Pastoral?* (Chicago: University of Chicago Press, 1996), 182–3. Cheney argues that Colin's progression mirrors Spenser's Orphic patterning of the career of the poet, 77–9 and 107–10.

'Litle herd gromes piping in the wind'   49

> That kepen bestis in the bromes
> Ther saugh I than Atiteris
> And of Athenes Daun Pseustis. (1217–28)

Next up are:

> [...] Marcia that lost her skyn,
> Both in face, and body and chyn,
> For that she wolde envien, loo,
> To pipen bet than Appolloo.
> Ther saugh I famous, olde and yonge,
> Pipers of the Duche tonge,
> To lern love-daunces, sprynges,
> Reyes, and these straunge thynges. (1229–36)

After the pipers come those that make bloody sound in trumpet, horn and bugle. Virgil is one of their number (1244). And then, in other seats, numbering more than the stars in heaven, are those who play on a variety of instruments which the narrator is unable to name (1250–6). These players are followed by magicians, enchanters, witches and sorceresses who make men famous (1259–74). Last to be named is:

> [...] Colle tregetour
> Upon a table of sycamour,
> Pleye an uncouth thyng to telle –
> Y saugh him carien a wynd-melle
> Under a walsh-note shale. (1277–81)

This enormously long-winded list of musicians both adheres to decorum and flouts it. Stringed instruments are followed by woodwind, woodwind by brass. Percussion, which presumably includes 'Colle tregetour' playing a windmill under a walnut shell on his sycamore block, comes last. Closer inspection, however, shows that this apparently hierarchical description of musical sound is far from decorous at all. Rather, it is a frantic medley.[36] Following each of the star performers, those named by names are all the sycophants and counterfeiters who attempt to compete with the great and the good with inferior instruments. Pipers of name (Atiteris, Pseustis, Marsyas and Apollo) come between the bagpipes and shawms of a nameless horde (including those little herdgrooms), and a flurry of wind that might be Dutch, German or Flemish. The brass players, including Virgil and his epic sounds, are succeeded by Joab who blew his trumpet after killing King David's son, Theodomas, a Theban soothsayer, and unnamed trumpeters from Catalonia and Spain. In amongst the fray are tricksters, illusionists and con-artists. The apparently orchestrated consort of musicians mangles nations and

---

36 Cheney regularises the order and also, significantly, leaves out the percussion in his comparison of the musicians in the *Calender* to this passage, 60.

generations as it confounds pioneers with apeists, names with non-entities, and generic sonority with percussive dead wood.

Those little herdgrooms, and their 'bergerie' are quite overwhelmed. Hard on their heels are the pipers Atiteris and Pseustis whose foreign names and half rhyme jangle the octosyllabic verse. Pseustis, whose name means Falsehood, appears to be a character from Theodolus's ninth-century eclogue. But who is Atiteris? 'A corruption of Tityrus' suggests the gloss in the *Riverside Chaucer*.[37] What happens when we say 'Atiteris' out loud? A titeris? Tityrus Proper becomes tityrus indefinite: any old pastoral singer; one of many. Accompanying the herdgrooms (and falsehood), is the mispronounced shepherd singer of Virgil's first eclogue. A 'tityrus' is a poetic role that anyone could inhabit. There are many more unnamed 'titeri' to come. Amongst them, the double Tityri of the *Calender*: Kentish Chaucer and Romish Virgil. E.K., with his compulsive tic of Tityrus checking, already has his 'schollerly' work cut out for him.

Tityrus is not the only *Shepheards Calender* name that gets heard in and between the 'February' eclogue and *The House of Fame*. The very last musician is 'Colle tregetour'. A 'tregetour' is a person somewhere between a tricksy entertainer and a traitor.[38] And Colle? As seen in the only other place where Colle appears in Chaucer's oeuvre, the name of a dog that joins the widow's household going in chase of a cockerel that has been snatched by a fox at the end of the *Nun's Priest's Tale* (VII.3383), Colle is a diminutive of Colin. A little clout of Colin turns up in *The House of Fame* even before the *Calender* harks back to him. For all of E.K.'s arrangement of company for Colin Clout with Skelton, Marot, Virgil and Tityrus (Gloss to 'January' line 1), to Chaucerian ears, hearing Colin in its clouted form from *The House of Fame*, summons, not a consummate pastoral piper on the move to patroned poetic responsibility, but Colin the uncouth con-man, bringing up the rear of a resounding rabble with noisy obscurity.[39] How can those little herdgromes, and their precociously vulnerable green pipes survive to become perfect patterns of poets?

If you have the pipes from *The House of Fame* ringing in your ears when reading the shepherd's pipes in the *Calender*, it makes it hard to take their role in the proper education of a poet seriously. For the pipers in that long list of musicians have already been upstaged and their endeavours overtaken. At the beginning of Book II of *The House of Fame* an eagle swoops into the verse in an off-duty moment from Dante's *Divina Commedia* to rescue the poem from poetic impasse.

---

37 The explanations of Pseustis and Atiteris are from *The Riverside Chaucer*, 986. Pseustis is the name Wyclif gives to Fallacious Unbelief his *Trialogus*; see *Trialogus cum supplementi Trialogi*, IV.40, ed. G. Lechler (Oxford: Clarendon Press, 1969), 390–1.
38 *MED* 'tregetour' (n.) (a) An entertainer, a sleight-of-hand artist, a juggler, an illusionist, etc.; (b) one who practices black magic, a sorcerer; ~ ayen laue, a heretic [quot. a1400, Vsp vr.; prob. from erroneous transposition with traitour n.]; (c) a deceiver, charlatan; (d) as surname.
39 Harry Berger Jr.'s reading of the *Calender* in *Revisionary Play: Studies in Spenserian Dynamics* (Berkeley: University of California Press, 1998), stresses its more ludic qualities, describing Spenser's rhetorical buffoonery at the expense of his pastoral puppet Colin (388), and he compares the *Calender* poet to Ovid's Mercury, a trickster whose 'art lulls asleep those auditors who fail to heed the subtextual warnings about the limits of its pastoral enterprise' (442).

Dangling from the eagle's claws in mid-air, the narrator is treated to a very lengthy disquisition on the origins of sound:

> Soune is noght but eyre ybroken,
> And every speech that ys yspoken
> Lowde or pryvee, foule or faire
> In his substaunce it is aire [...]
> But this may be in many wyse,
> Of which I wil the two devyse.
> As soun that comth of pype or harpe.
> For whan a pype is blowen sharpe,
> The air is twist with violence,
> And rent; lo, this is my sentence;
> Eek, whan men harpe-stringes smyte,
> Whether hit be moche or lyte,
> Lo, with the strook the air to-breketh;
> Right so hit breketh whan men speketh.
> Thus wost thou wel what thing is speche.
> 'Now hennesforth I wol thee teche,
> How every speche, or noise, or soun,
> Through his multiplicacioun,
> Thogh hit were pyped of a mouse,
> Moot nede come to Fames House. (765–86)

The eagle argues that *every* speech, *every* sound, be it foul or fair, has its natural place in air, and *every* 'voys, or noyse, or word, or soun' (819) is moved by the reverberation of the air until it comes to the House of Fame. Voice, noise, word and sound are rattled out indiscriminately as if one were the equal of another: even the pipe. The symbol of pastoral woodwind is matched with a harp in the wrong order, and described with percussive brutality: 'sharpe'; 'twist'; 'violence'; 'smyte'; 'stroke'; and 'breketh'. Break comes twice. But this is not the plangent broken pipe of a desolate young shepherd in January or the abandoned instrument of a disconsolate poet in December; this is a pipe that breaks wind (765 and 775). Its sounds will, indiscriminately, come up to the House of Fame with no less or more distinction than the piping of a mouse (785). Not so much of a pipe then; more of a peep. The sound of an ancient poet's verse almost whole unleashes a Chaucerian piping in the ears that engulfs the pastoral agenda of the *Calender*. Its broken pipes and wintery blasts are already burdened with the mouse-squeaking fartery of the *House of Fame*. The *Calender*'s insistent recall of Titeri and pipes is sustained to the bitter end: '[d]are not to match thy pype with Tityrus his style' (*Epilogue*, 9). To din this collocation into the ears of a reader of *The House of Fame* causes comic confusion. Whether from *The House of Fame* (or indeed from anywhere in Chaucer's oeuvre), pipes are consistently associated with discord, or something dubious.[40]

---

40 Alongside the Miller's brazen bagpipes (I.565), Theseus tells Palamon and Arcite in the *Knight's Tale* that since they both can't marry Emelye, one of them will have to go and pipe in an ivy leaf

And if you have Chaucerian wind in your ears, it interferes with the pitch of Colin's pastoral resignation in 'December':

> Here will I hang my pype upon this tree,
> Was never pype of reede did better sounde.
> Wynter is come, that blowes the bitter blaste. ('December', 141–3)

Colin's final gesture in hanging up his pipe heralds a new kind of poetic endeavour: the pastoral reed, so vulnerable and easily broken, yields to the trumpet of epic. As Louis Montrose observes, these lines reprise the triumphant act of Sannazaro's 'Mantuan Tityrus' who left the woods and his pipes for the fields, the city and a sonorous trumpet:

> Which reed (when having abandoned his goats he set himself to instruct the rustic tillers of the soil, perhaps, with a hope of later singing with more sonorous trumpet in the arms of Trojan Aeneas) he hung up there where now you see it, in honour of this God who had shown him favour in his singing. After him came never a soul to these woods that has been able to play it with accomplishment, though many, spurred by ambitious daring, have attempted it oftentimes and attempt it still.[41]

Colin's ambitiously poetic transition, a gestural rite of passage from humble pipe to resounding trumpet, presages the opening stanza of *The Faerie Queene*:

> Lo I the man, whose Muse whilome did maske,
> As time her taught in lowly Shepheards weeds,
> Am now enforst a far vnfitter taske,
> For trumpets sterne to chaunge mine Oaten reeds,
> And sing of Knights and Ladies gentle deeds;
> Whose prayses hauing slept in silence long,
> Me, all too meane, the sacred Muse areeds
> To blazon broad emongst her learned throng:
> Fierce warres and faithfull loues shall moralize my song. (*The Faerie Queene*, I.proem.1)[42]

If, however, you are following this poetic line of succession with an earworm from *The House of Fame*, orderly poetic progression and ambition are rumbled. First,

---

(I.1838), a proverb that recurs just as snibbingly in *Troilus*, V.1433. The Reeve lists piping along with poaching as one of Simkin the miller's dubious accomplishments (I.3927). In *Thopas*, while the giant announces the presence of the Faerie Queen with harp, pipe and symphony, she never appears (VII.2005); that is, until Spenser rescues her.

41 Louis A. Montrose, '"The perfecte paterne of a poete": The Politics of Courtship in *The Shepheardes Calender*', in *Edmund Spenser*, ed. Andrew Hadfield (Harlow: Longman, 1996), 30–63 (57). The quotation is from Sannazaro, *Arcadia and Piscatorial Eclogues*, trans. Ralph Nash (Detroit: Wayne State University Press, 1966), 104–5.

42 Quoted from *Spenser: The Faerie Queene*, ed. A.C. Hamilton (London and New York: Longman, 1977). Montrose argues that in all of Spenser's work where he appears, Colin Clout embodies a Spenserian motive that can be identified variously as desire, ambition or aspiration: see 'The perfecte paterne of a poete', 51. Staley Johnson argues for a more disjointed reading of the relationship between Spenser and Colin, pointing towards Colin's narcissistic stylistics and artistic

from the resonance of the collocation of 'pipe', 'wynd' and 'blasts' in the 'December' lines themselves. Second, from the resonance of pipes and trumpets. The first musical instrument sounded in the *Calender* is not the pipe but the trumpet. This is what the dedicatory epistle has to say about the future of the uncouth, unkissed, new poet:

> so soone as his name shall come into the knowledg of men, and his worthines be sounded in the tromp of fame, but that he shall be not onely kiste, but also beloved of all, embraced of the most, and wondred at of the best. (dedicatory epistle, 13–17)

The trumpet of Fame does not have to be Chaucer's (it could be Virgil's), but it is hard not to hear a Chaucerian resonance because even before the 'February' eclogue, echoes of *The House of Fame* can be heard in the preface to the *Calender*:

> But if that any aske thy name,
> Say thou wert base begot with blame:
> For thy thereof thou takest shame. ('To His Boke', 13–15)

The tripping triplets of the rhymes on 'name', 'shame' and 'blame' recall the structural rhyming refrain of *The House of Fame*.[43] Taking full advantage of the chimes of octosyllabic couplets, the dominant rhyme pattern plays off name and fame, with name and shame, and name and game, and fame and blame.[44] The phoneme [ɑːmə] is a persistent acoustic that collapses distinction between them all. The *Calender*'s opening apologia re-sounds a key Chaucerian rhyme that resonates mischievously with the dedicatory epistle's 'trompe of fame'. For in *The House of Fame*, the trumpet's laudatory role is loudly debased. Far from heralding a serious change of poetic register, the blast of the trumpet confounds distinction itself.

The narrator recounts how groups of petitioners approach Lady Fame to beseech her to announce their glory throughout the world. Each group has their worth proclaimed by the blast of a trumpet; but the choice between the trumpet of praise or the trumpet of shame is unpredictably unmotivated. Eolus, the god of winds, has a 'clarioun' that is 'ful dyvers of his soun' (1573–4). Eolus blows 'Clere Laude' or 'Sklaundre' in total disregard of the suitors' worth (1575–80). One example of the extended trumpet ritual must suffice. The first group that approaches Lady Fame claims that they are of 'good name' in honour and 'gentillesse' and deserve 'good loos'. Fame dismisses their suit out of hand. They shall have 'a shrewed

---

isolation, 130–9. For Berger, Colin is the poet's puppet, an image of the fledgling imagination who disports purely in the garden of literary convention and artifice, reluctant to pass through the gate into the world, 339 and 317. Bernard calls Colin a 'perfect poetic windbag', 75.

43 Berger proposes that these triple rhymes suggest caricature, 327.

44 Thomas C. Kennedy, 'Rhetoric and Meaning in *The House of Fame*', *Studia Neophilologica*, 68 (1996), 9–23, discusses how the reduction of language to sound is illustrated by random patterns of rhyme. He mentions name/fame etc. but does not list the occurrences. They are: Name/fame (305–6; 1145–6; 1153–4; 1275–6; 1311–12; 1405–6; 1411–12; 1489–90; 1555–6; 1609–10; 1619–20; 1695–6; 1715–16; 1735–6; 1761–2; 1871–2; 1899–1900; 2111–12). Fame/game (663–4; 821–2; 1199–1200; 1473–4). Shame/name (557–8; 1815–16). Shame/diffame (1581–2).

fame', 'wikkyd loos' and 'worse name' (1615–21). She commands Eolus to take his trumpet 'Sklaundre' and to 'trumpe alle the contrarye / Of that they han don wel or fayre' (1625–30). So Eolus takes his black trumpet of brass, and blows so hard that it seems that the whole world should come to an end. The blast sounds like the firing of a cannonball. Smoke billows out of 'his foule trumpes ende' (1646):

> Blak, bloo, grenyssh, swartish red,
> As doth where that men melte led,
> Loo, al on high fro the tuel […]
> And hyt stank as the pit of helle.
> Allas, thus was her shame yronge,
> And gilteles, on every tonge. (1647–56)

Thus are the praiseworthy heralded. The stinkiest fart in all Middle English literature is none other than the Last Judgement wake-up call. Overwhelming not just the petitioners but the whole poem, Eolus's trumpet voluntary takes nearly three hundred lines. Its indiscriminate noteworthiness is made all the more frangible by the post-dated revelation that all sounds which enter the House of Fame have been wafted from the wicker house of Rumour. Eolus does not even blow his own trumpet. All poetic aspiration to be lauded by the trump of Fame is blown to smithereens.[45]

In sum then, I am suggesting that to hear resonances of *The House of Fame* in the *Calender* ruins it. Whilst, *in situ*, those 'bergerie' lines in 'February' might be highly appropriate as a stage in the perfect patterning of a new poet, when we hear more of *The House of Fame* then that pattern comes unstuck. Chaucerian pipes are anything but decorous: a mouse squeak is indistinguishable from the pipe of a titeris, or from the sound of an uncouth instrument of a little clout of Colin. The progression from pipe to trumpet, cued by the Preface to the *Calender* and Colin's final gesture towards the opening of *The Faerie Queene*, cannot withstand the force of Chaucerian flatulence. If the swartish trump of fame makes no distinction between fame and shame, noise and word, then future claims to blazon forth its stern notes become futile. Blown about with the winds of rumour, the insouciant caprice of Chaucerian parping swallows up all pipes and instruments of poetic renown into an urban smog of black stink.

Herdgrooms in 'La Compleynt'

While it could be objected that such a reading is simply in bad taste, it is a reading that E.K.'s commentary prompts. If, however, we want to 'rescue' the new poet's endeavour, and take it seriously, there remains the option of thinking that E.K.'s

---

45 Richard Helgerson argues that although E.K. delivers a clarion blast about the arrival of a new poet, the poems themselves fail to deliver it: see *Self-Crowned Laureates: Spenser, Jonson, Milton and the Literary System* (Berkeley: University of California Press, 1983), 72. This is not, however, because of the poems' incongruous relationship to Chaucer (70), but because of the withered state of laureate poetry in England (78).

gloss to 'February' may not be to *The House of Fame* at all. Perhaps he was thinking of Chaucerian lines that Chaucer did not write. If Spenser/E.K. had herdgrooms playing in broom bushes in his ears, from 'La Compleynt', then he was hearing a poem far more fitting to the 'Loadsterre' of our language than either the farting trumpet of *The House of Fame*, or indeed, Pandarus's 'brocage' with Troilus. Running to 628 lines, 'La Compleynt' is literally fitting to 'Lidgate' in so far as it concludes *The Temple of Glass* in MS CUL Gg. 4.27 and MS BL. Additional 16165. In neither instance is it clear that the scribes knew that the poem had been written neither by Lydgate nor by Chaucer. Voiced by a male speaker who is distraught with unrequited love for Margaret, 'La Compleynt' is an appeal to his lady to take pity on him, and to read the little book he has prepared for her to attempt to win over her heart. Calendar time features prominently. The speaker bemoans the fact that it is March and the sunny beams of Phoebus are so out of season with the dark heaviness of this heart. The spring month mocks his grief even as its changeability matches the cruel vicissitudes of love. The speaker prays that April will bring a change to his plight and his lady will return. The little herdgrooms play their flutes all day long 'in aprylle and in may' (419-10). To situate the narrative in March, April and May sounds far more like Chaucer than the *Calender*'s choice of February and June; indeed far more decorous than Chaucer's own choice of December for *The House of Fame* (63). The conclusion of the complaint returns, as does the *Calender*, to the whole cycle of the year. Whatever change may bring, the speaker promises Margaret that he will be 'youre man fro yere to yere' (628).[46]

The herdgroom lines form part of the narrator's appeal to Fortune to take pity on his plight. Margaret is also a version of the daisy from *The Legend of Good Women* (F.40-83/G.40-60). The green corn pipes of *The House of Fame* become recorders, reeds and flutes (reminiscent, perhaps of *The General Prologue* Squire (I.91-2)). The 'bergerie' vignette in 'La Compleynt' is part of an idyllic seasonal spring time; an idealised landscape of harmless love from which the narrator is excluded. With its insistent recall of Chaucerian love poetry and complaint, 'La Compleynt' is a fine exemplar of mainstream sixteenth-century responses to Chaucer. The presence of the daisy, appeals to Fortune, the woodland setting and the formality of the verse make it a piece with the anthologised Chaucerian shorter poems, especially those in John Stow's 1561 edition; the volume of Chaucer's poetry that is thought to have influenced Spenser.[47] To have this work ringing in your ears when encountering

---

46 Intriguingly, that final line is an almost verbatim echo of the 'Balade of Complaint', a poem Shirley also copied into MS BL Additional 16165. Skeat thought it was Chaucer's and it is still printed in the Riverside edition in the section on poems not attributed to Chaucer in the manuscript. The prefatory note remarks that 'there is no persuasive reason for the attribution; it is a good example of pedestrian verse, heavily indebted to Chaucer but far from attaining his standard' (*The Riverside Chaucer*, 637). The poem is printed on 660, and concludes with the line 'Sith I yow serve, and so wil yeere by yere' (21).
47 Close analogues to the tone and temper of 'La Compleynt' in John Stow's 1561 edition include the fourth stanza of 'A goodlie balade of Chaucer' with its praise of the daisy closing its eye in the darkness of 'rude night' (fol. llxa); 'A Ballade', which includes the lines: 'O we for to worship the lustie floures alwaie / And in especiall one is called ee of the daie / The Daisie a floure white and rede / And in Frenche called La Bele Margarete' (fol. cccxliii).

the herdgrooms in 'February' is congruent with the progression towards maturity, patterned in part through Cuddie. The idealised innocence of the vignette in this anonymous complaint, and the self-indulgent, private nature of the lover's grief patterns out the portrait of a poet not yet matured and publicly responsible.

It would be attractive to 'save' the *Calender*'s decorum through resort to a poem that Chaucer did not write. But to do so would be to flatten the texture of Spenser's whole poem just as 'La Compleynt', and other sixteenth-century Chaucerian poems, flatten Chaucer's oeuvre.[48] Seen in miniature with the replacement of pipes by flutes, reeds and recorders, 'La Complaynte' attenuates Chaucer's characteristic tonal variety. Given that it does, nonetheless, recall the herdgrooms from *The House of Fame*, one could choose to read cacophony and black flatulence back into the new poem. To do so would be wilfully to ignore how 'La Compleynt' drowns the pitch of *The House of Fame* in its recall of *The Prologue to the Legend of Good Women* and in its insistent sixteenth-century Chaucerian diction. Its Chaucerian resonance is tone deaf. Even more tellingly, there is no annotator to supplement and to re-predicate Chaucerian echo. There is no 'schollerly' apparatus, with E.K.'s mischievous mis-directions, to tempt us into remembering that Chaucer wrote more than the *Calender* explicitly contains.

Rehearsing dissonance

'La Compleynt' offers a counterpoint to the work of Chaucerian resonance in the *Calender*; its monovocality helps us to hear far more clearly how the background interference of *The House of Fame* amplifes the dissonance that the *Calender* already contains. That dissonance takes various forms. It is not just Chaucer's musical instruments that get muddled. The woodcuts that form part of the learned apparatus in the *Calender* picture instruments that do not match the words of the text. January's broken pipe is not an oaten reed; it is a bagpipe whose association with male genitalia suggests not poetic disconsolation but castration. Elisa's ladies are said to be playing violins ('April', 104); the woodcut shows them with a viol, harp, lute and flute. Colin plays, not a pipe, but a shawm or clarion. The 'bloody sound' of brass gets pictured in pastoral.[49] The Virgilian paradigm of the October woodcut, with Piers as Virgil and Cuddie as a budding new poet, is undercut by substituting panpipes for pastoral reeds, while Orpheus/Cuddie has no instrument at all; he holds a sheep-hook.[50] Colin's wailful woe in December as he hangs

---

48 Miskimin argues that the polyvocal 'I' of Chaucer's poetry gets lost from view in the sixteenth century, 91.
49 Staley Johnson observes the relationship between bagpipes and castration, and that the fragments that lie near Colin's right foot may be a broken pipe, 107 and 108. Cheney argues that since Colin is playing the cornet in April, a Renaissance instrument used for royal salute in situations inappropriate for the [epic] trumpet, Spenser advertises his own ability to write epic: see Patrick Cheney, 'Spenser's Pastorals: *The Shepheardes Calender* and *Colin Clouts Come Home Againe*', in *The Cambridge Companion to Spenser*, ed. Andrew Hadfield (Cambridge: Cambridge University Press, 2001), 79–105, 90.
50 Jonathan Goldberg offers a brilliant deconstruction of the 'October' woodcut in *Voice, Terminal Echo* (New York and London: Methuen, 1986), 61–2.

his pipe on the tree, his renunciation of pastoral as a prelude to the embracement of epic, rings hollow when we notice that the woodcut shows shards of broken pipe next to his right foot. The perfect pattern of the poet has not progressed at all; not from pastoral to epic, maybe not even from January to December. Ceci n'est pas une pipe?[51] Like E.K.'s commentary, the woodcuts that accompany the verse play truant.

Sonic errancy pervades the verse itself. Spenser revels in the play of sound. Puns, polyphony and parallelisms provide a rich score that collapses distinctions between the learned and the ludic. Sounds and echoes of sounds feature prominently in 'November'. 'Hearse' echoes 'verse'. '[G]yrlond' (76), fuses female and flower in Spenser's own take on 'marguerite'. 'Dido/died, O' (37–8, 57–9) dies in lamentable repetition.[52] But when the name of Colin Cloute enters this choric elegy for a lost presence, we hear a key change into something more ludic. Elisa, we learn, fostered 'the simple shepheardes swaine'

> For she would cal hem often heme
> And give hem curds and clouted Creame.
> O heavie herse,
> Als *Colin cloute* she would not once disdayne.
> O carefull verse. ('November', 98–102)

Geffrey in *The House of Fame* might be fat and stuck for words, but in the *Calender*, the patch of Colin under which the new poet not so secretly shadoweth himself is indistinguishable from clotted cream. Not even Chaucer, with all his fun and games with smelly sounds, turns his portly self – or his con-artist Colin – into a pudding.[53]

Spenser's persistent quibbles on the sounds of ancient poets cause serious interference with their pastoral aspiration. If we recall that those 'February' herdgrooms, so bitterly chidden by Thenot, were crowing in pipes of green corn, then the Orphic pattern of poetic flight is in danger of being utterly grounded. 'December' returns to the sound of 'crow'. Here are the lines on the very last bird that the *Calender* names:

> The carefull cold hath nypt my rugged rynde,
> And in my face deepe furrowes eld hath pight:
> My head besprent with hoary frost I fynde
> And by myne eie the Crowe his clawe dooth wrighte. ('December', 132–6)

---

51 René Magritte, 'The Treachery of Images'.
52 M. Craig, 'The Secret Wit of Spenser's Language', in *Elizabethan Poetry*, ed. P.J. Alpers (London: Oxford University Press, 1967), 447–73, and A.C. Hamilton, 'Our New Poet: Spenser: "well of English undefyled"', in *A Theatre for Spenserians*, ed. J.M. Kennedy and J.A. Reither (Manchester: Manchester University Press, 1973), 101–23 offer acute analysis of Spenser's work with sound and sense.
53 Clout also turns up as a bandage on the leg of the ewe who falls into a dell in 'March' (50) and on the back heel of the fox disguised as a papistly-inflected, predatory travelling salesman in 'May' (243).

Deeply harrowing though these lines be, with poetic 'wrighting', turned into wrinkles, their tone is troubled by the recall of Cuddie's crowing pipe. While we may hear the echo to return to the transformation of Cuddie-as-Colin from fond fly to sage, its resonance is much darker. Pastoral poetry has turned ugly. Its silly pipe has become a corvid claw, and the Orphic wings of a swan, with all their metrical flights of fancy, are become the feet of a crow.[54]

Spenser is not the first writer to debase poetic birds: Baldwin got there before him when, in a blend of the *Manciple's Tale* with *The House of Fame*, he turns Chaucer's Dantean eagle into a crow that falls down a London chimney.[55] And if we 'thenk upon the crowe' (*Manciple's Tale*, IX.362), we start to hear not just crowing herdgrooms from *The House of Fame*, but the Manciple's Ovidian story in which Apollo, the God of Poetry, kills a crow because it taunts him with the sound of 'cokkow' (cuckoo or cuckold, IX.243).[56] Better not to have that sound in your ears when trying to take the poetic ambitions of the *Calender* seriously. So perhaps the 'merry tale' of the crow was one that E.K. skipped? Or passed over deliberately? In returning to the commentary's diversionary Chaucerian references, I want to pose a question that so far I have refrained from asking outright. How much of the sonic mayhem that is cued by resonances of 'Chaucers verse almost whole' would Spenser have wanted us to hear? To admit some turbulence could be seen to lend comic gravitas to the poet's flighty aims.[57] A modicum of merry byplay fits the witty game played between apparatus and commentary, poem and patronage. Framing, or allowing the *Calender* to be framed, with misleading commentary, glosses and woodcuts takes the edge off blazoning the naked ambition of poetic pride.[58]

But if we are alert to E.K.'s suppression of the title of Chaucer's verse, and hear rather more of it than simply its 'bergerie' vignette, then Spenser's jostle with Kentish Tityrus threatens the novelty of the new poet's work. E.K. starts to show uncanny resemblance to the man of 'gret auctorite' that Chaucer's narrator cannot make out, and whom he is unable to name (*The House of Fame*, 2155–8). The end of Chaucer's dream vision pre-empts the cloudiness of the name 'Immeritô' and all of those other names that may or may not belong to 'different persones'. Colin's missing emblem at the end of 'December' supplies a visual blank for the

---

54 Cheney traces the transcendent poetic career of Colin Clout through analysis of extended metaphors of flight and birds. On the crow, he notes that 'Colin has been written by the year' (107), but that the poet Spenser, by the end of the poem, has proved his tender wings, 110. Goldberg, in contrast, notes that swans cannot fly, 57.

55 William Baldwin, *Beware the Cat*, ed. William A. Ringler Jr. and Michael Flachman (California: Huntingdon, 1988), 33, though Chaucer precedes him when he compares previous poets to a nest of confused rooks in a tree (*House of Fame*, 1514–19).

56 Chaucer also plays on the reputation of Apollo as God of Poetry in *The House of Fame*, with the mischievous scansion and rhyme between 'loo' and 'Appolloo' (1231–2).

57 Berger sees the poem as a self-amused pastoral, a critical and comically squint re-enactment of attitudes, topics and norms characteristic of a traditional literary mode, 277.

58 Bart van Es discusses the inherent instability between the missing emblem, glosses, and verse, asking whether E.K.'s gloss to the absent emblem is meant to be richly ironic, giving voice to the silence of Colin's mutable text. Does it get to the heart of Spenser's imitation, or is it spectacularly wide of the mark? 'Works Published before 1589', in *A Critical Companion*, 116–38 (138).

uncertainty over where *The House of Fame* stops. The 'uncouth' poet and his 'schollerly' amanuensis have already been upstaged by Geffrey's sport with poetic resonance.[59]

E.K. shilly-shallies between admitting some parts of Chaucer and keeping the rest at bay in order to tamp the sound of the competition, not (I think), out of fear of Chaucerian seriousness; but anxiety about Chaucerian fun. Explicitly to name *The House of Fame* would be to risk unseemly comparison between comic inventions. To protect his poetic greenery from unruly gales of laughter Spenser primes E.K. to mute Chaucerian uproariousness. Like fragile corn pipes, however, will o' the wisp commentary is susceptible to bursts of rude wind. So, as a last ditch defence, Spenser provides the *Calender* with its concluding sound barrier. The twelve-line twelve-syllable square poem grounds Chaucer so that the *Calender* gets its free 'passeport'. Only, if we cannot expel our Chaucerian earworm, Chaucer gets the last laugh. The very strain of Spenser's efforts recalls Chaucer's own version of arithmetically proportioned poetry: the squire's 'ars-metrike' in the *Summoner's Tale* that is also divisible by twelve (III.2222 and 2257–70). Would Spenser have been pleased to have his perfectly articulated syllables dispersed in the resonance of a churl's neatly divided fart? To hear the sounds of 'auncient' Chaucer in *The Shepheards Calender* helps us to see that in contrast to those Chaucerian poets of love and complaint, Spenser, like Gascoigne before him, saw that Chaucer's poetry was funny. To keep hearing more and more of Dan Geffrey however, blasts the new poet out of his chosen waters.[60]

---

59 Goldberg's hauntingly lyrical deconstruction of the *Calender* argues that Colin, the shepherds that repeat his songs, and Immeritô, are all part of a chain of deferred meaning that leads ultimately to a disembodied voice. E.K. is just another voice in the text. Not quite a proper name, E.K.'s status cannot be distinguished from the text or its apparatus. He is just one of an endless chain of signifiers that fail to arrive at ultimate signification, 64. Goldberg's reading is much darker than my own, but his argument that pastoral poetics leads to loss and death iterates the *Calender*'s (and *The House of Fame*'s) dispersal of words into air: 'Sike prayse is smoke, that sheddeth in the skye / Sike words bene wynd, and wasten soone in vayne' ('October', 35–6).

60 Anne Lake Prescott notes that Spenser praises Chaucer with watery metaphors: 'June', 93–4; *Faerie Queene*, IV.ii.32 and VII.vii.9, 'Sources' 98. Lydgate anticipates Spenser in 'The Life of Our Lady', commending Chaucer as 'the nobyll rethoricien and poet of Gret Bretayne', the first to 'distyll and reyne / The gold dew dropys of speche and eloquence / In-to Englyssh tong'.

3

Diverse pageants: normative arrays of sexuality

Helen Cooper

Chaucer is the only one of Spenser's English predecessors whose influence on him is regularly acknowledged, and indeed, given Spenser's own recurrent invocation of him, it would be perverse not to take note.[1] Understanding just how that influence works, however, is a more complicated matter. Harold Bloom famously defined the relationship between a poet and his great predecessors as one of Freudian anxiety, as expressing an oedipal need to eliminate the father.[2] If ever there was a poetic father, however, Chaucer stood in that relationship to Spenser; but with them, the Bloomian model does not work, and I suspect that it is rather less generally useful as a principle of literary criticism than Bloom supposed. Freud was talking about the father you are born to; but poetic fathers are not like that. The Freudian model is often (not always) a false analogy – for you can *choose* your own poetic father.[3] In many cases, including Spenser's, the choice is made in order to assert not independence but filiation or descent. At the simplest level, Spenser takes that to the point where he repeatedly asserts Chaucer's greatness; in *The Shepheardes Calender* he famously has him replace Virgil as the 'god of shepheards Tityrus', appropriating the name that the great classical master-poet had chosen for himself for his own English master-poet.[4] Whereas in the *Calender*, however, he expresses the wish that some drops of Chaucer's genius would fall on him, by the time he was writing *The Faerie Queene* he was claiming something much more ambitious:

> [...] through infusion sweete
> Of thine owne spirit, which doth in me suruiue,

---

1 John A. Burrow's article 'Chaucer, Geoffrey', in *The Spenser Encyclopedia*, ed. A.C. Hamilton et al. (Toronto: University of Toronto Press, 1990), contains an admirable outline of Chaucer's multifaceted influence on Spenser; and see also the survey by Anne Higgins, 'Spenser Reading Chaucer: Another Look at the *Faerie Queene* Allusions', *Journal of English and Germanic Philology*, 89 (1990), 17–36.
2 Harold Bloom, *The Anxiety of Influence: A Theory of Poetry*, 2nd edn (New York: Oxford University Press, 1973; repr. 1997), though medieval poetry falls outside his range of reference.
3 Helen Cooper, 'Choosing Poetic Fathers: The English Problem', in *Medieval and Early Modern Authorship*, ed. Guillemette Bolens and Lukas Erne, *Swiss Papers in English Language and Literature*, 25 (Tübingen: Narr, 2011), 29–49.
4 'June' 81, in *Edmund Spenser: The Shorter Poems*, ed. Richard A. McCabe (London: Penguin, 1999).

> I follow here the footing of thy feete,
> That with thy meaning so I may the rather meete.[5]

Chaucer, at the end of *Troilus and Criseyde*, had asked his book to kiss the steps of the five great classical authors, 'Virgile, Ovide, Omer, Lucan, and Stace', but however ambitious the implied comparison, his position was explicitly one of subjection.[6] In setting out to follow Chaucer's steps, Spenser claims to bring him back to life, to be a companion with him in a shared 'meaning'.

That meeting, that commonality, of meaning that Spenser proposes is a reinterpretation based on a deep understanding. It does not, of course, suggest that he imitates Chaucer in any slavish, or even obvious, way. When he imitates Marot, Ariosto, Tasso, or even Virgil or Ovid, he does so tacitly;[7] only Chaucer is called in as an explicit presence in his poetry. When he does invoke him, however, readers are commonly baffled by the mismatch between what he claims and what he does. The gap in 'February' between the tales of love and chivalry that he has Thenot describe Chaucer as telling and the example he gives, the fable of the oak and the briar, is an obvious example, stirring E.K. himself to complain about the lack of similarity; and the episode in *The Faerie Queene* that he introduces as the completion of the *Squire's Tale* fails to match up with its original in any straightforward way. That the *Squire's Tale* was unfinished left readers tantalised – Milton famously wanted to 'call up him who left halftold / The story of Cambuscan bold', and John Lane, a friend of Milton's father, attempted to complete it in twelve books that, like Spenser's supplement, left Chaucer far behind.[8] Classical and early modern theories of *imitatio* insisted on difference rather than similarity alone: a writer should aim to emulate the best features of his master, not to copy him, and he should emulate in such a way that the imitation never intrudes. Spenser's imitations of Chaucer run the gamut from direct citation or quotation to much more subtle kinds of influence. For him as for all English writers through the 1570s and 1580s, Chaucer was acknowledged as the primary poet of England, the god of English poetry; but that does not prevent any of them from forging their own way. Spenser's encounters with Chaucer's meanings are liberating, opening up opportunities for him beyond anything that his master does.

Those principles of imitation, revivification or commonality of meaning thus go well beyond the places where he cites Chaucer by name, though those

---

5 *Edmund Spenser: The Faerie Queene*, ed. A.C. Hamilton, 2nd edn (Harlow: Longman, 2001), IV.ii.34; hereafter *FQ*. All quotations from the poem will be taken from this edition.
6 *Troilus and Criseyde* V.1792, 1790, in *The Riverside Chaucer*, general ed. Larry D. Benson (Boston: Houghton Mifflin, 1987; Oxford: Oxford University Press, 1988). All quotations from Chaucer will be taken from this edition.
7 The nearest thing to an exception is the reference to '*Virgils* spirit' in the *Ruins of Rome*, itself taken from du Bellay (*Shorter Poems*, ed. McCabe, no. 25, 347); others occur in E.K.'s notes to *The Shepheardes Calender*.
8 *Il penseroso* 109–10 (with a summary to line 115), *John Milton: Complete Shorter Poems*, ed. John Carey (London: Longman, 1968); *John Lane's Continuation of Chaucer's 'Squire's Tale'*, ed. Frederick J. Furnivall (London: Kegan Paul for the Chaucer Society, 1888, 1890) (its first publication).

moments carry particular weight and have received particular attention. As Judith H. Anderson argues elsewhere in this volume, the reflections and refractions of Chaucer's meanings can take many forms; and even when Spenser does not explicitly name his predecessor, his references to him are usually clearly intended to be recognised by his readers. The richness and breadth of allusions to Chaucer's work across the Elizabethan era show how deeply the earlier poet was embedded in the culture:[9] he was part of the library of the mind that Anderson describes, and so Spenser could set up resonances between his own work and that of the earlier poet without the need to name him through authorial intervention. A particularly important example is the near-quotation from Chaucer that he inserts at a crucial point in *The Faerie Queene*, in the first speech given to Britomart after she enters the poem in Book III. First speeches always carry a particular weight of definition; here, she is urging the superiority of faithful over compelled love, and concludes,

> Ne may loue be compeld by maistery;
> For soone as maistery comes, sweet loue anone
> Taketh his nimble winges, and soone away is gone. (III.i.25)

Spenser does not name his source here – indeed, he could not, since the words are spoken by the pre-Chaucerian Britomart, not the post-Chaucerian poet – but they are so closely borrowed from the *Franklin's Tale* as to be immediately recognisable:

> Love wol nat been constreyned by maistrye.
> Whan maistrie comth, the God of Love anon
> Beteth his wynges, and farewel, he is gon![10]

Editions regularly note Spenser's Chaucerian source, but the lines have received less attention than the places where Spenser names Chaucer explicitly. They deserve more discussion, both because they constitute the most extensive quotation from Chaucer in the whole of Spenser's works, and because Britomart is the central heroine of Books III–V: half of the poem, in fact. As her first words, they are defining for her, and also for the books in which she appears – especially the books of Chastity, in its sense of lifelong fidelity in the form of passionate and unflinching adherence to one lover, and Friendship. They suggest that the Chaucerian connections of those books deserve more attention in terms of what both authors make of those ideas of love and friendship more widely; and they raise the question of why Spenser looked to Chaucer to kick-start his whole exploration of varieties of love and sexuality.

---

9 The richness of their knowledge, in both number and range, is indicated by the allusion indexes of Jackson Campbell Boswell and Sylvia Wallace Holton, eds, *Chaucer's Fame in England: STC Chauceriana 1475–1640* (New York: Modern Language Association of America, 2004) (printed material only), and by Caroline Spurgeon, ed., *Five Hundred Years of Chaucer Criticism and Allusion 1357–1900*, 3 vols (Cambridge: Cambridge University Press, 1908–17; repr. 1925).
10 *Canterbury Tales* (hereafter *CT*), V.764–6.

It is those *varieties* that link the poets particularly closely – hence the title of this chapter. As Spenser puts it,

> Wonder it is to see, in diuerse minds,
>   How diuersely love doth his pageants play,
>   And shewes his powre in variable kinds. (III.v.1)

In both poets, these 'variable kinds' of love, the diverse pageants it plays, encompass the whole range of human (and, on occasion, non-human) attraction from 'sensuall desire' to 'goodly fire' (III.v.1.6, 8). The 'normative arrays' of the subtitle are in effect a paraphrase of that, using a term coined by Judson Allen as the equivalent of the medieval *distinctio*, a method of analysis whereby 'a single idea or thing is examined by subdividing it into its kinds, or parts'.[11] In Chaucer and Spenser, the dominant such array is that of all forms of sexuality, covering not only human love and lust but generative love in all its forms: a range that itself often stands in for broader patterns of moral and political action and social relations. For both poets, generative love includes the cosmic principle that keeps the whole natural world in being, and in continuation. Chaucer's invocation to Venus as the metonym for love in the proem to Book III of *Troilus* is one of his finest examples: he presents her as the principle of that love that runs throughout the cosmos from grass to God, taking in humanity along the way:

> In hevene and helle, in erthe and salte see
> Is felt thi myght, if that I wel descerne;
> As man, brid, best, fissh, herbe, and grene tree
> Thee fele in tymes with vapour eterne.
> God loveth, and to love wol nought werne;[12]
> And in this world no lyves creature
> Withouten love is worth, or may endure. (III.8–14)

Spenser's induction to *The Faerie Queene* III.iii does something similar, though he starts with God and works down to humankind:

> Most sacred fire, that burnest mightily
>   In liuing brests, ykindled first aboue,
>   Emongst th'eternall spheres and lamping sky,
>   And thence pourd into men, which men call Loue [...] (III.iii.1)

He does not at this point extend the principle to birds and beasts and grass, as Chaucer does, though he does so in the Garden of Adonis (III.vi.30, 35). Instead,

---

11 Judson Boyce Allen and Theresa Anne Moritz, *A Distinction of Stories: The Medieval Unity of Chaucer's Fair Chain of Narratives for Canterbury* (Columbus: Ohio State University Press, 1981), 86.
12 'Werne' means 'refuse': a significant alteration from Boccaccio's original, where the reference is to the pagan gods feeling the effects of love.

we are given an immediate recognition of the generous potential of such love to be corrupted in the fallen world:

> Not that same, which doth base affections moue
> In brutish mindes, and filthy lust inflame,
> But that sweete fit, that doth true beautie loue,
> And chooseth vertue for his dearest Dame,
> Whence spring all noble deedes and neuer dying fame. (III.iii.1)

Spenser posits here a disjunction between good love and bad lust, but across the whole poem things are not always quite so simple: not only may they be mistaken for each other (as his vices are experts in fraudulently imitating the good), but there is sometimes an overlap between them, or at least conversion may be possible. Chaucer's representations of love present a similarly full array. At one extreme, there is immutable divine love; at the other, human sexuality divorced from love, the selfishness of lust for its own sake. In between are the operations of generative sexuality within the natural world; love as the good relationship between men and women; and models of sustained or broken friendships.

An important point of entry into the whole topic is where Spenser starts in that verse with which he opens III.iii, with love as taking its origin from God. It is a strongly neoplatonic idea – and neoplatonism is something we associate with Spenser more than Chaucer. Ways of thinking about love and sexuality were however strongly continuous from the twelfth to the nineteenth centuries, or indeed from Boethius's fifth-century *Consolation of Philosophy* forward. One of the foundational texts of neoplatonism, the work both developed and transmitted some of Plato's key ideas in Latin for a mixed pagan and Christian audience, and Chaucer, who knew it with the thoroughness accorded to the translator, is much more neoplatonic than we usually allow. The tradition of this kind of neoplatonic love as it was known in the Middle Ages runs from Ovid through Boethius, Alan of Lille and the *Romance of the Rose*; and to those, Spenser added not only some of the more recent Italian writers on the subject, but Chaucer himself. He could have got to know Boethius at first hand (the text was widely accessible), but there is no decisive evidence for that; he could have got most or all of his knowledge of the *Consolation* through Chaucer's translation, and through the Boethian ideas that appear in many of his poems. Boethius's ideas of harmony, or indeed disharmony, were crucial to both poets. That the work is the consolation of Philosophy rather than Faith gives it an additional value for them: for Spenser, because he does not need to break the ostensible classicism of the surface of *The Faerie Queene* with too much overtly theological or confessional detail; and for Chaucer, because Boethius allows him to place key statements about the ordering of the world in the mouths of a number of his pagan characters. One of the fullest expressions of that comes in Troilus's great hymn to love at the end of *Troilus* Book III, the book in which the lovers consummate their affair in the highest moment of joy in the poem. The lines are sung by Troilus, but they are borrowed by Chaucer from the *Consolation*, where they are spoken by Philosophy – and it is a good rule of thumb that if a Chaucerian character quotes or adapts speeches of Philosophy's rather than her misguided interlocutor's, he is getting something right. The lines are not something that can be dismissed as emanating simply from Troilus's self-delusion, as our suspicious and cynical age sometimes likes to argue.[13]

> Love, that of erthe and se hath governaunce,
> Love, that his hestes hath in hevenes hye,
> Love, that with an holsom alliaunce
> Halt peples joyned, as hym lest hem gye,
> And couples doth in vertu for to dwelle,
> Bynd this acord, that I have told and telle.
>
> That that the worlde with feith, which that is stable,
> Diverseth so his stowndes concordynge,
> That elementz that ben so discordable
> Holden a bond perpetuely durynge,
> That Phebus mote his rosy day forth brynge,
> And that the mone hath lordshipe over the nyghtes, –
> Al this doth Love, ay heried be his myghtes!
> [...]
> So wolde God, that auctor is of kynde,
> That with his bond Love of his vertu liste
> To cerclen hertes alle, and faste bynde,
> That from his bond no wight the wey out wiste. (III.1744–57, 1765–8)

It is important to remember too that in so far as *Troilus* resembles an opera more than it does a novel, it is Troilus who has all the great music, the great arias. This is one of them; and that matters for how we should read the poem.

In the fifteenth century, Chaucer was thought of as a great love poet – the greatest to have written in English. That idea tended to be overridden by the Reformation view of him as a proto-Protestant, though that was important in encouraging the Elizabethans to regard him as a foundational poet for England. Chaucer, it seemed, had correct views on God and the Church, even if many of those views were ascribed to him on the basis of works he did not in fact write, such as the *Plowman's Tale*. It was in Spenser's own time, the end of the sixteenth century, that people first began to associate Chaucer primarily with his bawdy sections: what one might call the *Miller's Tale* syndrome. In the nineteenth century his works were read and admired as if they were naturalistic novels, and the critical priorities moved to praising his drawing of characters. That in turn led to Kittredge's twentieth-century invention of the 'marriage group', which came to define him at the cost of almost everything else. More recently, we have had the orthodox Catholic Chaucer, the feminist

---

13 The fashion was set by D.W. Robertson Jr., who argued it on the basis of both Boethian philosophy and Augustinian theology: see *A Preface to Chaucer: Studies in Medieval Perspectives* (Princeton: Princeton University Press, 1962), 472–502. Among the many objections to his interpretation is that his views do not allow for the possibility of Chaucer's engaging in a serious dialogue with the *Consolation*.

Chaucer, the Lollard Chaucer, and the New Historicist and political Chaucer (exemplified, for instance, by D.W. Robertson Jr., Carolyn Dinshaw, Alan J. Fletcher and Paul Strohm), and his views on love more broadly have tended to disappear from sight. That Spenser was a great poet of love remained central for much longer; his works include the sonnets, hymns and marriage songs, he comments on love more often and more explicitly, and if one read *The Faerie Queene* for its narrative, as many people did, that meant giving priority to its 'Knights and Ladies gentle deeds' (I.Pro.i). A century ago, the poem was part of the standard reading for boys, alongside the quests and adventures of Malory's *Morte Darthur*. It was largely only from the 1930s, and C.S. Lewis's *Allegory of Love*, that its place in the neoplatonic tradition was recognised: a recognition taken much further in Robert Ellrodt's *Neoplatonism in the Poetry of Spenser*.[14] That kind of criticism has in turn been overtaken by the massive investment given by New Historicism in Spenser's relations with Elizabeth and with Ireland, and that has largely overwhelmed the earlier neoplatonic, transhistorical approaches to his poetry; but just for those reasons, we need to revisit them. Of course Spenser's presentations of love have a strong historicist element: it is about as explicit as it could be in Gloriana and Belphoebe and Timias and the other familiar figures we read through to their historical equivalents. But in contrast to his wrestling with problems of Reformation theology and Irish politics, or with the problems of English foreign policy in Book V, love and sexuality (as distinct from the theologies of sex and the practice of marriage) are in his conception most noted for their transhistorical qualities, and New Historicism is not good at dealing with the transhistorical. It has difficulty even in thinking about sources, when to do so involves dealing with two different ages at once. The central books of *The Faerie Queene*, III and IV – central both in structure and in Spenser's vision for the work – sideline the political for much of the time: there is plenty of it there, but that is not what impels those books forward. That is something much larger, and (I would argue) much more Chaucerian: big ideas about love driving the universe, and also, at the micro level, of love and its opposites and failures expressed in human terms.

Not that Chaucer always considers love in human terms: sometimes avian terms can make things clearer. *The Parliament of Fowls* offers, not exactly an allegory, but a normative array of analogies, for human mating patterns. It seems to be a zoological fact that birds do indeed offer the closest parallels to humans, from lifelong pair-bonding to random promiscuity; but in the *Parliament*, all of them can be portrayed as part of that God-ordained pattern of regenerative creation under the aegis of Nature, 'The vicaire of the almyghty Lord' (379). She is given a description heavily indebted, as Chaucer notes, to Alan of Lille's 'Pleynt

---

14 C.S. Lewis, *The Allegory of Love: A Study in Medieval Tradition* (Oxford: Oxford University Press, 1936) (numerous reprints); Robert Ellrodt, *Neoplatonism in the Poetry of Spenser* (Geneva: Droz, 1960). Thomas Bulger points out how different Spenser's neoplatonism is from Chaucer's, 'Platonism in Spenser's *Mutabilitie Cantos*', in *Platonism and the English Imagination*, ed. Anna Baldwin and Sarah Hutton (Cambridge: Cambridge University Press, 1994), 126–38; and see also Yasunari Takada, 'Chaucer's Use of Neoplatonic Traditions', in the same volume, 45–51.

of Kynde', his *De planctu Naturae*; and Spenser in turn bases his own Nature of the Mutabilitie Cantos on Chaucer's, complete with a reference to 'that old *Dan Geffrey*' (VII.vii.9), on which more below. The *Parliament* was clearly a work that Spenser knew well, and the poem makes a good entry point for thinking about those diverse pageants of different kinds of love. The first of those pageants consists of the human lovers painted on the walls of the temple of Priapus and Venus, who have died of frustrated desire (246–94), and who form a group distinct from the noisy and lively crowd of birds clustering around Nature. The birds' own array ranges from the high courtly service of the eagles to the undying faithfulness of the turtle-dove to the random promiscuity of the lesser birds, the goose and the cuckoo and the duck. They operate in effect as an analogy for the range of heterosexual love offered in the *Canterbury Tales*, from the courtly suffering and service of the *Knight's Tale* down to the frolickings of the fabliaux – though in the *Tales*, since human beings have a dimension beyond the body such as is not granted to animals, Chaucer also adds the divine love of St Cecilia in the *Second Nun's Tale*. Across all his works, he offers a strikingly similar range to what Spenser offers in the middle books of *The Faerie Queene*. He covers immutable divine love, as in God's refusal to cease from loving in the *Troilus*'s invocation to Venus quoted earlier, in Troilus's Boethian hymn, or in the reminder to the audience of Christ's enduring faithfulness at the end of the poem (V.1842–8) – a reminder unavailable to the pagan characters within the narrative. He shows the operations of generative sexuality within the natural world, as in the description of the eternal influence, the 'vapour eterne', of Venus, or in the *Parliament* itself. He considers what should constitute the ideal relationship between 'frendes', as in the lines from the *Franklin's Tale* quoted by Britomart, which are expanded in Chaucer with an insistence that they apply as much to men as to women and to friends as well as lovers (*CT* V.761–87).[15] The lines are thus not just about heterosexual love in either Chaucer's or Spenser's use of them; in Spenser's case, they also make an intervention in the contemporary debate, going back to Cicero's *De amicitia*, about whether it was possible for friendship to exist between men and women.[16] The woman warrior Britomart can enjoy a full friendship with the knights with whom she rides, in a conflation of heterosexual and homosocial relationships. She does not go on to quote the Franklin's further lines about the need for forbearance between friends:

> On every wrong a man may nat be wreken.
> After the tyme moste be temperaunce
> To every wight that kan on governaunce; (V.784–6)

---

15 Spenser's re-use of the lines is a useful reminder that there is nothing ironic about them, as has sometimes been argued; again, the move was deeply influenced by Robertson, 470–2.
16 The case is extensively argued in Edmund Tilney's much-reprinted *The Flower of Friendship* (first edition, 1568); for its place in the debate, see Valerie Wayne's introduction to her edition of the work (Ithaca and London: Cornell University Press, 1992). See further Jean H. Hagstrum, *Esteem Enlivened by Desire: The Couple from Homer to Shakespeare* (Chicago: University of Chicago Press, 1992), especially 319–24.

But after she has unhorsed Guyon, he is persuaded to make peace with her 'through goodly temperaunce' and become friends with her, in a practical expression of just such a principle (III.i.12, iii.14). Homosocial friendship is at the core too of the *Knight's Tale*, though there it is a friendship that goes badly wrong. Spenser pays another extended homage to Chaucer when he offers his completion of the *Squire's Tale*, with its homage to 'Dan *Chaucer*, well of English vndefyled' (IV.ii.32) in his Book of Friendship.[17] Both poets also make space for virginity as a special option within their arrays of sexuality. Chaucer's is overtly Catholic, in St Cecilia, as Spenser's could not be; but with virginity as a religious virtue disallowed by the Reformation, Spenser gives a political counterpart in Belphoebe, though his narrative acknowledges the complications resulting from its reflection in the Queen. At the other end of the spectrum of sexuality there are the 'filthy lusts' of the jealous old man with a young wife, in the *Merchant's Tale* or the story of Malbecco and Hellenore; or of sex purely as gratification, in Chaucer's fabliaux, or Spenser's Squire of Dames. Both authors are careful to distinguish that kind of purely personal, selfish desire from what Spenser calls 'virtuous love', a love that should, as in the *Franklin's Tale*, be freely given and taken in full respect for the other person.

Those overlaps still leave plenty of room for differences in the treatment of love in the two poets. It is the larger ideas of love as a divine or neoplatonic influence that encourage Spenser to allegorise the right relationship between virtues – truth and holiness, or equity and justice – as companionship or love; or conversely, to show the relationships of the vices as fellowship or friendship or sexual associations that go wrong. The poets give very different emphases to how they analyse and attempt to understand all such relationships. We think of Spenser as writing in abstractions, and Chaucer as writing in terms of characters in a much more modern sense; but it is also evident that in the central books, Spenser moves some way away from personification allegory to produce a much more exemplary kind of narrative, a 'romance of types', and those types too are representative of the 'diverse pageants', a normative array.[18] Many of those types, and the structures that contain them, are more obviously Ariostan than Chaucerian. All those factors might appear to leave too large a gap between Spenser's not-quite-personifications in Books III and IV and the array of characters in the *Tales*, but the gap is not as large as it might appear. The structure of *The Faerie Queene* is most often based on a model of imperfect human virtue in male form, in the central knight of each book (Holiness, for instance), struggling to attain the principle of that virtue in its female form (Una) and choosing 'vertue for his dearest Dame' (III.iii.1). The virtues as abstractions, in other words, are represented as ladies. That representation has a long tradition behind it, closely connected with the fact that abstract nouns in Latin and other romance languages normally gender their abstract nouns as feminine. Humilitas,

---

17 'English vndefyled' refers primarily to the belief that Chaucer's English was uncorrupted by the wholesale Elizabethan import of 'inkhorn terms', but Spenser may also be suggesting a rescue of the poet from his increasingly common association with bawdiness.
18 The term 'romance of types' was popularised by Lewis, 417.

Castitas, Iustitia and so on come as ready-made feminines, and so are ascribed female attributes; and while it is true that the vices are also gendered feminine, it had long been the practice in art to represent the vices as male *exempla*. Gluttony, for instance, would be represented by a bloated male figure exemplifying the glutton, typically in the process of drinking; Avarice was represented as a miser with moneybags. Spenser follows this pattern in his procession of the vices in I.iv, where only the 'mayden Queene' Pryde is female. The English language lost its gender system early, so it was not bound to follow that pattern – and indeed it does not always do so: Langland strikingly rethinks the genders of his personifications from scratch, but he does so to a degree very rarely followed by later writers, Spenser included.[19] Even now, we give virtue names to girls, not boys: names such as Hope, Constance, Prudence or Faith.

That principle is present in Chaucer too. Denise Baker argued that four of Chaucer's key heroines are closely associated with the four cardinal virtues:[20] Prudence, so named in 'Melibee', who comes close to being a personification rather than a person; Constancy, or Fortitude, in the courageous endurance of undeserved suffering by the Custance of the *Man of Law's Tale*; Temperance, in the Virginia of the *Physician's Tale*, whose 'attempraunce', 'abstinence', 'mesure' and avoidance of drink and parties are described in detail for over thirty lines (*CT* VI.39–71); and Justice in Griselda. The equation for Griselda may seem an oddity, but she is an exemplar of justice in the dominant element of its medieval definition as rendering what is due, in her case of obedience to her husband, backed by her truth to her sworn promise. She is also supreme in her exercise of justice in her husband's absence, when she executes

> juggementz of so greet equitee
> That she from hevene sent was, as men wende,
> Peple to save and every wrong t'amende. (IV.439–41)

One Italian manuscript of a vernacular translation of the Latin work of Petrarch's that Chaucer had used as his source shows her in the full iconography of Justice, complete with sword and scales.[21] In addition, the Prologue to the *Second Nun's Tale* analyses St Cecilia's name into a demonstration of a whole basket of virtues, including the three theological ones of faith, hope and charity.[22] With the partial exception of Prudence, all those women are presented as much too fully rounded individuals to be personifications (and one wonders indeed if Chaucer changed

---

19 See Helen Cooper, 'Gender and Personification in *Piers Plowman*', *Yearbook of Langland Studies*, 5 (1991), 31–48.
20 Denise N. Baker, 'Chaucer and Moral Philosophy: The Virtuous Women of *The Canterbury Tales*', *Medium Ævum*, 60 (1991), 241–56. Custance and Virginia both take their names in part from their fathers, but the moral implications are unmissable. On the place of Chaucer's women within ethical schemes, see Alcuin Blamires, *Chaucer, Ethics and Gender* (Oxford: Oxford University Press, 2006).
21 K.P. Clarke, *Chaucer and Italian Textuality* (Oxford: Oxford University Press, 2011), 112.
22 See *CT* VIII.85–119, especially 92–3 and 100 on the hope of heaven; 110, on faith; and 118, on charity. As the text notes, the passage is a translation from the *Golden Legend*.

Custance's name from the 'Constance' of his source to make her more of an individual), but the parallels are none the less good to think with: those personified heroines of Spenser are perhaps not so far from Chaucer's women – or Chaucer's not so far from them – as we might at first think. How far Spenser would have invested in the Chaucerian parallels with the virtues remains a matter for speculation, but his alertness to the ethical potential of both narrative and names strongly suggests that he would have drawn similar conclusions. Chaucer finds these five names already there in his sources, and with the exception of the elaborate etymologising given to Cecilia, they work by association (Virginia with temperance, and so on); Spenser prescribes what his characters are (or, in the case of vices disguised as virtues, what they are pretending to be) by means of the names he gives them.[23] *The Faerie Queene* does on occasion allow its characters to escape from their nominative determinism: if Griselda's name has nothing of equity about it, neither does Britomart's, though that is the equation Spenser makes for her in Book V. The women of the *Tales* do however serve as a warning against assuming that Chaucer had no moral compass, that every one of the *Canterbury Tales* is judgement-free, or works independently of contemporary moral schemes – an assumption that is itself partly a backlash against earlier criticism that tried to turn all the tales into warnings against various sins, culminating in the *Parson's Tale*. In these tales of good women, at least, virtue, not sin, is at the centre, and the women are crucial to those schemes.[24]

Spenser thus need not be leaving Chaucer so far behind in constructing his exemplary 'romance of types'; but neither poet consistently writes to formula. The Dorigen of the *Franklin's Tale* is a notable exception to any tendency towards abstraction in Chaucer's more serious tales, in that it is impossible to essentialise her, even though the tale itself has a strong ethical grounding in an exposition of human relationships both social and heterosexual. Britomart, who marks her connection with the story of Dorigen in that opening speech of hers, is also one of the most Chaucerian of Spenser's heroines in the sense of being most fully human. Her name stresses that she has a function in the larger political and nationalist allegory of the poem, as the martial ancestress of the British line, but that does not limit her to any single form of moral representation. Her characterisation takes her beyond the political and ethical meanings that Spenser has her represent, in that she becomes part of a love story of the sort found in non-allegorical romances, and a love story that generates a good deal of audience sympathy. She forms an unusually broad number and variety of relationships: with various knights errant, starting with Arthur, Redcross and Guyon; with various women, not least Amoret; and ultimately with the man she has seen in the mirror and is questing for, Artegall. He may be the Justice to her Equity, or a Leicester figure given a place in the British genealogy of which she will become a part (Artegall being a name held by one of

---

[23] See Herbert Marks and Kenneth Gross, 'Names, Naming', in *The Spenser Encyclopedia*, ed. A.C. Hamilton *et al.* (Toronto: University of Toronto Press, 1990), 494–6.

[24] It should be noted that the Ovidian heroines of the *Legend of Good Women* do not share these Christian ethical models: they are 'good' principally by comparison with the men who wrong them.

the traditional ancestors of the earls of Warwick, a title held by the Dudleys),[25] or the equivalent to Arthur to enable the descent of the English royal house despite Arthur's own childlessness; but their love-story has its interest primarily because it is just that, an engaging story in its own right. In addition, Britomart helps to generate other stories that in turn comment on other relationships. Scudamour acknowledges that his abduction of Amoret from the Temple of Venus was against her will, with much more of the 'maistrie' about it such as Britomart disavows in her opening Chaucerian speech than the free action that her lines advocated:

> But yet for nought,
> That euer she to me could say or doe,
> Could she her wished freedome fro me wooe. (IV.x.57)

It needs Britomart to release Amoret from that compelled yielding before she is able to love him freely, as an autonomous individual – and for once, the phrase 'autonomous individual' makes sense within a moral allegory.

Spenser's use of the lines from the *Franklin's Tale* to define Britomart makes it clear that he took them absolutely seriously: that he regarded them as normative in that medieval-early modern sense of expressing the norm of *how things ought to be*. The aphorism demands additional assent too from the fact that it originates with Chaucer, the father of English poetry. The omission of any origin for it other than its speaker herself allows it to carry full weight within its new context, of Britomart as the poem's representation of married chastity – that is, of lifelong and passionate fidelity. The passion, with all its denotations of sexuality, is important, though it is something Britomart shares less with Chaucerian heroines than with those of Middle English romance, and of Shakespeare.[26] This is the kind of love that properly overcomes even temperance; which is why, in contradiction of Spenser's general principle of the virtues fighting the vices or the vices quarrelling with each other, Britomart's first and defining *action* is unhorsing that embodiment of Temperance, Guyon. The enchanted spear of good love is impossible to resist, although, in accordance with the Franklin's later lines, it is also imperative on friends to bear with each other, and the knights accept Britomart into their company. The principles she embodies – freedom in love, mutual obedience, faithfulness – serve as a standard to measure all the rest of the *exempla* of attraction in these more social books. The fact that she is a woman in man's armour further implies that those principles are gender-inclusive. Negatively, those principles serve to condemn the figures who do attempt to compel love by *maistrie*: Radigund, Malecasta, Poeana among the women; or the men who try to force women, Scudamour at the mildest, the attempted rapes of Belphoebe by Braggadochio and of Florimell by the fisherman (for which there

---

25 It first appears as 'Arthgall Cargueirensis, quae nunc Warwic appellatur' in Geoffrey of Monmouth, *The History of the Kings of Britain*, ed. Michael D. Reeve, trans. Neil Wright (Woodbridge: Boydell Press, 2007), 211. The title of earl of Warwick was held by Leicester's elder brother.
26 Helen Cooper, *The English Romance in Time: Transforming Motifs from Geoffrey of Monmouth to the Death of Shakespeare* (Oxford: Oxford University Press, 2004), 218–68.

is again a Chaucerian parallel, in the attempted rape of Custance at sea).[27] Her generous faithfulness similarly condemns Malecasta's promiscuity and Malbecco's jealousy. Positively, it approves friendship, in the basic narrative pattern of the poem by which the virtues accompany and support each other, and, when the principles of virtue are at issue, promise to marry each other – though the actual marriages are most often postponed, as being beyond fulfilment in the world as it is. At the level of the individual episode, her principles are expressed again in the story of Cambello, Canacee, Triamond and Cambina, who end up not only as paired brothers and sisters but as friends with each other and also as happily married couples,

> So all alike did loue, and loued were,
> That since their days such louers were not found elswere. (IV.iii.52)

As Anne Higgins noted, in many ways the episode is more reminiscent of the *Knight's Tale* than the Squire's, from the echo in its opening line forward ('Whylome as antique stories tellen vs', IV.ii.32) through its strongly martial emphasis.[28] The reminiscence shows too in its rewriting of relationships: Palamon and Arcite are cousins, sworn brothers and friends, and all three bonds break down drastically in the course of the tale through their rivalry for Emily. Spenser reinstates and strengthens the relationships, turning the cousinship and the sworn brotherhood into closer bonds, resolving the enmity of Cambell and Triamond in time to give them a happy ending, and adding a second woman to resolve the triangle into a foursquare stability.

There is one other love-relationship in *The Faerie Queene* that is drawn from Chaucer, and that is at once the most famous, or infamous, and the most baffling. Arthur's dream of his fairy queen and his subsequent quest for her borrows from Sir Thopas's dream of his elf-queen: the most visionary of all the episodes of falling in love in Spenser's work, and the most bathetic of Chaucer's. Spenser cannot have taken *Sir Thopas* as other than comic – at least, no one else in the sixteenth century seems to have done[29] – though that would not rule out a desire on his part to recuperate for seriousness a moment in his forebear's work that has generous poetic potential. The borrowing perhaps makes best sense in terms of those 'diverse pageants'. It adds a new and different kind of initiation into love, one that goes beyond the usual human processes of attraction. Gloriana is beyond normal reach, not least because she never appears in the poem as we have it, and it is hard to imagine how she might ever have been represented. In Arthur's dream, however, she is more than just a solely spiritual or imaginary being: she is material enough to leave her impression in the 'pressed gras' after he has woken (I.ix.15). There is a strong hint too of potential sexuality in the 'goodly glee and louely

---

27 *FQ* II.iii.42, III.viii.25–9, *CT* II.904–24.
28 Higgins, 22–4. Compare 'Whilom, as olde stories tellen us' (*CT* I.859) – perhaps the closest verbatim quotation from Chaucer after Britomart's opening speech.
29 See J.A. Burrow, 'Sir Thopas in the Sixteenth Century', in *Middle English Studies Presented to Norman Davis*, ed. Douglas Gray and E.G. Stanley (Oxford: Oxford University Press, 1983), 69–91.

blandishment' (I.ix.14) she accords him all night long, though Spenser never quite commits the couple to going beyond amatory conversation. She is thus both a creature within the world of nature, appearing in conjunction with the favour of 'the fields, the floods, the heauens' (I.ix.12); but in her visionary status, she exists outside that too. There is no equivalent to such a mate in the array of sexuality presented by Nature in the *Parliament of Fowls*, nor could there be. To search for a woman perceived only in vision invokes a sublimated sexuality of a kind that goes well beyond avian analogies, and indeed beyond Britomart's glimpse of Artegall in her magic mirror: his reflection gives her an image of a 'real' person, whereas Gloriana participates in a state beyond quotidian reality.[30] In terms of that normative array of desire that the poem sets out, the love between herself and Arthur (and it is important that she initiates it) is at a point of the spectrum that none of the other characters matches.

If Spenser looks to Chaucer for some of his key stories, his final vision in the Mutabilitie Cantos is likewise not so different from the older poet's – and it is worth remembering that Chaucer was the first recorded person to use the word 'mutability' in English. Those cantos pick up from the '*Foules parley*', not this time for its array of mating patterns, but for its reach beyond those to the principles of a regenerating Nature, lifted from

> That old *Dan Geffrey* (in whose gentle spright
> The pure well head of Poesie did dwell). (VII.vii.9)[31]

And Spenser echoes the *Parliament* again at the very end of the work, when Nature pronounces how all things will finally turn 'to themselues at length againe' (VII.vii.58) and change will cease as everything works towards its perfection (VII. viii.2). Chaucer envisions a very similar process in the proem to his work, in his summary of the 'Dream of Scipio', when 'every sterre shuld come into his place / Ther it was first', and the change and mutability of the cosmos will be over.[32] The end of *Troilus* likewise moves beyond change, when at his death Troilus is allowed to leave behind the mutable world of Fortune to enjoy a harmonious Boethian vision of the concord of the created world, 'this litel spot of erthe, that with the se / Embraced is', an experience enhanced by the music of the spheres (*TC* V.1815–16, 1812–13). As Troilus is a pagan, Chaucer cannot go so far as to offer him salvation; but he does allow him the Boethian next best thing. He offers his Christian readers something better, in the unfailing love of Christ (V.1842–8). At the end of the *Canterbury Tales*, the vision of a world beyond time is again made

---

30 It is worth remembering too that the best-known mirror in English romance before Britomart's was Canacee's, in the *Squire's Tale*, though that reveals fickleness in love (*CT* V.137–41).
31 See further Craig Berry's chapter in this volume; Robert Lanier Reid, 'Spenser's Mutability Song: Conclusion or Transition?', in *Celebrating Mutabilitie: Essays on Spenser's Mutabilitie Cantos*, ed. Jane Grogan (Manchester: Manchester University Press, 2010), 61–84 (65–6); and Glenn A. Steinberg, 'Chaucer's Mutability in Spenser's Mutabilitie Cantos', *Studies in English Literature 1500–1900*, 46 (2006), 27–42, who points out the discontinuities between the two accounts.
32 *PF* 67–70, with the implication of the restoration of cosmic harmony throughout the universe.

fully Christian, in the Parson's account of 'the endelees blisse of hevene, ther joye hath no contrarioustee of wo ne grevaunce' (X.1076–7). Spenser prays to 'great Sabaoth's God' that he may be granted 'that Sabaoth's sight' (VII.viii.2); Chaucer prays that he may be 'oon of hem that at the day of doom that shulle be saved' (X.1092). There is nothing in *The Faerie Queene* to match Chaucer's expression of repentance in the *Retractions*, as he prays for forgiveness for 'many a song and many a leccherous lay' (X.1087), but he does offer something comparable in his 'Hymne of Heavenly Love':

> Many lewd layes (ah woe is me the more)
> In praise of that mad fit, which fooles call loue,
> I haue in th'heat of youth made heretofore,
> That in light wits did loose affection moue.
> But all those follies now I do reproue.[33]

The moral allegory of *The Faerie Queene* enables Spenser to write of love with the aim of encouraging virtue, an approach not so easy in Chaucer's more naturalistic mode. The comparisons are none the less a useful reminder of how crude are our generalisations about periodisation, when the humanist early modern poet is more homiletic than the medieval, and when the Protestant writer is concerned about the need for repentance just as the Catholic one is. We are accustomed to talking of Renaissance humanism and the Reformation as the great dividing lines in English cultural history; but in their conceptions of life both in this world and the next, Chaucer and Spenser are not so different from each other.

---

33 'An Hymne of Heavenly Love' 8–12, in *Shorter Poems*, ed. McCabe.

4

The source of poetry: Pernaso, Paradise and Spenser's Chaucerian craft

Claire J.C. Eager

The June eclogue of *The Shepheardes Calender* is famous for its homage to Chaucer as 'the God of shepheards *Tityrus*' (81), marking the poem as an explicit site for Spenser's thinking about his project of making poetry and its relation to an English literary past.[1] The lament for Tityrus in 'June' offers precise insights into the role Chaucer played in Spenser's early-career ambitions for his poetry, which this chapter explores by examining the spatialised poetics of 'June' alongside Chaucer's similar project in the *Franklin's Tale*. Colin Clout's situation in 'June' resembles that of Dorigen in the tale. Both poems stipulate a similar setting for the main character's emotional predicament: a *locus amoenus* described in terms of Paradise. In each case a despairing emotional state prevents the character from experiencing the joys of the paradisal space; each poem links this situation to a spatialised account of poetic making that locates literary failure, inspiration and achievement within its imagined geography.

This chapter investigates resonances between the two poems and their implications for Spenser's Chaucerian poetics.[2] Staging a character's isolation from the ultimately pleasant place serves to highlight problems associated with poetic inheritance and ambition and to frame the solutions both poems contemplate. 'June' figures Colin's problem as despair over love, which excludes him from the shepherd Hobbinol's pleasant retreat. E.K., the *Calender*'s purported editor, explains that Hobbinol represents Spenser's friend Gabriel Harvey and Colin (*inter alia*) is a 'shadow' for the poet himself ('September', 176, gloss; 'Epistle', 134). Similarly, Colin's 'love' and its consequences stand in throughout the *Calender* for a set of artistic and political problems facing Spenser and his England: concerns that monarchs and clergy will abuse their power and that poets will fail to receive the

---

1 In *The Shorter Poems*, ed. Richard A. McCabe (London: Penguin, 1999), 87–94. See Clare R. Kinney, 'Marginal Presence, Lyric Resonance, Epic Absence: *Troilus and Criseyde* and/in *The Shepheardes Calender*', *Spenser Studies*, 18 (2003), 25–39, and '*The Shepheardes Calender* (1579)', in *The Oxford Handbook of Edmund Spenser*, ed. Richard A. McCabe (Oxford: Oxford University Press, 2010), 160–77 (168–9, 173); John N. King, *Spenser's Poetry and the Reformation Tradition* (Princeton: Princeton University Press, 1990), 20–31.
2 For more on 'resonance' and intertextuality, see chapters by Judith H. Anderson and Helen Barr in this volume. See also Wai Chee Dimock, 'A Theory of Resonance', *PMLA*, 112.5 (1997), 1060–71.

recognition, patronage and remuneration they deserve.[3] In 'June', Tityrus's poetic authority and skill offer Colin – and, by extension, Spenser – a way to address the problems they face. Close analysis of the eclogue's resonances with similar passages of the *Franklin's Tale* reveals Chaucer's role as symbolic inspiration, practical guide, and, in the spatialised poetics of the June eclogue, material source for Spenser's lofty literary goals.

'But if on me some little drops would flowe': Spenser in search of solutions

Edmund Spenser was a poet whose greatest personal and public literary goal – building a commonwealth where poetry and virtue might thrive – was often expressed as his deepest fear: that false art, corrupt power, inexorable time or wilful ignorance would instead wreak destruction.[4] The crimes of Archimago and the Blatant Beast in *The Faerie Queene*, the anxieties of *Amoretti* 75 and *A Vewe of the Present State of Ireland*, demonstrate this fear. At decisive moments, however, glimpses of the goal itself appear. Julia Reinhard Lupton has analysed passages in which 'Spenser's created "home" is [...] poetry itself, a *locus amoenus* established as both compensation for and critique of the public world'.[5] Such moments, I find, are often signalled by settings and images that invoke 'Paradise' as a site of divine art and virtue, and a refuge for deserving poets, albeit a fragile one. For Spenser and his contemporaries, importing classical and Christian images of paradise into the landscape of English poetry seems to require a series of moves amounting to colonisation: an existing place is found to be inadequate; a promising addition is identified and then incorporated; its new identity overwrites its previous affiliation and inhabitants.[6] Such actions, as Spenser himself would later learn only too well, may produce art, but rarely virtue, for their practitioners.[7] 'If poetry is finally the home which Spenser creates for himself', Lupton observes, 'it is an abode built with costs to others'.[8] At the start of his career, however, the aesthetic and ethical horizons seemed clear and inviting, offering bountiful solutions to Spenser's poetic problems, if only those problems could be properly framed.

The frame for 'June' is that of a paradise – present, but paradoxically unfulfilling. The eclogue constructs a detailed three-dimensional setting of earthly perfection, yet Colin Clout is excluded from its sensory pleasures. Somehow this paradise does not work for him. It fails to function as it ought to. In the eclogue's opening stanza

---

3 See Annabel M. Patterson, *Pastoral and Ideology: Virgil to Valéry* (Berkeley: University of California Press, 1987), 118–32; McCabe, 'Introduction'; 'The Shepheardes Calender', in Spenser, *The Shorter Poems* xi–xxi; 514n–74n. For E.K. and his place in Spenser scholarship, see Megan Cook's and Barr's chapters in this volume.
4 Richard Helgerson makes related but distinct claims in his examinations of 'kingdom', 'empire', 'nation-state' and 'power'. See *Forms of Nationhood: The Elizabethan Writing of England* (Chicago: University of Chicago Press, 1992), 1–4, 295–301.
5 Julia Reinhard Lupton, 'Home-Making in Ireland: Virgil's Eclogue I and Book VI of *The Faerie Queene*', *Spenser Studies*, 8 (1987), 119–45 (140).
6 See ibid., 138.
7 See Andrew Hadfield, 'Postcolonial Spenser', in *The Oxford Handbook of Edmund Spenser*, 792–805.
8 Lupton, 141.

Hobbinol welcomes his friend Colin to his 'pleasaunt syte', what the accompanying editorial gloss explains is his 'situation and place' (1). That 'situation' appears at first to be a physical setting. With a density of spatially deictic and place-oriented words and phrases – 'here the place', 'pleasaunt syte' and so forth – that is unusual for the *Calender*, which by definition tends more often to mark itself in time, the poem signals that the nature of its space is something to pay attention to:

> Lo *Colin*, here the place, whose pleasaunt syte
> From other shades hath weand my wandring mynde.
> Tell me, what wants me here, to worke delyte?
> The simple ayre, the gentle warbling wynde,
> So calme, so coole, as no where else I fynde:
> The grassye ground with daintye Daysies dight,
> The Bramble bush, where Byrds of euery kynde
> To the waters fall their tunes attemper right. (1–8)

Cool air, gentle breezes, grass, flowers, birds and musical water: these are familiar ingredients of the conventional pleasant place or *locus amoenus*, often implicitly or explicitly reminiscent of an earthly Paradise. In fact, Colin says so himself, before beginning a complaint about his own status: 'O happy *Hobbinoll*, I bless thy state, / That Paradise has found, whych *Adam* lost' (9–10). All the sights, scents and 'tunes attemper right' for a full-sensory experience echoed in the poetry itself (8). Judicious alliteration and dense rhyming add to the initial sense of fullness and repose to create the harmonious setting that 'From other shades hath weand [Hobbinol's] wandring mynde' (2). The eight-line stanza contains only two alternating end-rhymes, which in this case use the same vowel sound. Yet the enveloped scheme ends not on a couplet but on a cross rhyme that suspends poetic closure, and Hobbinol's cheery 'mynde' may have more of an impact on his surroundings than first appears.[9]

Elsewhere in the *Calender*, the eclogues set in winter suggest relationships in the pathetic mode between weather and personality, mental state or time of life. In 'Januarye' Colin appears alone, mourning the loss of his unfaithful love, Rosalind, and breaking his musical pipe in despair. Hobbinol's happiness in summer accords with this model, but the pleasant world of 'June' is simply inaccessible to Colin. Hobbinol may have found Adam's lost Paradise, 'But I vnhappy man', Colin continues, 'Can nowhere fynd, to shroude my lucklesse pate' (14, 16).

The woodcut that accompanies the poem shows a central Hobbinol, clad in rags befitting a shepherd but with gesture and stance suggesting openness and relaxation (see Figure 4.1). Faraway birds suggest light streaming down from the bright zodiac-inscribed cloud above. In the middle distance, scantily clad mowers build haystacks (the usual labour of June in medieval calendars), and in the high distance a pavilion or castle adds a touch of elegance and loftiness to the scene.[10] Colin's cramped third of the image, in contrast, is dark and busy with clumps

---

9 See McCabe's similar analysis of *Daphnaïda*, in *Shorter Poems*, 642n.
10 Colum Hourihane, ed., *Time in the Medieval World* (Princeton: Index of Christian Art, 2007), lvii.

Figure 4.1 The woodcut at the opening of 'June' (F2v)

of sheep and hatchings of hills and water. Overshadowed by a tree, Colin is still bundled in his winter garments and seems to huddle into them, wringing his hands with cold or pain as he cradles his drooping staff. Hobbinol's upright crook divides the world into unequal parts. One part is joyous and 'June'-like; the other is broken like the pipe of 'Januarye' still lying on the ground, upended by Colin's grief, stuck in the shadows of winter without a possibility of being 'weand' from them to enter his friend's 'pleasaunt' shade. It is graphically clear that Hobbinol's 'Paradise' is a personal and not a general one. The wall of this garden may be invisible, but it is still there, constructed out of Colin's own despair.

Colin is disconsolate over the double loss of his lover Rosalind and his own poetic talent. Towards the end of the poem, his despair modulates into a lament:

> The God of shepheards *Tityrus* is dead,
> Who taught me homely, as I can, to make.
> He, whilst he liued, was the soueraigne head
> Of shepheards all, that bene with loue ytake:
> Well couth he wayle hys Woes, and lightly slake
> The flames, which loue within his heart had bredd,
> And tell vs mery tales, to keepe vs wake,
> The while our sheepe about vs safely fedde.
>
> Nowe dead he is, and lyeth wrapt in lead,
> (O why should death on hym such outrage showe?)
> And all hys passing skil with him is fledde,
> The fame whereof doth dayly greater growe. (81–92)

The source of poetry

E.K. informs readers 'That by Tityrus is meant Chaucer' (81, gloss). However, this gloss does not go far towards explaining the terms of Colin's characterisation of Tityrus and his poetry, or the stakes of that identification. Two features of the lament are of paramount significance. First, Colin's grief for Tityrus is raw and fresh, suggesting that his death has only recently occurred. The tone and syntax strongly resemble passages from Thomas Hoccleve's *Regiment of Princes* (c. 1411; common in manuscript), which record a genuinely recent loss as well as a desire to trade on Hoccleve's self-proclaimed Chaucerian lineage.[11] Second, Tityrus's poetic talent is figured as a 'spring' (93–6). While the metaphor naturally leads to comparisons with the '*Chaucer*, well of English vndefyled' of the future *Faerie Queene* (IV.ii.32), more resonant connections emerge from the headwaters of Spenser's literary past.[12] The image may originate in John Lydgate's own lament for Chaucer in 'The Floure of Curtesye' (printed in William Thynne's editions of Chaucer's works, including apocrypha and tributes, between 1532 and 1561): 'The welle is drie with the lycoure swete, / Bothe of Clye and of Caliopé' (241–2).[13] Yet, unlike Chaucer's younger contemporary, Colin claims Tityrus's well is *not* yet dry; he hopes to partake of its 'drops' (93). Tityrus as spring, we shall see, represents Colin's personalisation of the fountain of Helicon on the muses' Parnassus. This locus of poetic inspiration emerges both in the *Franklin's Tale* and elsewhere in 'June' as the symbol of a Chaucerian craft Spenser seeks to master. In the spatialised poetics of the June eclogue, Parnassus also becomes a territory Colin might claim to solve the problems of poetic and political exclusion.

'Who taught me homely, as I can, to make': Tityrus as/and Chaucer

While the June eclogue offers the most sustained engagement with 'Tityrus', that person or concept appears seven times in the *Calender* to varying effect.[14] The slippery attribution refers sometimes to Chaucer and sometimes to Virgil, as E.K. professes to explain in the 'Epistle' that introduces the book: 'Chaucer: [...] whom our Colin clout in his Æglogue called Tityrus the God of shepheards, comparing hym to the worthines of the Roman Tityrus Virgile' (2–7). E.K. frequently muddies the waters in his subsequent glosses. Nonetheless, when referring to Chaucer, the eclogues consistently assert Tityrus's nearness to the poet-shepherds in time and space, and thus his accessibility as a poetic model. In his commentary on 'June', E.K. notes 'That by Tityrus is meant Chaucer, hath bene already sufficiently sayde, and by thys more playne appeareth, that he sayth, he tolde merye tales. Such as be hys Canterburie tales' (81, gloss). In his edition of the *Calender*,

---

11 Thomas Hoccleve, *Regiment of Princes*, ed. Charles R. Blyth (Kalamazoo: Medieval Institute, 1999), 1958–74, 2077–107, 4982–98; 'Introduction', 12–14. See also A.C. Spearing, *Medieval Autographies: The 'I' of the Text* (Notre Dame: University of Notre Dame Press, 2012), 129–31.
12 See Kinney, 'Marginal Presence', 34–5; King, 20.
13 In *The Chaucerian Apocrypha: A Selection*, ed. Kathleen Forni (Kalamazoo: Medieval Institute, 2005), 83–92.
14 Barr's elucidation in this volume of the comic effects of E.K.'s Tityrus commentary is congenial to the following analysis.

Richard McCabe sees through such bland transparency: 'lurking in the background is the figure of Virgil'.[15] As the most famous of Virgil's pastoral characters, Tityrus in the Renaissance was understood to be a mouthpiece for the Roman writer's political commentary.[16] Virgilian references in 'June' point to the abovementioned political causes of Colin's despair. The presence of Tityrus-Chaucer, I will demonstrate, offers poetic solutions to those political problems.

The identification of Tityrus with Chaucer in the *Calender* as a whole is intermittent rather than obviously 'sufficient'. E.K.'s 'already' in the 'June' gloss refers (with circular logic) to his assertion in the 'Epistle'. Yet E.K. in 'Januarye' reiterates 'Tityrus' as Virgil's shadow persona, analogous to the shepherd Colin Clout for 'this Poete' (1, gloss).[17] The only other mention of Tityrus prior to 'June' appears in 'Februarie'. Using the words 'tale', and 'Kent', the shepherd Thenot clearly refers to Chaucer (91–3). However, E.K.'s doubtful 'I suppose he meane Chaucer' makes his subsequent confidence in the 'June' gloss all the more strange (92, gloss). After the lament of 'June', the poet-cowherd Cuddie in 'October' specifies a 'Romish *Tityrus*', whom E.K. confirms is 'wel knowen to be Virgile' (55, gloss) – and explicitly connected to the political and patronage issues McCabe highlights. In 'December' Colin's 'Tityrus' is glossed once again as 'Chaucer: as hath bene oft sayd' (4, gloss). Finally, the closing *envoi* in the voice of the New Poete himself would seem to use the name to distinguish between Virgil and Chaucer – or else to enshroud the latter in a series of layered personas: '*Dare not to match thy pype with Tityrus hys style, / Nor with the Pilgrim that the Ploughman playde a whyle*' (9–10).[18] Unencumbered by the decorous 'errour of shepheards vnderstanding' proper to the eclogues ('Julye', 65, gloss), the New Poete uses 'Tityrus' for Virgil and 'the Pilgrim' for Chaucer, although at this point it may be impossible to entirely disentangle the two.[19] Throughout the *Calender* the name Tityrus is associated with Chaucer and Virgil in equal and often alternate measure.

Virgilian political dissatisfaction is important to any thorough understanding of the *Calender*. However, the glosses' misdirections can obscure what is actually a fairly consistent usage of Tityrus within the eclogues themselves, as interpreted by the 'Epistle': in 'Februarie', 'June' and 'December', Tityrus to Colin and his fellow shepherds signifies Chaucer. The exception in 'October' is the one occasion to explicitly identify its Tityrus as 'Romish'. All other references to Tityrus as Virgil occur in E.K.'s 'Epistle' and glosses, or in the New Poete's *envoi*. Each time Chaucer-Tityrus is mentioned, he appears as a renowned teacher and direct antecedent of *these* shepherd-poets and their art. 'December' praises Colin by way of this association: 'which wel coulde pype and singe, / For he of *Tityrus* his songs did lere' (3–4). Similarly, in 'Februarie' the 'olde Shepheard' Thenot 'cond' his tale 'of *Tityrus* in my youth' (Argvment; 92). For all E.K.'s reluctance to confirm Chaucer's presence

---

15 *Shorter Poems*, 540n.
16 See Patterson; Patrick Cheney, *Spenser's Famous Flight: A Renaissance Idea of a Literary Career* (Toronto: University of Toronto Press, 1993), 67.
17 John Skelton and Clément Marot also 'lurk' in the vicinity (1, gloss).
18 *Shorter Poems*, 574n. William Langland, of course, may also be present.
19 See Kinney, '*Shepheardes Calender*', 169.

in 'Februarie', he ends by affirming, 'whose prayse for pleasaunt tales cannot dye, so long as the memorie of hys name shal liue, and the name of Poetrie shal endure' (92, gloss). Colin's 'June' lament extends this praise of Chaucer's art across many elegant lines, including a modest anticipation of the 'December' reference: 'Who taught me homely, as I can, to make' (82). However godlike in his art, Tityrus is nonetheless local and thereby accessible to Colin and his compatriots. Thus it is possible to define the 'June' Tityrus precisely as a renowned shepherd-poet of living memory. Tityrus-Chaucer offers the authority of English poetry and is sufficiently near at hand to directly confer that authority upon his self-nominated follower. Colin-Spenser requires Chaucerian authority, and Chaucerian craft, if he is to successfully address the problems the *Calender* presents.

'Wolde han maked any herte lighte': the emotionally inaccessible paradise

In the opening stanzas of 'June' Colin labels Hobbinol's 'pleasaunt syte' a Paradise, an Eden temporarily un-lost, but one that he, Colin, cannot access – despite the fact that he seems to be physically located within it – because he is stuck in a personal microclimate of wintry depression. Hobbinol's private paradise is constructed out of familiar cultural referents drawn from Chaucer and other literary forebears. Colin invokes Adam's Christian Paradise of Eden; E.K. adds etymological and possibly classical sources:

> A Paradise in Greeke signifieth a Garden of pleasure, or place of delights. So he compareth the soile, wherin Hobbinoll made his abode, to that earthly Paradise, in scripture called Eden; wherein Adam in his first creation was placed. Which of the most learned is thought to be in Mesopotamia, the most fertile and pleasaunte country in the world […] (10, gloss)

E.K. hints that Colin's sense of deprivation has to do with the shepherds' current situations in life; Hobbinol has employment and Colin seeks it (1, 18, glosses). In the world the poem constructs, however, this 'situation or place' is spatial and experiential. Colin's central problem is the failure of his poetry, whether this is due to lovesickness, politics or unemployment. 'June' transforms this literary problem into a set of symptoms in Colin's body and an incongruity with his surroundings. Colin inhabits the type of setting I call an 'emotionally inaccessible paradise', as distinguished from other instances of paradise inaccessible because of temporal or spatial distance.[20] The Paradise he refers to at the June eclogue's opening, the 'pleasaunt syte' of his friend Hobbinol, is one Colin cannot access owing to his despairing emotional state.

Colin's situation is analogous to that of Dorigen in the *Franklin's Tale* as she sinks into despair over her beloved husband's long sojourn overseas. Dorigen's

---

[20] See Alessandro Scafi, *Mapping Paradise: A History of Heaven on Earth* (London: British Library, 2006).

friends seek to distract her with sensory pleasures, arranging an outing to a garden on the sixth of May:

> Which May hadde peynted with his softe shoures
> This gardyn ful of leves and of floures;
> And craft of mannes hand so curiously
> Arrayed hadde this gardyn, trewely,
> That nevere was ther gardyn of swich prys
> But if it were the verray paradys.
> The odour of floures and the fresshe sighte
> Wolde han maked any herte lighte
> That evere was born, but if to greet siknesse
> Or to greet sorwe helde it in distresse,
> So ful it was of beautee with plesaunce. (907–17)[21]

Longing for her absent husband, and terrified of the 'grisly rokkes blake' that in her mind represent his peril at sea (859), Dorigen suffers from 'to greet sorwe', which prevents her from enjoying the paradisal garden. The multisensory charms of this garden – leaves, flowers, lovely odours and fresh 'sighte' – strongly resemble those of 'June' and, like 'June' for Colin, fail to operate properly upon Dorigen's emotions, to make her 'herte lighte'. Like Colin's, Dorigen's despairing emotional state bars her from the pleasures of a garden whose powers approach those of 'the verray paradys'. Chaucer's pleasure-garden setting cues his readers to be prepared for a courtly encounter or a temptation scene, and they find both in the person of the amorous squire Aurelius. Above all, the marvellous but ineffectual garden points out the dangerous state of Dorigen's passions. The rest of the plot is quite different from that of 'June', but the terms of the scene are almost identical: sensory pleasures arrive at eyes, ears, and nostrils to work an overpowering emotional transformation for all – except for those for whom they do not work, the ultimately distressed.

It is this strange failure that distinguishes these two situations, and a few others I have studied, within the broader traditions of the *locus amoenus* and its subsidiary, the *hortus conclusus*.[22] To call a conventional *locus amoenus* 'paradise', and moreover to signal that that 'paradise' is no idle metaphor but a specific invocation of the superlative delights and moral tensions of the Christian Eden, as both poems do, is to dramatically raise the stakes for claiming that – somehow – the protagonist remains unsatisfied therein.[23] Milton understood this: to remain unhappy in 'Paradise [...], whych *Adam* lost' is, potentially, to align oneself with

---

21 In *The Riverside Chaucer*, ed. Larry D. Benson, 3rd edn (Boston: Houghton Mifflin, 1987), 178–89.
22 This chapter is part of my work in progress on paradisal spaces in Renaissance literature.
23 As noted above, Colin specifically invokes Adam; the moral stakes of Dorigen's garden are discussed further below. Their situations contrast with familiar *hortus conclusus* settings in the *Knight's Tale* (1030–122) and the *Kingis Quair* (211–466), which do not mention paradise and in which overt lovesick despair takes place not in the garden but in the towers above (in *Riverside*, 37–66; *The Kingis Quair and Other Prison Poems*, ed. Linne R. Mooney and Mary-Jo Arn (Kalamazoo: Medieval Institute Publications, 2005), 31–79). Compare also *The Romance of*

Satan – or to deny the affective power of unfallen creation, which amounts to the same thing.[24]

Analysis of Spenser's project in the *Calender* has tended to focus on his complex engagement with the pastoral mode.[25] However, the June eclogue's insistence on paradisal – and, by extension, horticultural – settings suggests that an alternative lens for understanding Spenser's ideal of poetic making is appropriate. The 'curiously' crafted garden of the *Franklin's Tale* offers such an alternative (909); considering the two poems together serves to illuminate more clearly the poetic spaces each works to build. Resonance with the June eclogue runs beyond similarities of setting and emotional predicament; just as 'June' cryptically offers Tityrus as the solution to Colin's poetic problems, critics have long identified the *Franklin's Tale* as a site of Chaucer's own thinking on the relations amongst art, nature, and poetry.

'I sleep nevere on the Mount of Pernaso': siting Chaucerian poetics

A focus on the poetic implications of the garden topos allows me to take up some of the 'rokkes' V.A. Kolve left unturned in his analysis of the *Franklin's Tale* as Chaucer's presentation of the aesthetics and ethics of his art.[26] Kolve analyses the tale as a function of three settings. The rocks are a psychological figure for harsh reality; the garden is their opposite, the place of sweet illusion (174–8). The third setting Kolve examines is the study of the Clerk of Orleans, a magician Aurelius visits in the hope of holding Dorigen to her rash promise, made in the garden,

---

the *Rose*, trans. Frances Horgan (Oxford: Oxford University Press, 1994), the source of so many of these conventional settings, in which the delights of a '*parevis terrestre*' do work as expected on the emotions of the young man (633–740). In any case, the *Romance* here remains resolutely secular: 'the Dreamer [...] does not identify the garden with the garden in Eden and risk the doctrinal and artistic consequences', as A. Bartlett Giamatti explains in *The Earthly Paradise and the Renaissance Epic* (Princeton: Princeton University Press, 1966), 62–3. For evidence of Spenser's ethical engagement with the *Franklin's Tale* in *The Faerie Queene*, see Helen Cooper's chapter in this volume and Anderson, *Reading the Allegorical Intertext: Chaucer, Spenser, Shakespeare, Milton* (Fordham University Press, 2008), 70–8.

24 See John Milton, *Paradise Lost*, ed. Alastair Fowler, 2nd edn (New York: Routledge, 2006), IV.152–9.
25 See Patterson; Cheney; Paul J. Alpers, *What Is Pastoral?* (Chicago: University of Chicago Press, 1996); John D. Bernard, '"June" and the Structure of Spenser's "Shepheardes Calender"', *Philological Quarterly*, 60.3 (1981), 305–22; Ted Brown, 'Pride and Pastoral in *The Shepheardes Calendar*', in *Subjects on the World's Stage: Essays on British Literature of the Middle Ages and the Renaissance*, ed. David C. Allen and Robert A. White (Newark: University of Delaware Press, 1995), 100–115 (105–7); David R. Shore, *Spenser and the Poetics of Pastoral: A Study of the World of Colin Clout* (Montreal: McGill-Queen's University Press, 1985), 74–80. Harry Berger productively reads the 'paradise principle' of the *Calender* and 'June' through a pastoral lens ('Mode and Diction in *The Shepheardes Calender*', *Modern Philology*, 67.2 (1969), 140–9; 'Orpheus, Pan, and the Poetics of Misogyny: Spenser's Critique of Pastoral Love and Art', *ELH*, 50.1 (1983), 27–60 (27, 43ff.); *Revisionary Play: Studies in the Spenserian Dynamics* (Berkeley: University of California Press, 1988), 432–41); here I propose instead a horticultural refraction as offering a clearer vision of the poetics of 'June'. See also A.C. Hamilton, '"The Grene Path Way to Lyfe": Spenser's *Shepheardes Calender* as Pastoral', in *The Elizabethan Theatre VIII*, ed. George R. Hibbard (Port Credit: Meany, 1982), 1–21 (9); 'The Argument of Spenser's *Shepheardes Calender*', *ELH*, 23.3 (1956), 171–82 (176).
26 V.A. Kolve, 'Rocky Shores and Pleasure Gardens: Poetry Versus Magic in *The Franklin's Tale*', in *Telling Images: Chaucer and the Imagery of Narrative II* (Stanford: Stanford University Press, 2010), 171–98.

to love him if he can make the rocks disappear. Kolve claims the Clerk's magical study as the source of art or illusion that can mediate the other two settings, for good or ill. He argues that Chaucer recognises dangerous similarities between the Clerk's magic and his own poetry, and that he seeks to define himself against such false art, both aesthetically and ethically (189–93). However, the garden setting is more significant for the tale's poetics than Kolve's reading will allow.

Central to my reading of the tale is a sense that its narration is of a distinctly Chaucerian flavour, and thus that its account of rhetorical art is one the poet would own. Such passages as the *occupatio-cum-diminutio* that claims 'I ne kan no termes of astrologye' – and then deploys such terms for thirty lines (1266–96) – remind this reader of the studied ignorance elsewhere in Chaucer's work of such 'gentil' matters as love:

> What shulde I speke more queynte,
> Or peyne me my wordes peynte
> To speke of love? Hyt wol not be;
> I kan not of that faculte. (*House of Fame*, I.245–8)[27]

This and other examples suggest that the 'I' of the tale's text, when present, speaks in an authorial voice, signalling Chaucerian instances of what A.C. Spearing has termed 'autography'.[28] The heightened authorial attention implicit in the 'craft' of the garden description and other moments of narrative 'rethorik', I argue, points readers to the tale's articulation of its poetics (909, 719).

Such moments first appear in the tale's introductory frame. 'The Prologe of the Frankeleyns Tale' briefly claims the Breton *lai* as its literary antecedent and then apologises for any lack of rhetorical skill:

> I lerned nevere rethorik, certeyn;
> Thyng that I speke, it moot be bare and pleyn.
> I sleep nevere on the Mount of Pernaso,
> Ne lerned Marcus Tullius Scithero.
> Colours ne knowe I none, withouten drede,
> But swiche colours as growen in the mede,
> Or elles swiche as men dye or peynte.
> Colours of rethoryk been to me queynte;
> My spirit feeleth noght of swich mateere. (719–27)

This explicit invocation of rhetorical principles, shrouded in comic renunciation, is designed to frame reception of the tale itself. The 'rethorik' *diminutio* resembles

---

27 In *Riverside*, 348–73.
28 Spearing cites the tale as an example of Chaucer's 'normal narrative manner throughout his work', in *Textual Subjectivity: The Encoding of Subjectivity in Medieval Narratives and Lyrics* (Oxford: Oxford University Press, 2005), 126. The 'I' need not be either an autobiographical Chaucer or a fictional Chaucer-pilgrim. Instead, such moments are consistent with the poetic persona who occasionally appears in the course of Chaucer's autographic passages. See Spearing, *Autographies*, 40; 33–51.

those noted above in structure and diction; Chaucer also rhymes 'peynte' with the distancing 'queynte' in the deprecatory passage from the *House of Fame* (I.245-6). Later in the same poem, he refers to poetic inspiration in terms similar to those of the 'Prologe'. The Proem to Book II calls on the muses:

> And ye, me to endite and ryme
> Helpeth, that on Parnaso duelle,
> Be Elicon, the clere welle. (II.520-2)

The 'rethorik' *diminutio* in the 'Prologe' uses the terms of this invocation to deny its efficacy, averring that 'I sleep nevere on the Mount of Pernaso' (721).

'But swiche colours as growen in the mede': Chaucer's verray crafted paradise

It is well known, of course, that the claim of the 'Prologe' is as much a misdirection as any of E.K.'s glosses.[29] Spearing highlights the skill of the last few lines of the prologue: its ostentatious plainness; its denial of the rhetorical colours ('ne knowe I none') in favour of those 'as growen in the mede', which may in turn be linked with the artfully crafted flowers in Dorigen's garden. 'Perhaps', Spearing speculates, 'the Orleans Clerk should be thought of as a gardener-poet'.[30] This gentle rebuttal to Kolve's indictment of the Clerk may be elaborated, I hope, into two points central to my analysis of the Chaucerian poetics as implied in the tale. First, I interrogate the elegant simplicity of Kolve's dichotomy between the Clerk and Chaucer as bad and good models for the poet as illusion-maker. Second, it is Dorigen's garden rather than the Clerk's study that in my reading illuminates the tale's poetics, as I find paradise rather than pastoral does for 'June'.

The Clerk of Orleans is one of the candidates for the 'mooste fre' in the tale's closing riddle asking listeners who has shown the greatest generosity and mercy (1622). As the sole representative of a less than 'gentil' middle class, he might be expected to stand in for either the Franklin's or Chaucer's perspective on the avoidable predicaments the gentry seem to find themselves in over love. However, the Clerk is often read as unsympathetically inscrutable.[31] Kolve's reading condemns him outright, finding him in the study deliberately deceiving Aurelius with his magic and then exacting 'a ruinous price' for his art, the self-serving act of 'a shrewd business man' (192).

But what if our reading of the Clerk himself is more 'fre'? Kolve cites the line, 'On which hymself he [Aurelius] daunced, as hym thoughte' (1201), as evidence of the false art of the Clerk's confidence scheme as it entraps his mark in the engrossing illusion of dancing with his lady. It is Aurelius, however, who tracks down the Clerk in the first place, and the line may describe Aurelius's own self-deception. Could

---

29 See Spearing, *Autographies*, 229-30.
30 'Introduction', in Chaucer, *The Franklin's Prologue and Tale*, ed. Spearing, rev. edn (Cambridge: Cambridge University Press, 1994), 1-76 (76).
31 See Spearing, 'Introduction', 66; Sherron Knopp, 'Poetry as Conjuring Act: *The Franklin's Tale* and *The Tempest*', *Chaucer Review*, 38.4 (2004), 337-54 (338-9, 351n7, 351n10).

the Clerk's 'ruinous price' perhaps be designed to save Aurelius from his own foolish desires, or at least to exempt the Clerk from being implicated in them – a sort of rash promise of his own, designed to be rejected? 'He made it straunge' (1223) – in unsympathetic readings a demurral serving to drive up the price – tersely covers a range of possible reactions, including an astonished disbelief not unlike Dorigen's at Aurelius's original declaration of love: ' "Nevere erst", quod she, "ne wiste I what ye mente" ' (981). And since he forgives Aurelius's debt so quickly, having only belatedly learned the real moral stakes of a job he has undertaken on false pretenses and nonetheless faithfully performed (1587–602), might not the Clerk be arguably 'mooste fre'? 'He made it straunge' falls in the same line as 'so God hym save', which Spearing identifies as 'the only specifically Christian phrase' spoken in the tale.[32] In a world of mostly virtuous pagans hampered by their lack of grace, such words seem unlikely to be spoken by the villain. Indeed, while drawing on Kolve's analysis, Spearing reads the possible identification of Chaucer with the Clerk in a less sinister light.[33] This would appear to put him in company with Shakespeare, whose appropriation of 'Al oure revel was ago' for *The Tempest* suggests that he, too, sees the Clerk less as Mephistophilis than as Prospero (1204).[34]

Denying the Clerk the status of villainous foil opens up possibilities for other instances of poetic modelling elsewhere in the tale. Aurelius composes a love 'pleynt' in his prayer for aid and another in his confrontation of Dorigen in the temple (1029–79, 1311–38), and Dorigen also voices 'hire compleynt' at the cruelty of fortune in her lengthy contemplation of suicide (1354–456). Although William Woods convincingly describes a Chaucerian 'spatial poetics' in which central characters 'define' the setting that surrounds them, this diffusion of poetic endeavour suggests that it is not in any single character that this tale locates its spatialised poetic claims.[35] Focusing on the garden as a site not only of pleasure but also of moral testing, as in Eden, and of poetic art, as in the 'craft of mannes hand' that built it, produces an alternative account of poetic making to any one character's embodiment thereof, be it the Clerk's dangerous wish-fulfilment, Aurelius's glorious self-deluding complaints, or Dorigen's inventive despair.

The garden explicitly evokes 'the verray paradys' (912), a place of testing, fall and judgement – not (merely) softness and pleasure – and functions as such a place throughout the tale.[36] Dorigen is wrong to find her plight 'to greet' and in the garden opens herself up to the error of emotional excess. The events set in motion there lead directly to Aurelius's subsequent error of greedy misperception

---

32 'Introduction', 68.
33 Ibid., 66–8. See also Spearing, 'Classical Antiquity in Chaucer's Chivalric Romances', in *Chivalry, Knighthood, and War in the Middle Ages*, ed. Susan J. Ridyard (Sewanee: University of the South Press, 1999), 53–73 (66–7).
34 See Knopp, 338–41, 350n1, 351n10.
35 William Woods, *Chaucerian Spaces: Spatial Poetics in Chaucer's Opening Tales* (Albany: University of New York Press, 2008). See e.g. 38, 51, 133, 139–40, 146.
36 See Derek Pearsall, 'Gardens as Symbol and Setting in Late Medieval Poetry', in *Medieval Gardens*, ed. Elizabeth Blair MacDougall (Washington, DC: Dumbarton Oaks, 1986), 235–52 (247).

in the study. The garden is both the actual site of Dorigen and Aurelius's original encounter and the anticipated final setting towards which all their thoughts and actions tend, only averted at the last minute by a chance meeting as they make their way 'to the gardyn-ward' (1505). As in 'June', the paradisal garden serves as the posing of a problem – and governs the aesthetic and ethical space of the poem long after the action has departed from it. Chaucer's garden presents virtue on trial and ultimately redeemed by the 'sentence' and 'solaas' of the tale's poetry.[37] This presentation of the aesthetics and ethics of his art may constitute an attempt to shape or construct his own future memory. The tale seems to be one of the sites where Chaucer as poet-retractor was concerned with the judgement of future audiences, and perhaps also with that of potential poetic followers, such as Colin and Spenser claim to be.[38]

Like 'June', the tale highlights the garden-paradise as a central locus of poetic making. The *diminutio* of the 'Prologe' explicitly links the powers of Parnassus to the flowers of rhetoric *and* of horticulture. The rhetorical appeal to real flowers in turn primes the tale's listeners or readers to be sensitive to the art that has 'arrayed' Dorigen's garden 'so curiously': the 'craft of mannes hand' that planted it but also the hand that wrote it – Chaucer's. It is in the garden, not the study, that the art of poesy reaches its full potential. This is an ethical as well as an aesthetic claim. Conventional medieval gardens are always potentially spaces of danger, but also – therefore – always potentially spaces of high morality and miraculous transformation.[39] In the garden passage the flaunting modesty of the narrative does not shy away from likening the pleasant place it builds unto 'the verray paradys'. The poetry aligns itself not merely with human artistry but also, by implication, with the craft of *goddes* hand. Poetry, Philip Sidney reminds his own readers, is next to godliness. Its greatest achievement, he suggests, is just such a paradisal reinscription as Chaucer's garden: 'pleasant rivers, fruitful trees, sweet-smelling flowers' – by these shall ye know the 'golden' world.[40] Vatic status confers legitimacy on grateful (or duplicitous) poetic disciples; Spenser learns from Sidney and Chaucer as Chaucer (more surreptitiously) 'lerned' from 'Scithero' and 'Pernaso'.[41]

'I neuer lyst presume to *Parnasse* hyll': Chaucerian misdirection

One thing Colin seems to have 'lerned' from Tityrus is, like the 'Prologe', to lay claim to Parnassus obliquely by denying it outright:

> Of Muses *Hobbinol*, I conne no skill:
> For they bene daughters of the hyghest *Ioue*,

---

37 *General Prologue* (798). Kolve makes a similar claim from other evidence (196).
38 See Kolve, 171.
39 See Pearsall, 237.
40 'The Defence of Poesy', in *Sir Philip Sidney: The Major Works*, ed. Katherine Duncan-Jones, rev. edn (Oxford: Oxford University Press, 2002), 212–50 (183–5).
41 As Craig A. Berry notes, Chaucer's strategy here resembles E.K.'s (private communication).

> And holden scorne of homely shepheards quill.
> [...]
> I neuer lyst presume to *Parnasse* hyll [...] (65–70)

Colin's Chaucer-like demurral is nonetheless the third time 'June' seeks to import Parnassus and its denizens into the landscape it constructs. Alongside Hobbinol and Colin, a cast of mostly classical characters also physically inhabits the eclogue's poetic space.

The first Parnassus reference in 'June' appears in Hobbinol's elaboration on the delightful pleasures of his 'syte'. Colin claims he is hounded by 'angry Gods' (15); Hobbinol assures him that 'Here' he will find 'Graces, / And lightfote Nymphes', who

> chace the lingring night,
> With Heydeguyes, and trimly trodden traces,
> Whilst systers nyne, which dwell on *Parnasse* hight,
> Doe make them musick, for their more delight:
> And *Pan* himselfe to kisse their christall faces,
> Will pype and daunce, when *Phœbe* shineth bright:
> Such pierlesse pleasures haue we in these places. (23, 25–32)

By way of their vivid verbs, the mythical ladies partaking of 'A country daunce or rownd' (27, gloss), along with Pan to 'pype and daunce' – and 'kisse' – all appear to be acting within the space of the poem, rather than above or behind it where one might expect the gods to be. Hobbinol's 'syte' is very near the home of the muses, the 'systers nyne, which dwell on *Parnasse* hight', for their 'musick' is within earshot for the nymphs to dance to (28–9). Parnassus seems to be as close to the shepherds in space as Tityrus is in time.

The incorporation of Parnassus and its inhabitants into the space 'June' builds is different from an earlier invocation to the muses in 'Aprill': 'And eke you Virgins, that on *Parnasse* dwell, / Whence floweth *Helicon* the learned well, / Helpe me to blaze [...]' (41–3). This is the apostrophe of a confident poet, Colin before his despair, to distant patrons. It is analogous to, and syntactically reminiscent of, the passage from the *House of Fame* quoted above (II.520–2).[42] In 'June', however, both Hobbinol's description and Colin's denial imply that the poet could 'presume' to physically approach Parnassus, if he dared. Here the June eclogue is more like the *Franklin's Tale*; the line 'I sleep nevere on the Mount of Pernaso' implies spatial access to Parnassus, even in the course of renouncing it. This sense of Parnassus being near to, but not quite present within, Hobbinol's 'syte' complicates the paradisal nature of the scene described by Hobbinol and labelled by Colin. As a holy mountain, source of art and learning, Parnassus can encode a classical Golden Age paradise.[43] It also stands in metonymically for a complex of classical symbols for poetic inspiration, often conflated, as E.K. illustrates in his gloss to 'Aprill':

---

42 *Shorter Poems*, 532n.
43 See Giamatti, chap. 1.

Helicon) is both the name of a fountaine at the foote of Parnassus, and also of a mounteine in Bæotia, out of which floweth the famous Spring Castalius, dedicate also to the Muses: of which spring it is sayd, that when Pegasus the winged horse of Perseus (whereby is meant fame and flying renowme) strooke the grownde with his hoofe, sodenly thereout sprange a wel of moste cleare and pleasaunte water, which fro thence forth was consecrate to the Muses and Ladies of learning. (42, gloss)

Parnassus-Helicon/Helicon-Castalius is a source of both 'water' and 'learning', multiply or redundantly sacred to the muses. Although E.K. withholds a direct connection between Parnassus and Paradise, his gloss describes the sacred spring in 'pleasaunte' terms that associate it with Hobbinol's 'syte' and thus with a paradise setting.[44] In Hobbinol's account, however, Helicon remains a distinct if nearby location. Within the geography of the poem Hobbinol may have 'found' Adam's paradise, but Apollo's remains farther off. A space that is merely Edenic in its pleasures may appear incomplete to an aspiring poet with classical ambitions. Perhaps this is why Hobbinol's 'syte' fails to comfort Colin. The inspired poetry of the muses is at hand, but not present – at least not in the present time and place of Hobbinol and Colin's dialogue.

'To heare thy rymes and roundelayes': recreating Paradise, remembering song

Part of what makes Hobbinol's 'syte' so pleasant is that he can hear the muses playing 'on *Parnasse* hight'. But Hobbinol also recalls a time when Colin's music was so beautiful that the muses themselves left Parnassus to seek him out. For there is another *locus amoenus* in the poem, a few lines later, described in almost identical terms to Hobbinol's 'pleasaunt syte'. This one, however, is set not in Hobbinol's present but in Colin's past, and recalls some prior occasion upon which a (presumably happy) Colin created a *locus amoenus* out of his own poetic song:

> *Colin*, to hear thy rymes and roundelayes,
> Which thou were wont on wastfull hylls to singe,
> I more delight, then larke in Sommer dayes:
> Whose Echo made the neyghbour groues to ring,
> And taught the byrds, which in the lower spring
> Did shroude in shady leaues from sonny rayes,
> Frame to thy songe their chereful cheriping,
> Or hold theyr peace, for shame of thy swete layes. (49–56)

---

44 Both water and poetry served as paradisal symbols in Renaissance Italian Parnassus fountains (Claudia Lazzaro, *The Italian Renaissance Garden: From the Conventions of Planting, Design, and Ornament to the Grand Gardens of Sixteenth-Century Central Italy* (New Haven: Yale University Press, 1990), 132–4; see also Cheney, 9. Interchangeable with 'springs' in natural contexts ('fountain, n., 1.a.', *OED*), fountains as upward jets of water did not arrive in England until around 1590. See Andrew Eburne and Richard Taylor, *How to Read an English Garden* (London: Ebury, 2006), 188.

Even the muses paid attention, claims Hobbinol:

> And from the fountaine, where they sat around,
> Renne after hastely thy siluer sound.
> But when they came, where thou thy skill didst showe,
> They drewe abacke, as halfe with shame confound,
> Shepheard to see, them in theyr art outgoe. (60-4)

The wording of Hobbinol's description links his 'syte', where muses sing and nymphs dance, to the similar sensory effects of Colin's past 'songe'. This is a complex moment of poetic making, unique in the *Calender* for its attempt to recreate the experience of prior song without presenting the song itself. Hobbinol (re)constructs an episode from Colin Clout's happier days, when he was 'wont on wastfull hylls to singe'.[45] Elsewhere in the *Calender* songs appear as directly reproducible within the 'Æglogues', E.K.'s so-called goatherd dialogues ('Generall argument', 3-8). Hobbinol presents an old 'laye' of Colin's in 'Aprill' (33) and the singing contest in 'August' concludes with Cuddie's doing the same (149).[46] Distinguished by changes in form within a given eclogue, these quoted or performed songs imply that the balance of the *Calender*'s poetry, not marked as formal singing, is to be read as (comparatively) informal conversation. The moment of remembered song in 'June', however, does not alter the form of its intricately rhymed stanzas, which persist throughout the eclogue. The consistency of form makes the verbal and sensory parallels with the opening stanza clear. These poetic echoes further highlight the psychological and temporal distinctions between Colin's present despairing emotional state, Hobbinol's equally present 'Paradise', and Colin's own strikingly similar past experience.[47] Exploring the formal construction of this paradisal past, memorable yet seemingly inaccessible – in time as well as in affect – helps to characterise Spenser's engagement with his own literary past and his ambitions for a personal and national poetic future. A Chaucerian strategy of spatialising the locus of poetic thought enables 'June' to work through literary source material while renewing its availability to Colin and Hobbinol within the imagined space the poem builds for itself.

In Hobbinol's memory, Colin's past music shames the natural as well as the supernatural musicians into silence, but it also recreates – or anticipates – the harmony of the opening stanza: birds, groves and air in the guise of Echo all

---

45 For entirely different readings, also highlighting this episode's significance for Spenser's poetic project, see Cheney (92-8) and Rebeca Helfer, *Spenser's Ruins and the Art of Recollection* (Toronto: University of Toronto Press, 2012), 114-17.
46 See Heather Dubrow's work on audience inclusion and distancing in the fictive world of 'Aprill' and its subsequent reception, with implications for voice and autography, in *The Challenges of Orpheus: Lyric Poetry and Early Modern England* (Baltimore: Johns Hopkins University Press, 2011), 57-62.
47 The vivid distinctions fostered by similarities in the form and language of 'June' might be added to the formal and indexical distancing effects Dubrow further discusses. See '"A Sheapherdess Thus Sayd": Immediacy and Distance in the Early Modern Lyric', in *Something Understood: Essays and Poetry for Helen Vendler*, ed. Stephen Burt and Nick Halpern (Charlottesville: University of Virginia Press, 2009), 60-82 (62, 66-9).

'Frame' themselves to his song. The diction of the stanza echoes the sensory plenitude of the opening even in those images that are not strictly part of the scene: neither 'larke' nor 'Sommer' is necessarily present 'on wastfull hylls', but they are in the text beside them. E.K's gloss 'Spring) not of water, but of young trees springing' is nonetheless a sort of liquid *occupatio* (53, gloss), and the birds' 'shady leaues' recall Hobbinol's superlative 'shade'. The passage also closely recalls the first recorded Spenserian *locus amoenus*, in the opening half of Epigram 3 in *A Theatre for Worldlings*:

> Then heauenly branches did I see arise,
> Out of a fresh and lusty Laurell tree
> Amidde the yong grene wood. Of Paradise
> Some noble plant I thought my selfe to see,
> Suche store of birdes therein yshrouded were,
> Chaunting in shade their sundry melodie.
> My sprites were rauisht with these pleasures there. (1–7)[48]

Here again are 'shade', 'birdes [...] yshrouded' singing, 'yong' trees, and ravishment for the June eclogue's 'delyte' (3) – a 'Paradise' or garden of 'pleasures' indeed. Thus Hobbinol's memory of Colin's 'songe' is also Spenser's memory of his own youthful work as a translator for the project of Dutch poet Jan Van der Noot. The implications of this direct connection between the *Theatre* and the *Calender* serve to illuminate more precisely the June eclogue's status as protest literature, posing personal and public problems and seeking solutions for them by way of its literary source material.

'A Spring of water mildely romblyng downe': the source of Spenser's Parnassus

The 1569 English edition of the *Theatre* opens with commendatory poems and a dedication to Queen Elizabeth. The main text consists of a series of six 'Epigrams', not-quite sonnets which a very young Spenser translated from Clément Marot's French (itself translated from Petrarch's Canzone 323), and then a longer series of fifteen 'Sonets' translated in blank verse, eleven from Joachim Du Bellay's *Songe* (inspired by the same *canzone*) along with four by Van der Noot, the *Theatre*'s principal author and project mastermind. Each short poem faces an emblematic image illustrating its subject, often including before-and-after scenes.[49] The remainder and bulk of the work comprises Van der Noot's religious commentary on the poems.

Before he even gets to his commentary, Van der Noot has dramatically altered the meaning of the Petrarch by its context. The Epigrams remain very close to the original Italian text, presenting six beautiful visions – of a deer, a ship, a tree, a spring, a phoenix and a lady – that are suddenly ruined or destroyed. Petrarch's visions, of course, all signify in the first instance his beloved Laura, with other important

---
48 In *Shorter Poems*, 1–22.
49 The first du Bellay sonnet is unillustrated and faces a quatrain *envoi* to the Epigrams.

resonances in the complex relationship amongst love, art and ambition.[50] Van der Noot's book, however, makes the Epigrams about the transitory nature of earthly pleasure, a generalised frame for Du Bellay's sonnets, understood in the *Theatre* to be specifying grave problems in the contemporary Church of Rome. Each and all of these meanings held significance for Spenser throughout his career.[51] Most resonant for my reading of 'June' is the way Petrarch's *canzone* poses and perhaps originates a version of Spenser's anxiety, articulated at the beginning of this essay, concerning how art and virtue can face up to the destruction of the beauty that inspires them, whether from the ravages of time or the more sinister works of humankind. Such problems, in a more pointedly Reformation context, seem also to have been deeply felt concerns for Van der Noot and his collaborators on the *Theatre* project.

That Spenser in 'June' was thinking closely and precisely about his prior work with the *Theatre* is clear not only from the textual echoes of these passages but also from the parallels of setting and, for lack of a better word, of plot. Recall that in Hobbinol's account the muses are within hearing of Colin's 'groue' from where they 'sat around' a spring, presumably – with help from E.K.'s 'Aprill' gloss – Helicon or Castalia on Parnassus. In the *Theatre*, Epigram 3 presents the 'yong grene wood' with its birds and paradisal laurel. To accord with the episode in 'June', a spring must be within shouting, or singing – or page-turning – distance. In fact, as presented overleaf in Epigram 4, it may be the same spring:

> Within this wood, out of the rocke did rise
> A Spring of water mildely romblyng downe,
> Whereto approched not in any wise
> The homely Shepherde, nor the ruder cloune,
> But many Muses, and the Nymphes withall,
> That sweetely in accorde did tune their voice
> Vnto the gentle sounding of the waters fall.
> The sight wherof dyd make my heart reioyce. (1–8)

A spring, in or hard by a paradisal *locus amoenus*, where muses and nymphs congregate but shepherds 'approched not', sounds a great deal like the remembered past of 'June'.[52] Colin creates such a paradise with his pipe, so marvellous that the muses seek it (60–1). Hobbinol's two eight-line pentameter stanzas describing the numinous scene take up almost identical poetic time and space as the portions of the *Theatre* sonnets quoted above. Their semantic fields are strikingly similar. And they occur in the same order, with the place and moment of paradise first

---

50 The *Theatre* is only one example of Canzone 323's long afterlife in visionary European art. See Julia Conaway Bondanella, *Petrarch's Visions and Their Renaissance Analogues* (Madrid: J. Porrúa Turanzas, 1978); Charles Roger Davis, 'Petrarch's Rime 323 and Its Tradition Through Spenser' (unpublished doctoral thesis, Princeton, 1973).
51 See Tom MacFaul, 'A *Theatre for Worldlings* (1569)', in *The Oxford Handbook of Edmund Spenser*, 149–59.
52 And a bit like the *Parliament of Fowls* (183–210, in *Riverside*, 385–94), whose vocabulary Spenser deploys here and in 'June'. Anderson discusses the poem's subsequent 'refractions' in the *Faerie Queene* (*Reading the Allegorical Intertext*, chap. 9).

established through shade, birds and multi-sensory attunement, and then a scene shift to the nearby water and muses in the next epigram or after the stanza break.[53]

In the *Theatre* an earthquake subsequently destroys the spring, whereas Colin's playing only makes the muses draw 'abacke', but it seems clear that Spenser had these passages in mind as he was crafting the world of the June eclogue, where amongst so many other echoes Hobbinol, along with his birds, 'To the waters fall their tunes attemper right' (8). Thus Petrarch's Canzone 323, via the *Theatre*, is the direct model for the Spenserian *locus amoenus* as presented in 'June' – and, subsequently, in shorthand or elaboration, for pleasant places throughout Spenser's career.[54] Petrarch's pleasant place combines with the spatialised poetics of the *Franklin's Tale* to allow this literary source to appear as a specific location within the eclogue.

'June' adds to Dorigen's Edenic space the classical feature of the muses' Helicon, the fountain of poetic inspiration featured in both Spenser's Petrarchan and Chaucerian sources. This classical addition would seem to be a quintessentially 'Renaissance' move on Spenser's part, but it is one that Chaucer has made earlier in his backhanded invocation of 'Scithero' and 'Pernaso'. Like the 'Prologe', Colin also denies Parnassus, rejecting Hobbinol's recollection. Colin's muse-charming song, he claims, is irrevocably lost: 'I neuer lyst presume to *Parnasse* hyll' (70). This Chaucer-like *diminutio* would appear to cut off all access to Parnassus in the poem's present. In an architectonic sense, however, the remembered episode and Colin's response to it are central to the June eclogue – seventh to ninth of 15 stanzas – just as Epigrams 3 and 4 are the middle two of six. Indeed, Spenser places Helicon in the central couplet of the poem: 'And from the fountaine, where they sat around, / Renne after hastely thy siluer sound' (60–1). Lest any reader miss its significance, E.K. notes 'Thys [eighth] staffe is full of verie poetical inuention' (57, gloss). From this epicentre the poem sends out a shockwave with enough power to relocate the source of poetic inspiration. Unlike the antecedent 'Prologe', in this instance, the classical muses are leaving their fountain to seek the English poet.[55]

'Of that the spring was in his learned hedde': Chaucer as Helicon

Spenser inscribes the muses' Helicon within the bounds of the poem's paradisal space as part of his declaration of poetic importance as well as independence from

---

53 A further link emerges from close scrutiny of the Epigram 4 images alongside the *Calender* woodcut for *Aprill*. In the lower left corner of each scene is the strikingly similar form of a spring, its water streaming out of a rock or miniature escarpment in a narrow curving arc. Where the muses sat in the Epigram, a standing shepherd now pipes, in keeping with *Aprill*'s more confident framing of images and ambitions that motivate Colin's despair in *June*.
54 See Claire Eager, '"The sacred noursery / Of Vertue" – and Violence: Plotting Spenser's *Locus Amoenus*', unpublished talk, abstract in 'Spenser in Dublin Abstracts', *Spenser Review*, 45.2, www.english.cam.ac.uk/spenseronline/review/45/452/abstracts/spenser-in-dublin-abstracts [accessed 15 October 2015]. These echoes appear, in whole and in part, in such thoroughly pleasant places as Mount Acidale as well as in suspect or damaged settings such as the Bower of Bliss and the (now-) ruined Helicon of 'The Teares of the Muses'. Richard Danson Brown discusses the latter in '*The New Poet*': *Novelty and Tradition in Spenser's Complaints* (Liverpool: Liverpool University Press, 1999), chap. 4.
55 Hamilton notes a similar episode in 'December' ('"Grene Path Way"', 5).

his lesser compatriots and forebears. Later in 'June', however, Spenser re-figures the muses' fountain as Tityrus himself, whose 'little drops' could restore the transformative poetic power that Colin has lost:

> But if on me some little drops would flowe,
> Of that the spring was in his learned hedde,
> I soone would learne these woods, to wayle my woe,
> And teach the trees, their trickling teares to shedde. (93–6)

Another spring, another (hypothetical) wood transformed by the power of poetry: and this performance Colin might consider worthy of the muses' notice, since it would be fully efficacious in representing the depths of his despair. Tityrus offers Colin what Geffrey in the *House of Fame* seeks from the inhabitants of Parnaso: a wellspring of poetic inspiration. In so doing, Tityrus makes what has been inaccessible available once again. Parnassus and Eden are on the same continuum, as classical and Christian versions of paradise, and Chaucer and Spenser share a similar sense of their poetic tools and projects. Spenser posits poetry, and specifically Chaucerian poetry, via the classical Helicon, as a route back to paradise for poets like Colin and, by implication, for himself.

Regardless of whether or not a true or 'verray' paradise is actually available to anyone in the worlds of these poems, they dramatise a troubling situation in which something paradise-like ought to function but cannot, deploying different aspects of this now-familiar situation for their own purposes. Dorigen's sorwe-ful state of mind prevents her from bodily experiencing the garden the way her friends do; Colin has lost his ability to share the landscape embodiment of Hobbinol's joyful state of mind. Whereas the despair of gendered loss and anxiety that cuts Dorigen off from paradise *is* the problem to be solved or warded off in the *Franklin's Tale*, Colin's discontent may be an appropriate response to the personal and political situations facing him – or the poet he stands in for. Colin is the canary in the coal mine, what biologists call an indicator or sentinel species, alerting readers to the risk of a broader affective climate change if the *Calender*'s hyperbolised winter of social corruption and poetic devaluation spreads.[56]

In 'June', the solution to this problem is (unsurprisingly) poetry. Colin still aspires to a 'passing skil' that might come to him from his own personal Helicon – Tityrus, 'Of that the spring was in his learned hedde' (91, 94). If so, he can force the world into his own pathetic accompaniment, such as Dorigen could only imagine (95–6):

> Then should my plaints, causd of discurtesee,
> As messengers of all my painfull plight,
> Flye to my loue, where euer that she bee,
> And pierce her heart with poynt of worthy wight [...] (97–100)

---

56 Such consequences, Danson Brown suggests, are spelled out in 'The Teares of the Muses' (133, 145–54, 165–7; private communication).

Such poetry might make even Rosalind listen. Such poetry might also, quite literally, create a paradise – for it already does create one, earlier in 'June' as in the *Franklin's Tale*, by building the pleasant passages I analyse above. Hobbinol ventriloquises Colin's song in remembering (and re-membering) it for him. And, lest we forget, 'happy *Hobbinoll*', despondent '*Colin*', and the words they speak, all come from the same poetic brain.

They also, of course, represent real people, or so E.K. claims, as apparently do others of the characters and allusions in the *Calender*. Spenser and Harvey were corresponding and inventing new forms for English poems – and English Poesy – while the *Calender* was under construction. Whether all the words in the book are Spenser's, or E.K. is partly Harvey or some other person, Spenser's first 'independent' publishing product is clearly in truth a collaboration amongst printer, visual artists and poets as much as the *Theatre* was.[57] These poetic collaborators may be contemporaries like Harvey, but they may also be literary forebears, such as Petrarch and Chaucer. This model of collaboration, learned from Spenser's earliest publishing experience, is one he carried with him in various ways throughout his career, from the paratexts of the *Calender* and *The Faerie Queene* to the composite *Complaints* and multi-authored 'communal grief' for Sidney following *Astrophel*.[58] Through works that celebrate poetic skill in such collaborative and meritocratic settings, I argue, Spenser sought to found a *republic* 'of our own language' over the course of his career.[59] Parnassus, transplanted into the landscape of English poesy, offers the territory for that poets' sanctuary.[60]

So, can supremely skilful poetry, in the hands of a 'happy' poet (with the help of his literary, artistic and publishing collaborators) charm the politics as well as the literature of England into a more pleasant course? Such is the lofty claim of 'June', however much Colin protests that he 'neuer lyst presume to *Parnasse* hyll / [...] Ne striue to winne renowne' (70, 74). Paradise can be approached, Spenser's work suggests, through poetic inspiration, assiduous effort, and collaboration with other like-minded artists. The moment of *The Shepheardes Calender* was an exciting one for Spenser; his career lay ahead and full of promise. It is important for critics to honour that moment, even as we may be aware of the frustrations and failures that lie in the poet's future.[61]

The republic of our own language

Along with their characters' emotional, aesthetic and ethical relationships to Paradise, the eclogue and the tale also resonate in their invocations of Parnassus.

---

57 *Shorter Poems*, 516n; see this author, '"So many strange things hapned me to see": Myths and Mysteries in the Illustrations of *A Theatre for Worldlings*', unpublished paper, abstract at rarebookschool.org/admissions-awards/fellowships/rbs-uva/prize/ [accessed 31 August 2015].
58 McCabe, in *Shorter Poems*, 662n.
59 Compare Helgerson, 25ff.
60 See Lupton, 138–40.
61 See note 54 above. Cheney also argues against discounting the precise ambitions of the *Calender*, claiming their promise was as precisely fulfilled (3, 46, 52–6, 75–6).

Both poems present the home of the muses as a place their poets explicitly refuse, although they have physical access to it. Both nonetheless implicitly lay claim to a Parnassian inspiration and authority.[62] Colin Clout takes his implicit claim a step further by transforming Chaucer himself into a fountain, a material source for Colin's poetry. Colin believes that 'if on me some little drops would flowe, / Of that the spring was in his learned hedde', then his work will succeed. Throughout the eclogue, Spenser asserts himself in a Chaucerian tradition of 'sentence' *through* 'solaas', a goal also espoused by the *Calender*'s dedicatee Sidney and, later, in Spenser's 'Letter to Ralegh'. 'June', however, further asserts the *nearness* of Tityrus, placing him temporally within living memory and spatially as a fountain within the landscape of the poem, and thereby increasing the legitimacy of Spenser's own claims to poetic authority.[63] A Chaucerian poetics grants him access to the hitherto-inaccessible Paradise.

Each poem claims some new ground to help address its version of the emotionally inaccessible paradise, staking out territory for its poetic art in response to the problem of accessibility it presents. This is, formally, a colonising move. The poem sets up a local problem – affective and personal – for which the response is expansive, or expansionist – poetic and territorial. Chaucer does it more gently, claiming the space of the *Franklin's Tale* as one for thinking explicitly about the ethics of making poetry, from the reference to Parnassus in the 'Prologe' to the 'craft of mannes hand' in the garden. The June eclogue, I suggest, specifically claims the power of *Tityrus as Helicon* for the English vernacular. Focusing on the vehicle of this metaphor gives concrete shape to the familiar argument that Spenser asserts the authority of Chaucer to provide an established poetic tradition, giving legitimacy and cover to his poetic followers.[64] Still more artfully, Spenser claims Chaucer himself as the material source of poetry in English, a fountain future poets can draw upon for their own poetic making.

Chaucer is the font and fountain of Spenserian poetry, the dominant poetic source Colin seeks. But Spenser's assertion of a continuous, unitary Chaucerian authority partially conceals a further shared feature of the poetics implied by the two poems. 'June', like the tale, partakes of the humanist project of assimilating many literary and cultural antecedents into a new work, including in this case Petrarch, Van der Noot, and the anonymous woodcut artists, along with Chaucer himself. Both poems also spatialise this transmission, encoding their borrowings into the geographies of their settings and characters. This spatialised poetics in turn enables a uniquely powerful access to the literary past. When Paradise is here, now, a poetic character has the ability to repudiate its charms, to be in but not of them, to hold out for a better offer – or a worse, as Dorigen finds,

---

62 For further authoritative strategies, see Berry's chapter in this volume.
63 It is possible to reconcile this claim with Danson Brown's and Cook's conclusions in this volume. In those cases, 'Chaucer' indexes a formal practice to be renovated or a body of received text to be framed as archaic. Here 'Chaucer' is a mythical figure, a model of poetic making to be drawn and held close.
64 In contrast, Berger's otherwise exemplary reading of the eclogue (concretely) envisions a decapitated Tityrus whose head is translated, Bottom-like, to Colin's 'own shoulders' (*Revisionary Play*, 435).

and Milton's Satan after her. When Parnassus is just over there, its territory and thus its inspirational authority are available for poetic conquest. Chaucer writes Christian, classical, Celtic and contemporary matters into the physical and moral landscapes of coastal Brittany, clerkly Orleans and crafted garden. Spenser's Hobbinol stands 'Here', the vernacular fairies dance nearby and the muses play over there, while Rosalind as a vision of personal or political happiness remains out of reach. Together, these figures in their connected but distinct spaces serve to entwine Virgilian aspirations and current politics with the material of an English literary past. The Chaucerian technique of planting varied sources to shape one (heterogeneous) literary garden, practised in 'June', will enable Spenser to build his Faerie Lond.

5

Chaucer in Ireland: archaism, etymology and the idea of development

William Rhodes

The references to Geoffrey Chaucer in *A View of the Present State of Ireland* seem surprisingly minor if we compare them to the older poet's looming presence in Spenser's verse. Chaucer appears only twice in Spenser's prose dialogue on Irish colonial reform. In each case, his writings serve as a source of lexical evidence about contemporary Irish material and legal culture. Hardly comparable in scope and significance to Spenser's emulation of and competition with Chaucer in his poetry, these references nevertheless suggest a strong continuity between Spenser's approach to literary history and his approach to Irish history. When Spenser links Irish clothing and colonial legal reforms to England's medieval past via Chaucer, he makes Ireland a living continuation of England's past, separating Ireland from the 'now' of England, while also suggesting Ireland's amenability to England's developmental path. This tendency to look to the past in order to imagine new forms defines Spenser's poetic relationship to Chaucer, which finds exemplary expression in the continuation of the *Squire's Tale* in Book IV of *The Faerie Queene*. Not coincidentally, the *Squire's Tale* is also the source for Spenser's most consequential citation of Chaucer in *A View*. In this chapter, I hope to show how Spenser uses Chaucer to mediate between past, present and future in Ireland by first considering the reference to *Sir Thopas* in Irenius's discussion of Irish clothes, before turning to the crucial legal-lexical debate between Eudoxus and Irenius about the word 'borrough'. These Chaucerian citations demonstrate how Spenser's innovatively retrospective use of literary history in his poetry shapes his vision of Ireland's colonial reformation.

Checklatoun: the untimeliness of Irish clothes

During the course of Irenius's frequently digressive report on the problems with Irish laws, customs and religion, each of which he intends to anatomise in turn before proposing schemes for reform, he and Eudoxus eventually turn to 'the Customes of the old Englishe which are amongst the Irish'.[1] The Old English, the

---

1 Edmund Spenser, *The Works of Edmund Spenser: A Variorum Edition*, ed. Edwin Greenlaw *et al.*, 11 vols (Baltimore: Johns Hopkins University Press, 1932–49), X: *Spenser's Prose Works*, ed. Rudolf

descendants of English nobility who settled in Ireland after the conquest of Henry II, are as much a part of Ireland's problems as the Irish, according to *A View*. Irenius emphasises their adoption of Irish customs as a factor in their resistance to New English dominance. The less-expert Eudoxus assumes that the Old English use Irish speech and dress because of civilisational degeneration caused by 'evill Customes [...] beinge borrowed from the Irishe' (118) – a belief consistent with what Irenius has already said about the Old English, who 'are degenerated and growen allmoste meare Irishe' (96). This opinion assumes that Englishness and Irishness are timelessly distinct, forming a synchronic opposition of civilisation and barbarity immune to the vagaries of historical change. However, when 'theire apparrell theire language theire riding and many other the like' (118) come up, Irenius makes a surprising retreat from his earlier, essentialist emphasis on Old English degeneration into Irish barbarity. Instead, the Old English may not have sunk from civilised English manners to bad Irish ones, because English manners in the time of Henry II may well have been as 'barbarous' as Irish customs seem to them now. Irenius takes this perception of historical change within England from the twelfth to the sixteenth centuries and reinscribes that temporal distinction upon the geography of the Atlantic Isles:

> for weare they at the beste that they weare of olde when they weare broughte in they shoulde in so longe an alteracion of time seme verye straunge and vncouthe for it is to be thoughte that the vse of all Englande was in the Raigne of Henrye the Seconde when Irelande was firste planted with Englishe verye rude and barbarous so as if the same shoulde be now vsed in Englande by anye it would seme worthie of sharpe Correccion and of new lawes for reformacion but it is but even the other daye since Englande grewe Civill. (118)

Since it may be impossible to tell the difference between current Irish customs and English practices from the time of Henry II, Irenius declares that he 'will not haue regarde wheather the beginninge thearof weare Englishe or Irishe' (118). Irenius shifts his emphasis from the timeless division of Irishness from Englishness (so familiar since Giraldus Cambrensis) to a gradual historical divergence of Irish and English culture.[2] In so doing, he opens up the possibility that they can now be re-aligned.

The claim that Old English customs, similar to Irish manners as they may seem, are not degenerations of ancient English practice, but are continuations of it, emphasises England's progress after 'so longe an alteracion of time'. But the length of time is not so great that Ireland cannot soon follow in England's path, since 'it is but even the other daye since Englande grewe Civill'. Of course, this could also mean that England's progress is recent enough to be vulnerable to reversal

---

Gottfried (Baltimore: Johns Hopkins University Press, 1949), 113. All references to *A View* are from this edition, with page numbers following quotations.

2 On Giraldus, see John Gillingham, 'The English Invasion of Ireland', in *Representing Ireland: Literature and the Origins of Conflict, 1534–1660*, ed. Brendan Bradshaw *et al.* (Cambridge: Cambridge University Press, 1993), 24–42.

if Irish instability spreads to England, a fear Irenius expresses at the beginning of the dialogue (44). England's past haunts the present of Spenser's Ireland, which makes Irish culture amenable to English-style reforms in *A View*, but which also exposes the fragility of England's ostensibly linear, progressive development, and causes Spenser to imagine the harshest means to prevent England's contagion by Irish unrest.

This vascillation between looking to the past as a distant origin for the present, and as a living agent that can affect the future frames Spenser's turn to Chaucer as a source of lexical evidence about Irish clothing. The allusions to England's poetic patriarch, the 'well of English vndefild',[3] at once so familiar and increasingly strange to sixteenth- and seventeenth-century poets,[4] both brings Ireland closer to England through an ostensibly shared history, and estranges Ireland by making it the location of England's archaic past. This dynamic of familiarity and estrangement makes Ireland the barbaric, diminutive island in need of English correction, amenable to English law, customs and religion. Spenser constructs an image of Irish backwardness that also suggests its potential for reform on the basis of a pre-established sequence. Spenser's early anthropology functions through the same 'trick' of modern anthropology identified by Johannes Fabian, where 'research involving personal, prolonged interaction with the Other' gives rise to 'a discourse which construes the Other in terms of distance, spatial and temporal'.[5] According to Doreen Massey, who builds on Fabian's work, this process of spatial and temporal distancing also creates a place for 'the meeting and the nonmeeting of the previously unrelated and [is] thus integral to the generation of novelty'.[6] *A View* exemplifies how temporal and spatial estrangement also creates the conditions for new cultural combinations. The citations of Chaucer in *A View* reveal the parallels in this colonial dynamic of estrangement and familiarity with the backward-looking innovation of Spenser's poetry, where other times and places provide the matter for a new poetic language. As Catherine Nicholson argues, style that evokes a distant time and place was a defining component of vernacular eloquence in Renaissance England, as poets exploited the frisson between the familiarity of English and the strangeness of ancient and foreign rhetoric.[7] Spenser did the same by turning to, in Paula Blank's words, 'contested boundaries within the national language' itself, using the geographically uneven diffusion of linguistic change in England to create his own form of avant-garde literary value.[8] In both

---

3 Edmund Spenser, *The Faerie Queene*, ed. A.C. Hamilton, 2nd edn (London: Longman, 2007), IV.ii.32. All references are to this edition, with book, canto and stanza numbers given after quotations.
4 Lucy Munro, *Archaic Style in English Literature, 1590–1674* (Cambridge: Cambridge University Press, 2014), 71–8.
5 Johannes Fabian, *Time and the Other: How Anthropology Makes Its Object* (New York: Columbia University Press, 2002), xli.
6 Doreen Massey, *For Space* (London: Sage Publications, 2005), 71.
7 Catherine Nicholson, *Uncommon Tongues: Eloquence and Eccentricity in the English Renaissance* (Philadelphia: University of Pennsylvania Press, 2014), 11–12.
8 Paula Blank, *Broken English: Dialects and the Politics of Language in Renaissance Literature* (New York: Routledge, 1996), 104.

his poetry and *A View*, the history embedded in Chaucerian words allows Spenser to cut up time and space in order to recombine the parts in the pursuit of novelty, either poetic or legal and political.

For example, the discussion of certain outlawed garments adopted by the Old English from Irish dress allows Irenius to expand upon the relationship between ancient English customs and current Irish ones. According to Irenius, the Irish persist in wearing the mantle, 'the Leather quilted Iacke', linen head wraps, and other traditional garments, because laws against Irish clothes are not enforced (120). This alarms Eudoxus because, as he claims, 'theare is not a litle in the garment to the fashioninge of the minde and Condicions' (121). Irenius seems to think there is something essentially Irish lurking in the folds of these strange garments, and by continuing to allow them to be worn, the English authorities are all but assuring the continued intransigence of the Irish national character. As Mercedes Camino has argued, these garments block the 'all-seeing imperial eye', but Irenius and Eudoxus's analysis of these garments shows that even an obfuscating object can generate a kind of fantastical knowledge rooted in the study of the past.[9] In this, Eudoxus is perfectly in line with other claims in the dialogue about the importance of material practice for mental disposition, such as Irenius's observation about the dangers of English mothers using Irish nursemaids because 'the minde followeth muche the Temperature of the bodye' (119). But in the case of Irish garments, as Irenius reveals, such clothes are not, in fact, 'fashions of the Irishe Wede', but rather English:

> for the quilted leather Iacke is olde Englishe for it was the proper wede of the horsemen as ye maye reade in *Chaucer* wheare he describeth: *Sr Thopas* apparell and armour when he wente to fighte againste the Geaunte which Checklaton is that kinde of gilden leather with which they vse to imbrother theire Irishe Iackes and theare likewise by all that discripcion ye maye see the verye fashion and manner of the Irishe horsemen moste livelye set forthe in his longe hose, his Rydinge shoes of Costelye Cordwaine his hacqueton and his habericion with all the rest thearevnto belonging. (121)

Against the incredulous Eudoxus's emphasis on the strangeness of Irish dress and manners of riding, Irenius maintains that they are, in fact, 'native Englishe and brought in by the Englishemen firste into Irelande' (122). The current Irish fashion, then, is a direct continuation of the style of dress worn by the horsemen of Ireland's first English invaders, which is the same as that which Chaucer describes when Sir Thopas suits up for battle against the giant Olifaunt. In the very obscurity of the reference, Irenius performs the license of the coloniser to fill gaps in knowledge created and exemplified by the inscrutable Irish clothes. The strange homeliness of archaism was a ready-to-hand, familiar method for Spenser to both

---

9 Mercedes Camino, '"Methinks I See an Evil Lurks Unespied": Visualizing Conquest in Spenser's *A View of the Present State of Ireland*', *Spenser Studies*, 12 (1991), 169–94 (175). See also her article '(Un)folding the Map of Early Modern Ireland: Spenser, Moryson, Bartlett, and Ortelius', *Cartographica*, 34.4 (1997), 1–17.

exoticise and imaginatively domesticate the garments of the Irish.[10] For Irenius, Chaucer helps to prove that the English past lives in the Irish present through the 'untimely matter' of Irish clothes.[11] This does not make Irenius any less sensitive to the 'inconvenience' (118) of these warlike Irish forms of dress (122), but it does promise the suitability of Irish customs to an accelerated version of English development since the time of Henry II.

In point of fact, Spenser misquotes and seems to misunderstand Chaucer here, despite 'the ease, detail, and pervasiveness of his borrowings' from *Sir Thopas* throughout his oeuvre.[12] He conflates stanzas and fumbles Chaucer's vocabulary, but this is because the philological details do not matter to Spenser as much as the structure of historical periodisation that such citations allow. He gets 'his hacqueton and his habericion with all the rest thearevnto belonginge' from Chaucer's account of Thopas dressing for battle: 'And next his sherte an aketoun, /And over that an haubergeoun / For percynge of his herte; / And over that a fyn hawberk' (860-3).[13] 'Aketoun' here means the quilted jacket that goes under armour, which Spenser conflates with the 'syklatoun' of the earlier stanza describing Sir Thopas's unarmed dress (730-5). Sir Thopas's 'syklatoun' means some kind of fine fabric, like 'patterned silk', as the editors of the *Riverside Chaucer* guess (918). Taking the word 'syklatoun', with its suggestion of finery, and the meaning of 'aketown', Spenser arrives at 'Checklaton' as 'that kinde of gilden leather with which they vse to imbrother theire Irishe Iackes'. The finery seems to be picked up again and conflated with the 'quilted leather Iacke' in Book VI of *The Faerie Queene* when Disdaine's dress is described: 'But in a Iacket quilted richly rare, / Vpon checklaton he was straungely dight' (VI.vii.43). In *A View*'s account of Irish clothing, Spenser quotes the description of Sir Thopas's 'shoon of cordewane', as well as his 'hosen' and 'His robe [...] of syklatoun' (732-5). That these Chaucerisms would also appear in Book VI of *The Faerie Queene*, which concludes in a recognisably Irish setting, suggests the close affinity between the material traces of English history in Spenser's account of the Irish present, and the poetically generative traces of linguistic history in Spenser's Chaucerian diction.[14] Checklatoun, this obscure Chaucerian word, knits together Spenser's explicit, prosaic description of Irish culture and his poetic treatment of Irish matter in Book VI, a connection that allows us to see how the multi-temporality of Spenser's

---

10 On Spenser's *unheimlich* Ireland, see Kenneth Gross, *Spenserian Poetics: Idolatry, Iconoclasm, and Magic* (Ithaca, NY: Cornell University Press, 1985), 79.
11 Jonathan Gil Harris, *Untimely Matter in the Time of Shakespeare* (Philadelphia: University of Pennsylvania Press, 2009). For Harris, 'untimely matter' describes the propensity for all objects to 'collate many different moments', and in the process, 'prompt many different understandings and experiences of temporality' (4).
12 Judith H. Anderson, *Reading the Allegorical Intertext: Chaucer, Spenser, Shakespeare, Milton* (New York: Fordham University Press, 2008), 57.
13 All references to Chaucer are from *The Riverside Chaucer*, ed. Larry D. Benson, 3rd edn (Boston: Houghton Mifflin, 1987).
14 'Checklatoun' has also proved important for the recent debate, now resolved, about Spenser's authorship of *A View*. See Carol Kaske, 'The Word "Checklaton" and the Authorship of *A Vewe of the Presente State of Ireland*', Spenser Studies, 13 (1999), 267.

poetic style informs the clash of historical epochs in his account of Irish material culture, replete with untimely survivals from Scythia to England.[15]

Using Chaucer to assert the English origins of Irish dress points to the ways in which space and time are mutually implicated in questions of both poetic diction and material history. Poetic theorists of the sixteenth century assume that regional English dialects preserve archaic English words, just as Spenser believes that Irish clothing preserves archaic English fashion.[16] The further one gets from the civilisational centre, the further one goes back in time. Linguistic and material histories merge for Spenser in their purported ability to reveal the sedimented histories that tie England and Ireland together in relationships of uneven development. Ireland's alterity consists in its 'medieval' cultural hangovers, but these hangovers also make Ireland familiar, legible to the historically minded colonist, and, promisingly (to Irenius's mind) suggest that there may be grounds to think that Irish culture can be made to 'fit' English law, the main desideratum for much of the remainder of the dialogue.[17] When Eudoxus and Irenius turn to the legal reform of Ireland's territorial organisation, the question of the fit of English law to Ireland ends up relying heavily on an etymological question to which Chaucer provides crucial evidence for Irenius's answer.

Borough: land, law and language

The second invocation of Chaucer occurs when Irenius and Eudoxus discuss the reform of Ireland's political organisation, with the goal of eliminating the decentralised authority of the sept and replacing it with a hierarchical division of the Irish populace into manageable units, answerable to English authority. After having demonstrated to Eudoxus's satisfaction the necessity of supporting a large force of English troops to subdue the Irish completely so that 'they will and muste yealde to anie ordinaunce that shalbe given' (198), Irenius lays out his plans to 'establishe suche an order of gouernement [...] meteste for the good of that Realme' (198). This requires not the total replacement of the legal code with something uniquely fitted to Ireland's situation, but rather the installation of an English style of government, since New English settlers will not accept any other system, and 'the Irishe will better be drawen to the Englishe then the Englishe to the Irishe

---

15 David Wallace notes the Ovidian and Petrarchan resonances of the Scythian imaginary, a literary historical formation that 'allows Spenser to suppose that the Irish are too western and too eastern at one and the same time'. See *Premodern Places: Calais to Surinam, Chaucer to Aphra Behn* (Oxford: Blackwell, 2004), 193.
16 Munro, 172–3.
17 On the legal theoretical sense of 'fit' in *A View*, see Elizabeth Fowler, 'The Rhetoric of Political Forms: Social Persons and the Criterion of Fit in Colonial Law, *Macbeth*, and *The Irish Masque at Court*', in *Form and Reform in Renaissance England: Essays in Honor of Barbara Kiefer Lewalski*, ed. Amy Boesky and Mary Thomas Crane (Newark: University of Delaware Press, 2000), 70–103. The metaphor of clothing implied in the fit between a people and their government is made explicit in Thomas Smith's *De Republica Anglorum* in an illuminating passage, which Jeffrey Griswold discusses in relation to *A View* in 'Allegorical Consent: *The Faerie Queene* and the Politics of Erotic Subjection', *Spenser Studies*, 29 (2014), 219–37 (225–6).

gouernemente' (199). As Irenius goes on to explain, 'sithens we Cannot now applie Lawes fitt to the people as in the firste institucion of Comon wealthes it oughte to be we will applie the people and fitt them to the Lawes as it moste Convenientlye maye be' (199). In this consequential formulation, Irenius shows why even the minor detail of the garments of Irish horsemen matter for his vision of Irish reform, as any clue to the historical conjuncture of Irish and English culture suggests that the Irish may one day 'fit' English government. To discover Chaucer in Ireland's material culture – and to use his lexicon to understand England's ancient legal system to which Ireland must conform – goes beyond antiquarian citation and performs the assumption that Ireland's potential capacity for Englishness warrants Irenius's plan to institute an English form of government there.

Among the first political reforms Irenius proposes is to establish the laws of King Alfred, who pacified Anglo-Saxon England before the Norman Conquest by, according to Irenius, dividing the realm 'into shieres and the shieres into hundredes and the hundreds into Lathes or wapentackes and the wapentackes into tythings' (201). Here, Irenius invokes the mythic wellhead of English legal history in pre-Norman times. This origin story helped define the common law as an essentially English institution, and Irenius invokes it in order to justify its application to Irish culture in the present.[18] A sceptical Eudoxus, remembering the aspects of Irenius's account that emphasise Ireland's otherness, wants to know how Irenius 'woulde transfer a principall institucion from Englande to Irelande' (202). Irenius's answer invokes the same comparative historical method that brought Chaucerian knights to bear on the analysis of contemporary Irish horsemen. England's past is similar enough to Ireland's present to justify Irenius's belief that Ireland may be rapidly pacified, as the pre-Norman English had been under the guidance of Alfred:

> This Lawe was made not by the *Norman* Conquerour but by a Saxon kinge at what time Englande was verie like to Irelande as it now stands. ffor it was (as I tolde youe) annoyed greatly with Robbers and outlawes which troubled the wholle state of the Realme euerie Corner hauing a Robin hoode in it that kepte the woodes and spoiled all passengers and inhabitantes as Irelande now hathe so as me semes this ordinaunce woulde fitt very well and bring them all into Awe. (202–3)

English common law's pre-Norman origin, the crucial factor that made it so essentially English to Elizabethan Anglo-Saxonists like Laurence Nowell and William Lambarde, paradoxically allows Irenius to assert its transferability to Ireland based on the fact that Ireland appears to be a living continuation of ancient English conditions, as if crossing the Irish Sea also meant returning to England before the invasion of 1066.[19] With a 'Robin hoode' in every Irish woodland, Spenser's legal antiquarianism joins with an imagination shaped by romance, using medieval

---

18 'Perhaps more than in any other arena, the study of law in the later sixteenth century increasingly posited the Anglo-Saxon period of history as the essential, foundational time for English identity.' See Rebecca Brackmann, *The Elizabethan Invention of Anglo-Saxon England: Laurence Nowell, William Lambarde, and the Study of Old English* (Cambridge: Brewer, 2012), 191.
19 On the relationship between *A View* and the work of Nowell and Lambarde, see ibid., 178–85.

poetic fictions to fill out his vision of Ireland's physical and political geography.[20] This tendency to find English antiquities in Irish culture positions Ireland as historically belated, inviting correction by a strong English government.

This colonial aim of accelerated development necessarily involves reconfiguring both space and time, and Renaissance poetics and rhetorical theory provided a model for conceiving of the relationship between geographical marginality and historical belatedness. If language is essentially bound to history and geography, then style offers a way to think about change over time.[21] Indeed, as Jenny Mann has shown, the figure of Robin Hood haunts English poetic and rhetorical treatises in the period as an ineloquent trace of England's geographical, temporal and artistic distance from classical civilisation, which suggests another reason, beyond associations with mobility and violence, why Spenser would transfer this English sign of civilisational delay to Ireland: Robin Hood is not just a criminal, but a figure of vernacular resistance to civilising language.[22]

So it is fitting that, shortly after Irenius explains his plan to 'fitt' ancient English government to Ireland in order to 'bring them all into Awe', Eudoxus's interrogation takes a lexical turn; 'what do youe meane by your hundred and what by your Burroughe', he asks (212). Eudoxus assumes that these terms refer only to geographical units, like plowlands and towns: 'by that which I haue red in ancient recordes of Englande, an hundred did Containe an hundred villages or as some saie an hundred plowlandes [...] and by that which I haue read of a Burrroughe it signifyethe a free Towne' (212). Irenius corrects him, and in so doing, names Chaucer a second time: a hundred means one hundred people pledged to an alderman, and

> Likewise a burroughe is as I heare vse it and as the olde lawes still vsed it, is not a Burroughe Towne as they now Call it That is a ffranchise Towne but a main pledge of C free persons therefore Called a freburroughe or (as youe saie) *Franciplegium* for *Borh* in old *Saxon* signifyethe a pledge or suertye and yeat is so vsed with vs in some speches, as *Chaucer* saithe St. Iohn to borrowe that is for assurance and warrantye. (213)[23]

---

20 Tamsin Badcoe, '"The compass of that Islands space": Insular Fictions in the Writings of Edmund Spenser', *Renaissance Studies*, 25.3 (2010), 415–32 (421–3).
21 Recent studies of Renaissance poetics and their relation to historical and spatial alterity include Nicholson; Munro; Jenny C. Mann, *Outlaw Rhetoric: Figuring Vernacular Eloquence in Shakespeare's England* (Ithaca: Cornell University Press, 2012); Blank; David Scott Wilson-Okamura, *Spenser's International Style* (Cambridge: Cambridge University Press, 2013). Matthew Harrison notes how with a stylistic term like 'rudeness', 'Spenser finds a way of thinking formally about historical difference'. See 'The Rude Poet Presents Himself: Breton, Spenser, and Bad Poetry', *Spenser Studies*, 29 (2014), 239–62 (253).
22 Mann, 1–28. As Patricia Palmer notes, 'Irish became synonymous with the political and religious dissidence to which it gave voice'. See *Language and Conquest in Early Modern Ireland: English Renaissance Literature and Elizabethan Imperial Expansion* (Cambridge: Cambridge University Press, 2001), 97.
23 The *Variorum* reads 'bothe', but I have followed the variant reading of 'borh', recorded in Ware's edition (1633); British Museum, Harleian MS 1932; Public Record Office, State Papers 63.202, pt. 4, item 58; Trinity College, Dublin, MS E.3.26; and the Arthur A. Houghton MS.

Irenius's corrections draw a distinction between the meaning of 'hundred' and 'burroughe' as geographical units, on the one hand, and political units, on the other. A 'Burroughe Towne' or 'ffranchise Towne' signifies a bounded space with certain legally recognised privileges, but the meaning that Irenius emphasises is the formation of a polity through pledges, affirmed by a handshake ('main pledges'), amongst a hundred 'free persons'. In order to authorise this semantic shift from geography to political allegiance, Irenius turns to Chaucer, quoting a line from the *Squire's Tale*.

Irenius hopes Chaucer proves the meaning of one of the key legal terms that will define his preferred form of government. As early modern legal scholars knew, understanding what words meant was necessary for interpreting the law, and this knowledge required etymological and historical research.[24] Irenius's citation of Chaucer not only clarifies his intended meaning, but also suggests the similarities between the English past and the Irish present. Chaucer serves as the shuttle between a lost Anglo-Saxon world and a contemporary Anglo-Irish one that allows Irenius to weave together England's past and Ireland's future.

Scholars have long studied the temporal and historical contortions that mark Spenser's engagement with Chaucer in his poetry.[25] This ambivalent enterprise of simultaneous innovation and retrospection, so evident in his poetry, also structures Spenser's approach to the reformation of Ireland. The 'tension between practical and poetic purposes', or 'the impulse to *make* meaning out of Irish antiquity, rather than simply record what is directly relevant to a historical point', as Judith H. Anderson describes it, emerges in *A View* because the investigation of the Irish past activates the same desire to merge archaism and novelty that marks Spenser's poetry.[26] Chaucer's appearance in Spenser's colonial Ireland suggests that the poetic project of bending the arc of literary history through the combination of Chaucerian diction and bold experimentalism has a surprising affinity with the practical, colonial project of radically transforming Ireland's contemporary political and spatial organisation by applying the lessons of English linguistic and legal histories. Where power and language intersect in the law, the temporal dimension of linguistic research takes on spatial force as it is applied to the physical existence of imaginatively distanced colonial subjects. As we know from George Puttenham's famous remarks on the unacceptably dated language of Middle English poets, the speech of 'Northern men', and 'any speech used beyond

---

24 Brackmann, 189. On the convergence of lexical research and legal language in Spenser's poetics, see Andrew Zurcher, *Spenser's Legal Language: Law and Poetry in Early Modern England* (Cambridge: D.S. Brewer, 2007).
25 Alice S. Miskimin, *The Renaissance Chaucer* (New Haven: Yale University Press, 1975); A. Kent Hieatt, *Chaucer, Spenser, Milton: Mythopoeic Continuities and Transformations* (Montreal: McGill-Queen's University Press, 1975); A.C. Spearing, *Medieval to Renaissance in English Poetry* (Cambridge: Cambridge University Press, 1995); Theresa M. Krier, ed., *Refiguring Chaucer in the Renaissance* (Gainesville: University Press of Florida, 1998); Anderson; Megan L. Cook, 'Making and Managing the Past: Lexical Commentary in Spenser's *Shepheardes Calender* (1579) and Chaucer's *Works* (1598/1602)', *Spenser Studies*, 26 (2011), 179–222.
26 Anderson, 158.

the river of Trent', the normative study of language involves dividing up both space and time.²⁷

At issue when Irenius describes the pre-Norman system of tythes, hundreds and boroughs is the 'fit' between a culture and a legal and political constitution, and it cuts directly to the problem of establishing the relationship between human bodies, the land they live on, and the language used to define the social and material links among them. Irenius confronts the problem of social personhood, which, as 'personifications of social relations', cannot be reformed just through applying new names to forms of social organisation, but through 'penetrating the social bonds underneath the language, the networks embodied in the persons'.²⁸ This is what the debate about the meaning of the word 'borrough' brings out, as a proper understanding of the new governmental terminology leads to the transformation of Irish social organisation, territorial division and political community.

The Anglo-Saxon terms Irenius uses are unclear in a way that further underscores the distinction between physical place and the networks of social persons that Irenius wants to disrupt.²⁹ Do these words describe measures of land or groups of people? Eudoxus reports,

> that which I haue red in ancient recordes of Englande an hundred did Containe an hundred villages or as some saie an hundred plowlandes [...] and by that which I haue rede of a Burroughe it signifyethe a free Towne which had a principall officer called a headburoughe to become ruler and vndertake for all the dwellers vnder him havinge for the same franchises and priviledges graunted them by the kinge wheareof it was Called a freburoughe of the Lawyer *Franciplegium*. (212–13)

Eudoxus, while right about the importance of the pledge in this system, thinks the terms Irenius has introduced to the discussion could be plotted on a map as groups of plowlands and towns populated with free people beholden to a leader accountable for them before the sovereign. Irenius corrects this partial accuracy: 'for that which ye speake of devidinge the Countrye into hundredes was a divicion of the Landes of the Realme but this which I tell was of the people who weare thus devided by the poll so that a hundred in this sence signifyethe C pledges' (213). The confusion over whether 'burrough' meant a town or a pledge arises from the similarity between the Old English '*borg*', meaning a surety or pledge, specifically a 'group of householders standing in pledge for each other in law, tithing' – and the Old English '*burh*' as a word for a fortified town.³⁰ This similarity meant that they are conflated in Eudoxus's and Irenius's dialogue, with

---

27 George Puttenham, *The Art of English Poesy*, ed. Frank Whigham and Wayne A. Rebhorn (Ithaca, NY: Cornell University Press, 2007), 229.
28 Fowler, 72, 76.
29 On the importance of the separation of people from land in colonial ideology, especially in Elizabethan Ireland, see Ken Hiltner, *What Else is Pastoral? Renaissance Literature and the Environment* (Ithaca: Cornell University Press, 2011), 156–73.
30 'Borg', sense 3.a.ii.b and 'burh', sense B in *Dictionary of Old English: A to G* online, ed. Angus Cameron *et al.* (Toronto: Dictionary of Old English Project, 2007) http://tapor.library.utoronto.ca/doe/index.html [accessed 1 July 2015].

the former assuming that a town is the primary meaning (albeit a town peopled with inhabitants pledged to a ruler), while the latter asserts that 'burrough' primarily means a pledge between people, separate from any fixed geographical unit like a town. Spenser had used this latter meaning in *The Shepheardes Calender*, as Hannah Crawforth points out, 'in this specifically Anglo-Saxon sense' of a pledge in order 'to evoke a pre-Conquest legal system not based upon feudalism but rather dependent upon exactly the principles of self-control, moderation, and communal responsibility' that characterised the ideal English church, but which also, in *A View*, represent the principles that the Irish social structure, as Irenius describes it, most desperately lacks.[31] Spenser's poetic archaism in the *Calender* here presages the power that old words can possess in the historical imagination of the colonial reformer.

Eudoxus and Irenius debate not just a point of linguistic antiquarianism in the discussion of 'burrough', but rather the force such linguistic knowledge can exert on Ireland's population and the land which ensures its survival. In Andrew Zurcher's terms, regulating 'the flow of power' in *A View* involves both physical control over the landscape and 'control over allegiances'.[32] Irenius argues that the shifting, untraceable connections between clan leaders and their territory will be bureaucratically fixed in place once people are divided into hundreds and boroughs and pledged to an alderman who has been appointed for his loyalty to the English. Irenius hopes to use the principles of English law to correct the alleged failings of Irish law. According to Brackmann, Laurence Nowell argued that 'English law concerned itself greatly with property – protecting the rights of landowners, recognising lawful heirs, and ensuring that land stayed in the hands of those who (under the law) were entitled to it. Irish custom […] did none of these things'.[33] Eudoxus's lexical turn is consistent with the legal antiquarianism of early modern Anglo-Saxonists, like Nowell, whose maps and descriptions of Ireland, collected with his maps of England and research into Old English place names in BL Cotton Domitian xviii, contained 'tactical information crucial to a military campaign' in Ireland.[34] As Nowell and Spenser knew, research into ancient words can take on material force when they guide legal institutions backed up with military action. England's past not only lives in Ireland's present, as Irenius's citations of Chaucer are meant to show, but the desire to delve into that past is motivated by reformist ambition in the present.[35] This ambition means, paradoxically, that the imposition of Anglo-Saxon legal structures on the undeveloped, living historical relic that is Elizabethan Ireland results in a novel governmental structure that replaces the feudal 'honour communities of the nobility and gentleman' with 'a distinct new

---

31 Hannah Crawforth, 'Strangers to the Mother Tongue: Spenser's *Shepheardes Calender* and Early Anglo-Saxon Studies', *Journal of Medieval and Early Modern Studies*, 41.2 (2011), 293–316 (302).
32 Zurcher, 191.
33 Brackmann, 167.
34 Ibid., 163.
35 As Crawforth shows, this motivated, reformist research into Anglo-Saxon language and history was a crucial activity of a circle of Elizabethan Protestant intellectuals that was important to Spenser's early development (293–316).

hierarchy of civil servants and crown-oriented administrators'.[36] By going back to the pre-feudal legal culture described by Anglo-Saxonist research, Spenser articulates a post-feudal future that divides Irish communities into hierarchies that descend from and lead back to the queen. Just as Spenser imagines an Ireland pacified by the construction of new roads and garrisons that divide and regulate Ireland's terrain, he also uses the periodic division of history to imagine Ireland's accelerated repetition of English political development.

Irenius's legal and governmental reforms deploy historical knowledge in order to create political concord out of orderly division, where previously there had been only unstable and shifting allegiances. In this new system, friends and enemies can be easily identified through an elaborate system of pledged accountability, organised around a new conception of Ireland's territorial structure. Given this goal, the source of Irenius's citation of the phrase 'St. John to borrow' in Chaucer's *Squire's Tale* takes on ironic significance once returned to its original context in a narrative of broken faith and the failure of friendship, the guiding virtue of Book IV of *The Faerie Queene*, where Spenser continues the Squire's unfinished narrative. The phrase 'St. John to borrow' occurs when Canacee, thanks to the properties of her magic ring, converses with a falcon who has injured herself in sorrow over her betrayal by a tercelet. The falcon describes the fatal moment in which they pledge love to each other: 'As I best myghte, I hidde fro hym my sorwe, / And took hym by the hond, Seint John to borwe, / And seyde hym thus: "Lo, I am youres al; / Beth swich as I to yow have been and shal"' (595–8). The tercelet replies fairly, but acts otherwise, eventually leaving the falcon for a kite. Spenser's citation of this passage as a witness for his etymology of 'borough' as a pledge or surety ironically refers to a scene of broken truth due to fickleness. Perhaps this explains the choice of this instance of 'borrow' as an illustration of what a pledge might mean in a country that has a power to so quickly 'alter mens natures', as Eudoxus laments (210).

In Book IV, by contrast, poetry's formal properties have the power to 'alter mens natures' for the better. This power of correcting vice and re-ordering social relations based on virtue depends in part on poetry's ability to recover 'antique stories' and use them for the present (IV.ii.32). But even 'Dan *Chaucer*, well of English vndefyled, / On Fames eternall beadroll worthie to be fyled' (IV.ii.32), is threatened by the depredations of 'wicked Time', which has effaced Chaucer's tale and requires Spenser's efforts to continue it (IV.ii.33). As Spenser sets out to repair poetic history, the periodising assumptions that underlie Spenser's citations of Chaucer in *A View* find their complement in the poetic desire to bring the past into the present through an 'infusion sweete' of antiquity that inspires the creation of new forms (IV.ii.34).

This convergence of innovative archaism in Spenser's poetry and his political theory is made explicit here, as he prepares to complete the *Squire's Tale* and praises poetry's Orphic and Davidic power to create concord from discord, two musical terms that also apply to Spenser's vision of governmental reform. He describes this poetic capacity thus:

---

36 Zurcher, 194, n. 28.

> Such Musicke is wise words with time concented,
> To moderate stiffe minds, disposd to striue:
> Such as that prudent Romane well inuented,
> What time his people into partes did riue,
> Them reconcyld againe, and to their homes did driue. (IV.ii.2)

Spenser invokes Meninus Agrippa and his fable of the social body, wherein he figuratively 'did riue' the populace into representative body parts in order to show the complementarity of their interests and to moderate the desires of the mob. In this sense, he exemplifies the task of finding words that agree with 'time', or the proper occasion to deliver moderating speech. But 'wise words with time concented' also refers to the rhythm of the poetic song. Spenser reveals the common vocabulary that joins poetic making with social ordering, and in each case, manipulating experiences of time is paramount – the time of the poetic line, and the historical time with which 'wise words' must fit. The image of the people riven 'into partes' and then 'reconcyld' and driven home has an uncanny resemblance to what Irenius hopes to achieve in Ireland, where 'Tythinge the polls', or the division and subdivision of the populace into accountable units, means that 'the people are broken into manie smalle partes like little streames that they Cannot easelye come togeather into one heade' (205). This is the first step to ensuring that the cattle-herding Irish will settle into fixed addresses in farm towns as either free-holders or tradespeople (215–17).

The riparian metaphor for the division of the Irish populace also recalls the catalogue of neatly ranked English and Irish rivers at the marriage of Thames and Medway (IV.xi). These rivers and nymphs come together but retain their separate identities, avoiding the prospect of unruly, combined powers that animates Irenius's fear of Irish convocations.[37] The rivers gather in an ordered, hierarchical procession, as Irenius hopes the Irish will for the annual assemblies meant to re-count and re-order the tythes of the Irish under Alfred's style of government; they do not 'come togeather into one heade'. The etymological characterisation of each river and its nymphs in the catalogue, as Judith H. Anderson reminds us, exhibits the same 'expansiveness' that marks Spenser's etymological treatment of Irish names in *A View*, as emplacement in a social hierarchy is imaginatively achieved through the knowledge of the past embedded in the history of names and words.[38] Etymology thereby becomes a tool in the colonial project of reordering society and its government, suggesting the deep association in Spenser's colonial thought between social relations and the words used to designate and define them. Hence the importance of Spenser's insistence on the 'old Saxon' and Chaucerian sources for the terms through which he means to reform the Irish government and fit Ireland to English law. Discovering old words and imagining their origins is a powerful tool for re-making the present and shaping the future, as Spenser repeatedly asserts in his poetic and prosaic citations of Chaucer.

---

37 On convocations, see Zurcher, 189–90.
38 Anderson, 157.

This path of innovative retrospection is fraught with ambivalence about the risk that England's past can not only guide Ireland's present, but also come back to transform England's future should the fear of contagion by Irish unrest prove true (44). In Book IV, not only does Spenser explicitly lament the effects of 'wicked Time' on past knowledge, he also implicitly points to the dangerous limitations of martial roughness inherent in the incompletely civilised cultures of the British past. For Spenser, the 'warlike numbers and Heroicke sound' of 'Dan *Chaucer*' meant that 'Chaucer's meter sounded strong and energetic but also harsh and undisciplined. Like the overeager martial tendencies that must be brought into concord in Book IV, Chaucer's rough verse must be tamed and put to work in the service of the virtue of friendship'.[39] As Irenius claims, the Irish, too, manifest the martial vigour of their ancient, Scythian roots, which in turn resemble England's mythic period of pre-Norman bellicosity. Each one is admirable in its warlike strength, but only as long as this strength is subjected to the harsh discipline of civilising development.

The intertextual suture between Book IV and *A View* created by the shared reference to the *Squire's Tale* points towards the significance of Chaucer's otherwise minimal presence in Spenser's Irish dialogue. The allusions to Chaucer in *A View* show Spenser adapting the poetic process of backward-looking innovation to the legal and material development of Ireland. Just as the ostensibly rough metres of Chaucer's 'martiall numbers and Heroicke sound' indicate both an appealing vigour and a rough incompleteness that must be smoothed within a tale of virtuous concord, so too does the persistent ferocity of the Irish provoke both admiration and the desire for correction and domestication. Dividing the Irish population 'into small parts like little streams' is an image that conveys both the threatening strength of a gathering Irish force, as well as a wishful vision of future harmony arising from well-ordered division. Extending the musical metaphor of concord and discord to the ordering of a population puts the New English colonial reformer in the position of David and Mennius Agrippa, who, with 'Music [and] wise words with time concented [...] moderate stiffe minds, disposd to striue'. When, thirty stanzas later, Spenser describes Chaucer's inflowing spirit overcoming the ravages of time, he connects poetry's ability to mould its hearers with its power to shuttle between antiquity and the present. Chaucer functions much the same way in *A View*, authorising Irenius's attempt to bring England's ancient legal regime and material culture to life in the Irish present.

Critics like Andrew Zurcher and Hannah Crawforth have called for renewed attention to Spenser's care with linguistic history as a crucial element of his poetics, a concern that is directly related to his knowledge of legal language and the historical scholarship that supported its interpretation.[40] This legal and lexical background is just as central to *A View*'s attempt to guide Ireland's future with the aid of knowledge extracted from the sedimented histories of key English and Irish

---

39 Craig Berry, '"Sundrie Doubts": Vulnerable Understanding and Dubious Origins in Spenser's Continuation of "The Squire's Tale"', in Krier, ed., 106–27 (116–17).
40 Zurcher; Crawforth.

words. Spenser's use of Chaucer as a witness for the continuity of English antiquity in Ireland exemplifies how the division of past from present in the construction of colonial models of material development is intertwined with the poetic project of remaking the past in the present through the imaginative recovery of linguistic origins.

6

Wise wights in privy places: rhyme and stanza form in Spenser and Chaucer

Richard Danson Brown

In the late 1960s, the poet Hayden Carruth captured some of the challenges *The Faerie Queene* poses for modern readers:

> The greatest difficulty was with the rhymes [...] Sometimes I thought that if another stanza rolled into view with hight/pight/wight/night or sayd/ayd/apayd/upbrayd for its terminations, I'd heave the book in the fire.[1]

As the *Concordance to the Rhymes of The Faerie Queene* (which I wrote and edited with Julian Lethbridge) demonstrates, though Carruth's clusters are plausible, Spenser uses the second one only once (III.vi.21) and the first one not at all.[2] Carruth furnishes metaphors for the experience of reading Spenser, while correctly identifying some of his favourite rhymes. *Hight* lies just outside the top ten with a score of 121, making it *The Faerie Queene*'s fourteenth commonest rhyme; even the most recherché of Carruth's rhymes, *apayd*, is used seven times in all.[3] Some of these terms are suggestively Chaucerian. The *hight: wight* cluster is used in moments of contrasting stress in Book IV of *Troilus and Criseyde*, first when Troilus assures Pandarus of his amatory steadfastness: 'sens I haue trouth her hight / I wol nat ben untrewe for no wight'.[4] Then with bitter irony Criseyde recycles the same pairing as she reassures Troilus of her ability to escape the Greek camp:

> I am nat so nyce a wight
> That I ne can ymagynen a way
> To come ayen that day that I haue hyght
> For who may holden a thyng that wol away

---

1 My thanks are due to the editors of this volume, and to Craig A. Berry and Claire Eager for their supportive comments on the draft.
   Hayden Carruth, 'Spenser and his Modern Critics', *Hudson Review*, 22.9 (1969), 139–47 (141).
2 Richard Danson Brown and J.B. Lethbridge, *A Concordance to the Rhymes of 'The Faerie Queene'* (Manchester: Manchester University Press, 2013), 7.
3 See ibid., 424–31.
4 All quotations from Chaucer are from *The Works 1532 with supplementary material from the Editions of 1542, 1561, 1598 and 1602*, ed. D.S. Brewer (Ilkley: Scolar, 1976), unless otherwise stated. I also provide book and line references checked against *The Riverside Chaucer: Third Edition*, ed. Larry Benson *et al.* (Boston: Houghton Mifflin, 1987). Sig. Nn2ʳ; IV.445–6.

> My father naught/ for al his queynte play
> And by my thrift/ my wendyng out of Troye
> Another day shal turne vs al to ioye. (sig. Oo3r; IV.1625–31)[5]

Though Spenser typically uses *hight* in the sense of 'to call' or 'agree' rather than 'to promise' in the following example, his usage is congruent with Chaucer's.[6] Here Aemylia tells of her abortive elopement:

> Thenceforth I sought by secret meanes to worke
> > Time to my will, and from his wrathfull sight
> > To hide th'intent, which in my heart did lurke,
> > Till I thereto had all things ready dight.
> > So on a day vnweeting vnto wight,
> > I with that Squire agreede away to flit,
> > And in a priuy place, betwixt vs hight,
> > Within a groue appointed him to meete;
> To which I boldly came vpon my feeble feete. (IV.vii.17)[7]

In each stanza, a female speaker sets up an assignation which either will not happen or which turns to disaster; the *wight: hight* rhyme signals the tensions between normative social obligations and the promises between the lovers. As Criseyde brags of her ability to fool Calcas, so Aemylia is over-confident of her ability to 'worke / Time to my will' and to keep her affairs secret, 'vnweeting vnto wight'. Similarities like this open up the question of Spenser's technical debt to Chaucer. I illustrate the rhyming relationship between the two poets to dramatise the culture of formal assumptions in which *The Faerie Queene* originally circulated. One strand of my argument queries David Scott Wilson-Okamura's contention that Spenser's style is best understood in terms of the continental Renaissance.[8] My approach owes more to Ants Oras's study, which argues that Spenser's rhyming practice derives more from the English tradition than the Italian.[9] Oras suggests that Spenser's rhymes mutated between the two installments of *The Faerie Queene*: from a traditional, Chaucerian model, heavily reliant on *rime riche*, to something which is more like the rest of 1590s poetry. This is not to advance a Little Englander Spenser, much less a UKIP Spenser. It is rather to reassert that while his reading

---

5   Chaucer plays continuously on *wight* through Book IV. Troilus's lines rebuke Pandarus's earlier jocose suggestion 'god forbyd alway that eche plesaunce / In o thyng were / and in non other wight [...] selde seynge of a wight / Done olde affections al ouer go' (sig. Nn2ʳ; IV.407–23).
6   'hight, v.1', compare definitions 2 and 4 in the *OED Online* (Oxford: Oxford University Press, 2014). Note that Speght's edition glosses both senses of 'hight', sig. Ttt6ʳ.
7   All quotations from *The Faerie Queene* are from Edmund Spenser, *The Faerie Queene: Revised Second Edition*, ed. A.C. Hamilton with Hiroshi Yamashita, Toshiyuki Suziki and Shohachi Fukuda (London: Pearson Longman, 2001; repr. 2007).
8   David Scott Wilson-Okamura, *Spenser's International Style* (Cambridge: Cambridge University Press, 2013). Though he includes some discussion of English influences, he does not consider *Troilus and Criseyde* as a precedent for *The Faerie Queene*: see 43–4.
9   Ants Oras, 'Intensified Rhymes Links in *The Faerie Queene*', *Journal of English and Germanic Philology*, 54 (1955), 39–60 (57).

was international, his forms remain rooted in domestic models, amongst whom Chaucer remains in Puttenham's phrase, 'the most renowned of them all'.[10]

A further strand in my argument is that rhyme can be read semantically. In his paradigm-shaking essay, Lethbridge suggests that 'rhyme often disappears into the page, and the verse appears to aspire to the condition of blank verse'.[11] My position is that even the most formulaic of rhymes can tell us much about the intertextual meaning(s) Spenser continues to find in his formal patterns.[12] Aemylia's phrase 'vnweeting vnto wight' is not simply poetic filler, but anticipates the different 'priuy place' of Lust's Cave in which she finds herself. Like Criseyde's 'I am nat so nyce a wight', the phrase makes discriminations and establishes aspects of character and disposition which will be turned to advantage later. The rhymes throughout this stanza emphasise Aemylia's hidden 'intent', the wishful chanciness of the assignation she sets up. Rhyme is itself a cultural process 'betwixt us hight' – an agreed function of language, which may be at once conventional, consensual, or in this context, 'ready dight' to emphasise aspects of the text in hand.[13] Pursuing these poetic agreements enables a clearer view of those aspects of Chaucer's poetic praxis which Spenser followed, and those which he critically adapted. My concern with rhyme as an aesthetic and sonal process is related but different to the (sometimes) cacophonous soundscape recorded by Helen Barr in her chapter.

In making these comparisons, I privilege *Troilus and Criseyde*, because of its centrality to the sixteenth-century understanding of Chaucer, and because it is written in what Puttenham called the 'meter heroical' of rhyme royal stanzas.[14] A related facet of the Renaissance Chaucer which isn't often remarked on is that sixteenth-century editions have the effect of making him seem a more stanzaic poet than modern collected editions. Kathleen Forni observes that the majority of William Thynne's non-Chaucerian selections in the 1532 folio are 'composed in rhyme royal'.[15] Seen in the material contexts of the great folios, it is Chaucer's rhyming couplet poems which are eccentric. So the decision to use rhyming stanzas for an epic is less surprising than Wilson-Okamura suggests. Finally, I explore the extent to which the Spenserian stanza not only attempts to 'ouergo'

---

10 George Puttenham, *The Art of English Poesy*, ed. Frank Whigham and Wayne A. Rebhorn (Ithaca, NY: Cornell University Press, 2007), 149. On Spenser's library, see Andrew Hadfield, *Edmund Spenser: A Life* (Oxford: Oxford University Press, 2010), 227–30.
11 Brown and Lethbridge, 109. See also Wilson-Okamura's related argument that Renaissance style is primarily ornamental and does not necessarily have a relationship with meaning (140–79).
12 In this context, see Judith H. Anderson, *Reading the Allegorical Intertext: Chaucer, Spenser, Shakespeare, Milton* (New York: Fordham University Press, 2008).
13 For discussion of 'dight' in Spenser, see Lucy Munro, *Archaic Style in English Literature 1590–1674* (Cambridge: Cambridge University Press, 2013), 204–16.
14 Puttenham, 149–50; see Craig A. Berry, '"Sundrie Doubts": Vulnerable Understanding and Dubious Origins in Spenser's Continuation of the Squire's Tale', in *Refiguring Chaucer in the Renaissance*, ed. Theresa Krier (Gainesville: University Press of Florida, 1998), 106–27 (108), for Puttenham's ambivalence about Chaucer.
15 Kathleen Forni, *The Chaucerian Apocrypha: A Counterfeit Canon* (Gainesville: University Press of Florida, 2001), 90. For the full canon of apocrypha, see xv–xviii, 44–87.

Ariostan *ottavo rima*, but rebuilds Chaucerian rhyme royal to produce a hybrid English form.[16]

Seen/unseen: *rime riche* in context

Rime riche was something of a calling card for both Chaucer and Spenser. Consider a rhyme on different meanings of *wise* from Book I of *Troilus and Criseyde*; this is the kind of rhyme Oras calls 'linkings of cognate words of identical sound but different semantic functions':[17]

> The wyse eke seyth/ wo him that is alone
> For and he fall/ he hath none helpe to ryse
> And sythe thou haste a felowe/ tell thy mone
> For this nys naught certayne the next wyse
> To wynnen loue/ as techen vs the wyse
> To walowe and wepe/ as Niobe the quene
> Whose teeres yet in marbel ben ysene (sig. Hh6ʳ; I.694–700)

The first line quoted here incidentally dramatises the metrical uncertainty which surrounded Chaucer in the sixteenth century. All earlier printed editions (and the *Riverside*), read 'The wyse seyth/ woo hym that is alone'; Thynne's addition of 'eke' shows both a failure to hear the final -e and a desire to produce a text of decasyllabic regularity.[18] Spenser repeats the same rhyme cluster in his continuation of the *Squire's Tale* in Book IV:

> Which whenas *Cambell*, that was stout and wise,
> Perceiu'd would breede great mischiefe, he bethought
> How to preuent the perill that mote rise,
> And turne both him and her to honour in this wise. (IV.ii.37)

In the deep Chaucerian context of the Cambell-Canacee narrative, such formal proximity is unsurprising.[19] The *rime riche* pairings are formulaic: both 'stout and wise' and 'in this wise' satisfy the metrical contract while advancing the narrative. Spenser's adoption of Chaucerian technique is less semantically purposive than Pandarus's playing on notions of wisdom and expedience in love in *Troilus and*

---

16 See Edmund Spenser, *The Prose Works*, ed. Rudolf Gottfried (Baltimore: The Johns Hopkins Press, 1949), 471, for Gabriel Harvey's 1580 letter to Spenser which reports the latter's ambition 'to emulate, and hope to ouergo' the *Orlando Furioso* with 'that *Eluish Queene*'.
17 Oras, 42.
18 See Chaucer, *Troylus and Creseyde* (Westminster: William Caxton, 1483), sig. B3ʳ; *The noble and amerous au[n]cyent hystory of Troylus and Cresyde* (London: Wynkyn de Worde, 1517), sig. C1ʳ; and *The boke of Troylus and Creseyde* (London: Rycharde Pynson, 1526), sig. A5ᵛ.
19 The other *wise: wise* clusters in *The Faerie Queene* are I.i.50b and IV.ii.9c; see Brown and Lethbridge, 344. Chaucer rhymes on *wyse* three times in the *Squire's Tale*, but not as a *rime riche*; see 375–6 (*ryse: wyse*), 627–8 (*wyse: servyse*) and 705–6 (*wyse: suffyse*). See also the *Knight's Tale*, 1739–40 (*juwise: wise*), printed 'iewyse' and 'wyse' by Thynne, and 1803–4 (*servyse: wyse*), in Chaucer, *The Works*, sig. C6ʳ.

Criseyde, where the coupling of 'the wyse' with 'the next wyse / To wynnen loue' hints at the rooted pragmatism of his advice. Yet the fact that this instance of *rime riche* is formulaic does not mean that Spenser's usage invariably follows this pattern. Earlier in the same canto, the pairing is used to describe the false Florimell and Blandamour:

> Sometimes estranging him in sterner wise,
> That hauing cast him in a foolish trance,
> He seemed brought to bed in Paradise,
> And prou'd himselfe most foole, in what he seem'd most wise. (IV.ii.9)

Such rhymes show Spenser directly following the footing of Chaucer's 'feete': as the stanza enacts the dance of the false Florimell's flirtation, so the *wise: wise* pairing points to the folly of the 'wise' in which Blandamour is behaving. Illusory wisdom and delusive behaviour – the fool's 'Paradise' of Blandamour's erotic pursuit of an insubstantial illusion – are juxtaposed through identical rhyme. As Oras suggested, the value of this device is the 'gradation' it implies between cognate yet subtly different terms.[20] The richness of this rhyming lies in the complex blending of sonally identical yet semantically distinct terms to create 'sound-metaphors'.[21] In other words – by means of *not* choosing other words – for both Chaucer and Spenser *rime riche* is a provocation to rereading. Rather than the more 'speedy' reading proposed by Lethbridge, Spenser's fondness for this device is indicative of a felt need to make the reader register similarities and differences between rhymes.[22] *Rime riche* impedes forward momentum, and retards fluency of movement by the very fact of its rich like-not-like repetitions. It insists on what might be called the *versiness* of stanzaic rhyming as the repetitions are underlined by *mise-en-page*. For example, the *seene: vnseene* rhyme in the third stanza of the Proem to Book II is hard to overlook (see Figure 6.1).

Syntactically, the pause at the end of the fifth line is strongly marked by the question, while the anaphoristic openings of the sixth and seventh lines ('What if within [...] What if in') encourage the reader to note the complex reciprocities between line ends and line beginnings.[23] In the poetic context of Spenser's meditation on the murky visibility of faerie land – 'all these were when no man did them know' – the *seene: vnseene* rhyme is anything but unseen.[24] It flaunts

---

20 Oras, 59. Spenser may have remembered some of Chaucer's uses of 'paradys'; see *Troilus* 4.864: 'Her face lyke of paradys the ymage / Was al ychaunged in another kynde'; and the *Merchant's Tale*, 1265–6: 'That in this world it is a paradise / Thus seyde the olde knyght, that was so wise', sigs. Nn4ᵛ, H3ᵛ.
21 W.H. Auden, *Prose and Travel Books in Prose and Verse 1926-1938*, ed. Edward Mendelson (London: Faber & Faber, 1996), 20.
22 Brown and Lethbridge, 94–6. Lethbridge evokes Spenser's 'speed of movement' (94) impressionistically. This is a useful characterisation of the experience of reading *The Faerie Queene*, but it does not register the ways in which Spenser's verse may deliberately impede the reader.
23 See Paul J. Alpers, *The Poetry of The Faerie Queene* (Columbia: University of Missouri Press, 1967; repr. 1982), 70–95, for the sovereignty of the individual line in *The Faerie Queene*.
24 Compare VII.vii.46b (*seene: weene: vnseene: beene*), which similarly depends on the reader registering a disjunction between appearance and reality ('*Death* with most grim and grisly visage seene [...] Yet is he nought [...] but like a shade to weene, / Vnbodied, vnsoul'd, vnheard,

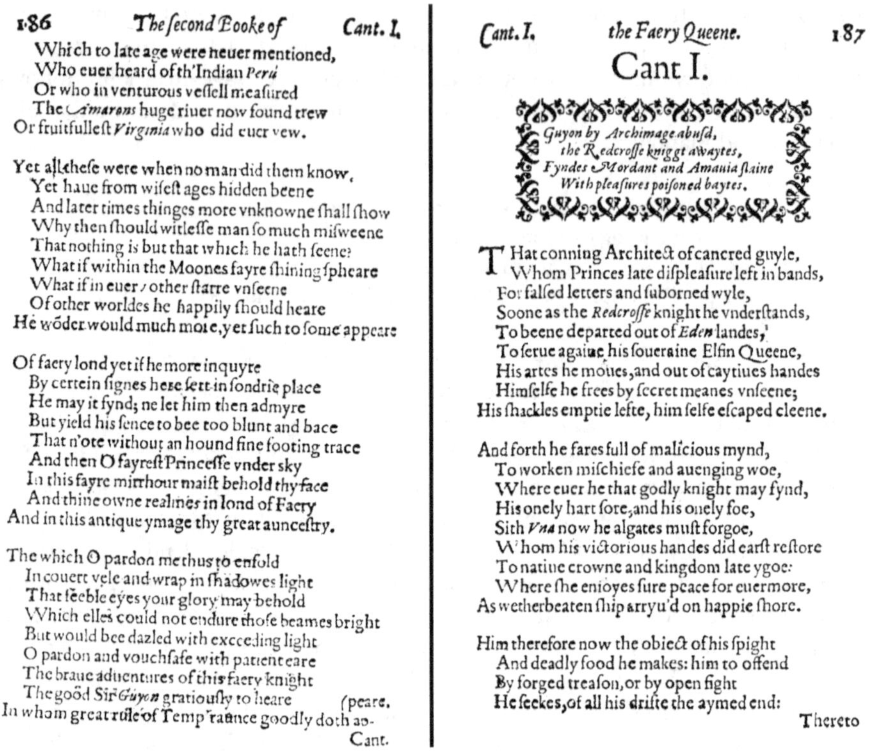

186 *The ſecond Booke of* *Cant. I.*

Which to late age were neuer mentioned,
Who euer heard of th'Indian *Perú*
Or who in venturous veſſell meaſured
The *Amarons* huge riuer now found trew
Or fruitfulleſt *Virginia* who did euer vew.

Yet all theſe were when no man did them know,
Yet haue from wiſeſt ages hidden beene
And later times thinges more vnknowne ſhall ſhow
Why then ſhould witleſſe man ſo much miſweene
That nothing is but that which he hath ſeene?
What if within the Moones fayre ſhining ſpheare
What if in euery other ſtarre vnſeene
Of other worldes he happily ſhould heare
He wõder would much more, yet ſuch to ſome appeare

Of faery lond yet if he more inquyre
By certein ſignes here ſett in ſondrie place
He may it fynd; ne let him then admyre
But yield his ſence to bee too blunt and bace
That n'ote without an hound fine footing trace
And then O fayreſt Princeſſe vnder sky
In this fayre mirrhour maiſt behold thy face
And thine owne realmes in lond of Faery
And in this antique ymage thy great aunceſtry.

The which O pardon me thus to enfold
In couert vele and wrap in ſhadowes light
That feeble eyes your glory may behold
Which elles could not endure thoſe beames bright
But would bee dazled with exceeding light
O pardon and vouchſafe with patient eare
The braue aduentures of this faery knight
The good Sir *Guyon* gratiouſly to heare
In whom great rule of Temp'raunce goodly doth ap- (peare.

Cant.

Cant. I. *the Faery Queene.* 187

Cant I.

Guyon by Archimage abuſd,
the Redcroſſe knight awaytes,
Fyndes Mordant and Amauia ſlaine
With pleaſures poiſoned baytes.

THat conning Architect of cancred guyle,
Whom Princes late diſpleaſure left in bands,
For falſed letters and ſuborned wyle,
Soone as the *Redcroſſe* knight he vnderſtands,
To beene departed out of *Eden* landes,
To ſerue againe his ſoueraine Elfin Queene,
His artes he moues, and out of caytiues handes
Himſelfe he frees by ſecret meanes vnſeene;
His ſhackles emptie lefte, him ſelfe eſcaped cleene.

And forth he fares full of malicious mynd,
To worken miſchiefe and auenging woe,
Where euer he that godly knight may fynd,
His onely hart ſore, and his onely foe,
Sith *Vna* now he algates muſt forgoe,
Whom his victorious handes did earſt reſtore
To natiue crowne and kingdom late ygoe:
Where ſhe enioyes ſure peace for euermore,
As wetherbeaten ſhip arryu'd on happie ſhore.

Him therefore now the obiect of his ſpight
And deadly food he makes: him to offend
By forged treaſon, or by open fight
He ſeekes, of all his drifte the aymed end:

Thereto

Figure 6.1 Page spread from 1590 *Faerie Queene* showing Proem to Book II

its salience to the matter in hand as it teases the reader about his or her ability *witlessly* to 'misweene' that which is 'hidden' yet hovering on the fringes of what may 'to some appeare'. *Rime riche* here is emphatically something which is both 'seene', and, 'happily', heard, as interlocking, epistemological rhyme words play on what is perceived where and how.

Yet there are many ways in which Spenser's practice appears more Chaucerian than in fact it is. This is due to changes in English pronunciation between the fourteenth and sixteenth centuries.[25] Consider rhymes on *creature*. Spenser uses this as a rhyme on two occasions.[26] *Creature* is always a feminine rhyme, where

vnseene'). See also II.i.1c (*Queene: vnseene: cleene*) and II.i.21b (*seene: vnseene: beene: teene*), both from the canto immediately following the Proem.

25 See April McMahon, 'Restructuring Renaissance English', in *The Oxford History of English*, ed. Lynda Mugglestone (Oxford: Oxford University Press, 2006; 2012), 189–218, for the historical complexity of describing these changes.

26 The rhymes on *creature* are IV.ii.44b and IV.vi.17b: note that the a-rhyme of the latter, *endure: impure*, with the emphasis on the second syllable, half rhymes with the *creature: nature: feature: defeature* cluster; as Hamilton notes, this 'rare duplication' of a- and b-rhymes 'seems designed to highlight' (453) a crucial moment in the relationship between Britomart and Artegall. There is a single rhyme on *creatures* in the Mutabilitie Cantos: *creatures: features* (VII.vii.4a), which is linked to the next a-rhyme of *Nature: stature* at VII.vii.5a.

the stress falls strongly on the first syllable. Though such rhymes are virtually excluded from the 1590 *Faerie Queene*, he then 'flood[s] the second installment' with them.[27] In total, there are around 169 such rhymes. There is an ongoing debate about why Spenser made this change. Wilson-Okamura argues that he intended to produce a 'big, fat sound' in imitation of the poets of the Pléiade and Medieval Latin, whereas I have suggested that the 1596 installment aligns *The Faerie Queene* with contemporaneous long English poems: it is the rhyming practices of the 1590 edition which are more eccentric than those of 1596.[28] Chaucer's practice is very different. He rhymes on *creature* relatively frequently: there are at least 20 separate instances in *Troilus and Criseyde*. He scanned the word as a tri- or quadri-syllable, if the final e- is sounded. This pattern is followed in each of the twenty rhymes I have looked at,[29] as in this description of Criseyde:

> She nas nat with the moste of hire stature
> But alle hire lymmes so wel answeryng
> Weren to womanhode/ that creature
> Was neuer lasse mannysshe in semyng (sig. Hh3ᵛ, I.281-4)

The *stature: creature* cluster has a parallel in *The Faerie Queene* in the description of Agape:

> all the powres of nature,
> Which she by art could vse vnto her will,
> And to her seruice bind each liuing creature;
> Through secret vnderstanding of their feature.
> Thereto she was right faire, when so her face
> She list discouer, and of goodly stature (IV.ii.44)

This is an example of the 'foot surgery' which Craig Berry diagnoses in Spenser's continuation of the *Squire's Tale*: 'a poet such as Spenser – with an unusually fine ear but a sixteenth-century understanding of Middle English pronunciation – could not help but feel a roughness in Chaucer's versification', and, I would add, in some of his rhyming.[30] Spenser's 'creatures' are those of early modern English: in a Chaucerian narrative context, Chaucerian rhymes are updated. Spenser's language again proves to be less archaic in practice than its reputation suggests.[31] The verse mimics Agape's practice by using poetic art to

---

27 Wilson-Okamura, 162; see also Brown and Lethbridge, 22. The precise figure is ambiguous because of the uncertain status of words like *powre*, which could be realised either as mono- or di-syllables.
28 Wilson-Okamura, 177 (and 161–77); Brown and Lethbridge, 47–57.
29 The full list is: I.104; I.116; I.283; I.570; II.417; II.717; III.13; IV.252; IV.386; IV.756; IV.767; IV.1679; V.154; V.210; V.241; V.384; V.714; V.808; V.832; V.1701.
30 Berry, 116.
31 See Manfred Görlach, *Introduction to Early Modern English* (Cambridge: Cambridge University Press, 1991), 144, 202; Andrew Zurcher, 'Spenser's Studied Archaism: The Case of "Mote"', *Spenser Studies*, 21 (2006), 231–40; Zurcher, *Spenser's Legal Language: Law and Poetry in Early Modern England* (Cambridge: D.S. Brewer, 2007), 31–2; Wilson-Okamura, 58–62; Munro, 204–36, and

'bind each living' syllable into cogent rhyming clusters with appropriate metrical values. Early in his career, Spenser famously demanded of Harvey 'why a Gods name may not we [...] haue the kingdome of our owne Language [...]?' in the context of the doomed enterprise of making English behave metrically like Latin.[32] Harvey's reply stresses the durability of linguistic custom and the tyranny of Spenser's proposals to 'vsurpe [...] vpon a quiet companye of wordes', yet Spenser's updating of Chaucerian rhymes suggests a deeper sensitivity to the mobility of linguistic usage.[33] Words are not 'quiet' creatures: they move, and the way they will work in verse shifts with time and changes in pronunciation; as Edmund Waller would lament 'who can hope his lines should long / Last in a daily changing tongue?'[34] Spenser's double-edged diction – alluding to a fantasy time while holding the 'relationships between past, present and future' unsettled – manifests this tension.[35]

Leak, spill and interconnected rhyme

I turn now to a particular technique which I have argued is widely used in *The Faerie Queene*: interstanzaic knitting. This device uses the same or related rhyme words within episodes to make connections between different parts of the same narrative action.[36] This device is a facet of the extreme technical restrictions of the Spenserian stanza. The Spenserian is a restrictive grid, which repeatedly requires the poet to come up with new rhymes.[37] Rather than following this prompt towards lexical novelty, Spenser restricts himself further (as Catherine Addison demonstrates) by his fondness for verbal rhymes, and interstanzaic repetitions.[38] Chaucer again provides a precedent: Spenser would have found many rhymes across stanzas in *Troilus and Criseyde*, such as the *hight: wight* clusters cited earlier.

---

my review: Richard Danson Brown, 'Lucy Munro, Archaic Style in English Literature, 1590–1674', *Spenser Review*, 44.2 (Fall 2014), www.english.cam.ac.uk/spenseronline/review/volume-44/442/reviews/munro-lucy-archaic-style-in-english-literature-1590–1674 [accessed 19 November 2018].

32 Spenser, *Prose Works*, 16. See Derek Attridge, *Well-Weighed Syllables: Elizabethan Verse in Classical Metres* (Cambridge: Cambridge University Press, 1974), 146–9, for Harvey's horrified reaction. See Richard Helgerson, *Forms of Nationhood: The Elizabethan Writing of England* (Chicago: Chicago University Press, 1992), 1–18, for a political reading of the question.

33 See Spenser, *Prose Works*, 473–4, for Harvey's reservations about Spenser's proposal to elongate the central syllable of *carpenter*.

34 Edmund Waller, 'Of English Verse', 5–6, in *Seventeenth-Century Poetry: An Annotated Anthology*, ed. Robert Cummings (Oxford: Blackwell, 2000), 245.

35 Munro, 5.

36 See Brown and Lethbridge, 60–3, for commentary on the Book I Proem, and Richard Danson Brown, '"I would abate the sternenesse of my stile": Diction and Poetic Subversion in *Two Cantos of Mutabilitie*', in *Celebrating Mutabilitie: Essays on Edmund Spenser's Mutabilitie Cantos*, ed. Jane Grogan (Manchester: Manchester University Press, 2010), 282–3, for interstanzaic knitting in the Mutabilitie Cantos.

37 I borrow the term 'grid' from Anne Carson, *Red Doc>* (London: Jonathan Cape, 2013), 77; see below.

38 Catherine Addison, 'Rhyming Against the Grain: A New Look at the Spenserian Stanza', in *Edmund Spenser: New and Renewed Directions*, ed. J.B. Lethbridge (Madison: Fairleigh Dickinson University Press, 2006), 337–51.

He would also have learned much about this from the Chaucerian tradition.[39] His use of the device is more extreme, partly because the grid of the Spenserian stanza is more restrictive than that of rhyme royal: because the Spenserian is intrinsically more repetitive, repetitions between stanzas are felt more vividly, more intrusively, than they are in a poem like *Troilus and Criseyde*.[40]

There is a related factor in play here. Wilson-Okamura contrasts the 'hermetic box [...] syntax' of *The Faerie Queene* with the 'leaking' stanza form preferred by Tasso and others, in which syntax flows from one stanza to the next. Arguing that Spenser exhibits English distaste 'for stanzas that will not stay shut', he finds only four such stanzas in *The Faerie Queene*. Though he recognises that Chaucer and 'his disciples in the Renaissance' are an exception, he proposes that sixteenth-century English practice is uptight, with the suggestion of an almost anally retentive resistance to 'leak and spill'.[41] Though the observation usefully signals the restrictions on *The Faerie Queene*'s syntax, the generalisations are precarious, particularly in relation to the Chaucerian tradition. Read in Thynne's edition, with its minimal punctuation (carried forward in later sixteenth-century editions), almost any stanza of the *Troilus and Criseyde* could be seen to 'leak' into the next (see Figure 6.2).

Chaucer's syntax is usually constrained within stanzas, but this is by no means an invariable rule. In the extract from *Troilus and Criseyde* Book IV reprinted from Thynne overleaf, the sixteenth-century text leaves everything unpointed, except caesural virgules, which are vestigial pointers to lineal shape rather than syntax. Thynne avoids full points at the end of stanzas, with the result that a reader could infer that there is a continuation of related ideas in the first two stanzas: 'And thynketh wel/ that somtym it is wyt' readily follows on from 'Sens to be true/ I haue you plight my trouth'. Similarly, the syntactic gap between the second and third stanzas is less definitive than the full pointing given to it in *The Riverside Chaucer*, which reads ' "Or here my trouthe: I wol naught lyve tyl morwe. // "For if ye wiste how soore it doth me smerte' (559).

In apocryphal poems like *The Floure and the Leaf* and *The Court of Love*, leakage is extremely common to the extent that the relationship between stanza form and syntax can become uncertain as sentences – to vary the liquid imagery – meander from stanza to stanza.[42] The opening ten stanzas of *The Floure and the*

---

39 *The Floure and the Leafe* has six rhyming clusters which include *wight* in its 595 lines; see 13–14 (*wight: light*); 16–19 (*night: might: wight*); 36–8 (*sight: wight*); 69–70 (*wight: might*); 310–13 (*bright: might: wight*) and 433–4 (*wight: sight*). Though most of these are formulaic variations on patterns such as 'any wight' and 'earthly wight', they demonstrate that such repetitions were an intrinsic part of the Chaucerian tradition. See *The Floure and the Leafe, The Assembly of Ladies, The Isle of Ladies*, ed. Derek Pearsall (Kalamazoo: TEAMS, 1990), 4–19. The poem only appears in the 1598 and 1602 Speght folios, and was read there by Gabriel Harvey; see Forni, 128.
40 Carruth's comments quoted above usefully articulate the readerly frustration inherent in a form which requires four-fold repetitions.
41 Wilson-Okamura, 29–31. See also Brown and Lethbridge, 106–7, for Lethbridge's suggestion that the punctuation in the early editions is unreliable as a guide to Spenser's own punctuation: 'that the majority of Spenser's stanzas end with a full stop does not entail that the majority of the stanzas end with the end of the sentence' (107).
42 For *The Court of Love*, see Forni, 7–45. The poem was first added to Chaucer's *Works* by Stow in 1561.

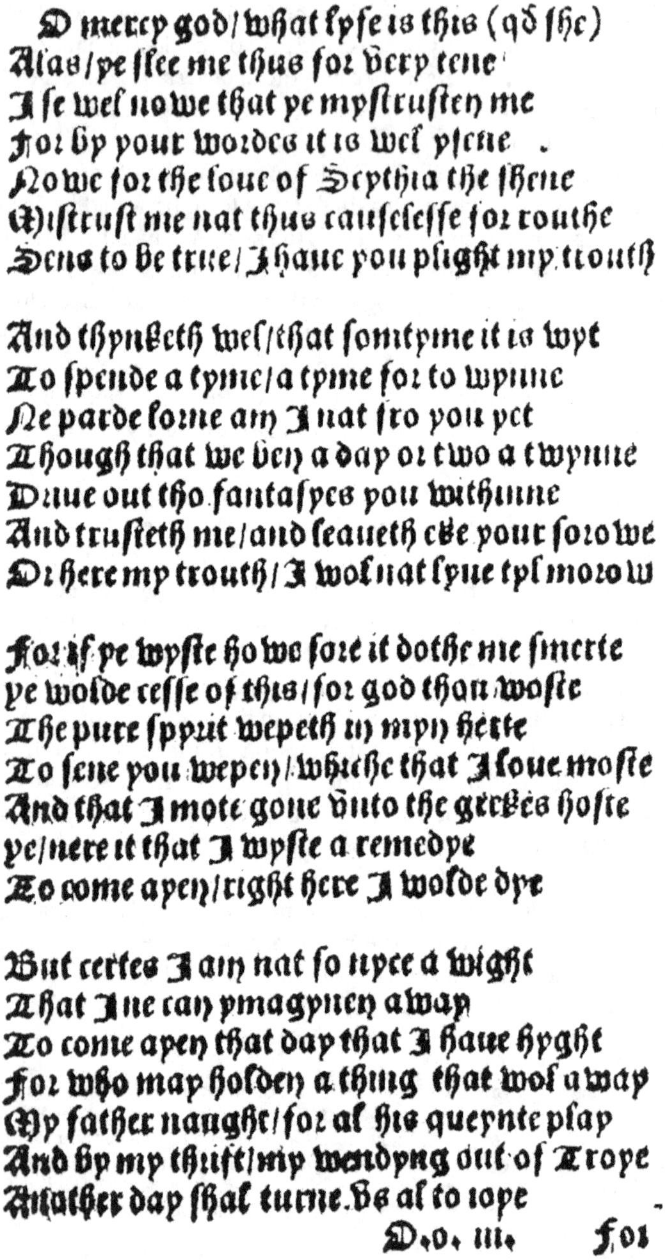

O mercy god/ what syse is this (qd she)
Alas/ye slee me thus for very tene
I se wel nowe that ye mystrusten me
For by your wordes it is wel ysene
Nowe for the loue of Cythia the shene
Mistrust me nat thus causelesse for routhe
Sens to be true/ I haue you plight my trouth

And thynketh wel/ that somtyme it is wyt
To spende a tyme/ a tyme for to wynne
Ne parde forne am I nat fro you yet
Though that we ben a day or two a twynne
Driue out tho fantasyes you withinne
And trusteth me/ and seaueth eke your sorowe
Or here my trouth/ I wol nat lyue tyl morow

For if ye wyste howe sore it dothe me smerte
Ye wolde cesse of this/ for god thou woste
The pure spyrit wepeth in myn herte
To sene you wepen/ whiche that I loue moste
And that I mote gone vnto the grekes hoste
Ye/ nere it that I wyste a remedye
To come ayen/ right here I wolde dye

But certes I am nat so nyce a wight
That I ne can ymagynen away
To come ayen that day that I haue hyght
For who may holden a thing that wol away
My father naught/ for al his queynte play
And by my thrift/ my wendyng out of Troye
Another day shal turne.Vs al to ioye
                        O. O. iiii.   fo₁

Figure 6.2 Troilus and Criseyde IV.1604–31 in Thynne's edition, showing minimal punctuation between stanzas

Leaf show little pressure to match stanza with sentence form; even those stanzas where there is a conjunction of the two in Pearsall's modern edition might just as easily be read as continuations of related ideas, as in the minimally punctuated Speght edition. Pearsall has a full stop at the end of the third stanza, yet the connective which begins the fourth stanza indicates the relative lightness of the pause: 'for I nad sicknesse nor disease. // Wherefore I mervaile greatly of my selfe'.[43] The printing of medieval stanzaic verse in the sixteenth century is more syntactically permissive than in modern editions, or indeed later verse texts like *The Faerie Queene*, where grammatical pointing tends to be more regularised.[44] Spenser was well read in these texts, so he was aware of the light connections between stanzas which such conventions afforded. This raises the connected problems of why *The Faerie Queene*'s *mise-en-page* tends to be different from that of the sixteenth-century Chaucer folios, and how to read Spenser's particular approach to interstanzaic linkages. My suggestion is that one of the main ways in which Spenser revises his Chaucerian inheritance is by making his forms more restrictive, more demanding: poetic excellence is a consequence of the intense technical demands of the stanza form. The look of the Chaucer Folios, and their suggestion of syntactic permissiveness, is therefore something which Spenser and his compositors wanted to resist and to correct in the printing of *The Faerie Queene*.[45] So although *The Faerie Queene* is more syntactically disciplined and regularised than the Thynne text of *Troilus and Criseyde*, it is not bound-in because of any connection between stanzaic form and 'national character'; Spenser in my view is not formally disciplined and repetitive because of his nationality – or indeed because of his psychology – but because of his interest in the poetic effects such devices might yield.[46]

The fight between Cambell and the Brothers 'Mond in Book IV canto iii exhibits a large number of interstanzaic rhymes in a Chaucerian narrative context. It features a (literally and metaphorically) striking coincidence between verbal patterning and the events narrated: as the fight seems unfinishable, so the verbal tricks Spenser uses imply stasis and a disquieting inability for the narrative to make progress. He goes out of his way to use samey devices: there are numerous

---

43 See Pearsall (ed.), *The Floure and the Leafe*, 4, ll.21–2. Pearsall comments 'The rhyme royal stanza is treated in a remarkably free and un-Chaucerian manner, with little attempt to match sense to stanza-unit or to natural divisions within the stanza', 3. See also Chaucer, *The Works*, sig. Ttt1ᵛ, where there is no punctuation. The poet's fondness for beginning stanzas with 'And [...]' further demonstrates the relative lightness of the stanzaic structure.
44 Although compare with Figure 6.1, where the punctuation of II.proem.ii is light in the Huntington Library copy, with only the comma (l.1) and question mark (l.5) as definitive line-end markers. The British Library and Folger copies (also on EEBO) show the same punctuation. The 1609 Folio, however, shows a much more 'modern' approach, with more interventionist marking at all line ends except the fourth and seventh lines; see Spenser, *The Faerie Queene* (London: Matthew Lownes, 1609), 59.
45 For the printing of *The Faerie Queene*, see Hiroshi Yamashita et al., *A Textual Companion to The Faerie Queene, 1590* (Tokyo: Kenyusha, 1993), Toshiyuki Suzuki, 'A Note on the Errata to the 1590 Quarto of *The Faerie Queene*', *Studies in the Literary Imagination*, 38.2 (2005), 1–16, and Andrew Zurcher, 'The Printing of the Cantos of Mutabilitie in 1609', in Grogan (ed.), 40–60.
46 Wilson-Okamura, 29.

anaphoras,[47] epic similes, which cumulatively become tropes of repetition by virtue of their frequency.[48] I begin with a description of three instances of interstanzaic linkage to map their place in this episode.[49]

(1) Simple linkage of disparate stanzas. Stanzas 6 and 11 share related, unusual B-rhymes: *abet* and *affret* are only used once or twice elsewhere.[50] The rhetorical variety of Spenser's practice is shown through the semantic variation: 'All arm'd to point his chalenge to abet' uses the rhyme word verbally; 'The meede of thy mischalenge and abet' is the unrelated noun meaning fraud. The clear similarity of wording means that stanza 11 recoils back to the formulation of stanza 6; this is the kind of effect close interstanzaic linkage generates.

(2) Direct linkage of neighbouring stanzas. Stanzas 10 and 11 show one of Spenser's favourite devices, where a C- rhyme produces the next A- rhyme, creating a five-rhyme form: *brake: shake: bespake* segues into *take: sake.*[51] The effect is to create a sequence of five rhymes binding two stanzas together sonally and semantically.

(3) More complex linkage of disparate stanzas. Stanza 23 uses an unusual two rhyme form, where the A- and C- rhymes are identical.[52] The B- rhyme of this stanza anticipates the C- rhyme of stanza 31, while the B- rhyme of 31 anticipates the C- rhyme of 33. In the space of ten stanzas, there is a remarkable coincidence of similar rhymes and identical forms, some of which are only used in this canto.

What are we to make of this? Firstly, the proximity of these interlaced rhymes underlines the endlessness of the fight between Cambell and his unkillable opponents. The *-ake* rhymes which link stanzas 10 and 11 accentuate the recurring gestures which constitute the fight; the alexandrine of stanza 11 captures the tension between renewal and weary repetition which lies at the heart of this episode as Priamond redoubles his efforts: 'And charging him *a fresh* thus felly him *bespake*'.[53] Five stanzas later, another *-ake* cluster verbalises a sense of poetic

---

47 See stanzas 11 ('thy meede […] The meede'); 12–13 ('wearie ghost'); 18 ('Where it *was ment*, so deadly it *was ment*'); 21 ('the lifelesse corse it left. // It left […]). Puttenham's description of anaphora as 'the Figure of Report' which 'lead[s] the dance to many verses in suit' (282) captures the slow-motion, balletic quality of these repetitions.
48 For the similes, see IV.iii.15, 16, 19, 23, 27, 15, 29, 39, 41.
49 Almost every stanza in this episode has rhymes which are in some ways related to others, so the following discussion is illustrative of broader tendencies.
50 For *abet*, see VI.v.22b; for *affret*, see the related IV.ii.15c and III.ix.16a. These are not always identical repetitions: in IV.iii.6, *abet* is an infinitive ('his challenge to abet'), while in IV.iii.11, *abet* is the unrelated noun meaning fraud ('thy mischalenge and abet'). See 'abet, n.', *OED Online* (Oxford: Oxford University Press, March 2014). For the data, see Brown and Lethbridge, 183, 185.
51 For other examples of a C- rhyme producing the next A- rhyme, see II.i.8–9, II.i.20–1, III.v.8–9, III.v.25–6. The latter both feature anaphoristic uses of identical rhyme ('but one, that *Marinell* is hight […] A Sea-nymphs sonne, that *Marinell* is hight'; 'that Squire liues with renowne […] takes small ioy of his renowne'). The device is common, and would repay more detailed study.
52 There are other examples of stanzas in this form in *The Faerie Queene*; see V.v.19–20 (two consecutive stanzas with two rhymes only) and my commentary in Brown and Lethbridge, 69–70.
53 My emphases.

stalemate: 'cruell battell twixt themselues doe *make* [...] So cruelly these Knights stroue for that Ladies *sake*' (IV.iii.16).⁵⁴ Cruel knights indulge in a cruel battle, but the logic underlying the struggle is curiously absent; what matters rather is the sense of impasse, which is stressed by the epic simile which compares the combatants with 'two Tygers prickt with hungers rage'.⁵⁵ As scholars like Berry and Anderson have observed, Spenser's version of the *Squire's Tale* threatens to reproduce the parent tale's endlessness; this interminability, I suggest, is audibly registered in these overlapping rhymes.⁵⁶

Secondly, through similar rhymes, Spenser constructs tropes of wonderment for these at once baffling, at once repetitious, deeds of arms. Virtuosity in rhyme is purposive inasmuch as it gives the reader ways of registering the amazement the narrator keeps trying to instil. Stanzas 23 and 31 illustrate this process of horrific wonder. Though rhymes on *–ight* terminals are common, that should not dilute the reader's sense of the technical accomplishment on display.⁵⁷ Stanza 23 invites the beholder's astonishment at Cambell's fortitude, and that wonder is made intelligible through the rhymes: the 'wounded [...] *Knight*' becomes in the process of these rhymes 'freshly [...] *dight*' like the snake; the internal rhyme focuses on the reader's astonishment at this spectacle: 'Some newborne *wight* ye would him surely weene'. Similarly, the recycling of the B-rhyme of 23 in the C-rhyme of 31 gives a jarring sense of circularity. In this fight, nobody properly dies, and every weary warrior starts up perkily from apparent defeat:

> But nathelesse whilst all the lookers on
>   Him dead behight, as he to all appeard,
>   All vnawares he started vp anon,
>   As one that had out of a dreame bene reard,
>   And fresh assayld his foe, who halfe affeard
>   Of th'vncouth sight, as he some ghost had seene,
>   Stood still amaz'd, holding his idle sweard;
>   Till hauing often by him stricken beene,
> He forced was to strike, and saue him selfe from teene. (IV.iii.31)

---

54 My emphases. Similar observations could be made about the shared A- and B- rhymes in stanzas 17 and 18, where rhymes on *–ent* relentlessly highlight the circularity of the conflict: 'Full many strokes that mortally were ment' threaten to resolve into a stroke from Diamond that would stint 'all strife incontinent', but Cambell's last minute swerve means that their 'fell intent' continues.
55 The tigers simile is literalised in stanza 39, describing the lions that draw Cambina's chariot. Where the warring tigers make 'cruell battel betwixt themselues' over 'some beasts fresh spoyle', the lions are tamed by Cambina's influence: 'Now made forget their former cruell mood, / T'obey their riders hest'.
56 Judith H. Anderson, 'Cambell, Canacee, Cambina', in *The Spenser Encyclopedia*, ed. A.C. Hamilton et al. (Toronto: University of Toronto Press, 1990; repr. 1997), 130. See Berry's related worries about Chaucer and Spenser's failure to address the question of Cambell's potentially incestuous love for Canacee, 118.
57 See Brown and Lethbridge, 424–31, for a frequency list of rhymes. *The Faerie Queene*'s dependence on these rhyming terminals is shown by the raw statistics: 'right', 'despight' (both 106 instances), 'hight' (121), 'fight' (153), 'light' (162); while 'sight' (199), 'knight' (204) and 'might' (259) are the three commonest rhymes of all. See also Brown, '"I would abate the sternenesse of my stile"', 281–2, on *–ight* rhymes in the Mutabilitie Cantos.

Readers and combatants are caught in a poetic feedback loop of astonishing events. Christopher Burlinson and Andrew Zurcher have commented on 'the conspicuously funny element of much of Spenser's violence' in *The Faerie Queene* in relation to what he experienced at first hand in Ireland.[58] Such obtrusive interstanzaic rhyming emphasises disquiet and unfamiliarity as preludes to the amity which these characters ultimately, and somewhat implausibly, symbolise. Such readerly suspension of incredulity is connected with Viktor Shklovsky's concept of *enstrangement*; in Shklovsky's terms, enstrangement occurs when 'an artifact [...] has been intentionally removed from the domain of automatised perception'.[59] A less sympathetic reading might be that Spenser desperately tries to inject some excitement into yet another battle scene which doesn't fully engage his imagination, yet the evident care with which he continues and develops this Chaucerian narrative tells against such a reading.[60] The 'lookers on', including the reader, who believed Triamond to be dead, are treated to a Zombie revival which, rather than crudely stretching, artfully extends, our credulity. It is also (as Burlinson and Zurcher suggest), and unlike its great precedents in the *Iliad* and the *Aeneid*, epic violence which is continuously teetering on the fringes of comedy: the image of Triamond being struck out of astonishment into self-defence encapsulates the at once bewildered and exhausted tone which the narrator adopts throughout an episode of 'perilous tumult' (IV.iii.37).

Wonderment is a component of the *Squire's Tale*, where both characters and narrator are repeatedly astonished by extraordinary events and objects such as the mechanical horse: 'euermore her moste wonder was / Howe that it couthe gon/ and was of bras' (sig. G6ʳ; 199–200). The narrator's topoi of rhetorical incapacity are part of what makes the fragment so enigmatic: is the narrator to be believed, or is Chaucer playing an elaborate game with the limits of what is credible?[61] Certainly, Spenser's continuation is radically unlike the parent tale in terms of mode of narration, despite the connections in terms of plot and some details of imagery.[62] Spenser is less interested than Chaucer in destabilising his narrator, and the artful linkages of overlapping rhymes can imply that he took the tropes of wonderment in Chaucer seriously and developed them without the patina of irony which is so characteristic of *The Canterbury Tales*. Once again, Spenser rewrites Chaucer in such a way as to correct aspects of his style and idiom which may have seemed unachieved or poetically incomplete.

---

58 Edmund Spenser, *Selected Letters and Other Papers*, ed. Christopher Burlinson and Andrew Zurcher (Oxford: Oxford University Press, 2009), lx.

59 Viktor Shklovsky, *Theory of Prose*, trans. Benjamin Sher (Champaign: Dalkey Archive Press, 1990), 12.

60 Compare Wilson-Okamura's exploration of *The Faerie Queene*'s failure to deliver on its promises of epic warfare, 184–93. As well as its debts to the *Squire's Tale*, there is a sense in which the fight between Cambell and the 'Monds gestures towards the endless battle scenes of *The Iliad*; for a recent discussion, see Adam Nicholson, *The Mighty Dead: Why Homer Matters* (London: Collins, 2015), particularly 198–207.

61 See 31–41, 67–75, 105–9, 245–6 and 341–2 in *The Riverside Chaucer*, 169–73. On the ambiguity of the narrator, see Berry, 110–23, and *The Riverside Chaucer*, 890–1, for an overview.

62 The big cat imagery of stanzas 16 and 39 has clear precedents in the *Squire's Tale*, 419–22 and 543–4, in *The Riverside Chaucer*, 174–5.

Stanzas 31 and 33 of Spenser's version demonstrate that Chaucer's diction is never far from the surface. Spenser's tropes of renewal point back to his miraculous recovery of Chaucer's lost tale 'through infusion sweete / Of thine owne spirit' (IV.ii.34), and the Chaucerian idiom is prominent in these interlaced rhymes. Cambell's *sweard* in stanzas 31 and 33 is a strikingly Chaucerian property, reminiscent of the knight's 'naked swerde' (sig. G5ᵛ; 84) in the *Squire's Tale*. These are the only rhymes on *sweard* – indeed, these are the only instances of the word in the poem. Spenser's usual term is the modern English *sword*.[63] Chaucer always uses *swerd*, so the signifier is an archiastic hallmark, similar to the parody of the opening line of the *Knight's Tale* at the start of the episode, 'Whylome as antique stories tellen us' (IV.ii.32).[64] 'Reaching forth his sweard' like Cambell, Spenser marks his verse with an indelibly Chaucerian patina which wittily reinforces the gestures of recovery with which the episode began (IV.iii.33).

Full of little snags: rebuilding rhyme royal

Spenser's rhyming strategies are thus profoundly Chaucerian.[65] This does not mean that there is any slavish following of Chaucer – as recent scholarship on Spenserian archaism suggests, his diction is very different from Thomas Wilson's satire of affected courtiers talking 'nothyng but Chaucer'.[66] It is more the case that Chaucer's influence can be felt in Spenser's adoption of devices like *rime riche* and interstanzaic knitting. Specific aspects of Chaucerian diction are recollected in rhyming positions, as if in the process of remembering Chaucer, Spenser flagrantly smuggles specific pieces of medieval lexis into the fabric of his verse. Rebeca Helfer's summary of the complex relationship between Chaucer and Spenser in *The Shepheardes Calender* is germane: 'as Cicero's *On the Orator* is dedicated to the memory of its interlocutors, so Spenser dedicates his work to Chaucer's memory'.[67] There is no more striking way of keeping this memory alive than with the 'sweard' that Cambell sneaks 'Close vnderneath' Triamond's shield (IV.iii.33).

Yet this leaves a broader question unanswered: to what extent is the Spenserian stanza endebted to Chaucer? Is it possible to read the invention of the Spenserian as being part of the process of keeping Chaucer's memory alive described by Helfer?[68] Such questions overlap with Wilson-Okamura's luminous discussion of why Spenser used stanzas for his epic. Wilson-Okamura offers two main conclusions: firstly, that 'we must not imagine [...] that Spenser was a mere puppet of Continental fashion'.

---

63 Brown and Lethbridge, 417, 427, 450. *Sword* is used as a rhyme eleven times.
64 For Chaucer's *swerd*, see Norman Davis, Douglas Gray, Patricia Ingham and Anne Wallace-Hadrill (eds), *A Chaucer Glossary* (Oxford: Clarendon, 1979), 148. See Berry, 116, for the suggestion that Spenser's replacement of 'antique' for Chaucer's 'olde' filters the Chaucerian text to a sixteenth-century readership.
65 'All full of litle snags' describes Impotence's staff at II.xi.23.
66 Thomas Wilson, *The Arte of Rhetorique* (London: Richard Grafton, 1553), sig. Y2ᵛ.
67 Rebeca Helfer, *Spenser's Ruins and the Art of Recollection* (Toronto: University of Toronto Press, 2012), 126.
68 For earlier discussion of the relationship between these forms, see Theodore Maynard, *The Connection Between the Ballade, Chaucer's Modification of It, Rime Royal, and the Spenserian*

The Spenserian is more than an expanded version of *ottava rima*, and is as much a product of English traditions as European ones.[69] Secondly, citing Erasmus's dictum that 'Beautiful things are difficult', Wilson-Okamura offers a salutary reminder of the cultural value across Renaissance Europe of artistic difficulty.[70] A demanding verse form enables the poet to showcase his or her virtuosic ability; the Spenserian stanza is a bravura exhibition of cultural capital through the successful subordination of language to formal constraint.[71]

There is no doubt that the Spenserian is a difficult form, and was almost always experienced as such. Yet difficulty, then as now, can be alienating as much as compelling. Alongside the celebrated early deniers of the Spenserian such as Jonson and Davenant,[72] Steven May has drawn attention to the Norfolk farmer Henry Gurney, who browsed a first edition of *The Faerie Queene* in the 1590s. Gurney voices a robust and bemused cultural resistance to artistic novelty. As May notes, though Gurney knew that *The Faerie Queene* had been 'highly acclaimed', his comments concentrate on the technical shortcomings he found in the poem:

> ould outworne wordes, this aucthor does observe
> And vsuall staff, or measure, doth reiect
> if praise or blame, therfor he do deserve
> I cannot Iudge, although I may suspect
>   that when a woorke is strang & new devised
>   the aucthor is Invyed, or dispised.[73]

Though modern scholarship queries the extent of *The Faerie Queene*'s reliance on 'ould outworne wordes', Gurney provides first-hand testimony to the groupthink which surrounded the poem.[74] Spenser was archaic partly because, as Helfer shrewdly diagnoses, E.K. had told everyone that the New Poet used 'olde and obsolete wordes'; this truism was clearly operative in Gurney's reading of *The*

Stanza (Washington, DC: Catholic University of America, 1934; repr. Folcroft: Folcroft Library Editions, 1973).
69 Wilson-Okamura, 28–32 (28).
70 Ibid., 36.
71 This remark places my discussion in relation to Stephen Greenblatt's claim that for Spenser 'the final colonialism [is] the colonialism of language'. Though Greenblatt's discussion reaches beyond formalism, his conclusion is partly arrived at through working with Paul Alpers's 'Narration in *The Faerie Queene*', *ELH*, 44.1 (spring, 1977), 19–39; *Renaissance Self-Fashioning: From More to Shakespeare* (Chicago: Chicago University Press, 1980), 192, 289.
72 See R.M. Cummings (ed.), *Spenser: The Critical Heritage* (London: Routledge and Kegan Paul, 1971), 135, 187–8, for Jonson and Davenant.
73 Steven W. May, 'Henry Gurney, A Norfolk Farmer, Reads Spenser and Others', *Spenser Studies*, 20 (2005), 183–223 (191).
74 This aspect is well caught in Everard Guilpin's remarks about Spenser's 'grandam words' in Satire VI of *Skialetheia* (1598). These lines are usually decontextualised to suggest that Guilpin disliked Spenser's diction, but the poem as a whole is a Stoic attack on the diversity of opinion; the remarks on Spenser are evidence of what the poem earlier calls 'The fickle censure of shallow neglect'. See *Skialetheia: or A Shadowe of Truth, in Certaine Epigrams and Satyres*, ed. D. Allen Carroll (Chapel Hill: University of North Carolina Press, 1974), 89–90; see also Cummings (ed.), 288, for an excerpted citation.

Faerie Queene.⁷⁵ The most intriguing aspect of Gurney's reaction, however, is his rejection of the Spenserian. The form of his 'Censure' is significant: it is written in the *Ababcc* sixain, a form which Spenser had used in *The Shepheardes Calender* and elsewhere, and which was one of the most popular stanza forms of the period.⁷⁶ Gurney's 'vsuall staff' may echo Puttenham's description of the sixain as 'not only the most usual [stanza], but also very pleasant to the ear'.⁷⁷ A conventional sixain rebukes the 'strang' form of the Spenserian with the imputation that it is a flawed novelty – the kind of formal gewgaw mocked in 'The Teares of the Muses' as 'fond newfanglenesse'.⁷⁸ Though this might be thought of as a provincial reaction to high culture (Gurney was lord of the manor in Great Ellingham, about seventeen miles from Norwich), its value lies in the way it articulates the confusion *The Faerie Queene* may have generated in its early readers: what *is* this stuff?⁷⁹ Why use this bizarre stanza form? Naive though these reactions may seem, there is a sense in which formal criticism of Spenser is still asking cognate questions.⁸⁰

Gurney would certainly not have reacted so negatively had *The Faerie Queene* been written in rhyme royal. As well as the many texts written in the form in the various editions of Chaucer's *Works*, it was used widely in compilations like *The Mirror for Magistrates* and *Tottel's Miscellany*.⁸¹ Where the Spenserian felt strange to some readers, rhyme royal would have been familiar and to an extent authorised by the practice of 'our Mayster and Father Chaucer'.⁸² At the same time, there is evidence that rhyme royal's heyday was waning during the 1590s.⁸³ As Puttenham demonstrates, rhyme royal was associated with Chaucer, and so by the early 1590s, it carries a certain aura of venerable desuetude. When he describes it as 'the chief of our ancient proportions used by any rymer writing anything of historical or grave poem, as ye may see in Chaucer and Lydgate', Puttenham's phrasing is at once

---

75 *The Yale Edition of the Shorter Poems of Edmund Spenser*, ed. William A. Oram, Einar Bjorvand, Ronald Bond, Thomas H. Cain, Alexander Dunlop and Richard Schell (New Haven: Yale, 1989), 14. See Helfer, 83.
76 See 'Januarye', 'December', 'The Teares of the Muses' (from *Complaints*), 'Astrophel' and 'The Doleful Lay of Clorinda', if the latter is indeed by Spenser. 'October' is a more exacting sixain form, rhyming *Abbaba*, perhaps chosen to emphasise the eclogue's concern with issues of poetics.
77 Puttenham, 155. 'Staff' is the habitual term used for stanza by Puttenham, Gascoigne and Webbe; see Whigham and Rebhorn's notes in Puttenham, 154, 447.
78 Spenser, *Shorter Poems*, 281; 'The Teares of the Muses', 327.
79 May, 183–4.
80 See David Scott Wilson-Okamura, 'The Formalist Tradition', in Richard McCabe (ed.), *The Oxford Handbook of Edmund Spenser* (Oxford: Oxford University Press, 2010) for the durability of formalist approaches and questions, 718–32.
81 See May, 194, for Gurney's praise of *The Mirror*. For Tottel, see *Tottel's Miscellany: Songs and Sonnets of Henry Howard, Earl of Surrey, Sir Thomas Wyatt and Others*, ed. Amanda Holton and Tom MacFaul (London: Penguin, 2011). This edition's 'Index of Verse Forms', 538–9, shows rhyme royal is used for eleven poems, while the sixain for thirty poems.
82 George Gascoigne, *Certayne Notes of Instruction*, in *Elizabethan Critical Essays*, ed. G. Gregory Smith (Clarendon: Oxford, 1904), two vols, I, 56.
83 Frank Whigham and Wayne A. Rebhorn adduce Drayton's revision of the rhyme royal *Mortimeriados* (1596) into the *ottava rima* of *The Barons' Wars* (1603) as 'marking the end of rhyme royal's dominance as the great heroic measure'. In Puttenham, 405.

respectful to the past and yet conscious of changes in fashion.[84] By implication, it is *only* the 'historical' Chaucer and Lydgate who still use this form. For sixteenth-century critics, Chaucer is always great, but he is also always old.

It is conceivable that the slow falling out of fashion of rhyme royal was associated with Reformation attitudes towards the medieval past. Steven Mullaney's retelling of the Protestant desecration of bones from St Paul's ossuary in 1549 describes an attempt to uproot the ancestral past: 'It was an effort to dislocate the dead from human feeling as well as local habitation; to root them out from the hearts and minds of the survivors.'[85] Though poetic forms are different from the bones of the dead, the comparison is not too far-fetched. As the medieval dead had become unacceptable to the Duke of Somerset's radical Protestant regime, so the 'grave' rhyme royal becomes less usable, less acceptable by the 1590s. Mullaney describes the opposite process to the one proposed by Helfer: instead of re-edifying the past in poetry, the Reformers worked to eradicate cultural memory through the spoliation of the bones of the dead. Poets did not stop writing poems in rhyme royal during the 1590s – Drayton's *Legends* and Shakespeare's *Lucrece* are the obvious exceptions – but the form becomes less often used at this time, in the same way that traditional religious practices went underground or died out during the Elizabethan period.[86] It is perhaps appropriate that Spenser's most antiquarian poem, 'The Ruines of Time', a text vested in and obsessed with the passage of time, should be written in rhyme royal.[87] The critical question for Spenser as he embarked on *The Faerie Queene* was conceivably less 'why stanzas for an epic?', but rather 'what sort of stanzas for an epic?'[88] Since *ottava rima* was associated with Ariosto and Tasso – poets Spenser consciously wished to emulate and surpass – while rhyme royal was 'Wasted [...] as if it never were',[89] Spenser's

---

84   Ibid., 155; see also 177. Puttenham echoes Gascoigne and James VI; see Smith (ed.), I, 54, 222. Puttenham also mirrors Sidney's backhanded compliment, where the excellence of *Troilus and Criseyde* is balanced with the assertion that Chaucer had 'great wants, fit to be forgiven in so reverent an antiquity', in *Miscellaneous Prose of Sir Philip Sidney*, ed. Katherine Duncan-Jones and Jan van Dorsten (Oxford: Clarendon, 1973), 112.
85   Steven Mullaney, *The Reformation of Emotions in the Age of Shakespeare* (Chicago: University of Chicago Press, 2015), 3.
86   Drayton's *Legends*, modelled on and sometimes included in the *Mirror*, were first published between 1594 and 1607; *Lucrece* was first published in 1594. Except for the poem on Piers Gaveston (which is in sixains), the other three *Legends* are all in rhyme royal. See Anne Lake Prescott, 'Drayton, Michael (1563–1631)', *Oxford Dictionary of National Biography* (Oxford: Oxford University Press, 2004; online edn, May 2015). For changes in ritual practice in the period, see Eamon Duffy, *The Stripping of the Altars: Traditional Religion in England 1400–1580* (New Haven: Yale University Press, 1992; repr. 2005).
87   See Helfer, 136–67, for 'The Ruines of Time' as a poem in dialogue with the processes of 'inevitable decay' (167). See Richard Danson Brown, *The New Poet: Novelty and Tradition in Spenser's Complaints* (Liverpool: Liverpool University Press, 1999), 99–132, for my earlier work on 'The Ruines of Time' as a transitional bridge between tradition and novelty. Spenser does not finish his experiments with rhyme royal with this poem: it is used in 'Fowre Hymnes' (1596), though he claims that the first two hymns were juvenilia, while *Daphnaïda* (1591) modifies the seven-line stanza into a new form (rhyming Ababcbc). See Spenser, *Shorter Poems*, 690.
88   Wilson-Okamura, 18.
89   'The Ruines of Time', 120, in *Shorter Poems*.

felt need was for a new stanzaic form, rooted in the past yet 'strang' enough to be remarkable.[90]

This is why it makes sense to think of the Spenserian as a rebuilding of rhyme royal. In the same way that 'The Ruines of Time' provides a 'memory theatre' for the vanished civic past of Roman Britain and laments the heroic dead of the Dudley clan, so the Spenserian takes elements from rhyme royal and recomposes them into a new, extended form.[91] At this point, I compare three different examples of these stanza forms in action. My purpose is not to suggest any direct relationship between them, though all three are in different ways concerned with Cupid. It is rather to illuminate the different structural relationships inherent in rhyme royal, *ottava rima* and the Spenserian. Such examples must carry a health warning: these are only specific realisations of the forms; they are not guides to every instance of those forms, which are always more flexible and contingent than isolated description may allow for.[92] In this context, Gascoigne and Puttenham's characterisation of rhyme royal as a grave, dated form needs qualification. Its essential spirit is better captured by Martin Stevens and T.V.F. Brogan: in Chaucer, it is 'a remarkably flexible form, used as widely and imaginatively as the couplet, in every sort of poetic context'.[93] Spenser wanted something of this flexibility for his new stanza form, while at the same adding complexity since – following Erasmus – 'beautiful things are difficult'. Although literary forms are contingent and their use is affected by changing tastes and fashions, those which are deployed in multiple contexts by different writers have to be flexible to survive.

The first example is the narrator's response to Troilus falling in love:

> For thy ensample taketh of this man
> Ye wyse/ proude/ and worthy folkes all
> To skornen loue/ which that so sone can
> The fredom of your hertes to him thrall
> For euer it was/ and euer it be shall
> That loue is he that althyng may bynde
> For no man may fordo the lawe of kynde (Hh3r; I.232–8)

Chaucer's stanza falls into two unequal portions: an *Abab* quatrain, and a *Bcc* tercet, amplifying the first four lines. The syntax aligns the fourth line with the first quatrain rather than the second; this is a common arrangement of rhyme

---

90 There are some twenty-eight poems in *ottava rima* in *Tottel's Miscellany*, all but two of which take the form of single-stanza *strambotti*; see Holton and MacFaul (eds), 399. 'Virgil's Gnat' and 'Muiopotmos' (both in *Complaints*), show Spenser's experiments with *ottava rima*, and the former is almost certainly early; see Brown, 39–62, and particularly 56–61.
91 Helfer, 137.
92 For similar anxieties about the deployment of closely read examples as generalisations which may stand for or displace the reading of longer poems, see Wilson-Okamura, 5, and Gordon Teskey, 'Thinking Moments in *The Faerie Queene*', *Spenser Studies*, 22 (2007), 103–24 (111).
93 Martin Stevens and T.V.F. Brogan, 'Rhyme Royal', in *The New Princeton Encyclopedia of Poetry and Poetics*, ed. Alex Preminger and T.V.F. Brogan (Princeton: Princeton University Press, 1993), 1066.

royal, but there are of course other available patterns.⁹⁴ The stanza is a compact exploration of the moral issues entailed by the narrative, moving from apostrophe ('Ye wyse') to a reminder of commonly accepted truths ('For euer it was'), and resolving on the reassertion of 'the lawe of kynde'. The architecture of rhyme royal is based on a contrast between the interlaced *Abab* quatrain – which may as in this example be felt as a coherent syntactic unit in itself – and the two couplet rhymes (*Bbcc*) which follow. As the fifth line is critical to the Spenserian, so the fourth is the hinge in rhyme royal as a unit which may be joined either to the first three or the last three lines.

Ottava rima enables different syntactic permutations. Wyatt's epigram 'Of his love that pricked her finger with a nedle' showcases one such realisation:

> She sat, and sowed: that hath done me the wrong:
> Whereof I plain, and have done many a day:
> And, whilst she heard my plaint, in piteous song:
> She wisht my hart the samplar, that it lay.
> The blinde master, whom I have served so long:
> Grudging to heare, that he did heare her say:
> Made her own weapon do her finger blede:
> To fele, if pricking were so good in dede.⁹⁵

Instead of the contrast between two unequal halves in rhyme royal, this stanza – despite the obtrusive punctuation – organises its syntax into groups of two.⁹⁶ Lines 1–2 outline the basic situation, lines 3–4 complicate this image, lines 5–6 introduce a further complication which clinches the obvious erotic joke of the final couplet, as the mistress is pricked by her own needle. Wyatt's syntax tends to conform to these groups of two, with an enjambment (again minimised by the punctuation) between lines 6 and 7. This structure is similar to the patterns used by Spenser in the climax of 'Muiopotmos' (377–440). Each of these eight stanzas broadly replicates, in a more fluid narrative context, the syntax described here. Though there are enjambments elsewhere, the tendency is for the sixth line to flow into the seventh.⁹⁷

In contrast, the Spenserian stanza is different again. Its syntactic structure is closer to rhyme royal both in its double couplet structure, and in the tension which it sets up between its two unequal halves. The decision to construct a stanza with an odd number of lines was crucial because it moves the Spenserian away

---

94 This is shown by *Riverside*'s punctuation, which has a semi-colon after the fourth line; 476. For a stanza where the fourth line is connected with the second half of the stanza, see I.218–24.
95 Holton and MacFaul (eds), 77.
96 Holton's and MacFaul's edition is more strongly pointed than the 1557 edition, which has no punctuation at the ends of lines 1 and 3. The contrast with the minimalist punctuation of the Chaucer folios is striking. See *Songes and sonettes, written by the right honorable Lorde Henry Haward late Earle of Surrey, and other* (London: Richard Tottel, 1557), sig. G4ʳ⁻ᵛ.
97 See 'Muiopotmos' 398, 406, 422, 430 and 438, in Spenser, *Shorter Poems*, 428–30. See also *Godfrey of Bulloigne: A critical edition of Edward Fairfax's Translation of Tasso's 'Gerusaleme Liberata' together with Fairfax's Original Poems*, ed. Kathleen M. Lea and T.M. Gang (Oxford: Clarendon, 1981), 62–4, for the Augustan regularity of Fairfax's *ottava rima*.

from the clearer allocations of syntax to line typical of both *ottava rima* and the *Venus and Adonis* sixain.[98] The odd number of lines reveals the root of the new structure in the paradigmatic shape of the rhyme royal stanza. William Empson's classic evocation of the Spenserian focuses on the fifth line as the stanza's key unit: 'stanzas may [...] be classified by the grammatical connections of the crucial fifth line, which must give a soft bump to the dying fall of the first quatrain, keep it in the air, and prevent it from falling apart from the rest of the stanza'.[99] Consider the description of Cupid in the House of Busirane:

> Blyndfold he was, and in his cruell fist
>   A mortall bow and arrowes keene did hold,
>   With which he shot at randon, when him list,
>   Some headed with sad lead, some with pure gold;
>   (Ah man beware, how thou those dartes behold)
>   A wounded Dragon vnder him did ly,
>   Whose hideous tayle his left foot did enfold,
>   And with a shaft was shot through either eye,
> That no man forth might draw, ne no man remedye. (III.xi.48)

The parenthetical line responds well to Empson's description of one realisation of the fifth line: 'it may add to the quatrain as by an afterthought, as if with a childish earnestness it made sure of its point'.[100] With more gravity than childishness, the parenthesis is a moralising apostrophe congruent with Chaucer's exclamation 'ensample taketh of this man / Ye wyse/ proude/ and worthy folkes all'. The structural debt to rhyme royal is evident: the fifth line demarcates the first quatrain (describing Cupid) from the second (describing the dragon). Such stanzas are balanced between related objects of description or narration, in which the odd number of lines allows for the compartmentalisation of the stanza into two different yet related halves. As in rhyme royal, this syntactic scheme is designedly at odds with a rhyme scheme which emphasises the reciprocities between the two parts of the stanza. The B-rhyme, with its attractive mixture of *rime riche* (*hold: behold*) and its concrete imagery of the Cupid idol and the dragon, threads through the stanza, linking what the reader beholds with the ongoing anxiety about how we – and Britomart – interpret what we see.[101] Empson's observation that the fifth line must avoid 'falling apart from the rest of the stanza' points to

---

98 For the syntax of the sixain, see the opening section of 'The Teares of the Muses' (1–54). This resembles *ottava rima*: syntax moves in groups of two or four lines; where there is enjambment, it is usually between the end of the fourth line (closing the *Abab* quatrain) and the fifth (introducing the couplet). Though 'The Teares of the Muses' is a processional, ritualistic poem, the same pattern is evident in Drayton's *The Legend of Pierce Gaveston*; Michael Drayton, *Poems [1619]* (Menston: Scolar, 1969), 353–69.
99 William Empson, *Seven Types of Ambiguity* (1930; rpt. London: Hogarth, 1984), 33.
100 Empson, 33.
101 See Brown and Lethbridge, 200, 232, 249, 259 for these rhymes. Their usefulness is shown by the widespread use of *gold*, *behold*, and *hold*, with respectively 32, 43, and 48 instances in the poem (431).

the skilful joining of cognate ideas which is common to both rhyme royal and the Spenserian.

The Spenserian resembles rhyme royal in having two rhyming couplets, yet this effect is subtly different in each form. Where rhyme royal resolves into the double couplet close of the second part of the stanza, the extra extension of the Spenserian means that the couplets are distanced from one another by the intervention of the first line of the C-rhyme and the recursion to the last line of the B-rhyme; the artistic problem is, as Empson indicates, ensuring that lines 7–9 do not become detached from lines 1–5. Spenser usually achieves this through semantic concentration and isolation; stanzas are concerned with coherent objects or sections of narrative. This stanza is a blazon of Cupid in which the dragon is a key part of the 'fowle Idolatree' embodied by Cupid and his worshippers (III. xi.49). Similarly, in IV.iii.31 (quoted above), the narrative focuses on closely related actions: Triamond seems dead, then amazingly recovers, then renews battle against an equally amazed opponent.

The closes of Spenserian stanzas seldom feel Chaucerian. 'Till hauing often by him stricken beene, / He forced was to strike, and saue him selfe from teene' emphasises the disjointed, antithetical ballet of striking and being struck which is an intrinsic part of the Cambell-Triamond fight. 'And with a shaft was shot through either eye, / That no man forth might draw, ne no man remedye' gnomically stresses the dragon's blindness (*why* is he blind?, the reader wonders), alongside the impossibility of providing 'remedye' for this grisly predicament. Though the reader wants to read on, in part to find out what happens and what these images might mean, Spenser's stanza closes tend to be at once emphatic and vertiginous. Theresa Krier has commented,

> Spenser carries the reader into stanzaic intervals, allowing brief moments of readerly drift, relinquishment of alert cognitive agency, while also keeping active our engagement with the story insofar as we continue to desire access to the internal structures of these events. In the stanza breaks, a reader experiences suspension, that great Spenserian-romance condition, but this is an active condition of change and novelty and surprise, not a static or somnolent condition. It's a sojourn.[102]

How is the reader carried? Simply enough, through the agency of the drifting alexandrine: by introducing this innovation, Spenser plumps up the closes of his stanzas with an extra foot.[103] They are like ostentatious conservatories added to the backs of suburban homes by status-conscious owners; or rather, like the enormous, costly panes of glass Robert Smythson put on the façade of Hardwick Hall in the late 1590s.[104] This is why I incline to trust the punctuation of the early editions: Spenser wants his rebuilt stanzas to close with aplomb – to finish with a

---

102 Theresa Krier, 'Time Lords: Rhythm and Interval in Spenser's Stanzaic Narrative', *Spenser Studies*, 21 (2007), 1–19 (5).
103 See John Hollander, 'Alexandrine', in *The Spenser Encyclopedia*, ed. Hamilton et al., 15–16.
104 Mark Girouard, *Hardwick Hall* (London: The National Trust, 1976), 19.

density of sound unknown in rhyme royal.¹⁰⁵ Thus the balanced alexandrine which closes this stanza – 'That no man forth might draw, ne no man remedye' – shuts with a magestic decisiveness which mirrors the horror of the monster described. That such balanced lines sound unChaucerian does not mean that the Spenserian as a whole should be read in this way. As I have argued, the stanza is a reclamation of the syntax and rhyme scheme of rhyme royal; a grandiloquent updating of the familiar into something knowingly 'strang'. In changed poetic and political contexts, Spenser rebuilds Chaucer's stanza according to his own dimensions.

Despite the decorous obeisance of the 'June' eclogue, Spenser's relationship to 'The God of Shepheards' is characterised by critical adoption and updating; devices like *rime riche* and the stringent development of interstanzaic devices show Spenser actively reshaping Chaucer's forms.¹⁰⁶ Rereading the fight between Cambell and the Brothers 'Mond, what we encounter is, rather than stanzaic leak and spill, flow and process within an episode through rhyming repetition between discrete stanzas. The Spenserian stanza demands to be read as a form which takes its syntactic impetus more from rhyme royal than elsewhere.

The broader question remains what do we do with rhymes? What sense should we make of them? In a brilliant essay, the linguist Guy Cook discusses the 'deviant language of poetry', in which rhyme figures as a randomiser, a force which implicitly problematises the critic's Aristotelian search for meaning. Poetic language by 'its very focus on form rather than meaning may create new meanings, by bringing together units which schematic thinking would often keep apart'.¹⁰⁷ Such inventiveness is apparent on almost every page of *The Faerie Queene*. To give one final example: the C-rhyme of III.xi.48, *ly: eye: remedye* is echoed by the B-rhyme of the next stanza (*bee: knee: Idolatree: satisfie*) and repeated in the A-rhyme of stanza 50 (*eye: spye*). What, like Britomart, are we *spy*ing here? Rhymes are generative in the sense that they organise related patterns of imagery and feeling and give impetus to Spenser's narratives. The *eye: remedye* couplet anticipates Britomart's 'busie eye', and 'Her greedy eyes' a few stanzas later (III.xi.53); what we see through the rhymes is the dangerous interpretative game in which the heroine is engaged in the House of Busirane.¹⁰⁸ In Anne Carson's brilliant poem-novel *Red-Doc>* – a text which is largely written in tightly organised prose rather than verse – one of the characters reflects on the value of rhyming tags used by a therapist:

> Tell me Pig
> Doc she says why I'm
> always stealing. Because

---

105 For largeness of sound, see Wilson-Okamura, 173–6. He argues that richness of sound is an end in itself (176); my point is that what he calls 'the project of making poetry more splendid' (174) is related to ideas of status, like the Hardwick Hall windows.
106 'June', 81, in *The Shorter Poems*, 112. See Helfer, 74, on E.K.'s attempts to erase Chaucer's influence on The New Poet.
107 Guy Cook, 'Genes, Memes, Rhymes: Conscious Poetic Deviation in Linguistic, Psychological and Evolutionary Theory', *Language and Communication*, 15.4 (1995), 375–91 (381, 389).
108 See Brown and Lethbridge, 235, 300. *Eye* is a common rhyme (seventy-one instances), while this is the only rhyme on *remedye*, though there are several on different spellings (361, 375).

> it's the opposite of *feeling*
> he says. She grins. Silly
> rhymer. Rhymes don't
> cure you. Yet it pierces
> her grid so she closes the
> grid with others of her
> own bad deal get real
> cucumber peel as he goes
> on.[109]

Carson's characters reflect modern attitudes towards rhyme. Intrinsically 'silly', coincidence of sound offers no 'remedye' to psychological disorder. Yet as this passage reflects, rhyming remains an affective practice, something readers enjoy for the suggestive pleasure of recurring sound and the connections those sonal accidents may facilitate. Counter-intuitively perhaps, rhyme remains as good a way of 'getting real' – or rather of getting *to* the real through the elaborate, creative and deviant practices of poetic language – as it did for Chaucer and Spenser.

---

109 Carson, 77.

7

Romancing Geoffrey: Chaucer and romance in the manuscript tradition

Gareth Griffith

Writing about romance in the *Canterbury Tales*, J.A. Burrow comments, 'It is as if Chaucer, who seems so much at home in the fabliau, the miracle of the Virgin, and the saint's life, felt less easy with the very genre which we regard as most characteristic of his period, the knightly romance'. He goes further in a comparison with Dante: 'it may be surmised that he, like Chaucer, regarded knightly romance as a form of agreeable light reading to which no serious fourteenth-century poet should devote more than passing attention.'[1] If what Burrow says is true, how could an admirer of Chaucer, such as Spenser, choose the 'knightly romance' form for his most important work, *The Faerie Queene*?

Certainly there is a pardonable overstatement in Burrow's words. Among Chaucer's works, the *Knight's Tale* is clearly a romance, but the tales of the Man of Law, Wife of Bath, Franklin, Squire and the *Tale of Sir Thopas*, as well as *Troilus and Criseyde* and *Anelida and Arcite*, also deserve consideration as romances (as does the possibly-Chaucerian translation of *The Romance of the Rose*).[2] Among these texts, the *Knight's Tale*, the *Franklin's Tale*, the *Man of Law's Tale* and of course *Troilus and Criseyde* draw deeply on the possibilities of the courtly romance, with principal characters who are 'knightly' in some way. The *Wife of Bath's Tale* is also set in this milieu, though, as Burrow notes, the opening lines serve to indicate some of Chaucer's (or the Wife's) unease about that world.[3] This type of serious, knightly romance is what Chaucer uses for some of his richest, most reflective and involved writing, producing far more than 'agreeable light reading'. Yet the *Tale of Sir Thopas*, in its peerless metrical jokes, and to some extent the *Squire's Tale*, in its profusion of supernatural elements and unfinished narrative threads, both poke fun at a wider popular tradition which sets its tales in the same noble milieu but which employed a different style, different metres and different emphases from the courtly mode. In the corpus of Chaucer's works now known to us, this popular mode of romance is thus largely present to be mocked, if affectionately.

---

1 J.A. Burrow, '*The Canterbury Tales* I: Romance', in *The Cambridge Companion to Chaucer*, ed. Piero Boitani and Jill Mann, 2nd edn (Cambridge: Cambridge University Press, 2003), 143–59 (143 and 146).
2 For a summary of scholarship on the authorship question, see 1103–4 in Larry D. Benson *et al.*, eds, *The Riverside Chaucer* (Oxford: Oxford University Press, 1987).
3 Burrow, 144.

Nevertheless, it is these more 'popular' romances that Spenser takes as his models, providing a continuation of the *Squire's Tale* in Book IV of *The Faerie Queene* and, as Judith H. Anderson shows, returning to *Sir Thopas* throughout the poem.[4]

This chapter proposes that part of the answer to this problem can be found in the way that romances linked to Chaucer appear in manuscripts of the fifteenth century.[5] It is not concerned to prove that Spenser read Chaucer in a manuscript context (although he could have done: medieval manuscripts continued to circulate in the era of print, especially among the well-connected). Instead, it will suggest that the presentation of Chaucer in manuscripts from this period shows the older poet becoming even more closely associated with romance after his death. In the process, the 'Chaucer' presented to early modern readers by the manuscript processes of insertion and excerption took on an increased interest in violence, anti-clericalism, games of incompleteness and imitation, and women suffering from male desire. In short, in significant respects, he became more Spenserian.

Defining romance

In recent decades, scholarly work on the popular romance in Middle English has been plentiful and rich, alongside continued interest in the more 'courtly' works associated with major canonical authors.[6] This scholarship has frequently found it necessary to establish a way or ways by which the category of romance could be defined. So, for example, W.R.J. Barron explored a variety of critical approaches to the question at the outset of his survey of Middle English romance.[7] One of these approaches to definition is derived from Aristotle, and uses the nature of the hero to distinguish between myth, romance and mimesis. In this schema, the romance hero is of the same kind as the other characters (he is not a god or other supernatural character, as he would be in myth), but superior in degree (often either in social status, or virtue, or both). A romance is thus structured around the story of someone nobly born, such as a king or knight. A second approach considered by Barron looks for the presence of one or more conventional motifs: the challenge,

---

4 Judith H. Anderson, *Reading the Allegorical Intertext: Chaucer, Spenser, Shakespeare, Milton* (New York: Fordham University Press, 2008), 27–31.
5 For details of all manuscripts containing works by Chaucer see M.C. Seymour, *A Catalogue of Chaucer Manuscripts – Vol 1: Works Before the Canterbury Tales* and *A Catalogue of Chaucer Manuscripts – Vol. 2: The Canterbury Tales* (Aldershot: Scolar Press, 1995/1997). Additional information is provided by Gisela Guddat-Figge's *Catalogue of Manuscripts Containing Middle English Romances* (Munich: Fink, 1976).
6 In a wealth of diverse scholarship, see especially: Raluca Radulescu and Cory James Rushton, eds, *A Companion to Medieval Popular Romance* (Cambridge: D.S. Brewer, 2009); Ad Putter and Jane Gilbert, eds, *The Spirit of Medieval Popular Romance* (Harlow: Pearson, 2000); Derek Brewer, 'The Popular English Metrical Romances', in *A Companion to Romance: Classical to Contemporary*, ed. Corinne Saunders (Malden: Blackwell, 2004), 45–64; Susan Crane, *Insular Romance: Politics, Faith and Culture in Anglo-Norman and Middle-English Literature* (Berkeley and Los Angeles: University of California Press, 1986); Roberta Krueger, ed., *The Cambridge Companion to Medieval Romance* (Cambridge: Cambridge University Press, 2000); K.S. Whetter, *Understanding Genre and Medieval Romance* (Aldershot: Ashgate, 2008).
7 W.R.J. Barron, *English Medieval Romance* (London and New York: Longman, 1987), 2–6.

the quest, the sight of the beloved, the victory against overwhelming odds.[8] Much more recently, Raluca Radulescu has noted that 'An attractive and, in some cases, defining feature of some popular medieval romances is (the intrusion of) the outrageous and the spectacular or unexpected, which unsettles the order of chivalric adventures encountered in these texts'.[9] Still other critics have drawn attention to a frequent preoccupation with heterosexual desire, something which tends to mark romance out from more homosocial traditions such as *chansons de geste*.[10]

There are obvious benefits to defining romance purely according to narrative or thematic content, but generic definition is also subject to historical change, especially as writers seek to exploit and develop the generic conventions they inherit, and subtle shifts take place in how texts are received. Andrew King has shown in detail the ways in which romance narratives from the late Middle English period bequeathed a wealth of matter and manner for the use of sixteenth-century romancers, with Spenser chief among them.[11] Chaucer's work, although not considered in detail in King's book, is also a part of that tradition of romance on which Spenser draws. As such, he too is also subject to redefinition over time; looking at the manuscript tradition makes it possible to see this process in action, and to bridge the gap between Chaucer and 'Chaucerian romance'.

The *Tale of Gamelyn*

The most notable example of the romance element in Chaucer's work being made more prominent after his death concerns the position of the *Tale of Gamelyn*.[12] This 898-line poem was not included in any printed copy of Chaucer's poems until John Urry's edition in 1721, but it survives in twenty-five manuscripts, more than any other popular romance in English from the Middle Ages. This remarkable apparent popularity is undoubtedly owed to its early association with Chaucer: in every single one of the manuscripts in which it survives, it is included in a copy of the *Canterbury Tales*. It is usually placed at the end of what is now called Fragment I, after the *Cook's Tale* breaks off. There is sufficient evidence for us to be confident that *Gamelyn* is not by Chaucer: the best and earliest manuscripts of the *Tales* do not include it; it uses a metre Chaucer never uses elsewhere;[13] and the use of tag

---

8 Ibid., 5.
9 Raluca Radulescu, 'Genre and Classification', in Radulescu and Rushton, eds, *Companion to Medieval Popular Romance*, 31–48 (31).
10 For an intensive discussion of these issues see Louise Sylvester, *Medieval Romance and the Construction of Heterosexuality* (New York: Palgrave, 2008).
11 Andrew King, *The Faerie Queene and Middle English Romance: The Matter of Just Memory* (Oxford: Oxford University Press, 2000).
12 The edition used here is that by Stephen Knight and Thomas H. Ohlgren in *Robin Hood and Other Outlaw Tales* (Kalamazoo: Medieval Institute Publications, 1997), available online at http://d.lib.rochester.edu/teams/text/tale-of-gamelyn [accessed 19 November 2018]. The earlier edition by W.W. Skeat (*The Tale of Gamelyn* (Oxford: Clarendon Press, 1893)) is still useful for linguistic matters.
13 So, of course, does the *Tale of Sir Thopas*, but this is with an intricately satiric intent, not present in the *Tale of Gamelyn*. See J.A. Burrow, '"Sir Thopas": An Agony in Three Fits', *The Review of English Studies*, 22 (1971), 54–8.

halflines and repetition, as well as the unsophisticated grammatical construction, all mark it out as distinct from his style. Historically, scholars such as W.W. Skeat have been concerned to establish this non-Chaucerian authorship and to account for the inclusion of the text so consistently in so many copies of the *Tales*. The most commonly accepted theory is that a copy of the poem was found among Chaucer's papers at his death, and for this reason included in an early copy of the *Tales*, perhaps to fill the lacuna left by the incomplete state of the *Cook's Tale*. Some suggest further, with Skeat, that Chaucer was planning to produce his own version of Gamelyn as part of the completed *Tales*, but died before he was able to do so.[14] If this were so, it would be a further sign of the interest that romance had for Chaucer, and hints that if the *Tales* had been completed, they might have included an even more multifaceted interrogation of the mode of romance.

However, if that tantalising prospect cannot be established for certain, the presence of *Gamelyn* in so many of the manuscripts shows that it was widely read as an integral part of the *Tales*. We now feel sure that it is not a poem by Chaucer; yet, early modern readers had no such distinction to help them in the manuscripts (unless they chose to make one on stylistic grounds). Most copies of the tale do not identify it with any particular pilgrim in an opening paratext, but some do provide an identification with the Cook, and a greater number have a closing paratext which connects the poem with that same pilgrim.[15] The visual presentation of the poem is therefore continuous with the larger Chaucerian collection. Thus for readers of Chaucer who relied on manuscripts, or who used manuscripts to supplement their print-reading of the poet, the *Tale of Gamelyn* was part of what 'Chaucer' meant. We know for certain that at least one sixteenth-century writer was reading Chaucer in manuscript in this way, and may even provide a link to Spenser. As already mentioned, the *Tale of Gamelyn* was not included in any printed editions of the *Canterbury Tales* available in the sixteenth century, but Thomas Lodge nonetheless knew the poem since he made it the basis of the first half of his prose romance *Rosalynde* (which in turn served, of course, as the source for Shakespeare's *As You Like It* at the end of the 1590s). *Rosalynde* was printed in 1590, the same year as the first edition of *The Faerie Queene*, and Lodge was evidently an admirer and imitator of Spenser as well as of the 'Chaucer' of the *Tale*

---

14 See Skeat's edition of the *Tale of Gamelyn* for his explanation of this theory (xiii–xvi). He had previously outlined the idea in the introduction to his edition of the *Prioress's Tale* (Oxford: Clarendon Press, 1893), xv. Knight and Ohlgren repeat the idea, without giving a reason or reference for it (http://d.lib.rochester.edu/teams/text/tale-of-gamelyn-introduction).

15 Manuscripts that explicitly link the tale to the Cook are: Cambridge University Library MS Ii.3.26, Cambridge Fitzwilliam Museum MS McClean 181*, Oxford Bodleian Library MS Laud misc. 600 (with opening paratext); Lichfield Cathedral Library MS 29, London British Library MS Egerton 2726, London British Library MS Egerton 2863*, London British Library MS Harley 1758, New York Pierpoint Morgan Library MS M 249, Oxford Bodleian Library MS Barlow 20*, Oxford Bodleian MS Hatton Donat. 1*, Oxford Bodleian Library MS Rawlinson poet. 149, Philadelphia Rosenbach Library MS1084/1 (with closing paratext); Glasgow Hunterian Museum MS U.1.1*, London British Library MS Royal 17 D.XV, London British Library MS Sloane 1686 (with both). Manuscripts marked here with a * (and Petworth House MS 7) also use a linking couplet to suggest that the *Tale of Gamelyn* continues from the genuinely Chaucerian fragment given to the Cook, and thus in the voice of that pilgrim.

of Gamelyn.¹⁶ Evidence of influence in the other direction is rather harder to find, although Lodge's biographer has suggested that he may be the model for Alcon in *Colin Clouts Come Home Againe*.¹⁷ Even if the chain from the *Tale of Gamelyn* in manuscript, through Lodge, to Spenser, ultimately breaks down, the poem is still a part of the poetic atmosphere in the years when the latter poet is at work.

The *Tale of Gamelyn* is in many ways a crude piece of work: crude not only in construction (it has a very limited vocabulary and a tendency towards repetition and the use of filler-phrases), but also in tone. It begins with a dying father seeking to divide his lands between his three sons according to merit, rather than primogeniture, and this lends an air of nobility to the tale which helps to qualify it as a romance (similarities to *King Lear* are obvious in the plot at least). Yet the physical prowess of the titular hero is coarse rather than courtly, often accompanied with a grim humour in the narrative voice, and this humour is perhaps the most sophisticated and rewarding aspect of the poem. The *Tale of Gamelyn* could thus put humour back into the notion of Chaucerian romance available to sixteenth-century poets, something notable given the long-standing critical interest in Spenser's comic wit.¹⁸

A central part of the humour in the *Tale of Gamelyn* is concerned with the theme of 'play', often in subversion of knighthood. This has a literal dimension: Gamelyn's first demonstration of his prowess comes not in battle, nor even in the play-battle of a joust (as his knightly rank might suggest), but in a wrestling competition, something altogether more immediate in its physicality. More pervasive than this literal dimension, however, is a verbal one, in the recurrent use of the word 'play' to mean 'fight', often in grimly ironic and graphically violent ways. Twice (lines 254 and 256) it is used of the wrestling itself, pointing up the half-serious nature of fighting as sport, but the word takes on darker overtones elsewhere in the poem. On his return from the wrestling competition, for example, Gamelyn is barred entry to the castle of his deceitful brother by its porter. This is only a temporary setback, as Gamelyn solves things with a blunt physicality: kicking in the castle door, he gives chase to the fleeing porter. He grabs him by the neck, breaking the bones, and then takes him by the arm and throws him into a well, seven fathoms deep. The narrator moves on from this incident with the line 'Whan Gamelyn the yonge thus had plaied his playe' (307). The darkly comic irony in this phrase, which describes the killing of the porter and the dumping of his body by the hero as a young man simply 'playing games', has been prepared in earlier

---

16 See Charles Walters Whitworth, Jr., 'Lodge, Thomas', in *The Spenser Encyclopedia*, ed. A.C. Hamilton *et al.* (Toronto: University of Toronto Press, 1990), 438.
17 N. Burton Paradise, *Thomas Lodge: The History of an Elizabethan* (New Haven: Yale University Press, 1931), 110–11.
18 For studies that consider humour in Spenser see particularly Judith H. Anderson '"A Gentle Knight was pricking on the plaine": The Chaucerian Connection', *English Literary Renaissance*, 15 (1985), 166–74, but also: Allan H. Gilbert, 'Spenserian Comedy', *Tennessee Studies in Literature*, 2 (1957), 95–104; Elizabeth Bieman, '"Sometimes I ... mask in myrth lyke to a Comedy": Spenser's *Amoretti*', *Spenser Studies*, 4 (1983), 31–41; Lauren Silberman, 'Spenser and Ariosto: Funny Peril and Comic Chaos', *Comparative Literature Studies*, 25 (1988), 23–34; Anthony Esolen, 'Spenserian Allegory and the Clash of Narrative Worlds', *Thalia*, 11 (1989), 3–13.

uses of the word. When Gamelyn remonstrates with his brother over the way he has been denied his inheritance, for example, the brother sets his servants to beat up Gamelyn, who easily retaliates with a pestle (itself a comic subversion of the knightly weapon) – as the poem puts it 'he gan to pleye' (130). Gamelyn himself uses the same language and the same tone, taunting his brother to come and fight him: 'And I wil teche thee a play at the bokelere' (136). This creates a telling ambiguity about the language used to describe the activities of the band of men who gather around Gamelyn in his exile in the forest. Returning there from his imprisonment in the court, he 'fonde ther pleying yenge men of pris' (768); the poem does not say explicitly what form this 'pleying' takes, or what 'good game' (772) they have at his return, but these words are, by now, loaded with violent undertones.[19]

The same sort of humour is found later at a feast, in the description of Gamelyn assaulting the assembled clergymen because they refused to show mercy and have him released from the undeserved bonds in which his brother has fettered him. He is eventually released from captivity secretly by his faithful servant, Adam the spencer,[20] and proceeds to take his revenge: 'Gamelyn spreyeth holy watere with an oken spire, / That some that stode upright felle in the fire' (499–500). Although he is literally beating the clergymen with an oak staff, the action is described as sprinkling them with holy water. This parody of sacred ritual is part of the poem's occasional anti-clerical tone, something that is again emphasised through comic violence. A few lines later, Adam sarcastically encourages Gamelyn to have reverence for the tonsure of these holy men, but to beat them anyway:

> 'Gamelyn', seide Adam, 'do hem but goode;
> Thei bene men of holy churche drowe of hem no blode
> Save wel the crownes and do hem no harmes,
> But breke both her legges and sithen her armes'.

This anti-clerical 'pleie' (as the narrator again describes it) clearly has the potential to appeal to post-Reformation readers with an anti-Catholic agenda.[21] There were certainly moves amongst some sixteenth-century writers to position Chaucer as a proto-Protestant author. In this way, the *Tale of Gamelyn* is comparable with the Wycliffite *Plowman's Tale* (sometimes known as the *Complaynte of the Plowman*) which survives in one manuscript (Library of the University of Texas at Austin MS 8) and which, after its first printing around 1536, was also included in Thynne's

---

19 See the *Middle English Dictionary*, s.v. 'game (n.)', especially senses 1, 2a and 3.
20 The name given to Adam's role (used eight times in the poem) is, of course, a pleasing coincidence given the concerns of this chapter, and perhaps an example of the kind of readerly mishearing that Helen Barr discusses elsewhere in this volume.
21 Recent scholarship has argued that Spenser's own religious affiliations are not straightforward; see John N. King, *Spenser's Poetry and the Reformation Tradition* (Princeton: Princeton University Press, 1990) and *English Reformation Literature: The Tudor Origins of the Protestant Tradition* (Princeton: Princeton University Press, 1982).

1542 edition of Chaucer.[22] As Andrew N. Wawn has shown, the *Plowman's Tale* was originally printed for 'a calculated and official propagandist purpose' at the height of the controversy with Rome.[23] Spenser alludes to the *Plowman's Tale* on a number of occasions in *The Shepheardes Calender*, but there is no such clear allusion to the *Tale of Gamelyn*.[24] Nevertheless, the latter text is a further example of a pseudo-Chaucerian text that could be used to make the older poet appear to anticipate the Protestant cause.

In spite of its metrical crudities and narrative abruptness, the *Tale of Gamelyn* does therefore contain sophisticated and imaginative elements, and its anticlericalism, blunt violence and dark humour might each, in different ways, find echoes in *The Faerie Queene*. As far as romance is concerned, it is not written in the 'high style' found in the *Knight's Tale*, the *Franklin's Tale* or Chaucer's other romances (apart from *Sir Thopas*), but this earthiness is not alien to Chaucer, of course. In the manuscript tradition *Gamelyn* extends the category of Chaucerian romance to the point where it begins to touch on the same tonal world as Chaucerian fabliau. As such, the traditional categories that medievalists use to read Chaucer begin to break down in the reading experience as suggested by the manuscripts. The focus on the body, especially in its uncourtly aspects, which fabliau always enjoyed, is made part of romance: an intermingling to which the context gives Chaucerian blessing.

The *Tale of Beryn*

Less well known than the *Tale of Gamelyn* is the *Tale of Beryn*, a much longer poem that exists in only a single manuscript, Northumberland MS 455: again, a copy of *The Canterbury Tales*.[25] Despite its location now, there is evidence to put the manuscript's origins in London or the south east of England. The dialect has been identified as from Essex,[26] and the scribe seems to have been a moderately

---

22 See further Andrew Wawn, '*The Plowman's Tale*', in *The Spenser Encyclopedia*, 548–9, and the edition in James M. Dean, *Six Ecclesiastical Satires* (Kalamazoo: Medieval Institute Publications, 1991), available online at http://d.lib.rochester.edu/teams/text/dean-six-ecclesiastical-satires-plowmans-tale-introduction [accessed 19 November 2018].
23 Andrew N. Wawn, 'Chaucer, *The Plowman's Tale* and Reformation Propaganda: The Testimony of Thomas Godfray and *I Playne Piers*', *Bulletin of the John Rylands Library, Manchester*, 56 (1973–4), 174–92 (175). See also Paul J. Patterson, 'Reforming Chaucer: Margins and Religion in an Apocryphal *Canterbury Tale*', *Book History*, 8 (2005), 11–36; Megan Cook, 'How Francis Thynne Read His Chaucer', *Journal of the Early Book Society for the Study of Manuscripts and Printing History*, 15 (2012), 215–43; and Brendan O'Connell's chapter in this volume.
24 See Wawn, '*The Plowman's Tale*', 548–9.
25 The edition used here is that by John M. Bowers in *The Canterbury Tales: Fifteenth-Century Continuations and Additions* (Kalamazoo: Medieval Institute Publications, 1992), available online at http://d.lib.rochester.edu/teams/text/bowers-canterbury-tales-fifteenth-century-interlude-and-marchants-tale-of-beryn [accessed 19 November 2018]. This supersedes Furnivall and Stone's 1909 edition for the Early English Text Society.
26 See the entry for this scribe in the online catalogue of scribal hands prepared by the universities of York, Oxford and Sheffield: www.medievalscribes.com/index.php?nav=off&browse=manuscripts&id=102 [accessed 19 November 2018].

prolific professional, whose other work includes copies of London chronicles.²⁷ Again, this is not to say that Spenser ever saw the manuscript, but it does make it more likely that it could have been seen by others in the London literary milieu.

The *Tale of Beryn* is very different in tone from *The Tale of Gamelyn*, and the poet responsible for *Beryn* and the 'Canterbury Interlude' which introduces it was in many ways more accomplished, certainly in the handling of metre and syntax, but also in bold characterisation and understated wit.²⁸ What immediately strikes the reader familiar with the *Canterbury Tales* is how well the poet has understood Chaucer's project, and how well he imitates and develops the tone and approach of the earlier text. In this sense, the *Tale of Beryn* would add little to the concept of 'Chaucer' given by the manuscript as a whole, simply because it fits in so well with the genuinely Chaucerian material. It is a different kind of romance from the *Tale of Gamelyn*, taking place not in an imagined English past, but in the more exotic locales of Rome and Egypt. In this way it has more in common with the *Squire's Tale* than with most other Chaucerian romances, and thus finds itself in tune with the Spenser who sought to complete this tale in Book IV of *The Faerie Queene*.

Yet perhaps the most illuminating light that the *Tale of Beryn* can offer on how Chaucerian and Spenserian romance relate to each other is in providing another example of the romance story-shape which is recognisable in spite of its difference of content and tone. Earlier in this chapter it was noted that among the conventional motifs often identified with the romance genre are the challenge and the quest; Radulescu develops this idea about 'popular' romance further to include 'the intrusion of the outrageous and the spectacular or unexpected, which unsettles the order of chivalric adventures encountered in these texts'.²⁹ Two refinements can be made to this suggestion: firstly to acknowledge that the notion of the 'challenge' to, or the 'unsettling' of, a courtly milieu can be found in both courtly and popular romances, and secondly to replace the idea of quest with broader ideas of journey and return. This latter definition specifically connotes a journey away from the 'home' location of the narrative in order to respond to or resolve the challenge or unsettling which is made apparent there, and then a return either once that challenge has been worked through, or indeed a return that is itself part of the process of working through the implications of the challenge.

These (admittedly loose) terms help to do justice to the ways in which texts that are in some ways very disparate nonetheless all come to be considered as romance, because they share some narrative contours. In *Sir Gawain and the Green Knight*,

---

27 See Simon Horobin, 'The Scribe of the Helmingham and Northumberland Manuscripts of the *Canterbury Tales*', *Neophilologus*, 84 (2000), 457–65; Linne R. Mooney and Lister M. Matheson, 'The Beryn Scribe and His Texts: Evidence for Multiple-Copy Production of Manuscripts in Fifteenth-Century England', *The Library*, 7th series, 4 (2003), 347–70; and Daniel W. Mosser and Linne R. Mooney, 'More Manuscripts by the Beryn Scribe and His Cohort', *The Chaucer Review*, 49 (2014), 39–76.

28 For a more extended discussion of the neglected merits of this poem, see J.A. Burrow, 'The *Tale of Beryn*: An Appreciation', *The Chaucer Review*, 49 (2015), 499–511.

29 Radulescu, 31.

for example, the application of this shape is clear: the Green Knight brings his challenge to unsettle Arthur's court, and Gawain journeys out to resolve in his own actions the tensions inherent in the values that he is pledged to uphold. Once these have been worked through to their logical conclusion, for good or ill, he returns to the court, which is subtly changed by the whole process. In the *Knight's Tale*, we might think of Emily as the unsettling of the enclosed 'court' kept by Palamon and Arcite in their cell. This unsettling has to be worked out through the departure of Arcite into banishment, which clarifies the nature of the challenge (which is better: freedom or the sight of your beloved?), but also through the process of return and final conflict. This narrative shape may also shed light on a popular romance such as *Sir Perceval of Galles*.[30] This poem is obviously based on the French and wider continental story of Perceval, but it adds an unusual twist. In the English poem, once Perceval has gone to Arthur's court to learn the ways of chivalry, and subsequently proved himself an exemplar of its values and actions, he does not remain there, but returns to a humble, obscure life with his mother. The 'quest' is not from the court of Arthur into the wilderness and back, but exactly the opposite. Nevertheless, the same shape is discernible.

This shape may be one of the things that Chaucer and Spenser found attractive about romance. It allows each poet to think through ideas – moral, emotional or philosophical conundrums – by having a protagonist journey away from their home location to work out the implications of a problem or paradox through lived experience or allegory, with the promise (often, in Spenser, continually deferred) of return, either after the problem is resolved or as part of the means of its resolution. This helps to place the *Tale of Beryn* in relation to romance. In this text, the eponymous character is born to Roman parents who take an indulgent view of his compulsive gambling (one mark of the anonymous poet's sophistication here may be the fact that the 'Interlude' that precedes the tale makes much use of the Pardoner, whose tale of course condemns this sin particularly). His mother dies, and his father remarries to a woman who is less tolerant of her stepson's besetting sin. After fighting with his father, Beryn refuses the offer of knighthood, a literal and symbolic rejection of the courtly, and instead sets off to Egypt in a new career as a merchant. He is blown off course, but arrives in a land where legal cases are decided not on the basis of truth, but on the basis of who lies best, a system of which he inevitably falls foul, by losing a bet on a game of chess, and finds himself in a state of peril from which his actual innocence, for once, is unable to rescue him. He is saved at the last minute by a jester who tells lies on his behalf that are more convincing than those told by the prosecution. As a result, he is acquitted and his possessions are restored to him.

It may stretch the definition of romance to include this text, but there are similar shapes here: the initial courtly milieu, the challenge to that milieu through the exposure of civilised corruption, and the journey away from the home location

---

30 Mary Flowers Braswell, ed., *Sir Perceval of Galles and Ywain and Gawain* (Kalamazoo: Medieval Institute Publications, 1995), available online at http://d.lib.rochester.edu/teams/text/braswell-sir-perceval-of-galles [accessed 19 November 2018].

in order to work out this problem. Yet there is no return, and Beryn's triumph comes not through abandoning his sin (although he is severely chastened) but by the use of another one: effective lying. This makes an unlikely link with the *Tale of Gamelyn*: both texts make playful use of romance convention to challenge the expectations of courtly romance. In the *Tale of Beryn*, this playfulness is evident not only in the anonymous poet's skilful use of themes and ideas from Chaucer's own *Tales* (of which the poem functions as an insightful critical appreciation), but also in one final in-joke. The jester who saves Beryn – that is, the professional provider of comic entertainment, the character who shows great dexterity at resolving narratives and inventing convincing untruths to defend the guilty – is called Geoffrey. This is surely a knowing, and admiring, riposte to Chaucer's own self-caricature as the naive, stumbling storyteller who can only recite *Sir Thopas* or offer the moral *Tale of Melibee*. In at least one manuscript context, therefore, the figure of Chaucer becomes not only a popular romancer and interrogator of the assumptions and values of courtly romance, but also an expert at the attractive lie. Had he read the poem, Spenser is unlikely to have approved of its moral shiftiness, but the *Tale of Beryn* does show another poet stepping in to fill the gaps left in the *Canterbury Tales*. He was one of many to do so: the same volume that contains John Bowers's edition of the *Tale of Beryn* also includes the work of at least four other late medieval poets who sought to fill gaps in the unfinished portions of the *Canterbury Tales*, not including the *Plowman's Tale* discussed above. Henryson's *Testament of Cresseid* is a continuation of that heroine's story, and therefore a form of post-Chaucerian gap-filling too. Spenser's gap-filling is the most famous, but it does not stand alone. It is a continuation of the tradition of continuations, and the *Tale of Beryn* is perhaps the most important example of this before Spenser.

Excerpting Chaucer

The shaping of the figure of Chaucer that takes place in the manuscripts into which his works were copied after his death does not take place only through insertion and addition. It is also brought about through excerption: the placing of one or more Chaucerian texts alongside a larger number of texts from other writers. In some cases, a collection of texts within a manuscript has a clear thematic focus. An example would be the Findern Anthology (Cambridge University Library MS Ff.I.6). The focus of the more than sixty items in this manuscript is clearly love, specifically heterosexual human love, and the mode of complaint. There are several anonymous love lyrics, as well as extracts from the *Confessio Amantis*, and Hoccleve's *Letter of Cupid*. Chaucer is present through a number of his complaint lyrics, but also the *Parliament of Fowls* and complaints extracted from longer works (Anelida's complaint, and the story of Thisbe from the *Legend of Good Women*). Roughly halfway through the manuscript is the romance of *Sir Degrevant*, which seems to have been chosen for inclusion because of its focus, once again, on love, as the titular character carries on a clandestine and chaste affair with Melydore, daughter of one of his neighbours. Although there is a clear codicological case for dividing the manuscript into discrete booklets, the thematic connections are very strong across these divisions, and the experience of reading the manuscript as a whole is thus strongly focused and tends to associate Chaucer with courtly love complaint.[31]

If that association seems natural to modern readers, a rather different connection is found in Trinity College Dublin MS 432 (or at least that part of it which is a medieval book – several later parts are bound together).[32] It is difficult to determine the original arrangement of the leaves in this manuscript, since the quires have now been broken up in rebinding, but as it stands it begins with Chaucer's *Lack of Steadfastness* and some proverbial verses, and is then followed by the *Knight's Tale*. This is followed immediately by *Robert of Sicily*, a romance entirely devoid of love interest, but concerned instead with the moral correction of a proud ruler through his replacement by an angel who takes on his appearance, leaving Robert to live among the dogs of the court for three years.[33] As in the *Tale of Beryn*, the movement away from court (to Rome, to meet the Pope and the Emperor) is part of the working out of Robert's correction, and eventually he returns to Sicily and to power, reigning and dying well. Yet if the romance outline is clear, the tone and theme are very different here. As the manuscript continues, it is clear that its twin concerns are miraculous happenings and the lives of saints (especially saints from the nobility) on the one hand, and the Yorkist cause on the other. There are obvious dangers in attempting to impose a reading of strict coherence on a miscellaneous manuscript whose ordering of texts is hard to determine, but this context raises the possibility that the story of Palamon and Arcite could be read in manuscript as an example of noble virtue, in some religious or political sense, giving it a greater kinship with the concerns of *The Faerie Queene*.

Palamon and Arcite is excerpted again in Longleat MS 257, where it follows Lydgate's *Siege of Thebes* (which is of course framed as a Canterbury Tale, and which engages in debate with the *Knight's Tale* on the subject of war), and is followed by the *Clerk's Tale*.[34] This in turn is followed by the prose version of *Ipomedon*, after which the manuscript seems originally to have been left blank, although later on two texts describing how one should serve in a noble household were added. As

---

31 For a fuller description of the manuscript, beside that in Guddat-Figge's catalogue (for which see fn. 10), see Rossell Hope Robbins, 'The Findern Anthology', *PMLA*, 69 (1954), 610–42. A facsimile is also available: Richard Beadle and A.E.B. Owen, eds, *The Findern Manuscript: MS Cambridge University Library Ff.1.6* (London: Scolar Press, 1977). A detailed discussion of how Chaucer may have been read in this context is given in Kara A. Doyle, 'Thisbe out of Context: Chaucer's Female Readers and the Findern Manuscript', *The Chaucer Review*, 40 (2006), 231–61.
32 Again, Guddat-Figge gives a useful description of the MS, but see also the editorial materials published as part of the online scholarly edition of *Robert of Sicily* by Joan Baker: www2.fiu.edu/~bakerj/RS/TrinDb432.htm [accessed 19 November 2018].
33 Available in Edward E. Foster, ed., *Amis and Amiloun, Robert of Cisyle, and Sir Amadace* (Kalamazoo: Medieval Institute Publications, 2007), and online at http://d.lib.rochester.edu/teams/text/foster-robert-of-cisyle [accessed 19 November 2018].
34 The most thorough scholarly description of the manuscript is Jordi Sánchez Martí, 'Longleat House MS 257: A Description', *Atlantis*, 27 (2005), 79–89.

Carol M. Meale notes, these and other indications suggest that this manuscript may have become associated with the nobility at some point in the late fifteenth century, or even later.[35] Once again, this collection of texts seems deliberately framed to interrogate a series of interrelated themes, but different ones this time. They include the question of whether there can be a just use of knightly violence, and if so what that might be; women suffering as the objects of male desire; and the ways in which violence and what we now call romantic love might relate to one another. All of these concerns are of course reflected and refracted many times over in *The Faerie Queene*.

The *Clerk's Tale* is found in other manuscripts that contain romance, notably the well-known Naples MS, Biblioteca Nazionale MS XIII.B.29.[36] This manuscript opens with a collection of medical recipes, but proceeds with copies of *Sir Bevys of Hampton, Saint Alex of Rome, Lybeaus Disconus* and *Sir Isumbras*, before a break after which Chaucer's poem is included. As I will argue in a forthcoming essay, there are codicological grounds to suggest that, in spite of the single scribal hand, the composition of this manuscript is in fact complex, and the juxtaposition of Griselda with these mostly knightly romance heroes may have been an afterthought. Nevertheless, once this manuscript was bound together (which happened early in its life), it placed Chaucer once again in a strongly romance-inflected textual environment. In different ways, these four manuscripts illustrate the way in which manuscript compilation can give clues to the ways in which Chaucer was being read in the fifteenth century, and thus presented to subsequent readers of the same manuscripts in the sixteenth.

The impression of Chaucer that one gets from reading his works in a modern scholarly edition such as the *Riverside Chaucer* is not the same idea of the poet that would have been available to audiences in the centuries immediately following his death. Rather, the presentation of Chaucer-as-text in the manuscript tradition does, in some striking ways, alter the prominence and significance of romance in his work.[37] This chapter has sought to uncover the nature of this alteration by looking at the textual company that Chaucer's texts keep in manuscripts of the fifteenth century, specifically the romances that are copied with texts by Chaucer and which thus come to be seen by fifteenth- and sixteenth-century audiences as in

---

35 Carol M. Meale, '"gode men / Wiues maydnes and alle men": Romance and Its Audiences', in *Readings in Medieval English Romance*, ed. Carol M. Meale (Cambridge: D.S. Brewer, 1994), 209–26 (215).
36 A concise description is in Guddat-Figge (see fn. 10). The most sustained essay on the manuscript as a whole is James Weldon, 'The Naples Manuscript and the Case for a Female Readership', *Neophilologus*, 93 (2009), 703–22, although the present author will take issue with the conclusions of that piece in a forthcoming article.
37 Other chapters in this collection touch on aspects of Chaucer's presentation in print in the sixteenth century, but see also Seth Lerer, *Chaucer and His Readers: Imagining the Author in Late-Medieval England* (Princeton: Princeton University Press, 1993), especially 147–208; Stephanie Trigg, 'Chaucer's Influence and Reception', in *The Yale Companion to Chaucer*, ed. Seth Lerer (New Haven: Yale University Press, 2006), 297–323; Siobhan Bly, 'From Text to Man: Re-Creating Chaucer in Sixteenth-Century Print Editions', *Comitatus*, 30 (1999), 131–65.

some sense Chaucerian. The purpose of this examination has not been to suggest any direct indebtedness on Spenser's part either to Chaucer or to these pseudo-Chaucerian texts, but rather to expand our idea of the extent to which Chaucer could be seen as a writer of romance, by audiences (including other writers) in the sixteenth century. In so doing, it sheds light on how 'Chaucerian' the very act of writing romance might have been to a poet like Spenser.

8

Cultivating Chaucerian antiquity in *The Shepheardes Calender*

Megan L. Cook

Chaucer's significance to Spenser is not news. It has been recognised at least since 1598, the year before Spenser's death, when the Francis Beaumont remarked in a prefatory epistle to Chaucer's collected works that Spenser's 'much frequenting of Chaucers antient speeches causeth many to allow farre better of [Spenser], then otherwise they would'.[1] Beaumont seems to have *The Shepheardes Calender* in mind in this passage, and this chapter follows suit, focusing on the specific ways in which Spenser's poetic debut puts the 'new Poete' in dialogue with his medieval predecessor.[2] But whereas Beaumont and many later commentators consider the ways that Chaucer influences Spenser, both in the *Calender* and in later poems, this chapter explores how the *Calender* reimagines Chaucer and his works. Specifically, this chapter aims to demonstrate that in the *Calender*, Chaucer has a dual authorising function. His 'aunciet' words ground him in the English past and equip Spenser with the linguistic resources to produce archaising effects in his own verse, but throughout the *Calender* Chaucer also functions as an authorial figure akin to Virgil himself. By classicising Chaucer in this way while retaining an investment in his identity as an English writer, the *Calender* works towards a synthesis of Latinate and vernacular poetic traditions, recasting the medieval poet as part of a literary genealogy that stretches back to classical antiquity and forward to the Spenserian present. This synthesis not only shapes the role that Chaucer plays in the *Calender* but, as I will argue, exerts a discernable influence on subsequent editions of Chaucer's own works published in 1598 and 1602.[3]

1 'F.B. to his very loving friend, T.S.', in *The workes of our antient and learned English poet, Geffrey Chaucer, newly printed* (London: Adam Islip at the Charges of Thomas Wight, 1598), a.iii.
2 This chapter builds upon and expands ideas presented in my 2011 *Spenser Studies* essay. See Megan L. Cook, 'Making and Managing the Past: Lexical Commentary in Spenser's Shepheardes Calender (1579) and Chaucer's Works (1598/1602)', *Spenser Studies*, 26 (2011), 179–222.
3 Studies of Chaucer's influence on Spenser are numerous and multifaceted, attending to Spenser's use of Chaucerian plot, language and authorial persona. While Spenser draws on Chaucerian material in the *Calender* (see Clarke Kinney, 'Marginal Presence, Lyric Resonance, Epic Absence: *Troilus and Criseyde* and/in the *Shepheardes Calender*', *Spenser Studies*, 18 [2003], 25–39), it is the last of these two categories that are most salient here. On Spenser's use of Chaucerian authorial persona, see especially Glenn A. Steinberg, 'Spenser's *Shepheardes Calender* and the Elizabethan Reception of Chaucer', *English Literary Renaissance*, 35.1 (2005), 31–51, which argues that Spenser follows Chaucer in adopting an ironically humble authorial persona. See also Anthony

The image of Chaucer that emerges in the *Calender* alongside Spenser's 'frequenting' of Chaucer's 'antient speeches' depends not only on the verse, but on the accompanying commentary attributed to a mysterious 'E.K.'[4] In his discussions of the medieval poet, E.K. presents Chaucer as a hybrid figure, an author aligned with classical antiquity even as he maintains his foundational position among English poets. While identifying Chaucer and his language as 'antient' or 'old' might at first seem to emphasise the distance between Chaucer and the *Calender*'s readers, doing so ultimately enhances Chaucer's stature. By associating him with a historically antecedent but culturally current poetic paradigm, E.K. represents Chaucer as a writer who proleptically embraces the literary values of his sixteenth-century admirers.

While E.K.'s discussion of Chaucer sets the tone for the more sustained exploration of the English literary heritage found in *The Faerie Queene* (as well as in the works of Spenser's contemporaries and near-contemporaries like Shakespeare, Nashe, and Greene), it also informs the way Chaucer is presented to his own readership post-Spenser. Most notably, E.K.'s views on Chaucer help to shape the first edition of Chaucer published after the appearance of Spenser's major works. First printed in 1598 and revised in 1602, *The Workes of Our Antient and Learned English Poet, Geffrey Chaucer* were prepared by London schoolteacher Thomas Speght and remained the edition of choice for more than a century.[5] Although Speght relies primarily upon previous editions of the *Works* for his text of Chaucer, his edition introduces a substantial and varied paratextual apparatus that includes a glossary, summaries of some of Chaucer's works, and several

---

M. Esolen, 'The Disingenuous Poet Laureate: Spenser's Adoption of Chaucer', *Studies in Philology*, 87.3 (1990), 285–311; David Lee Miller, 'Authorship, Anonymity, and the *Shepheardes Calender*', *Modern Language Quarterly*, 40 (1979), 219–36 and Alice E. Lasater, 'The Chaucerian Narrator in Spenser's *Shepheardes Calender*', *Southern Quarterly*, 12 (1974), 189–201. However, as John A. Burrow observes in his entry on Chaucer in *The Spenser Encyclopedia* (ed. A.C. Hamilton et al. [London: University of Toronto Press, 1990], 147), 'the task of proving that this or that word or form could only have come directly from [Chaucer] seems less easy the more one knows about other late-medieval and Tudor poetry'. Spenser's verse is shot through with Chaucerian resonances, and E.K. identifies a number of words in the *Calender* as having been taken from Chaucer. On Spenser's adaptation of Chaucerian language, see Edward Armstrong, *A Ciceronian Sunburn: A Tudor Dialogue on Humanistic Rhetoric and Civic Poetics* (Columbia: University of South Carolina Press, 2006) and Bruce Robert McElderry Jr., 'Archaism and Innovation in Spenser's Poetic Diction', *PMLA*, 47.1 (1932), 144–70. For more syncretic views of Chaucer's influence on Spenser, see especially the essays collected in Judith H. Anderson, *Reading the Allegorical Intertext: Chaucer, Spenser, Shakespeare, Milton* (New York: Fordham University Press, 2008) as well as Clare Kinney, *Strategies of Poetic Narrative: Chaucer, Spenser, Milton, Eliot* (Cambridge: Cambridge University Press, 1992) and A. Kent Hieatt, *Chaucer, Spenser, Milton: Mythopoeic Continuities and Transformations* (Montreal: McGill-Queen's University Press, 1975). Chaucer was, of course, not the only medieval poet whose work inspired and influenced Spenser, and *The Faerie Queene*, especially, has strong parallels with William Langland's *Piers Plowman*. See Judith H. Anderson, *The Growth of a Personal Voice: Piers Plowman and the Faerie Queene* (New Haven: Yale University Press, 1976) and Katherine Little, 'The "Other" Past of Pastoral: Langland's *Piers Plowman* and Spenser's *Shepheardes Calender*', *Exemplaria*, 21 (2009), 160–78.

4 Text and page numbers for *The Shepheardes Calender* are taken from *Edmund Spenser: The Shorter Poems*, ed. Richard A. McCabe (New York: Penguin, 1999).
5 Derek Pearsall, 'Thomas Speght (ca. 1550-?)', in *Editing Chaucer: The Great Tradition*, ed. Paul G. Ruggiers (Norman: Pilgrim, 1984), 91.

introductory epistles discussing Chaucer's language and versification, including the piece by Francis Beaumont mentioned above. While the more limited supplementary materials found in earlier editions of Chaucer's *Works* primarily celebrate Chaucer's Englishness, these new materials follow the precedent set by the *Calender* in presenting Chaucer as a writer who participates meaningfully in both classical and native English poetic traditions.

This essay considers how E.K.'s commentary represents Chaucer and situates him within the *Calender*'s multifaceted poetics, but also it attends to the ways that E.K.'s representation informs the 1598 and 1602 editions of Chaucer's *Works*. E.K.'s influence on the subsequent reception and representation of Chaucer's works might be considered an example of what William Kuskin describes as the recursivity of literary history, a process that he argues is best viewed not as a linear narrative but as an 'intertwined process of reading and rewriting'.[6] But the relationship between these two texts – the *Calender* and Speght's Chaucer – is complicated by the fact that while E.K. offers commentary on a self-consciously archaic work, the explanatory materials provided in Speght are intended to explicate the works of an actual fourteenth-century writer. E.K. comments on the text *as though* it is old; Speght comments on the text *because* it is old.

In this case, the intertextuality that links E.K.'s commentary and Speght's apparatus to Chaucer's *Works* blurs the line between poetic conceit and earnest scholarship. We may never know who 'E.K.' really was and to what degree he collaborated with Spenser when writing his commentary, but his notes and the *Calender*'s eclogues enter print circulation at the same time, and the total package announces to prospective readers that this poem is a kind of 'instant classic'. Speght, by contrast, recognises that he works at a historical remove when it comes to Chaucer. In his annotations, he takes as given Chaucer's foundational role in English literature, and his notes and other explanatory devices are clearly intended to help other readers better appreciate Chaucer's poetic accomplishments across a temporal and linguistic divide. This overlap between the scholarly and the poetic suggests that elements that Lucy Munro identifies as characteristic of literary archaism at the turn of the seventeenth century – particularly its concern with periodisation and national identity – might provide a useful framework for exploring other forms of the production of knowledge about the English past.[7]

Chaucer and his language in sixteenth-century England

Before turning to E.K. and the specific ways in which he discusses the antiquity of Chaucer and his language, it is useful to consider what Chaucer and his language might have meant to Spenser, and anyone else involved in the production of the *Calender* in 1579. I want to push back against the assumption that Chaucer's

---

6 William Kuskin, *Recursive Origins: Writing at the Transition to Modernity* (Notre Dame: University of Notre Dame Press, 2013), 7.
7 Lucy Munro, *Archaic Style in English Literature, 1590–1674* (Cambridge: Cambridge University Press, 2013), 12–30.

language would have been unintelligible to most readers by the second half of the sixteenth century, or that the definitions and glosses provided by E.K. were necessary in order that the *Calender*'s readers could understand the shepherds' archaic speech. Instead, I contend that E.K.'s commentary is viewed as a rhetorical intervention designed to situate Chaucer in a specific literary and historical context.

Chaucer died in 1400, almost 180 years before the publication of the *Calender*, and his language differed recognisably from Spenser's Tudor English. Difference, however, does not necessarily entail incomprehensibility, and there is considerable evidence to suggest that Chaucer's language remained accessible to a wide array of readers at least up until the final decades of the sixteenth century. Chaucer, Gower, Lydgate and Langland were all published in the 1550s or 1560s without special interpretive aids and without extensive commentary on the difficulty of their language. Indeed, although readers might comment on the increasingly obvious antiquity of these works, the first printed glossary to a Middle English text did not appear until 1561.[8] Middle English texts were still serving as the basis for adaptations like *Pericles* and *Two Noble Kinsmen* at the turn of the seventeenth century, and notes in surviving copies of Middle English texts suggest that these books were read and understood by a wide array of readers well into the seventeenth century.[9] While the occasional writer comments on the outdated or unfashionable qualities of Chaucer's language, the prefatory materials to printed editions of Middle English texts more often invoke the errors of earlier scribes and printers or the unwonted neglect of readers than outright linguistic obsolescence. For example, in an epistle to the readers in Thomas Marsh's 1555 edition of Lydgate's *Troy Book*, Robert Braham writes that,

> Neuertheles, lykewyse as it hapned ye same Chaucer to lease ye prayse of that tyme wherin he wrote beyng then when in dede al good letters were almost aslepe, so farre was the grosenesse and barbarousnesse of that age from the vnderstandinge of so deuyne a wryter. That if it had not bene in this our time, wherin all kindes of learnyng (thancked be god) haue as much floryshed as euer they did by anye former dayes within this realme, and namelye by the dylygence of one wyllyam Thi[nn]e a gentilman who laudably studyouse to ye polyshing of so great a Iewell, with ryghte good iudgement trauail, & great paynes causing the same to be perfected and stamped as it is nowe read, ye sayde Chaucers workes had vtterly peryshed, or at ye lest bin *so depraued by corrupcion of copies*, that at the laste, there shoulde no parte of hys meaning haue ben founde in any of them. Euen the same iniurye almost hathe happened to this wryter in this his Pamphlite of the euercio[n] of Troye: being printed about.xlii. yeares agoe, euen then in the tayle (as it hapned) of the dercke and vnlearned times, *suche was then the ignoraunce of bothe the prynter and correctour,*

---

8 The glossary explicates the short poem *Piers the Plowmans Crede*, which was appended to some copies of Owen Roger's 1561 edition of *Piers Plowman* (STC 19908).
9 On readers' use of early printed Chaucer, see Alison Wiggins, 'What Did Renaissance Readers Write in Their Printed Copies of Chaucer?', *Library*, 9.1 (2008), 3–36, as well as Antonia Harbus, 'A Renaissance Reader's English Annotations to Thynne's 1532 Edition of Chaucer's Works', *Review of English Studies*, 59 (2008), 342–55.

neyther of them as it shoulde seme eyther learned or [u]nderstandynge englishe, y^t ye same worke is so falsed in his verse by either lacke, folishe surplus, or displasinge of ye wordes, that thereby ye sentence and consequentlye ye historye is so confused and obscured, that in most places, there can be almost nothing gathered therof. (Emphasis added)[10]

Like other pre-*Calender* commentators on Middle English, Braham locates the responsibility for textual difficulty with those involved in the work's transmission, and sees the problem as an issue of poor workmanship rather than linguistic change.

Anglo-Saxon texts, some of which were also printed for the first time in the sixteenth century, provide a useful counterexample. As Jennifer Summit and other historians of early modern libraries observe, the Anglo-Saxon codices that survive the Reformation were largely preserved through the efforts of antiquarians, such as Archbishop Matthew Parker and the scholars in his circle, who operated with explicit religious and political aims.[11] Thus, while the writings of Ælfric and Alfred the Great are, like the work of Chaucer and his contemporaries, celebrated for their combination of Englishness and antiquity, the contexts in which these texts circulate and are discussed frequently foreground the content, rather than the language or the style, of their work.[12] Moreover, Old English could not be read by non-specialists and could not be printed using ordinary type.[13] While the study of Old English was based at the universities, printed editions of Middle English poetry continued to address themselves to a more general audience. Similarly, while antiquarian discourse on Anglo-Saxon often emphasised rediscovery, many references to Chaucer took as given his ongoing influence on or relevance to later writers. Even if his language may have required attention and, eventually, explication, Chaucer's stature as an English poet of unparalleled significance to sixteenth-century literary discourse was not in question.

---

10 *The auncient historie and onely trewe and syncere cronicle of the warres betwixte the Grecians and the Troyans* (London: Thomas Marsh, [1555]), STC 5580, [a].ii.
11 See Jennifer Summit, *Memory's Library: Medieval Books in Early Modern England* (Chicago: University of Chicago Press, 2008), 101–6, as well as Carl T. Berkhout and Milton McGatch, eds, *Anglo-Saxon Scholarship: The First Three Centuries* (Boston: G.K. Hall, 1982), x. For studies of the reformist agenda of the Parker circle, see Benedict Scott Robinson, '"Darke Speech": Matthew Parker and the Reforming of History', *The Sixteenth Century Journal*, 29.4 (1998), 1061–83 and Emily Butler, 'Recollecting Alfredian English in the Sixteenth Century', *Neophilologus*, 98.1 (2014), 145–59.
12 On Anglo-Saxon scholarship in early modern England, see Rebecca Brackmann, *The Elizabethan Invention of Anglo-Saxon England: Laurence Nowell, William Lambarde, and the Study of Old English* (Cambridge: Boydell & Brewer, 2012), as well as Hannah Crawforth, *Etymology and the Invention of English in Early Modern Literature* (Cambridge: Cambridge University Press, 2013). On Spenser's own engagement with Anglo-Saxon scholarship and its role in the *Calender*, see Crawforth, 'Strangers to the Mother Tongue: Spenser's *Shepheardes Calender* and Early Anglo-Saxon Studies', *Journal of Medieval and Early Modern Studies*, 41.2 (2011), 293–314.
13 On the development of an Anglo-Saxon typeface, see Peter J. Lucas, 'A Testimonye of Verye Ancient Tyme? Some Manuscript Models for the Parkerian Anglo-Saxon Type-Designs', in *Of the Making of Books: Medieval Manuscripts, Their Scribes and Readers*, ed. P.R. Robinson and Rikvah Zim (Aldershot: Scolar, 1997), 147–88.

This was possible, in part, because the traditional terms of Chaucerian praise foster an enduring sense of connection with Chaucer, even in the face of a changing vernacular. From the early fifteenth century, admirers like John Lydgate and Thomas Hoccleve associated Chaucer not only with the English language itself, but also with more abstract ideas like 'rhetoric' and 'eloquence'. Christopher Cannon notes that this customary yet abstract vocabulary for Chaucerian praise foregrounds terms that are flexible enough to adapt to changing aesthetic and poetic standards as well as the on-going evolution of the English language itself.[14] As Cannon observes, 'early definitional terms matter very much because they actually sketch out a typology into which almost every subsequent definition of Chaucer's achievement fits'.[15] This flexibility encourages the repetition of earlier praise, keeping Chaucer's close association with the English language intact in new historical contexts. This broad-based appreciation for Chaucer's 'eloquence' as a key step in the elevation of a national vernacular helps to explain, in part, why interest in his writing persisted into the sixteenth century even as the works of many of his peers were drifting into obsolescence.[16]

'Olde words and harder Phrases'

By the time Spenser began writing in the 1570s, however, Chaucer had one foot in the present and one in the past. His special status as a harbinger of poetic modernity was counterbalanced by assessment of the ways in which he failed to fully embody Renaissance precepts of eloquence. In his faults, Chaucer is seen as a victim of his historical moment; in his successes, he transcends it. Sir Philip Sidney acknowledges this duality in his *Defence of Poesy* (written shortly after the publication of, and with knowledge of, the *Calender*). Sidney first wonders whether 'to mervaile more, either that hee in that mistie time could see so clearly, or that wee in this cleare age, goe so stumblingly after him', but he also writes that Chaucer had 'great wants, fit to be forgiven in so reverent an Antiquitie'.[17] As work written 'in so reverent an Antiquitie', Chaucer's poems and the language they contain are at once both purer and less evolved than early modern English. While later poets might regard their own verses as eclipsing Chaucer's accomplishments, the works

---

14 Cannon writes 'both claims license their esteem for Chaucer by gathering all the objective license of historical fact to that esteem, but, inasmuch as these claims specify *by means* of praise, they finally leave obscure just what Chaucer did'. *The Making of Chaucer's English: A Study of Words* (Cambridge: Cambridge University Press, 2005), 11.
15 Ibid., 9.
16 Alexandra Gillespie's work on the early print history of Chaucer and Lydgate, whose reputation comes closest to rivaling Chaucer's own in the pre-Reformation period, provides an illustrative contrast, as do the essays contained in *Caxton's Trace: Studies in the History of English Printing*, ed. William Kuskin (Notre Dame: Notre Dame University Press, 2003). Of relevant interest is Jennifer Summit's discussion of the suppression of anonymous religious writing in her section on '*The Fifteen Oes* and the Reformation of Devotion', in *Lost Property* (Chicago: Chicago University Press, 2000), 111–26.
17 Sir Philip Sidney, *An Apology for Poetry*, ed. Forrest G. Robinson (Indianapolis: Bobbs-Merrill, 1970), 77.

of the poet whom Hoccleve calls 'the first fyndere of our faire langage' remain a necessary precursor to their efforts.[18]

Perhaps no work embodies this perspective quite as fully as the *Shepheardes Calender*. The general plan of the *Calender* is well known: a small book, published anonymously, it presents a series of eclogues, one for each month of the year, leveraging a dizzying array of poetic forms. Woodcuts at the opening of each poem evoke the humble English almanac; mottoes in Latin, Italian and French connect the project with continental literature; and the genre of the eclogue itself – announced on the title page – links the project with classical models and suggests the first step of the Virgilian *rota*.[19] Chaucer is not mentioned by name in the verse, although four of the eclogues ('Februarie', 'June', 'October' and 'December') make reference to his stand-in, Tityrus the god of shepherds. As the recently departed Tityrus, Chaucer is absent but still known personally to the shepherds – a scenario that recalls his standing among later-day English poets.

The *Calender* also includes a dedicatory epistle addressed to Gabriel Harvey, Spenser's close friend and former tutor; a short history of the eclogue; and numerous glosses, all attributed to E.K.[20] These glosses, which appear after each eclogue, range from one-word explanations for particularly obscure terms used in the verse, to longer entries that explore the etymology of certain words or purport to explicate specific aspects of the poem's allegory and classical allusions.[21] At the time of the *Calender*'s publication in 1579, such an apparatus for a work of English poetry was unprecedented, and E.K.'s notes would have evoked the commentary found in continental editions of authors like Virgil and Petrarch. Even if a reader were to skip or skim over the content of these notes, their presence in the *Calender* suggests that – despite its novelty and unknown author – this is a work worthy of serious scholarly attention.[22]

---

18 Thomas Hoccleve, *The Regiment of Princes*, ed. Charles R. Blyth (Kalamazoo: Medieval Institute Publications, 1999), 4978.
19 The influence of Virgil's career as a model for Spenser's has been well mapped by scholars; see M.L. Donnelly, 'The Life of Vergil and the Aspirations of the "New Poete"', *Spenser Studies*, 17 (2003), 1–35. On Virgil's specific influence in the *Calender* see studies by Nancy Lindheim, 'The Virgilian Design of the *Shepheardes Calender*', *Spenser Studies*, 13 (1999), 1–22; and Rebecca Helfer, 'The Death of the "New Poete": Virgilian Ruin and Ciceronian Recollection in Spenser's the *Shepheardes Calender*', *Renaissance Quarterly*, 56.3 (2003), 723–56 as well as Patrick Cheney, *Spenser's Famous Flight: a Renaissance Idea of a Literary Career* (Toronto: University of Toronto Press, 1993) and Merritt T. Hughes, *Virgil and Spenser* (Berkeley: University of California Press, 1929).
20 For an overview of the debates surrounding the identity of E.K., see Patsy Schere Cornelius, *E.K.'s Commentary on the Shepheardes Calender* (Salzburg: Institut für Englische Sprache und Literatur, 1974), 1–13, and Frances M. Malpezzi, 'E.K., a Spenserian Lesson in Reading', *Connotations*, 4.3 (1994–5), 181–91. See also Peter C. Herman, 'Poets, Pastors, and Antipoetics: A Response to Frances M. Malpezzi, "E.K., A Spenserian Lesson in Reading"', *Connotations*, 6.3 (1997), 316–25. On the significance of the glosses to the rhetorical work of the *Calender*, see Richard McCabe, 'Annotating Anonymity, or Putting a Gloss on *The Shepheardes Calender*', in *Ma[r]king the Text: The Presentation of Meaning on the Literary Page*, ed. Joe Bray, Miriam Handley and Anne C. Henry (Aldershot: Ashgate, 2000), 35–54.
21 On the importance of etymological thought in Spenser's *A View of the Present State of Ireland*, see William Rhodes's chapter in this collection.
22 Johan Kerling suggests that, 'the glosses, too, apart from actually helping the reader, also served to give greater weight to the poems by suggesting that the old words were authentic, and based on scholarly research, and thus helping to "promote" the book in academic circles'. See Kerling,

If the form of E.K.'s commentary suggests we are looking at a work within the classical tradition, its contents point towards a more complex mix of influences and models. E.K.'s notes frequently draw attention to the *Calender*'s use of conventions from Greek and Roman eclogues, and by explicitly connecting Chaucer and Virgil in the figure of Tityrus, E.K. invites readers to understand Chaucer as an analogue to the Roman *auctor* and a worthy progenitor to the *Calender*'s own classicising poet. At the same time, however, E.K. also discusses Chaucer's native 'antiquity'. His glosses for archaic words presume a substantial degree of linguistic and therefore historical distance between that 'new Poete' and Chaucer, whom E.K. calls 'that famous Olde poete' (25). The sharp distinction that E.K. draws here between 'Olde' and 'new' might consign Chaucer to an inert past, in which he serves as a passive resource to be drawn upon by, rather than as a literary model exerting active influence over later-day poets, but it is balanced by the active and animating connection to Virgil via Tityrus. Presented simultaneously in terms of his purported linguistic obsolescence and his affinity with classical models, Chaucer emerges as a hybrid figure, at once a source of 'pure' and native English words and a poetic forefather who can stand alongside the ancients.

E.K.'s commentary reveals the difficulty in disentangling all the sources and models from which 'our new Poete' constructs his poetic persona in the *Calender*. E.K.'s discussion of his glosses in the epistle to Harvey, in particular, reveals significant ambiguity around what constitutes an archaism in an English-language context – a position that reflects the uncertain status of Middle English more broadly at this time. E.K. tells his readers that the *Calender* is a work that 'hath laboured to restore, as to theyr rightfull heritage such good and naturall English words, as have ben long time out of use and almost cleare disherited' (27). The glosses thus offer English readers a much-needed lesson about their own linguistic past:

> Hereunto have I added a certain Glosse or scholion for thexposition of old wordes and harder phrases: which maner of glosing and commenting, well I wote, wil seeme straunge and rare in our tongue: yet for somuch as I knew many excellent and proper devises both in wordes and matter would passe in the speedy course of reading, either as unknowen, or as not marked, and that in this kind, as in other we might be equal to the learned of other nations, I thought good to take the paines upon me, the rather for that by means of some familiar acquaintaunce I was made privie to his counsell and secret meaning in them, and also in sundry other works of his. (29)

'English Old-Word Glossaries 1553–1594', *Neophilologus*, 63 (1979), 136–47 (140). Steven K. Galbraith argues that a similar impression of authentic Englishness and learned commentary is made through the use of black-letter for the verse of the eclogues and roman type for the surrounding commentary (see 'English Black-Letter Type and Spenser's *Shepheardes Calender*', *Spenser Studies*, 23 [2008], 13–40, as well as S.K. Heninger, Jr., 'The Typographical Layout of Spenser's *Shepheardes Calender*', in *Word and Visual Imagination: Studies in the Interaction of English Literature and the Visual Arts*, ed. Karl Josef Höltgen, Peter M. Daly, and Wolfgang Lottes [Earlangen: Univ.-Bibliothek Erlangen-Nürnberg, 1998], 33–71).

E.K. recognises the novelty of his approach, calling the annotations something 'straunge and rare in our tongue'. Nonetheless, he argues that a better knowledge of 'old words and harder phrases' is needed so that Englishmen 'might be equal to the learned of other nations'.

The project of annotating the *Calender*, as E.K. describes it here, is predicated on the importance of understanding the linguistic past, but he avoids stating clearly what, exactly, makes a word archaic. While E.K. expects that some of the words and phrases he glosses will be 'unknown' to readers of the *Calender*, others are simply 'not marked'. Thus, the reader is led to expect that, while some glosses will explain words and terms unfamiliar to sixteenth-century readers, others will draw attention to the antiquity or special meaning of terms still in regular use and hence liable to 'passe in the speedy course of reading'. Not all 'old words and harder phrases' are recognisable as such. Here, E.K.'s phrasing reveals what twenty-first-century literary historians will emphasise time and again: the establishment of any strict break between the 'old' and the 'new' requires rhetorical work and discursive intervention. In the case of the *Calender*, E.K.'s commentary will teach readers what linguistic antiquity looks like in an English context, and why it matters.

There are multiple reasons why an annotator like E.K. might wish to attend to the *Calender*'s use of 'old words and harder phrases'. Highlighting the poet's use of such terms establishes his interest in, and respect for, his native linguistic heritage. As E.K. writes, Spenser in the *Calender* 'hath labored to restore, as to theyr rightfull heritage such good and natural English words, as haue ben long time out of vse and almonst cleare disherited' (27). But the archaic terms associated with Chaucer also help Spenser to achieve a specific poetic effect, and to do so in a way that is explicitly endorsed in classical sources. In this scenario, readers need to understand Chaucer's linguistic antiquity in order to fully appreciate Spenser's classicising poetic accomplishments.

At the end of a long discussion of the eclogues' merits, E.K. turns to their lexicon, observing that,

> [...] the which of many thinges which in him be straunge, I know will seeme the straungest, the words them selues being so auncient, the knitting of them so short and intricate, and the whole Periode and compasse of speache so delightsome for the roundnesse, and so graue for the straungenesse. (25)

E.K. goes on to explain that the presence of these words in the eclogues is the result of the poet's extensive reading of older works, resulting in a kind of literary sunburn:

> I graunt they be something hard, and of most men vnused, yet both English, and also vsed of most Authors and most famous Poetes. In whom whenas this our Poet hath bene much traueiled and thoroughly red, how could it be (as that worthy Oratour sayde) but that walking the sonne although for other cause he walked, yet needs he mought be be sunburnt. (26)

This passage, with its focus on both continuity and difference within the English language, evokes the opening lines of the epistle, which describe Chaucer as the 'olde famous Poete' who is nonetheless the 'lodestar of *our* language'. Here, E.K. keeps the emphasis on Chaucer's language. Like that 'famous olde Poete', the 'old words and harder phrases' associated with him are familiar to E.K.'s audience, but also recognisably anterior to their own linguistic and literary moment. They are 'delightsome for the roundesse' and 'grave for the straungenesse' but they are also 'something hard' and 'of most men unused'; they are 'so auncient' but they are also 'still English'. Marking the antiquity of the words used 'of most Authors and most famous Poetes' fixes Chaucer as a foundational figure from the distant past, whose work can be mined by enterprising later writers like Spenser in search of an archaising turn of phrase.

By asserting the outdatedness of this language alongside its Englishness, E.K. lays the groundwork for a defence of archaic language. Such a defence, however, differs markedly from the terms in which Chaucer's poetry had historically been lauded. As he continues, E.K. praises the aesthetic effect produced by the poet's use of 'old words and harder phrases', declaring that, although such 'olde and obsolete wordes are most used of country folke', when applied according to rules of proportion and decorum, 'they bring great grace and, as one would say, auctoritie to the verse' (14). E.K. explains further:

> For albe amongst many other faultes it specially be obiected of Valla against Liuie, and of other against Saluste, that with ouer much studie they affect antiquitie, as courting thereby credence and honor of elder yeeres, yet I am of opinion, and eke the best learned are of the lyke, that those auncient solemne wordes are a great ornament both in the one and in the other [...] For if my memory fayle not, Tullie in that booke, wherein he endeuoureth to set forth the paterne of a perfect Oratour, sayth that ofttimes an auncient worde maketh the style seeme graue, and as it were reuerend: no otherwise then we honour and reuerence gray heares for a certein religious regard, which we haue of old age. (26)[23]

Following this analogy to its conclusion suggests a very different view of Chaucer's language than the one voiced by fifteenth- and sixteenth-century poets who celebrate Chaucer's 'eloquence'. In the section of the epistle from which this passage comes, Chaucer's 'auncient solemne words' (now appearing in the tongues of Spenser's shepherds) are described as 'fittest for such rusticall rudenesse of shepheards', of 'rough sounde' and 'olde and obsolete'.

---

23 The reference is to Cicero, *De Oratore*, III.153. James M. May and Jakob Wisse translate this passage as follows: 'In the category of individual words, then, there are three types that an orator can employ to lend brilliance and distinction to speech: unusual words, new coinages, and metaphors. Unusual words are, for the most part, archaic ones, words that have long since been abandoned in everyday language because of their antiquity. Their use is more open to the license of the poets than to us, yet a poetic word is, by way of exception, dignified in speech as well [...] When put in the right places, [unusual words] often tend to enhance the grandeur and antiquity of speech.' See *Cicero: On the Ideal Orator*, trans. and ed. May and Wisse (New York: Oxford University Press, 2001).

True, archaisms bring 'great grace and, as one would say, auctoritie to the verse', but this effect is largely a matter of contrast, rather than a quality of the words themselves. E.K. explains this, in part, using a visual analogy:

> But all as in most exquisite pictures they vse to blaze and portraict not onely the daintie lineaments of beautye, but also rounde about it to shadow the rude thickets and craggy clifts, that by the baseness of such parts, more excellency may accrew to the principall; for oftimes we fynde ourselues, I knowe not how, singularly delighted with the shewe of such naturall rudenesse, and take great pleasure in that disorderly order. Euen so doe those rough and harsh termes enlumine and make more clearly to appeare the brightnesse of braue and glorious words. (26–7)

While E.K. does not explicitly name Chaucer in this passage, most references to Chaucer in the monthly glosses do connect him with specific words. If we apply this conceit to the presence of Chaucerian words in the *Calender*, those words are 'rude thickets' and 'craggy clifts', 'natural rudeness' which may delight the viewer/reader but which ultimately serve to 'enlumine and make more clearly to appeare the brightnesse of braue and glorious words'. Those 'braue and glorious words' are Spenser's, not Chaucer's. From this perspective (and despite the epistle's endorsement of native English words), when it comes to contemporary poetic practice, Chaucer's antiquity and the attendant rudeness of his words are a means to an end, rather than an accomplishment in and of themselves. In this way, Chaucer provides Spenser with a 'well of English undefil'd' from which the later poet can draw.

E.K. departs from earlier encomia to Chaucer's language by suggesting Chaucer's words improve the *Calender* not by their presence alone, but more specifically through the contrast with the language of the 'new poet'. This claim does not depend on a sense of continuity and connection, anchored in a common understanding of style and rhetoric, between the medieval poet and his sixteenth-century successors.[24] Instead, E.K. here presumes a break, identifiable on linguistic grounds, between Chaucer and his successors. It is the 'new poet', who can skilfully deploy these archaisms, who benefits from this division.

If E.K. recasts Chaucer's words as 'rude' and 'base' in order to explain their role in Spenser's carefully archaic verse, his portrayal of Chaucer as an author figure seems designed to preserve Chaucer's position as a poetic exemplar. In the *Calender*, this praise of Chaucer is displaced from a vernacular context to a classical one, and Chaucer takes his place among the most revered poets of Latin antiquity. This is clear from the opening lines of E.K.'s epistle to Harvey, which begins,

> Uncouthe unkiste, Sayde the olde famous Poete Chaucer: whom for his excellencie and wonderfull skil in making, his scholler Lidgate, a worthy scholler of so excellent

---

[24] As A.C. Spearing notes, this sense of shared ground with Chaucer often depends upon a view of the medieval poet as exceptional figure, an 'inspired or divine poet mysteriously emerging in an age of darkness and barbarity'. See 'Renaissance Chaucer and Father Chaucer', *English*, 34 (1985), 1–38 (6).

a maister, calleth the Loadestarre of our Language: and whom our Colin clout in his
Æglogue calleth Tityrus the God of shepheards, comparing hym to the worthines of
the Roman Tityrus Virgile. (13)

This passage foregrounds vernacular connections through repetition of the archaic word 'unkent', which also appears in the opening lines of Immeritô's prefatory poem, printed on the opposing page (it begins 'Goe little booke: thy selfe present / As child whose parent is unkent [...]' [24]). The repetition not only links Immeritô and E.K., but also evokes E.K. and Immeritô's shared source, Chaucer's *Troilus and Criseyde*.[25] Yet these lines also anticipate the connection that the eclogues will draw between Chaucer and Virgil. As E.K. indicates here, the two figures are linked through use of the pseudonym Tityrus, Virgil's name for his own authorial persona in his *Eclogues* and the name used for Chaucer by Colin Clout and the other shepherds in the *Calender*.

It is important to note, however, that these parallels remain implicit within the eclogues themselves and that, like the identification of Chaucer's words as 'hard', the connection between Chaucer and Virgil is worked out primarily in the commentary. Neither Chaucer nor Virgil is mentioned by name in the *Calender*'s verse; as Colin Fairweather observes, the articulation of these literary historical relationships is left to E.K.[26] In his comments, E.K. mentions Chaucer by name sixteen times and Virgil twenty-three times (he also refers to Lydgate – whom he calls 'Chaucer's scoller' – and Cicero an additional four times each).[27]

In the eclogues, Chaucer is represented as Tityrus, the god of shepherds whose death Colin mourns in the 'June' eclogue, and from whom Thenot learned the fable of the oak and the briar recounted in the 'Februarie' eclogue. While, in a note to the 'Januarye' eclogue, E.K. connects Spenser's use of the 'Colin Clout' persona with Virgil's use of Tityrus in the *Eclogues*, most of his notes emphasise the Chaucer–Tityrus connection. In a note to the 'Februarie' eclogue, E.K. writes, 'I suppose he meane Chaucer, whose prayse for pleasaunt tales cannot dye, so long as the memorie of hys name shal liue, and the name of Poetrie shal endure' (48). In 'June', he makes a similar observation, highlighting the classical echoes: 'That by Tityrus is meant Chaucer, hath bene already sufficiently sayde, & by thys more playne appeareth, that he sayth, he tolde merye tales. Such as by hys Canterburie tales. whom he calleth the God of Poetes for hys excellencie, so as Tullie calleth Lentulus, Deum vitae suae.s. the God of hys lyfe' (93). And a third time, in 'December', Tityrus is 'Chaucer as hath bene oft sayd' (153). Meanwhile, 'the Romish Tityrus' that Cuddie mentions in the 'October' eclogue is, in E.K.'s words, 'well knowen to be Virgile' (135).

---

25 E.K. paraphrases *Troilus and Criseyde* I.809, while Immeritô evokes the envoy that appears at V.1786–98. See *The Riverside Chaucer*, ed. Larry Benson (Oxford: Oxford University Press, 1988).
26 Colin Fairweather, '"I suppose he meane Chaucer": The Comedy of Errors in Spenser's Shepheardes Calender', *Notes and Queries*, 46 (1999), 193–5.
27 William Kuskin discusses at length Spenser's use of Lydgate, and what it says about the relationship between fifteenth-century writing and early modern poetry. See *Recursive Origins*, 51–69.

These connections, and the degree to which E.K. treats them as obvious or familiar, take admiration for Chaucer and link it not with Chaucer's own words, but with the unquestionable cultural authority of Virgil. Rather than simply a native poetic forbearer, as a vernacular Tityrus to Virgil's 'Romish' exemplar, Chaucer is both English (like Spenser) and 'ancient' (like Virgil). While Chaucer's words are put into service as archaisms in the *Calender*, his persona remains a proximate (if recently departed) presence that both authorises the eclogues as vernacular experiments and links Colin/Spenser to the classical past.

In E.K.'s commentary, Chaucer and his words occupy two different, sometimes competing, concepts of antiquity, in ways that speak to Spenser's own efforts to synthesise these divergent models. On the one hand, Chaucer's language is consigned to a native, vernacular past that is both in need of restoration and available for appropriation. There is a twofold benefit to this characterisation: those old Chaucerian words provide evidence of the antiquity of the poetic tradition within which the *Calender* works, while Spenser's judicious use of archaic language enhances the *Calender* itself along classical models. On the other hand, there is the figure of Chaucer himself, namely Tityrus, whose stories are still told and whose death still impacts Spenser's shepherds, and who is situated in a distinctly Latinate past alongside Virgil himself. E.K.'s insistence that, within the world of the *Calender*, Chaucer is Tityrus and therefore Virgil rewrites Chaucer's own depiction of his work as 'subgit [...] to alle poesye'. While, in Book V of *Troilus and Criseyde*, Chaucer sends his 'litel book' off to 'kis the steppes, whereas thou seest pace / Virgile, Ovide, Omer, Lucan, and Stace', in the *Calender* Chaucer seems not merely to kiss those steps, but ascends to their summit.[28]

Our antient and learned English poet, Geffrey Chaucer

This bifurcated interest in Chaucer as an 'old' author emerges alongside what Catherine Nicholson identifies as a deep investment in estrangement at the heart of Renaissance ideas of eloquence.[29] By foregrounding Chaucer's distance from the present literary and linguistic moment, the *Shepheardes Calender* creates an intra-vernacular dynamic of old and new that parallels the Latin-vernacular relationship. References to Chaucer and Lydgate evoke the tropes of loss, displacement and exile that will be a theme throughout Spenser's career.

The *Calender*'s influence does not end with Spenser but continues into other areas of literary culture, including the ongoing work of editing and publishing Chaucer's collected works. Thomas Speght's 1598 edition of Chaucer's *Works* and its 1602 revision might initially seem to have little in common with the *Calender*. While the *Calender* heralds the debut of an 'unknown' poet in a small, almost ephemeral book, the *Works* represent the latest instalment in a series of handsome folio editions that bring together the writings of one of the best-known and most

---

28 See *Troilus and Criseyde*, V.1786–98.
29 See Catherine Nicholson, *Uncommon Tongues: Eloquence and Eccentricity in the English Renaissance* (Philadelphia: University of Pennsylvania Press, 2013).

uniformly celebrated English poets.[30] Both, however, share a deep concern with Chaucer's place in English literary history, and both use paratext and commentary to explore and explain his role.

Unlike previous editions of Chaucer, which provide a minimal amount of explanatory material, Speght's edition comes replete with interpretive aids. The ornate frontispiece to the 1598 edition announces that readers will find within 'his portraiture and Progenie shewed', 'His Life collected', 'arguments to euery Booke gathered', 'old and obscure words explaned', 'authors by him cited, declared' and 'difficulties opened'.[31] Perhaps the most conspicuous of Speght's additions is his glossary of 'the old and obscure words in Chaucer explaned'. While E.K.'s glosses are distributed throughout the *Calender*, Speght's hard word list appears at the back of the *Works*. Although it generally offers only short definitions, rather than the more wide-ranging commentary that appears in E.K.'s notes, in 1598, Speght's glossary occupies forty-four folio columns and includes more than two thousand terms; in 1602, it is revised and expanded, incorporating additional commentary and adding new information about the etymology of some words. In Speght, each headword is printed in black letter, while the short explanations are printed in Roman type. By leveraging the nostalgic associations of black letter, Speght creates a visual distinction between Chaucer's English and the contemporary English of E.K.'s notes.

Like the *Calender*, the *Works* also use black letter for the central text. While this follows the precedent set by earlier editions of Chaucer's *Works*, at the end of the sixteenth century Speght's use of black letter would have appeared as an example of what Zachary Lesser terms 'typographic nostalgia'.[32] As in the *Calender*, a combination of roman and italic type is used for the secondary commentary, creating a visual distinction between the archaic-seeming text and the scholarly apparatus. Because, even in 1598, the presence of a glossary and other explanatory devices remained highly unusual for the work of an English author, the explicatory materials perform a function similar to E.K.'s commentary in the *Calender*, evoking canonical works in Greek and Latin traditions (as well as continental vernaculars) and constituting a claim for Chaucer's ongoing significance to English language and literature.

In the prefatory materials prepared by Speght, it soon becomes clear that Spenser's poetry was well-known to those involved in the preparation of the *Works*, and that this knowledge extended to E.K.'s commentary on the *Calender*. This is especially evident in the epistle addressed to Speght and written by Francis Beaumont. Echoing the opening lines of E.K.'s epistle to Harvey, Beaumont writes,

---

30 Chaucer's works were first collected in a single-volume folio in 1532. That edition, produced by the courtier William Thynne and printed by Thomas Godfray, was reprinted in 1542 and c.1550. A subsequent edition, enlarged with new poems (mostly apocryphal) provided by the antiquarian John Stow, was published in 1561. This edition is the basis of Speght's.
31 On the place of Spenser in these materials, see Elisabeth Chaghafi's chapter in this volume.
32 Zachary Lesser, 'Typographic Nostalgia: Play-Reading, Popularity, and the Meanings of Black Letter', in *The Book of the Play: Playwrights, Stationers, and Readers in Early Modern England*, ed. Marta Straznicky (Amherst: University of Massachusetts Press, 2006), 99–126.

'so pure were *Chaucers* words in his daies, as *Lidgate* that learned man, calleth him The Loadstarre of the English language' ([a].v). While Beaumont inverts E.K.'s emphasis, praising Chaucer's purity rather than Spenser's ingenuity, the allusions, phrasing, and argument all evoke E.K. in the epistle to Harvey. In the 1598 version of the *Works*, Beaumont continues with the lines with which this chapter opens, drily noting that Spenser's 'much frequenting of Chaucers antient speeches causeth many to allow farre better of [Spenser], then otherwise they would' ([a. iii]) (these remarks may have less to do with Beaumont's honest assessment of Chaucer than with Spenser's highly antagonistic relationship with William Cecil, Lord Burghley and his son, Robert Burghley, to whom Speght's editions of the *Works* are dedicated).[33] The 1602 version of Beaumont's epistle, published after Spenser's death, offers a more moderate assessment of Spenser's accomplishments and Chaucer's place in them. Discussing Chaucer's words, it states that,

> [...] so good they are in our daies, as Maister *Spencer* (following the counsaile of *Tullie* in his third book *De Oratore*, for reviving of aunciente wordes) hath adorned his stile with that beautie and gravitie, that *Tullie* there speakes of: and his much frequenting of *Chaucers* auncient words, with his excellent imitation of diverse places in him, is not the least helpe that hath made him reach so hie, as many learned men doe thinke, that no Poet either French or Italian deserves second place under him. ([a].v.)

Even as it continues to subjugate Spenser's achievements to Chaucer's, this passage reflects the importance of classical poetic theory to an understanding of the relationship between Chaucer and Spenser. Like the epistle to Harvey in the *Calender*, Beaumont's letter explains Spenser's use of Chaucerian words in Ciceronian terms. As in the *Calender*, it is the fact that Chaucer and, by extension, his words are 'aunciaent' and therefore available for appropriation that enables a specific and classicising poetic strategy among later writers.

Elsewhere, Speght makes straightforward reference to *The Faerie Queene* and the *Calender*, as well as E.K.'s commentary on it:

> Master *Spenser* in his first Eglogue of his Shepheards Kalender, calleth him *Titirus*, the god of Shepheards, comparing him to the worthinesse of the Romane Titirus Virgil. In his Faerie Queene [...] he termeth him, Most renowmed and Heroicall Poet: and his writings, The works of heavenly wit: concluding his commendation in this manner:
>
> > Dan Chaucer, Well of English, undefiled,
> > On Fames eternall beadrole worthy to be filed.
> > I follow here the footing of thy feet,
> > That with thy meaning so I may the rather meet. (C.iii^v)

---

33 On Spenser's long and multifaceted conflict with Burghley, see Bruce Danner, *Edmund Spenser's War on Lord Burghley* (Basingstoke: Palgrave Macmillan, 2011).

Here, again, the commentary places emphasis on the ways in which Spenser's writings engage both Chaucer and classical literary figures. The mention of the Tityrus–Virgil–Chaucer connection might be particularly telling since, as discussed above, it is in E.K.'s commentary (rather than the verse itself) that this link is made explicit.

While moments like these make it clear that those responsible for the preparation of the *Works* in 1598 and 1602 were familiar with Chaucer's influence on Spenser, the *Works* as a whole demonstrate what might be called a Spenserian understanding of Chaucer. In the materials added by Speght, Chaucer appears as a figure at once both distant and familiar. Read in light of the *Calender*, it becomes clear that the *Works* seek to represent the medieval poet's writings as exemplifying the same kind of Latin-vernacular hybridity that E.K. celebrates in the *Calender*. Rather than simply epitomising all that is best in a distinctively native literary tradition, the *Works* treat Chaucer as a poet who combines vernacular poetry with a sophisticated adherence to ancient models. By pushing Chaucer back towards classical antiquity, Speght presents a figure with new relevance for a sixteenth-century audience. Like E.K.'s commentary, the explanatory materials found in the 1598 and 1602 editions of the *Works* mark Chaucer as both familiar and strange, a recognisable figure and yet also one in need of scholarly explication. That explication, like E.K.'s notes, is dedicated to cultivating in readers a proper sense of Chaucer's historical distance. In this, it mirrors broader trends in antiquarian scholarship that extend far beyond the literary realm. In the 1602 version of the dedicatory epistle to Robert Cecil, Speght surveys many improvements made to the *Works* and concludes that, 'I have reformed the whole Worke, whereby Chaucer for the most part is restored to his owne Antiquitie', a phrase that evokes both the *Calender*'s handling of Chaucer and William Camden's *Britannia*, which promises to restore 'Britaine to her antiquity, and antiquity to Britain'.[34]

A few examples illustrate this point: while previous editions advertise themselves as 'the Works of Geoffrey Chaucer', the frontispiece in Speght's edition announces 'the Works of Our Most Ancient and learned English poet, Geoffrey Chaucer'. 'English' explicitly links Chaucer with national identity, while 'Most Ancient' foregrounds Chaucer's antiquity. At the same time, it blurs the line between the classical past and the national past since the term could be used to refer to both classical antiquity and more recent and local history.[35] To call Chaucer, a post-Conquest writer who died in 1400, 'most ancient' asserts that Chaucer's 'then' is fundamentally different from the implied 'now' of the *Works*' readership. And yet

---

34 William Camden, *Britain, or A chorographicall description of the most flourishing kingdomes, England, Scotland, and Ireland, and the ilands adjoyning, out of the depth of antiquitie beautified vvith mappes of the severall shires of England*, trans. Philemon Holland ([London], 1637), [a].iii. Holland's translation is based on the 1607 Latin edition, published by John Norton and George Bishop, both of whom were also involved in publishing Speght's edition of the *Works*.
35 A similar blurring takes place in the Scene 1 of Shakespeare's *Pericles* (1607–8) in which 'From ashes ancient Gower is come', to tell a story set in the distant Mediterranean past. See *Pericles*, ed. Barabara Mowat (New York: Simon & Schuster, 2005), 7.

Chaucer shares his 'English' (and quite possibly also the 'learned') identity with his sixteenth-century readers, suggesting both continuity and change.

Speght explores Chaucer's combined Englishness and antiquity more fully in an epistle addressed to readers of the *Works*. Here, Speght's discussion of Chaucer's 'ancient'ness mirrors E.K.'s treatment of similar issues in the *Calender*. While E.K. uses classical rhetorical theory to explain Spenser's use of archaic words, Speght takes a slightly different approach in the *Works*, drawing on Latin and Greek authorities to explain aspects of Chaucer's language that might be off-putting for readers. Both men rely on comparisons to Greek and Latin literature as they defend Chaucer's poetic accomplishments and continued relevance to poetic discourse. Speght informs readers that they 'must not condemne in [Chaucer] as a fault' his unfamiliar versions of Latin and Greek names, such as 'Adriane' where readers might expect 'Ariadne' ([a].ii^v). Instead, Speght writes, Chaucer's non-standard spelling should be considered 'metaplasmus', a term Richard Mulcaster defines as 'alterations of the words form and favor' ([a].iii^v).[36] Chaucer's spelling, like Spenser's use of archaic English words, is read here as a sign of his compatibility with classical rhetorical precepts. Similarly, Speght identifies Chaucer's double negatives with the analogous grammatical construction in ancient Greek (a language Chaucer did not know): 'it is his manner likewise, imitating the Greekes, by two negatives to cause a greater negation: as, I ne said none ill' ([a].iii^v). In both cases, Speght defends Chaucer's 'old and obscure' words not by stressing their connection to present-day English or by faulting later readers for failing to recognise their excellence, but by framing his discussion of them in classical terms. This attempt to explain the vernacular writing of the past to the present by recourse to a common classical heritage recalls E.K.'s explication of classical tropes and allusions in *The Shepheardes Calender*. While E.K.'s focus is ultimately with the 'new Poete', Speght returns attention to Chaucer's language as he argues for a synthesis between the antique and the vernacular.

In the *Calender*, E.K. seeks to produce a more informed reading of Spenser's eclogues by educating its readers about their use of archaisms, both unknown and passed over. Speght, too, will educate the reader of the *Works* so that she or he can properly appreciate Chaucer's lines. This includes, in addition to materials like the glossary, a brief defence of Chaucer's metre, where in the 1602 revision Speght claims that the 'skilfull Reader' of Chaucer's verses can 'scan them in their nature' and find appropriate metre in them ([A.iii]). Any irregularities are the result of textual corruption due to the 'negligence and rape of Adam Scrivener'. In support of his claim, Speght cites Chaucer's own words from the fifth book of *Troilus and Criseyde*,

> And for there is so great diversitie
> In English, and in writing of our tongue,

---

[36] See Richard Mulcaster, *The first part of the elementarie which entreateth chefelie of the right writing of our English tung* (London, 1582), 142.

> So pray I God, that none miswrite thee,
> Ne thee mismetre for defaut of tongue, &c. ([a].iv)[37]

According to Speght, these lines are proof 'how fearfull [Chaucer] was to have his works miswritten, or his verse mismeasured', a comment that imagines Chaucer looking towards his own future reception, even as he recalls, in the preceding stanza of the *Troilus*, his debt to classical *auctores*.[38]

Comments like these, as well as the *Works*' larger paratextual apparatus, serve as analogues to E.K.'s commentary in the *Calender* and express a fundamentally Spenserian understanding of Chaucer and his language. Like E.K., Speght and Beaumont theorise Chaucer's importance by situating the medieval poet in relation to both contemporary and classical poetic practice. In the process, Chaucer and his language are definitively marked as 'ancient', but at the same time, Speght's comments on Chaucer's writing imagine an author who fully embodies a set of poetic values more closely associated with ancient Greek and Latin texts. Like the *Calender*, the Speght *Works* presents readers with a hybridised Chaucer who plays two distinct but complementary roles: on the one hand, he is the founder of a tradition of English eloquence; on the other, he carries forward a still older poetic tradition associated with figures like Virgil.

E.K.'s influence on the presentation of Chaucer at the end of the sixteenth century was not inevitable: Spenser was not the only poet mindful of the way that Chaucer shaped the tradition of English literature, and an edition of Chaucer's writings offering an extended explanatory apparatus would have appeared at some point regardless of Spenser's use of Chaucer in his own writings. Nonetheless, the timing of the *Calender*'s publication and the scholarly form that E.K.'s comments take mean that his perspective on Chaucer has much to do with the way that Thomas Speght and Francis Beaumont present Chaucer in the 1598 and 1602 *Works*. E.K.'s commentary performs a complex set of rhetorical negotiations, in which 'auncient' English words are portrayed as 'rusticall' and 'rough', but Chaucer re-emerges as an authorial figure on par with Virgil. While it may seem that, by putting Chaucer into dialogue with classical authorities like Virgil and Cicero, E.K. seeks to cast Chaucer back into a still-more distant 'antiquity', Speght's commentary shows how this same act of historical distancing can provide those responsible for presenting Chaucer in print with a rich new vocabulary for thinking and writing about 'the old Famous Poete'.

---

37 See *Troilus and Criseyde*, V.1793-6.
38 On these lines, see Spearing, 17-19.

9

Worthy friends: Speght's Chaucer and Speght's Spenser

Elisabeth Chaghafi

Speght's editions and Speght's 'additions'

Among early modern editions of Chaucer's works, Thomas Speght's 1598 *The Workes of our Antient and lerned English Poet, GEFFREY CHAVCER, newly Printed* stands out as the first to accompany Chaucer's text with supplementary materials. Speght, a schoolmaster and antiquary with a particular interest in heraldry, had prepared the edition with the help of his fellow antiquary and veteran Chaucer editor John Stow.[1] The supplementary materials added by Speght were 'The Life of Geffrey Chaucer', an overview of the 'Arguments to euery Tale and Booke', a glossary of over 2,000 'old and obscure words' used by Chaucer, translations of French phrases, a list of 'Most of the Authors cited by G. Chaucer', as well as some more detailed notes on Chaucer's text.[2] Apart from his own 'additions' (as he called them), Speght's edition also contained some paratextual materials: a dedicatory epistle to Sir Robert Cecil; a preface 'To the Readers'; a commendatory letter from Francis Beaumont, 'F.B. to his very louing friend, T.S.', dated 1597; a commendatory poem called 'The Reader to Geffrey Chaucer', signed 'H.B.' (tentatively identified by David Matthews as Beaumont's older brother, Henry); an engraved portrait of Chaucer based on the famous Hoccleve portrait; and the dedicatory epistle to Henry VIII that had originally been written for William Thynne's edition of 1532.[3] This chapter proposes that the additional materials were written or selected by Speght for his editions in order to highlight both Chaucer's datedness and his continued relevance. For this purpose, I begin by describing the paratextual and supplementary materials of the 1598 and 1602 editions. This is followed by a discussion of how these materials create a framework for early modern readers to regard Chaucer as an author firmly situated in the past but nevertheless still worth

---

1 Stow, who is now best known for his *Suruay of London* (also published in 1598), had published his own edition of Chaucer's works – the most recent one before Speght's – in 1561. Prior to his involvement in Speght's edition, he had also edited the *Pithy pleasaunt and profitable workes of maister Skelton, Poete Laureate* (1568).
2 Title page (1598).
3 David Matthews, 'Public Ambition, Private Desire and the Last Tudor Chaucer', in *Reading the Medieval in Early Modern England*, ed. Gordon McMullan and David Matthews (Cambridge: Cambridge University Press, 2007), 74–88 (77).

reading. The final section analyses how this double strategy of Speght's is exemplified in the way in which his editions frame the relationship between Chaucer and Spenser as an imaginary 'friendship' across the centuries.

The supplementary materials were Speght's main contribution to his edition, and through their sheer bulk they formed a contrast to all previous printed editions of Chaucer's works, which had reproduced the preface to Thynne's edition as the only introduction to Chaucer's text. In his preface, 'To the Readers', Speght claimed to have written his 'additions' only for the use of his 'priuat friends', who had urged him to have his collected glosses and explanations printed when an opportunity presented itself:

> But so it fell out of late that *Chaucers* Works being in the Presse, and three parts thereof already printed, not only these friends did by their Letters sollicit me, but certaine also of the best in the Companie of Stationers hearing of these Collections, came vnto me, and for better or worse would haue something done in this Impression. ('To the Readers' (1598), aij^v)

To sceptical readers, Speght's apology for 'publishing that which was never purposed nor perfected for open view' (a.ij^v) sounds less like a factual account than like a general disclaimer for potential inaccuracies and a modesty topos of the type favoured by early modern authors who did not wish to appear to be seeking the medium of print too eagerly. To lend further credibility to Speght's story, the preface was followed by a letter from such a 'priuat' friend – Francis Beaumont, father of the playwright of the same name. In that letter, Beaumont playfully threatens to have Speght's supplements to Chaucer's works published even against his will: 'If you will not put them abroad your selfe, they shall abroad whether you will or no' (Beaumont letter (1598), aiiij^r). Yet even this supporting evidence for Speght's account regarding the transition of his 'additions' to Chaucer from manuscript into print may need to be taken with a pinch of salt, because on closer inspection Beaumont's letter bears signs of editorial intervention, which Speght evidently did not regard as being at odds with the desire for factual accuracy expressed throughout his paratextual materials. Although Beaumont had died in 1598 – the letter is dated 1597 – the version of the letter printed in the revised 1602 edition contained substantial expansions and revisions that suggest Speght had adapted it to reflect what he would have liked Beaumont to have said, transforming the letter from a piece of supporting evidence into a second preface outlining the key ideas of his edition in somebody else's voice.[4] Speght also employs this strategy of adapting a source in order to express a point he wishes to make in a more fitting way in his other supplementary materials, most notably

---

4 Several decades later, the early modern biographer Izaak Walton used a similar strategy in his *Lives* to recreate the voices of his dead subjects from their own writings. So, for example, he merged several of John Donne's letters in order to create a 'typical' letter expressing Donne's state of mind at a particular point in his life.

in the 'Life of Chaucer' to create his fiction of a friendship between Spenser and Chaucer, discussed in detail in the final section of this chapter.

Speght evidently attached great importance to his 'additions'. This is clear from the numerous revisions and emendations he made to them for the 1602 edition, which reveal Speght's antiquarian thoroughness and love of detail.[5] Many of the actual changes Speght made to his 'additions' in the 1602 edition appear trivial at first sight, as they are merely small corrections regarding dates or the naming of sources, or additional passages cited in support of a point. Collectively, however, the changes show how seriously Speght took his annotations and glosses, and some of them suggest that he took pains to verify even minor points.[6] In the 1602 version of the dedication to Cecil – which is not so much a fresh dedication as a brief account of the improvements made to the supplementary materials – Speght announces the most visible change to the glossary of hard words: 'I haue [...] likewise proued the significations of most of the old and obscure words, by the tongues and dialects, from whence they are deriued' (Dedication (1602), aij^r).

Nevertheless, the changes to the glossary did not only concern additions. The 1602 glossary also merged multiple entries for the same words, while others were expanded or modified in an attempt to narrow down or correct the meanings of words given in the previous edition, or to provide more detailed descriptions. So, for example, the synonym given for 'arten' changes from 'constraine' to 'restraine' (Glossary (1602), Ttti^v), the entry for 'Besant' changed from simply 'a ducket' to 'a Greekish coyne called Bizantium, as *William Malmesburi* sayth, because it was the coyne of Constantinople, sometime called Bizantium' (Tttij^r), the new entry for 'cruil' read 'curled' instead of 'smooth' (Tttiij^v), and the definition of 'autentike' changed from 'of antiquity' to 'of authority' (Ttti^v). The numerous duplicate entries that are new to the 1602 version also indicate that the glossary went through multiple revisions and that Speght made an effort to realphabetise it afterwards – or at least instructed someone to do so. Additionally, some of the longer notes printed separately in the 1598 edition were incorporated into the glossary for ease of reference. Speght's main concern in his modifications to the glossary thus seems to have been to enhance the list's practical usefulness to readers rather than simply making particularly visible changes (such as doubling the number of entries) that could be advertised on the title page. In fact, although the glossary

---

5 In his preface to the 1598 edition, Speght had even gone as far as to actively invite readers to alert him to any remaining inaccuracies they happened to spot in the 'additions': 'I earnestly entreat all friendly Readers, that if they find anie thing amisse they would lend me their skilfull helpe against some other time & I wil thankefully receiue their labors' (aij^v–aiij^r). At least one of Speght's readers accepted this invitation to provide critical feedback: Francis Thynne sent him an open letter outlining some fifty errors in the 'additions' (*Animaduersions vppon the Annotacions and Corrections of some imperfections of impressiones of Chaucers workes*, published by the Early English Text Society in 1865). In the 1602 edition, Speght incorporated many of the changes suggested by Thynne. For a detailed account of Thynne's points of criticism and the marginalia he wrote on his copy of the 1598 edition, see Megan Cook's essay 'How Francis Thynne Read His Chaucer', *Journal of the Early Book Society*, 15 (2012), 215–43.
6 For example, in the 1602 version of the 'Life of Chaucer', Speght made several changes to a gloss describing John Gower's monument in Southwark. While his changes to the description of Gower's headdress are most likely owed to Francis Thynne's 'Animaduersions', Speght also changes the colour of Gower's 'habit of [...] damaske' (which Thynne had not commented on) from 'purple'

of the 1602 edition contains more changes than the 'Life of Chaucer', the 1602 title page begins with '1 In the life of Chaucer many things inserted', while the only change to the glossary referred to – in fourth place – is the new system of classifying words according to their language of origin.[7] Although this is the most noticeable difference between the two versions of the glossary, it is hardly the one most likely to help readers in understanding Chaucer's language. While Speght evidently took pains to make his glossary as practical and easy to use as possible, it would nevertheless be wrong to conclude that its sole function in the volume was to make Chaucer more accessible to readers.[8] It also played a key part in Speght's strategy of framing Chaucer as an ancient poet and reminding his contemporaries of how far removed Chaucer's age was from their own, as will be discussed in the next section.

The significance that the 'additions' held for Speght is also evident in the appearance of the volume itself. Rather than highlighting some of the contents to advertise the fact that the volume contained all of Chaucer's most famous and most popular works in a bid to attract buyers, as other contemporary editions of collected works did, the title page of Speght's 1598 edition began by listing the 'additions', of which only the last – 'Two Bookes of his neuer before printed' – concerned (unspecified) additional material by Chaucer (see Figure 9.1).[9]

The only piece of supplementary material in the 1598 edition not listed on the title page was a relatively short section towards the end of the book, called 'The French in Chaucer, translated', which provided translations of twenty-nine short French phrases (in the 1602 edition, this was expanded to 'The Latine and French, not Englished by Chaucer, translated').

In addition to the supplementary and explanatory materials supplied by Speght, the volume also contained several paratextual materials, such as dedications and prefaces, as well as images. While these were not strictly 'additions' to Chaucer's works in Speght's sense of the word, they had clearly been chosen with care and had a

---

to 'greenish'. This suggests that he either consulted additional sources or visited the monument himself to get a more accurate description. Either way, Speght seems to have gone to a lot of trouble, considering the appearance of Gower's monument is of little consequence to the 'Life of Chaucer' (let alone Chaucer's works). Ironically, in this case Speght's scrupulousness led him to introduce a new error: Gower's garment in the Southwark monument is blood-red, that is 'purple' 2c in the OED (rather fittingly, considering Speght's admiration for Spenser, the earliest example cited in the entry is from the 1590 *Faerie Queene*).

7 The remaining differences listed on the title page refer to the 'reforming' of the text through old copies (2), the addition of 'sentences and proverbs' (3), the translation of French and Latin phrases (5) and the addition of two (apocryphal) texts (6).

8 On the question of how obscure and obsolete Chaucer's language might have seemed to late sixteenth-century readers see Megan Cook's chapter in this volume.

9 The title of the first collected works of Sir Philip Sidney as given on its title page (*The Covntesse of Pembrokes Arcadia. Written by Sir Philip Sidney Knight. Now for the third time published, with sundry new additions of the same author*, also published in 1598) highlighted the fact that it contained Sidney's best known work. Similarly, the title page of the first complete edition of Edmund Spenser's works, published by Matthew Lownes from 1611 onwards, specifically referred to Spenser's most popular works: *The faerie queen: The Shepheards Calendar: together with the other works of Englands arch-poët Edm. Spencer*. Both of those were of course commercial editions in the broadest sense of the word (for the peculiar nature of the Spenser folio as a consumer product see Steven Galbraith's essay 'Spenser's First Folio: The Build-It-Yourself Edition', *Spenser Studies*, 11 (2006), 21–49). By contrast, the only indication that Speght may have targeted his editions at a wider audience is the fact that he offered translations for some French and Latin phrases in his additions.

Figure 9.1 Title page of Speght's 1598 edition of Chaucer's works

similar function for shaping both the *Workes* and their author, the 'Antient and lerned English Poet' Speght was hoping to introduce to readers of the edition. That is, like Speght's own 'additions', the paratexts by other authors also serve to frame Chaucer as either an ancient poet requiring explanation or as a poet whose works continued to be of relevance (occasionally even both, as in the case of Beaumont's letter).

It is of course impossible to know to what extent Speght's efforts were appreciated by his contemporaries (except for Robert Cecil, dedicatee of both of Speght's editions, who appears to have ignored both pleas for patronage). The study of paratexts can be instructive regarding what we might call 'editorial intention'; that is, it can help to reveal information about how the people who wrote or arranged them viewed the 'main' text and how they wanted their readers to read. Yet we must not make the mistake of assuming that this always corresponded to how the books in question were actually read. Thus the 'additions' and paratexts with which Speght supplemented Chaucer's works are fascinating in what they reveal about the amount of thought and scholarship he invested into the project, but it is nevertheless possible that at least some of the buyers of Speght's editions were primarily interested in owning and reading a classic text that had not been printed in several decades. So they may have glanced at the portrait of Chaucer, briefly skimmed the 'Life of Chaucer' and then turned straight to the *Canterbury Tales*, occasionally referring to Speght's most practical addition, the glossary, but otherwise largely ignoring the 'additions'. Yet even if Speght's editorial efforts may have gone unnoticed by his intended readership, they are nonetheless of particular interest. Collectively, the paratexts and additional materials provided by Speght reveal the peculiar double agenda that motivated him to re-edit the works of a poet who, though not forgotten, had gone out of fashion by the late sixteenth century.

'Antient' Chaucer

Fundamentally, Speght's 'additions' pursue two aims that would seem mutually exclusive: to present Chaucer as an 'antient' poet firmly situated in the past, but also to argue for his continued importance and relevance as an English classic. Thus they present a newly recovered, perhaps even 'modern' Chaucer to late sixteenth- and early seventeenth-century readers once they had managed to get past the 'old and obscure' language with the help of the 'additions'.[10]

The decades that had passed since the Chaucer editions of Speght's two predecessors, Thynne and Stow, had seen a shift in how Chaucer, and more specifically Chaucer's language, was perceived. In the preface to his 1532 edition, Thynne had still argued for Chaucer's significance as a poet by drawing attention to his services to the English language, which he described as 'fram[ing] a tongue before so rude and imperfite, to such a sweete ornature and composition' (quoted after 1598, ¶i^v). Towards the end of the sixteenth century, however, it was Chaucer's own language that was routinely referred to as 'rude' – most notably in the Epistle

---

10 See also David Matthews's essay, which argues that although the main aim of Speght's edition seems to lie in the recovery of a medieval author, it also presents readers with a 'contemporary' Chaucer.

of *The Shepheardes Calender*, where 'E.K.' had speculated that the poet may have chosen to include archaic-sounding, Chaucerian terms, 'thinking them fittest for such rusticall rudenesse of shepheards [...] for that theyr rough sounde would make his rymes more ragged and rustical'.[11]

At the same time, Chaucer's subject matter came to be regarded as rather vulgar and lacking refinement, as is apparent for example in the defence of Chaucer's 'broad' speeches in Beaumont's letter. In *Greenes Vision* (London, 1592), a pamphlet that humorously addresses the subject of authorial careers and explores the question whether an author should aim to do more than simply entertain his readers, Chaucer is famously portrayed as the jolly advocate of light entertainment.[12] Greene's portrayal of Chaucer is perhaps not to be taken entirely at face value given the context of *Greenes Vision*. It was written shortly after a mock-Chaucerian romance called *The Cobler of Caunterburie* (1590), 'a merry worke [...], conteining plesant tales, a litle tainted with scurilitie' (*Greenes Vision*, C2^r), had been falsely attributed to Greene.[13] Greene's description of Chaucer as an unabashedly trashy writer who encourages the narrator to continue writing in popular genres is clearly a comical exaggeration that may be explained by Greene's eagerness to deny authorship of the anonymous pamphlet and to distance himself from Chaucer as much as possible.[14] Nevertheless, the notion that forms the basis for Greene's exaggeration – that Chaucer stands for 'broad' language and light entertainment – seems like a typical example of the 'doubtfull coniectures' about Chaucer of which Beaumont's letter accuses his contemporaries.[15]

For late-sixteenth-century Chaucer enthusiasts like Beaumont and Speght, the easiest way of accounting for those perceived deficiencies of Chaucer's without calling his status as the 'Loadstarre of the English language' into question was simply to acknowledge his ancientness.[16] This offered a convenient excuse for any 'incivilitie' (by gently reminding readers that Chaucer had lived in a somewhat unrefined age), as well as for any real or imagined rudeness or archaism of language. Consequently, Chaucer's ancientness also forms the basis of Beaumont's defence in his letter, in which he not only observes that 'no man can so write [...],

---

11 Edmund Spenser, *The Shepheardes Calender* (London, 1579), ¶ij^r.
12 See *Greenes Vision*, C2^v–C3^r.
13 Although the frame narrative of *Greenes Vision* dates it to 1590 or 1591, it was only published following his death in 1592 (as one of several pamphlets purporting to be Greene's final work), most likely as a marketing ploy by its publisher, Thomas Newman, who sought to capitalise on the sudden demand.
14 Additionally, it is a key function of Chaucer's character in the text to act as a foil for his grave counterpart, Gower, who of course gives very different advice to the narrator.
15 Beaumont letter (1598), aiiij^r. For a different reading of Greene's portrayal of Chaucer, see Glen Steinberg's article 'Spenser's *Shepheardes Calender* and the Elizabethan Reception of Chaucer', *English Literary Renaissance*, 35 (2005), 31–51, which argues that it is an 'anti-literary [attack] on Chaucer's moral worth' (35).
16 The phrase is originally Lydgate's, and both Speght and Beaumont seem to have thought of it as a fitting way to describe Chaucer's role. Beaumont references it in his letter (aiij^v) and Speght cites the relevant passage in the 'Life of Chaucer' (cii^r). In both cases, this is closely followed by a reference to Spenser, perhaps in acknowledgement of the fact that the phrase had also famously been invoked in the first sentence of the Epistle of *The Shepheardes Calender* (¶ij^r).

as that all his wordes may remaine currant many yeares' but also cites Horace, an author even more ancient than Chaucer, in support of his claim.[17]

Yet even if Chaucer was already regarded as an 'antient' author by Speght's contemporaries, some of Speght's additions deliberately stress Chaucer's datedness and distance from the present in ways that earlier editions, such as Thynne's or Stow's, had not done. First there are two visual reminders of 'antient' Chaucer. The title pages – which differ between the surviving copies – have one thing in common: their elaborate frames featuring elements of classical architecture, perhaps a visual echo of the comparison between Chaucer and the classics made in Beaumont's letter.[18] Additionally, 'The Progenie of Geffrey Chaucer', an illustration inserted towards the beginning of the volume, depicted a family tree displaying numerous coats of arms connecting Chaucer to John of Gaunt, the tomb of Chaucer's son Thomas (also covered in coats of arms) and, at the centre of the image, a portrait of Chaucer, above the inscription 'The true portraiture of GEFFREY CHAUCER the famous English poet: as by THOMAS OCCLEUE who liued in his time, and was his Scholar' (see Figure 9.2).[19]

Although the image is indeed based on the famous Hoccleve portrait, the engraver has made two changes: Chaucer's right hand – which in the Hoccleve portrait points to the text – now grasps the inkhorn around his neck, and while the portrait in the Hoccleve manuscript ends at the waist, the engraver of the image used in Speght's edition has turned it into a full-length portrait by extending the folds of the garment and adding a pair of legs in quaint-looking pointed shoes.[20] The effect of both these changes is that unlike in the original portrait, the reader's view is directed away from Chaucer's face and towards his 'period' dress. In some surviving copies, Chaucer's image is facing the commendatory poem 'The Reader to Geffrey Chaucer', which begins with the following lines:

---

17 Beaumont letter (1598), aiij'. After this, the 1602 edition adds a quotation from *Troilus and Criseyde*, introduced by the phrase 'and *Chaucer* most excellently also himselfe in true foresight hereof in these verses of his' (Beaumont letter (1602), aiij'). Beaumont's – or, more likely, Speght's – use of the word 'foresight' seems peculiar here, given that he could hardly be regarded as having 'foreseen' Horace's observation. Arguably, the key difference between the quotations from Horace and Chaucer is that the passage from Horace is framing the fact that language ages as a general truth or a law of nature, while the Chaucer quotation specifically refers to a reader's sense of estrangement when encountering a sample of language current 'within a hundredth yeere'. Consequently, what Speght calls Chaucer's 'foresight' here is that the passage in a sense anticipates an early modern reader's view of his own language as 'straunge'. This in turn allows Speght to give his readers a glimpse of 'modern' Chaucer even in a passage that otherwise serves to highlight his datedness.
18 The title page designs seem to have been selected for their monumental appearance. At least one of them, which belonged to George Bishop, had been used before for two unrelated titles published by him (*Sermons of Master Iohn Caluin vpon the booke of Iob*, first published in 1574, and the 1587 edition of Holinshed's *Chronicles*).
19 'The Progenie of Geffrey Chaucer' (insert). The arrangement of the coats of arms in the image also serves to ennoble Chaucer and visually make him John of Gaunt's equal: their arms are depicted at equal height and distance from 'Payne Roet Knight', who is thus made to appear as a common ancestor to both – though Speght's account in the 'Life of Chaucer' reveals that this is only based on somewhat shaky evidence, which suggested that John of Gaunt and Chaucer became brothers in law through a second marriage ('Life of Chaucer' (1598), biij').
20 The shoes may have been suggested by Robert Greene's detailed description of Chaucer, which contains the line 'his shoes were corned broad before' (*Greenes Vision* (1591), C').

Figure 9.2 'The progenie of Geffrey Chaucer' (1602)

>   Rea.Where hast thou dwelt, good Geffrey al this while,
>   Vnknowne to vs saue only by thy bookes?
>   Chau.In haulks, and hernes, God wot, and in exile,
>   Where none vouchsaft to yeeld me words or lookes [...] ('Reader to GC' (1598), av^v)

The archaisms 'haulks' and 'hernes' are helpfully glossed by Speght in his own list of hard words as both meaning 'corners'. So while the situation described by Chaucer in the poem (not being considered worth a look or word by modern readers) was effectively remedied as soon as a reader of the volume opened it on that page, both the image and the poem present their 'true' Chaucer as firmly situated in the past: a figure in funny clothes and using old and obscure language.

Above all, the emphasis on 'antient' Chaucer is evident in the glossary, which by its sheer length suggests to readers that Chaucer's works are in need of significant amounts of explanation and annotation – even if some of the words explained are perhaps less 'old and obscure' than others. For example, it is hard to believe that the readers of Speght's edition really needed to be told that 'besiegeden' meant 'besieged' (Glossary (1602), Tttij^r), that 'beest' referred to 'a beast' (Tttij^r) and 'bole' to 'a Bull' (Tttij^v), or that 'but' could also mean 'except' (Tttij^v). What the inclusion of those seemingly unnecessary entries does, however, is to draw the reader's attention to old grammatical forms or old-fashioned spellings that, while they may not have been too 'old and obscure' to understand for Speght's contemporaries, are likely to have acted as constant reminders of the texts' age.

Even Speght's numerous references to the two older editions of Chaucer's works serve to highlight the distance between the readers of his editions and the 'antient' author. John Stow's 1561 edition is evoked by the reproduction of its title page (which had featured a large image of the Chaucer coat of arms, with the caption 'Vertue flourisheth in Chaucer still, / Though death of him hath wrought his will').[21] However, the edition that Speght refers to much more often is William Thynne's, which had first been published sixty-six years earlier, in 1532. In the 1598 edition, Thynne's edition is referred to in passing in the dedication to Cecil (in Speght's remark that 'this book when it was first published in print [...] was dedicated to the Kings most excellent Maiestie Henry the eight' (Dedication (1598), aij^r)), but 'that learned gentleman M. William Thynne' also heads the list of the 'men of later time' named in the 'Life of Chaucer' as having written favourably about Chaucer (ciij^r). The dedicatory epistle of the 1602 edition directly refers to 'Ma. William Thynne's praise-worthy labours' as a text Speght had consulted in order to 'reform' the text (Dedication (1602), aij^r) and contains additional references to Thynne via Speght's mentions of Francis Thynne and his plans to 'set out Chaucer with a Coment in

---

21 The 1598 edition used only the coat of arms on the page facing the beginning of the Knight's Tale. Speght may have selected it because of his heraldic interests. He also attached particular significance to Chaucer's arms when discussing the question of his origins in the 'Parentage' section of the 'Life of Chaucer', which contains a much less elaborate illustration. The 1602 edition reproduced the entire title page including the title and used it to introduce Lydgate's Siege of Thebes, which had been included in Stow's edition (and referred to in its title) but was a new addition to Speght's 1602 edition.

our tongue, as the Italians haue *Petrarke* and others in their language', using 'helps left to him by his father' (To the Readers' (1602), aij^v).[22] Most significantly, both of Speght's editions reprint the dedicatory epistle of Thynne's edition in full.[23] Unlike Stow, who in his 1561 edition had reprinted the epistle under the heading 'The Prologue' without further explanation, Speght in 1598 contextualised it by giving it the title '*The Epistle of William Thinne to King Henry the eight*' (the original title in the 1532 text is simply 'The Preface'), and also implicitly assigning the text its function as a voice from the past.[24] Although Speght's edition modernised the spelling of the epistle (converting Englysh into English), it nevertheless contains forms such as 'amonges', 'corrupcion' or 'Spanissh' that are likely to have struck readers as somewhat old-fashioned if not actually archaic in 1598 – if not in 1561.[25] However, while Stow's edition (like Thynne's) had used Tuke's epistle to the king strictly as a prologue – that is solely as an introduction to Chaucer's text in the absence of any other prefatory materials – Speght's inclusion of it framed by his own 'additions' recontextualises it as a historical document and a sort of testimony from a learned Chaucer reader who knew to appreciate him and did not consider his language to be 'rude'.[26] As such, it not only acts as proof of the excellence of Chaucer's language, but also reminds Speght's readers that until the recent past, that excellence had still been valued as it ought to be.

22 Francis Thynne's edition never seems to have been published, although he supplied a poem, 'Vpon the picture of Chaucer' for Speght's 1602 edition. Despite its title, and the fact that it was printed in the space originally intended for the image of Chaucer (facing 'The Reader to Geffrey Chaucer', that is), the poem is not concerned with Chaucer's picture but with Chaucer's status as a national poet whose skill exceeds that of other nations' great classics. The title may be explained through the fact that Speght's 1598 edition had been the first printed edition to contain the author's image. The same page in the 1602 edition (bj^r) also contains another (unattributed) poem by Thynne, called 'Of the Animadversions vpon Chaucer', a commentary poem for Speght's previous edition.
23 The epistle is attributed to Thynne himself, although it is now believed to have been written by Brian Tuke. For the attribution to Tuke see Greg Walker, *Writing Under Tyranny* (Oxford: Oxford University Press, 2005), 60–5.
24 In the 1602 edition, this additional line was removed again, perhaps in an attempt to save space. In the first edition, the epistle had taken up two and a half pages. The typesetter of the second appears to have aimed for a cleaner layout by using slightly smaller type and adding three lines to every column of text in order to make the epistle fit onto two pages and reserve the third for the table of contents. This attempt was unsuccessful, however, forcing the typesetter to add the table of contents directly after the last 21 lines of the epistle, without a separate heading to introduce it.
25 All of these forms show patterns of spelling that were common in Middle English but became rarer over the course of the sixteenth century (in the second edition, most of these are modernised). Stow's edition and both of Speght's editions all modified the spelling of the epistle. While the preferred spellings differ slightly between the editions – either due to different house styles or to the different typesetters involved – they all share a tendency to modernise the text's spelling by dramatically reducing the frequency of Ys in the place of Is and terminal '-es' for '-s' after consonants. Although both of these were of course still in use during the late sixteenth century and persisted especially in manuscript, books printed during the second half of the century tend to use those spellings far less frequently that those printed during the first half. So, for example, the very first words of the epistle, 'To the kynges hyghnesse' changes into 'To the kinges highnesse' in Stow's edition. Speght's 1598 and 1602 editions have 'To the Kings highnesse' and 'To the Kings Highnesse' respectively.
26 The association of Tuke's preface with the past is also visually reinforced by the choice of black-letter type, which the edition reserves for Chaucer's works and quotations from old (English) authors in the 'Life of Chaucer'. For the association between different types and different languages see Steven Galbraith's article '"English" Black-Letter Type and Spenser's *Shepheardes Calender*', *Spenser Studies*, 23 (2008), 13–40. In the 'Life of Chaucer', Hoccleve and Lydgate are quoted in

Chaucer the 'modern' classic

In highlighting Chaucer's 'antient'-ness and providing his works with so many paratextual and supplementary materials, Speght's 1598 edition was effectively the first to treat Chaucer as a 'medieval' poet. That is, Speght's edition frames Chaucer as a classic – a vernacular poet comparable to the ancients both in terms of literary significance and in terms of the datedness of his vocabulary – who can only be properly understood and appreciated by modern readers if they have the 'difficulties opened' to them with the help of glossaries, vocabulary notes and additional information about the historical context of the author and his works.[27]

At the same time, however, both the paratexts and the supplementary materials of Speght's edition collectively make a case for Chaucer's continued relevance. Speght's strategy as an editor is not exclusively to present his readers with an 'antient' medieval Chaucer. The 'additions' also evoke a Chaucer whose works are still worthy of being read by (early) modern readers – the Chaucer who, as 'The Reader to Geffrey Chaucer' claims, had been previously hidden from view 'In haulks, and hernes [...] and in exile' ('Reader to GC' (1598), av^v) but who could now, thanks to Speght's efforts, be directly accessed, and even addressed, by his modern readership. The first of the two additional poems included in the 1602 edition – Francis Thynne's 'Vpon the picture of Chaucer' – also contains this theme of a modern reader interacting with 'Chaucer' through reading Speght's edition. After listing several classic poets who immortalised the fame of other nations, the poem shifts its focus to Chaucer, who, unlike the other poets, is referred to in the present tense, echoing the idea that Chaucer – meaning Speght's newly recovered Chaucer – is still contributing to England's fame and continues to serve as an inspiration to future English writers:

> The same, and more, faire England challenge may,
> By that rare wit and art thou doest display,
> In verse, which doth *Appoloes* muse bewray.
> Then *Chaucer* liue, for still thy verse shall liue,
> T'unborne Poëts, which life and light will giue. ('Vpon the picture of
>   Chaucer' (1602), bj^r)[28]

---

black-letter, while quotations from authors writing in Latin – such as Camden – are printed in italic font; the quotation from Spenser, which I will discuss below, is the only one printed in roman font (like the rest of the 'Life'), which visually marks it as a quotation from contemporary source.

27 For a detailed account of how Speght's edition continually strives to establish Chaucer as both ancient and English see Megan C. Cook, 'Making and Managing the Past: Lexical Commentary in Spenser's *Shepheardes Calender* (1579) and Chaucer's *Works* (1598 / 1602)', *Spenser Studies*, 26 (2011), 179–222.

28 The final couplet is a revised version of the final lines of an elegy for 'Renowmed Spencer' which had featured in Thynne's poetic miscellany *Emblemes and Epigrames* two years earlier ('then live thou still, for still thy verse shall live, / to vnborne poets, which light and life will give.'). The added couplet takes the second stanza of 'Vpon the picture of Chaucer' from eight to ten lines, suggesting Thynne – or Speght – added them as an afterthought, because he thought it could be applied equally well to Chaucer.

The second poem added in the 1602 edition, the unattributed 'Of the Animadversions vpon Chaucer', is much shorter than the other two.²⁹ As in the other poems, the 'Chaucer' being contemplated is not the dead author but the one recently brought back to life by Speght's edition. In fact, in 'Of the Animadversions', Francis Thynne is so complimentary about the 'helpfull notes' of Speght's edition that Speght's 'peine' in preparing the edition takes centre stage, while Chaucer himself is all but reduced to a supporting role:

> In reading of the learn'd praise-worthie peine,
> The helpfull notes explaining *Chaucers* mind,
> The Abstruse skill, the artificiall veine;
> By true Annalogie I rightly find,
> *Speght* is the child of *Chaucers* fruitfull breine,
> Vernishing his workes with life and grace,
> Which envious age would otherwise deface:
> Then be he lov'd and thanked for the same,
> Since in his love he hath reviv'd his name. ('Of the Animadversions' (1602), bjʳ)

The image of Speght as Chaucer's brain-child is both paradoxical and peculiar. It serves not only to elevate Speght but also to illustrate Thynne's claim that for a reader of the 1598 edition, Speght's notes and his edition are inseparable from Chaucer himself, because they provide the only means of access to Chaucer's 'mind'. This is also expressed in the merging of '*Speght*' and '*Chaucer*' into a collective 'he' whose reference is not always entirely clear in the poem's final four lines.

The inclusion of Brian Tuke's sixty-six-year-old epistle also plays a key part within Speght's strategy to highlight Chaucer's reception by his contemporaries in his edition. In a sense, Tuke had been the first to argue for a 'modern' Chaucer. His epistle begins with the claim that the capacity for language is one of the characteristics in which we can see 'the similitude of man vnto Angels, and difference between the same and brute beasts' (quoted after 1598, ¶iʳ), before proceeding to chart the history of human language and the evolution of different languages, as well as that of written language. In his account of the confusion of tongues, Tuke follows a narrative that treats it as the beginning of a downward spiral in which all languages are inevitably moving away from the original language of man (which had been a God-given and consequently perfect form of expression) and towards linguistic corruption. The invention of written language, he argues, represents an effort on the part of man to counter that downward trend, and within that effort, poetry plays a special part:

> Herevpon ensued a great occasion and courage vnto them that should write, to compone and adorne the rudenesse and barbaritie of speech, and to form it to an eloquence and ordinate perfection: whereunto many, and many great Poets and Orators haue highly emploied their studies and corages, leauing therby notable Renoume of themselues, and example perpetuall to their posterity. (quoted after 1598, ¶iʳ)

---

29 Although no author's name was given for the poem in the 1602 edition, it can be attributed to Frances Thynne because his copy of the 1598 edition contains a draft version of it. I am grateful to Megan Cook for drawing my attention to this.

After defining poetry as an effort to counter the corruption of language, in an attempt to turn 'rudeness and barbaritie' into a good example for both contemporaries and future generations to imitate, Tuke turns to describing the quasi-miraculous advent of Chaucer as the saviour of the English language, reversing the downward trend and lifting the language out of a linguistic dark age:

> It is much to be maruailed, how in his time, whan doubtlesse all good letters were laid asleep throughout the world, as the thing, whych either by the disposition and influence of the bodies aboue, or by other ordinance of God, seemed like as was in daunger to haue vtterly perished, such an excellent Poet in our tong, should as it were (nature repugning) spring and arise. (quoted after 1598, ¶i^v)

What is peculiar about this passage is that in praising Chaucer's exemplariness, Tuke is also extracting him from his historical period. This extraction of Chaucer is particularly evident in the pronoun shift from '*his* time, whan doubtlesse all good letters were laid asleep' to 'such an excellent Poet in *our* tong, should […] spring and arise'. In his implicit assumption that the language of the writer and addressee of the epistle and the language of Chaucer can be collectively referred to as 'our tong', Tuke is effectively claiming Chaucer as the contemporary of his sixteenth-century readership.

Of course the central weakness in Tuke's 'Chaucer, Our Contemporary' argument immediately becomes apparent: notions of what constitutes 'fruitfulnesse in words well according to the matter and purpose, […] sweete and pleasaunt sentences [and] perfection in metre' (quoted after 1598, ¶i^v) inevitably change over time. Consequently, if Chaucer's merit as an author is exclusively defined through his exemplary language – that is, its function as a good example to be imitated by posterity – it means that as soon as his language stops being considered a perfect example of good English, his works are no longer worth reading. Francis Beaumont describes these consequences at the beginning of his letter to Speght, when outlining the two main prejudices commonly held against Chaucer in the late sixteenth century:

> First that many of his wordes (as it were with ouerlong lying) are grown too hard and vnpleasant, and next that hee is somewhat too broad in some of his speeches, and that the worke therefore should be lesse gratious. (Beaumont letter (1598), aiij^v)

In his letter, Beaumont proceeds to defend Chaucer against those charges, by arguing that, as was already known by the ancients, language is forever changing and 'no man can so write […], as that all his wordes may remaine currant many yeares' (aiij^v).

Worthy friends: Speght's Spenser and Speght's Chaucer

Speght's own strategy in arguing for Chaucer's 'worthinesse' (as he calls it) is more subtle than Tuke's claim that Chaucer speaks 'our tong' or Beaumont's defensive argument that anything that could be said against Chaucer could equally be said against the ancient classics. Instead of arguing for Chaucer's excellence purely on the merits of his language, as previous editors had done, Speght's strategy of presenting Chaucer as both 'antient' and of continued relevance to the present frames him not simply as an exemplary English poet but as an English classic, and thus provides his readers with a new reason for reading Chaucer.

Interestingly, Speght is modelling his idea of Chaucer the English classic not so much on the ancient classics (unlike Beaumont, who in his letter draws numerous comparisons between Chaucer and classical Roman and Greek authors) as on one of his own contemporaries: the poet Edmund Spenser. As Megan Cook has noted, there are striking parallels between the apparatus of Speght's Chaucer editions and that of *The Shepheardes Calender*, and Speght's notion of his role as an editor seems to be based on that of 'E.K.' – despite the fact that 'E.K.' had been glossing the work of an author who deliberately chose to employ archaic, 'Chaucerian'-sounding language for poetic effect, whereas Speght was of course dealing with the works of an actual medieval author.[30] Speght, however, is employing 'E.K.'s' strategies to do almost the exact opposite. The paratexts of *The Shepheardes Calender* had presented its readers with a narrative of the 'new' poet's authorial emergence and flight to fame that is really a narrative of the discovery of a fully-fledged classic – complete with an existing body of works that 'slepe in silence', as well as prefaces and glosses discussing 'Immeritô's' language and meaning as though he were dead and thus a fixed authorial entity to be given a final evaluation by his readers and commentators.[31] Speght's paratexts, by contrast, serve to demonstrate that the works of a poet who really is dead and buried and thought of less highly than he used to be (though not exactly 'slep[ing] in silence') still deserve a late sixteenth-century readership.

Speght's interest in Spenser and his high opinion of him are evident throughout his editions, and they are also central to his double agenda of presenting Chaucer as both ancient and modern. The result of Speght's persistent association of the two authors is not only a 'Spenserian' Chaucer (in the sense that he is substantially viewed through the lens of Spenser's works), but also inevitably a rather 'Chaucerian' Spenser, who is being defined in terms of his 'frequenting' of Chaucer. This is apparent in the two places in the *Workes* in which Spenser is directly invoked: Beaumont's letter and the 'Life of Chaucer'.

---

30 Cook, 'Making and Managing the Past', 179–222.
31 *The Shepheardes Calender*, 'Epistle', ¶iijʳ. Throughout 'E.K.'s' paratexts, there is no hint of any future works or work in progress by the 'new Poete', whose writing career is, after all, only beginning. Instead, 'E.K.' effectively behaves like an editor of a dead poet's remains. He only mentions unpublished and as yet unappreciated works (of whose existence there is no evidence beyond the titles alluded to in prefaces to Spenser's works, and which may well have been made up). In doing so, he also reframes the 'more' that is to be sent after the work ('To his Booke', 18) as extant but unpublished works rather than as yet unwritten ones. By contrast, the *Familiar Letters* (1580) between 'Immerito' and 'G.H.', which were published shortly after the *Calender*, present 'Immerito' as a living poet working on several poetic projects. Cf. my article 'Collaborative Spenser? Reading the "Spenser-Harvey Letters"', *Spenser Studies*, 33 (2019), 225–242.

Of the changes to Beaumont's letter in the 1602 edition, the one that most strongly suggests an intervention on Speght's part occurs in a passage that refers to Edmund Spenser's use of Chaucerian language. The 1598 version reads:

> But yet so pure were *Chaucers* wordes in his own daies, as *Lidgate* that learned man calleth him *The Loadstarre of the English language*: and so good they are in our daies, as Maister *Spencer*, following the counsaile of *Tullie in de Oratore*, for reuiuing of antient wordes, hath adorned his own stile with that beautie and grauitie, which *Tully* speakes of: and his much frequenting of *Chaucers* antient speeches causeth many to allow far better of him, then otherwise they would. (Beaumont letter (1598), aiiij^v)

Beaumont's main point here is no doubt that the beauty of Chaucer's language persists even into the 1590s, but what makes this passage interesting is his account of Spenser's use of Chaucer's language, which is at best ambiguously worded, perhaps even ambivalent: on the one hand, the fact that a major contemporary poet could be said to have 'adorned his own stile' with Chaucerian words is of course the best supporting evidence that someone arguing for Chaucer's continued relevance could wish for. On the other hand, the 'much frequenting of *Chaucers* speeches' by a poet whose main goal was not to repopularise Chaucer could also be regarded as an act of appropriation.

The ambiguity of the final 'him' – which may refer to either Spenser or Chaucer – further increases the passage's curious ambivalence towards Spenser. It can of course be read as referring to Chaucer, in which case Beaumont would be crediting Spenser with keeping Chaucer's literary reputation alive through his references and allowing readers to access Chaucer via the medium of Spenser's works. If the word 'him' is read as referring to Spenser, however, Beaumont's statement becomes evaluative, with a hint of disapproval of the fact that Spenser owed some of his success and his reputation as a poet to his borrowings from Chaucer, and that it was consequently Chaucer who deserved the credit for a good part of the 'beautie and grauitie' of Spenser's style. As a result of this ambiguity, it is not entirely clear whether Beaumont is merely commending Spenser for his revival of Chaucer or indirectly calling him derivative and overrated.

The ambiguity in Beaumont's letter may well have been unintentional (which would explain why Speght only removed it in the second edition). Nevertheless, Spenser's poetic achievement in relation to Chaucer was evidently a point that Speght felt needed not just disambiguation but further explanation. The 1602 version of the passage is not only free from (intended or accidental) slights against Spenser, but also uses the opportunity to praise him not purely as a successor to Chaucer but also in his own terms:

> Maister *Spencer* (following the counsaile of *Tullie* in his third booke *De Oratore*, for reuiuing of auncient wordes) hath adorned his stile with that beautie and grauitie, that *Tullie* there speakes of: and his much frequenting of *Chaucers* auncient words, with his excellent imitation of diuerse places in him, is not the leaste helpe that hath made him reach so hie, as many learned men doe thinke, that no Poet either French or Italian deserues a second place vnder him. (Beaumont letter (1602), aiiij^r)

The other modifications to Beaumont's letter in the 1602 edition do not significantly change its overall argument – apart from minor rephrasings they almost exclusively serve to provide additional illustrative examples.[32] This passage is clearly different, however, because here Speght's modifications transform both the way in which the letter describes Spenser's use of Chaucer, and the resulting conclusions drawn about Spenser's poetic career. The modified version of the letter turns Spenser from a mere vehicle for Chaucer's language (or an appropriator, if one adopts the less favourable reading) into a skilful imitator of 'diuerse places', highlighting Spenser's own poetic skill and achievement more emphatically than the 1598 version had done. Equally, Beaumont's point about the undiscriminating 'many', who he imagines would be apt to overlook Chaucer's significance for English literature, had it not been for Spenser's tributes to him (or are apt to overlook the extent of Spenser's indebtedness to Chaucer and rate him more highly as a poet than he truly deserves), is transformed into a direct tribute to Spenser. While the passage still refers to Spenser's use of Chaucer's works, the main emphasis is on Spenser's own achievement as a poet without equal, making him Chaucer's heir – our *modern* learned English poet, as it were. At the same time, the 1602 letter's claim that Spenser's drawing on Chaucer's language was 'not the leaste helpe that hath made him reach so hie' acknowledges the role of Chaucer as a predecessor to Spenser, but also stresses that Spenser is a great poet in his own right, by implying that his poetic achievements and his reputation as the foremost contemporary poet are not purely due to his borrowing from Chaucer. The effect of Speght's modifications to the passage in Beaumont's letter, then (a passage that occupies no very prominent place in its original context) is to shift the focus from Chaucer to Spenser, at a point where it is not strictly necessary to do so. This in turn prepares the ground for Speght's second reference to Spenser's indebtedness to Chaucer in a passage in the 'Life of Chaucer' that illustrates how eager Speght was to forge a close connection between the two poets.

Speght's 'Life of Chaucer' is believed to be the earliest biography of an English poet – yet it is rarely studied in much detail, since modern readers (and scholars of biography) tend to find it somewhat disappointing as a literary life. It is quite simply not the Life of Chaucer the poet. While it is carefully structured, that structure appears confusing at first sight, because it is at odds with modern ideas of biography in general and literary biography in particular. Apart from devoting a disproportionate amount of space to Chaucer's ancestry, Speght concerns himself almost exclusively with Chaucer's public life; the works only feature briefly in a short bibliographic note ('His Bookes').

Nevertheless, 'The Life of Geffrey Chaucer' is a very interesting text, especially its final section – also by far the longest in the Life – which is called 'His Death' but really

---

32 The only exception to this is a change of tense that most likely indicates that one of the Cambridge Chaucer enthusiasts mentioned in the letter, who had been educated by the same 'ancient, learned men' as Beaumont and Speght, had died between 1598 and 1602. The phrase 'one of them at that time was and now is (as you know) one of the rarest Schollers of the worlde' changes to 'one of them at that time, & all his life after, was (as you know) one of the rarest men for learning in the whole world' (Beaumont letter (1598), aiiij^v and Beaumont letter (1602), av^r). The 'scholler' in question has not been identified, although it may be a covert reference to the death of Spenser, who had been Speght's contemporary at Cambridge and had died in 1599.

deals with Chaucer's reception and poetic afterlife. In that section, Speght assembles a number of posthumous tributes to Chaucer written by other poets, ranging from Chaucer's contemporaries to 'men of later time'. The most recent example Speght quotes is taken from the 1596 *Faerie Queene*, published only two years before. The quotation concludes a paragraph on Spenser's praise of Chaucer, which runs as follows:

> Master *Spenser*, in his first Eglogue of his Shepheardes Kalender, calleth him *Titirus*, the god of Shepheards, comparing him to the worthinesse of the Romane Titirus Virgil. In his Faerie Queene in his discourse of friendship, as thinking himselfe most worthy to be Chaucers friend, for his like naturall disposition that Chaucer had, he sheweth that none that liued with him, nor none that came after him, durst presume to reuiue Chaucers lost labours in that vnperfite tale of the Squire, but only himselfe: which he had not done, had he not felt (as he saith) the infusion of Chaucers owne sweete spirite, suruiuing within him. And a little before he termeth him, Most renowmed and Heroicall Poet: and his Writings, The workes of heauenly wit: concluding his commendation in this manner:
>
> Dan Chaucer, Well of English vndefiled,
> On Fames eternall beadrole worthy to be filed.
> I follow here the footing of thy feet,
> That with thy meaning so I may the rather meet. ('Life of Chaucer' (1598), ciij^r–ciij^v)

When reading this passage from the 'Life of Chaucer', it is easy to pass over the quotation at the end without a second glance, because it is presented as a mere illustration of Speght's points. Yet while those lines sound Spenserian enough, there is something odd about the 'stanza' Speght quotes to illustrate Spenser's 'friendship' with Chaucer: the rhyme scheme is wrong. In the stanza form that *The Faerie Queene* is written in, there should be no two consecutive rhyming couplets.

Of course there is an easy explanation for this. On closer inspection, it turns out that despite implying that it is a verbatim quotation occurring at the end of the passage he is referring to, Speght has in fact taken the final couplets of two separate stanzas (stanzas 32 and 34 of Book 4, canto 2) and blended them together. Yet while it is evident *what* Speght has done, it is less clear *why* he has done it. One thing is certain, however: his condensation of three consecutive stanzas into two rhyming couplets cannot have been caused by space constraints: other authors are quoted at length in the same section, and the space left blank at the bottom of the page facing the Chaucer family tree, as well as the final page of the Life, would easily have been enough for Speght to quote the three stanzas from Book IV in full. What I would like to suggest, then, is that Speght's decision to reproduce just the two couplets and to print them as a stanza not only reveals something about how he viewed the relationship between Spenser and Chaucer, but the changes he makes to Spenser's text effectively create that relationship.

Speght's notion of the relationship between the two poets is characterised by the two operative terms he uses to describe and reinforce it through his account in the 'Life of Chaucer' – 'worthinesse' and 'friendship'. In the first sentence, the concept of 'worthinesse' is simply used to denote Spenser's reverence for 'Dan Chaucer', implied in the flattering comparison to 'Tityrus'. Yet as the next sentence indicates, 'worthinesse' is a quality that Spenser – according to Speght's reading – associates not only with Virgil (and Chaucer), but also with himself, turning a notion of reverence into one of respect among equals. Spenser, Speght claims, wrote the continuation of the *Squire's Tale* in Book IV 'thinking himselfe most worthy to be Chaucers friend, for his like naturall disposition that Chaucer had'. The idea of a 'friendship' between the poets is further reinforced by Speght through pointing out that the passage occurs in Book IV, whose alternate title is 'Of Friendship'.

A comparison of Speght's account of the relationship between the two great English poets and Spenser's own verse reveals how much the notion of a literary friendship or kinship owes to Speght's selective reading of Spenser. The relevant passage in Book IV of *The Faerie Queene* begins not directly with praise of Chaucer but with a literary joke: after spotting a pair of strangely harmonious knights and their ladies at a distance, the 'discordfull crew' led by Blandamour and Paridell send a squire – the Squire of Dames – 'afore, to vnderstand, / What mote they be' (IV.ii.31). The squire returns to report their names, but his report is cut short by the narrator, who, after having identified them as characters from the *Squire's Tale* (and noting that it is, sadly, a fragment), in a long digression continues their story until the point at which they entered the scene in IV.ii.30. So thanks to Spenser's narrator, this second squire's tale also remains a fragment. Stanzas 32–4 form an introduction, with stanza 32 acting as a respectful acknowledgement of 'Dan Chaucer' as the original source of the tale (or at least of the characters 'Cambell' and 'Canacee') and stanza 33 expressing the author's regret that the *Squire's Tale* has suffered the same fate as the records in the chamber of Eumnestes in that 'wicked Time [...] / that famous moniment hath quite defaste' (IV.ii.33). Chaucer himself is not addressed until stanza 34, in which the author implores the 'most sacred happie spirit' to forgive this 'revival' of his lost work, adding that he would not have dared to attempt it had he not – quite literally – felt inspired by Chaucer:

> [...] through infusion sweete
> Of thine owne spirit, which doth in me surviue,
> I follow here the footing of thy feete,
> That with thy meaning so I may the rather meete. (IV.ii.34)

Interestingly, then, the two key features of Speght's account – Spenser's confident assertion of his own 'worthinesse' to continue the tale and his claim to a friendship with Chaucer based on 'like naturall dispositions' – are absent from Spenser's verse and seem to be the product of an interpretive effort on Speght's part. The phrase 'most renowmed and Heroicall Poet' never appears at all but is a somewhat inaccurate paraphrase of lines 6–7 of stanza 32, which states that the tale of Cambell and Canacee was by

> that renowmed Poet [...] compyled,
> With warlike numbers and Heroicke sound,
> Dan Chaucer, well of English vndefyled,
> On Fames eternall beadroll worthie to be fyled. (IV.ii.32)

As these two longer quotations from stanzas 32 and 34 illustrate, Speght's blending of the two couplets not only gives the impression of a different rhyme scheme but also leads to a shift in meaning. The consequences of this shift are twofold: it modifies Spenser's stanza, while also supporting Speght's own reading of the close affinity (or 'friendship') between Chaucer and Spenser.

On one level, Speght's blending of the two couplets from *The Faerie Queene* into a single 'stanza' simply serves to make the quotation more memorable. Spenser, through his complex stanza form and his complicated syntax, is not the most aphoristic of poets. Consequently, his stanzas rarely express an idea in just one or two lines; they are far more likely to be spread across four or five. Even the final couplets do not tend to form self-contained units.[33] One effect of Speght's recontextualisation of the four lines, then, is to give at least the illusion of a self-contained unit of verse in which Spenser at once appears to declare his respect for Chaucer and his intention to follow in his 'footing' and be his poetic heir.

This in turn helps Speght's artificially created 'stanza' to support his main idea regarding the poetic 'friendship'. In their new context, the lines seem to be directly addressed to Chaucer and the action of Spenser following in his footsteps is no longer conditional on inspiration flowing from the 'well of English', but is made to sound like a poetic mission statement of sorts. In short, Speght is making Spenser declare himself Chaucer's heir not just in a single instance, by daring to continue a fragmentary Canterbury Tale but in general – a subtle but significant difference. In adapting Spenser in this manner, Speght is bringing the two 'friends' closer and making Chaucer more central to Spenser's poetry than is perhaps borne out by the poetry itself.

Finally, and perhaps most importantly, Speght's blending of the couplets serves to bring Spenser's *verse* closer to Chaucer's. One connotation of the phrase 'thy feet' in the line 'I follow in the footing of *thy feet*' is of course that of metre, implying that Spenser is following Chaucer not only in terms of contents (by completing the tale) but also in terms of form (by using iambic pentameter – although he does not follow his rhyme scheme). Speght's changes to Spenser's verse, then, have the effect of making Spenser follow Chaucer yet more closely, in converting Spenserian stanzas into rhyming couplets – the rhyme scheme of (among other things) the *Squire's Tale*.

Speght's manipulation both of his synopsis of *The Faerie Queene* IV.ii.32–4 and of the lines he quotes in his 'Life of Chaucer' thus to an extent cause what he claims to find in Spenser's verse: a close poetic affinity verging on a 'friendship' between Chaucer, the great English classic, and Spenser, the most celebrated contemporary poet, then at the height of his fame. This of course raises the question why Speght might have wanted to do that. I would like to suggest that, somewhat paradoxically, it is Chaucer – not Spenser – whom Speght is trying to

---

33 For the aphoristic quality of the rhyming couplet and its absence in *The Faerie Queene*, see J.B. Lethbridge's recent essay, which argues that poets writing in aphoristic couplets tend to 'put key terms at the ends of lines; Spenser, typically at any rate, not so'. J.B. Lethbridge, 'The Bondage of Rhyme in *The Faerie Queene*', in Richard Danson Brown and J.B. Lethbridge, *A Concordance to the Rhymes of The Faerie Queene* (Manchester: Manchester University Press, 2014), 67–180 (97).

elevate by presenting the relationship between the two poets as a particularly close one. More than any previous sixteenth-century edition, Speght's editions aimed to prove Chaucer's eminence as a poet in every possible way and also to justify his status as a classic still worthy of having his complete works published and read centuries later. Brian Tuke's preface had presented Chaucer as a pseudo-messianic saviour of the English language, whose emergence 'as it were (nature repugning)' constituted an act of divine intervention that halted the general trend of linguistic decline since classical times. Yet while Tuke had portrayed Chaucer as the epitome of good English, worth reading for his language alone, this perception of Chaucer had shifted since the 1530s, and by the end of the century, Chaucer's language was considered rough, archaic and in need of justification or explanation. So when Speght was preparing his own edition of Chaucer's works, he felt that it was necessary to highlight (and perhaps even deliberately exaggerate) Spenser's high opinion of and closeness to Chaucer, not so much to ennoble Spenser but to re-ennoble Chaucer and thus prove he was still worth reading.

10

Chaucer's 'beast group' and 'Mother Hubberds Tale'

Brendan O'Connell

At the heart of Spenser's *Complaints* (1591), clustered around the central 'Ruines of Rome', we find three examples of beast literature, which, taken together, might fairly be called a collection of animal fables: 'Virgil's Gnat', 'Prosopopoia, or Mother Hubberds Tale', and 'Muiopotmos'.[1] As Amanda Rogers Jones has noted, we are invited to read these works as a group because of their common features as beast poems, their physical proximity and the fact that beast fables were conventionally found in collections.[2] While the preface by William Ponsonby suggests that he, rather than Spenser, is responsible for the compilation of the works gathered in the *Complaints*, readers have found good reason to suspect that Spenser had a hand in preparing the work for publication.[3] Certainly the *Complaints* display signs of careful ordering, and Richard McCabe has drawn attention to a number of features that would indicate that Spenser envisaged publication, including details from the dedicatory sonnets and textual clues from 'Mother Hubberds Tale'.[4] Regardless of whether the order of the *Complaints* is authorial or editorial, however, it seems appropriate to consider the available models for the inclusion of the beast fables, especially when one of these works caused a major scandal on publication.[5] One such model, I argue, is the *Canterbury Tales*, which, in the editions Spenser is likely to have read, also featured a cluster of beast tales in a significant position

---

1 I am very grateful to Rachel Stenner, who first pointed out to me the central role of beast fable in the *Complaints* at the Chaucer and Spenser conference, *Dan Geffrey with the New Poete: Reading and Rereading Chaucer and Spenser* (Bristol, July 2014). The beast poems have rarely been discussed as a group, though Andrew Hadfield notes that much of the thematic unity of the *Complaints* centres on these texts: see *Edmund Spenser: A Life* (Oxford: Oxford University Press, 2012), 273.
2 Amanda Rogers Jones, 'Orderly Disorder: Rhetoric and Imitation in Spenser's Three Beast Poems from the *Complaints* Volume' (Unpublished Master's Thesis, Virginia Polytechnic Institute and State University, 2001), 2–4.
3 For discussion, see Richard Danson Brown, *'The New Poet': Novelty and Tradition in Spenser's 'Complaints'* (Liverpool: Liverpool University Press, 1999), 2–7; Bruce Danner, *Edmund Spenser's War on Lord Burghley* (London: Palgrave Macmillan, 2011), 15; Hadfield, 272–4.
4 Edmund Spenser, *The Shorter Poems*, ed. Richard McCabe (London: Penguin, 1999), 580–1. All quotations from the *Complaints* are from this edition.
5 The furore over 'Mother Hubberds Tale' is discussed in some detail by Hadfield (265–88), and extensively by Danner (1–17; 151–85), both of whom demonstrate conclusively that the beast fable was understood by Spenser's contemporaries as an attack on Lord Burghley.

(here the end, rather than the centre), each of which appears to have influenced one or other of Spenser's poems, and in particular his tale of the ape and the fox. In these works, Spenser found a powerful model for his literary re-appropriation of the beast fable in the *Complaints*, and particularly for the brilliantly savage satire of 'Mother Hubberds Tale'.

In her account of the beast fables in the *Complaints*, Jones argues compellingly that the three fables each represent Spenser's engagement with a different mode of poetic imitation and a different poetic model.[6] In 'Virgil's Gnat', Spenser is quite closely translating the pseudo-Virgilian *Culex*: as Jones points out, the work may be an early one, and represents quite a deferential engagement with the classical poet. The dazzling 'Muiopotmos', by contrast, offers a bolder and more assertive interaction with the poetic authority of Ovid, whose *Metamorphoses* are masterfully reworked by Spenser. Between these two poems, Jones argues, Spenser looks to the future, unleashing, in 'Mother Hubberds Tale', a modern poetic style that moves beyond classical models. While this interpretation is suggestive, it omits a crucial piece of the puzzle, namely the fact that in 'Mother Hubberds Tale' Spenser offers his most extensive and thoughtful engagement with his great vernacular literary forebear, Chaucer, whose beast fables all inform the poem to a greater or lesser extent.

In the following account, I first show that, despite being the result of distinct (and indeed unrelated) editorial decisions, the 'beast group' that emerged in early modern editions of the *Canterbury Tales* produced a surprisingly coherent exploration of the potential uses of beast literature and animal fable, which proved appealing to Spenser. As the second part of this study argues, Spenser responds to the beast group's deployment of beast literature as a satirical tool: in particular as a tool of estates satire and anticlericalism. Ultimately, I hope to show that Spenser found, in the talking birds of the Chaucerian beast group, a variety of models for the role of the poet. Spenser responds to these models by advancing the fox, and more particularly the ape, as figures of the poet against which he defines his own poetic role.

Spenser's Chaucer and the evolution of the 'beast group'

'Prosopopoia, or Mother Hubberds Tale' opens with an invalid narrator, surrounded by a group of friends who comfort him by telling stories, one of which (Mother Hubberd's tale of the ape and the fox) the narrator has singled out as worthy of remembrance. The beastly protagonists, unhappy with their current estate, resolve to seek better fortunes by mimicking those of better estate: first gaining employment from a farmer as a shepherd and his dog (281–342), then moving up the ladder to secure a place as a priest and his curate (552–74), before a stint at the royal court (655–942), after which they effect their most audacious move, taking the place of the Lion-king (949–1384). At each stage, their villainy is discovered, though not before they have achieved a surprising level of success;

---

6 Jones, 12–16.

ultimately, however, they incur the wrath of Jupiter and the Lion-king, and are hunted, captured and punished (1225–385). Taking only into consideration this plot summary, the poem would seem to have little debt to Chaucer, and yet the poem is arguably Spenser's most thoroughgoing attempt to come to grips with Chaucer's achievement in the *Canterbury Tales*.

Spenser signals this debt not only in the title, with its obvious nod to Chaucer's stories, but even in the poem's form, which replicates the decasyllabic rhyming couplets of so many of the *Tales*. Moreover, as Lauren Silberman has demonstrated, the opening of Spenser's poem features a remarkably assured series of Chaucerian allusions that effectively invert the opening of the *General Prologue*.[7] In Chaucer's poem, the elaborate astrological set-piece locates the action of the *Tales* in the aftermath of the sweet showers of April:

> Whan that Aprill with his shoures soote
> The droghte of March hath perced to the roote,
> And bathed every veyne in swich licour
> Of which vertu engendred is the flour;
> Whan Zephirus eek with his sweete breeth
> Inspired hath in every holt and heeth
> The tendre croppes [...]
> Thanne longen folk to goon on pilgrimages [...]
> The hooly blisful martir for to seke,
> That hem hath holpen when that they were seeke. (I.1–7; 12; 17–18)

Spenser's poem, by contrast, takes place at the tail-end of the summer, in the dog days of August:

> It was the month, in which the righteous Maide,
> That for disdaine of sinfull worlds vpbraide,
> Fled back to heauen, whence she was first conceiued,
> Into her siluer bowre the Sunne receiued;
> And the hot *Syrian* Dog on him awayting,
> After the chafed Lyons cruell bayting,
> Corrupted had th'ayre with his noysome breath,
> And powr'd on th'earth plague, pestilence and death. (1–8)[8]

The echoes of Chaucer's magnificent opening line are unsettling, as Spenser contrives to alter or invert their effect. The 'sweete breeth' of Zephirus, which had 'inspired' Chaucer's world, is here overpowered by a rank and 'noysome breath' that corrupts the very air. Instead of flowers engendered though the penetration of the parched earth by the moist 'licour' of April and the caress of the west wind, Spenser describes a fastidious Astraea (identified with a cold, disdainful

---

7 Lauren Silberman, The Hugh Maclean Memorial Lecture, 'Making Faces and Playing Chicken in *Mother Hubberds Tale*', *The Spenser Review*, 37.1 (2006), 9–20 (11).
8 All quotations from Spenser are from McCabe's edition of *The Shorter Poems*.

Virgo) recoiling from a licentious earth and returning to the hot, dry sphere where she was conceived. Even Time itself is a different beast in the later poem: where Chaucer evokes the constantly renewing cycle of the seasons, Spenser hones in on a seemingly specific astrological alignment that portends pestilence, death and ill-fortune.[9]

The movement from well-being to sickness in Spenser's poem also inverts Chaucer's opening, which culminates in the departure of pilgrims to seek out the shrine of the 'hooly blisful martir [...] That hem hath holpen whan that they were seeke' (I.17–18). Whereas Chaucer's robust and healthy pilgrims set out for Canterbury and agree to tell stories along the way, here a group of tellers gather around the narrator's sick-bed to tell a range of stories to comfort him:

> And sitting all in seates about me round,
> With pleasant tales (fit for that idle stound)
> They cast in course to waste the wearie howres:
> Some told of Ladies, and their Paramoures;
> Some of braue Knights, and their renowned Squires;
> Some of the Faeries and their strange attires. [...]
> Amongst the rest a good old woman was,
> Hight Mother *Hubberd*, who did farre surpas
> The rest in honest mirth, that seem'd her well. (25–30; 33–5)

The passage offers a richly textured pattern of literary allusion, as Spenser moves from a highly classicised opening through allusions to the great achievements of Italian Renaissance poets, to an evocation of a vernacular English tradition, of which Chaucer is root and Spenser crop. In its account of stories told during plague-time, there are obvious echoes of Boccaccio's *Decameron*, while the reference to tales of ladies, knights and squires, and of strangely attired 'Faeries' seems, at least in part, a self-referential allusion to the success of Spenser's *Faerie Queene*.[10] Yet even as he alludes to his own masterpiece, Spenser appears to acknowledge his debt to the knights, squires and fairies of the *Canterbury Tales*.[11] Furthermore, both the low social status of Mother Hubberd and the genre of her tale clearly evoke Chaucer's story collection, with its conscious effort to include representatives of lower-class men and women and to incorporate a wide variety of genres and styles, including 'lower' forms such as the beast fable.

If we are to look for models among the *Canterbury Tales* for stories in this genre, one very obvious candidate, the *Nun's Priest's Tale*, stands out. And yet,

---

9   Hadfield notes (268–9) that the astrological references in the passage, and their association with plague and pestilence, may have been intended to mock erroneous astrological predictions made by John and Richard Harvey, thus explaining why Gabriel Harvey, otherwise favourable to Spenser, took such a dim view of the *Tale*.
10 For the allusion to Boccaccio, see McCabe's note to lines 21–32 (611). The reference to Astraea in line 1 alludes to Queen Elizabeth, while lines 28–30 evoke Spenser's most famous work. Ponsonby's introductory letter to the *Complaints* assumes the reader's familiarity with *The Faerie Queene*.
11 Spenser is pervasively influenced by the tales of the Knight and Squire, while his Faerie realm owes an obvious debt to the elf-queene of *Sir Thopas*.

for late sixteenth-century readers, Chaucer was the author of a veritable 'beast group' among the *Canterbury Tales*. To understand this, it is necessary to put aside familiar notions about the order of the *Tales*, and to recognise that a reader such as Spenser would have encountered the texts in a different order, occasionally interspersed with apocryphal works. For a modern reader of the *Riverside Chaucer*, the order corresponds essentially to that of the Ellesmere manuscript: we read Fragment VII, culminating in the *Nun's Priest's Tale*, followed by Fragment VIII (the Second Nun's legend of St. Cecilia, and the Canon's Yeoman's tale of alchemical skulduggery), before the *Tales* are rounded out by Fragments IX and X (the *Manciple's Tale* and the Parson's penitential treatise). Yet from Caxton on, the earliest printed editions followed a variant order, which moves Fragment VIII to an earlier position in the *Tales*, before Fragment VI (the Physician's and Pardoner's tales).[12] For the present purposes, this has a twofold effect: it places the *Nun's Priest's Tale* much closer to the end of the Canterbury collection, and pairs it with another beast story, the Manciple's tale of the crow. The effect of pairing these two beast stories at the end of the collection was further amplified in 1542, when the revised William Thynne edition added another beast tale, the Plowman's debate between the Pelican and the Griffin, at the very end of the collection. The evolution of a clearly definable 'beast group' was complete in c.1550 when the *Plowman's Tale* was moved before the *Parson's Tale* to join the Nun's Priest's and Manciple's tales. This order (Nun's Priest–Manciple–Plowman–Parson) was preserved in the later edition of John Stow (1561), which is probably the edition Spenser knew; this order continued through the editions of Thomas Speght (1598 and 1602) and John Urry (1721), only changing in 1775 when Thomas Tyrwhit expunged the *Plowman's Tale* and moved Fragment VIII to its familiar, late, position.[13]

While the pairing of the Nun's Priest's and Manciple's tales almost certainly does not reflect authorial design, and the *Plowman's Tale* is unquestionably apocryphal, there is little reason to believe that readers of Chaucer from c.1550 on would have doubted that this grouping reflected Chaucer's design. While it does not effortlessly fit the framework, the *Plowman's Tale* was unquestionably adapted, by means of an effective (if somewhat artless) Prologue, to furnish a link with the Canterbury pilgrimage.[14] Once it came to be included in the *Tales*, it appears to have gained swift and wholehearted acceptance, presumably because its Lollard polemics were attractive for readers keen to claim Chaucer as a proto-Protestant critic of the Catholic Church, the fraternal orders and the papacy. Certainly, the decision to

---

12 This editorial practice follows a prominent manuscript tradition, which is usefully summarised by Helen Cooper in *The Canterbury Tales*, Oxford Guides to Chaucer (Oxford: Oxford University Press, 1989), 7.
13 It is not possible to definitively state which edition (or editions) of Chaucer's *Works* Spenser read. It could have been one of the Thynne editions (1532, 1542, c.1550), but it seems more likely to have been that of John Stow (1561), as A. Kent Hieatt argues in *Chaucer, Spenser and Milton: Mythopoeic Continuities and Transformations* (Toronto: University of Toronto Press, 1975), 19–23.
14 For a discussion of the process by which the *Plowman's Tale* came to be incorporated into the *Canterbury Tales*, see the introduction to *Six Ecclesiastical Satires*, ed. James M. Dean (Kalamazoo: Western Michigan University, 1991), and Darryl Ellison, '"Take it as a Tale": Reading the *Plowman's Tale* As If It Were', *Chaucer Review*, 49.1 (2014), 77–101. For more on the implications of this addition, see my 'Putting the Plowman in His Place: Order and Genre in the Early Modern Canterbury Tales', *Chaucer Review*, 53.4 (2018), 428–48.

move the tale to a position immediately prior to the *Parson's Tale*, along with the necessary alteration of the word 'Manciple' to 'Plowman' in the first line of the Parson's Prologue, reinforced the place of the apocryphal tale in the canon.[15] To date, critical attention on the addition of the *Plowman's Tale* has focused on attempts by early modern writers, including Francis Thynne, to identify Chaucer as a critic of a corrupt Catholic Church.[16] However, it is also of exceptional literary significance, as, grouped with the Nun's Priest's and Manciple's tales, it substantially alters the ending of the *Canterbury Tales*, establishing a very distinctive vision of Chaucer as a fabulist and satirist. Elsewhere in this volume, Gareth Griffith reflects on the ways in which the early modern understanding of Chaucer as a romance writer may have been shaped by the practices of excerption and insertion that led to Chaucer's romances being found in manuscript collections alongside non-Chaucerian romances; I would suggest that the early modern reception of Chaucer as an author of beast fable and satire must have been no less profoundly shaped by the presence of the beast group in the imposing Folio editions in which it is found.[17]

Perhaps unsurprisingly, the efforts of modern Chaucer scholars to define an authentic Chaucerian canon and construct an authoritative order for the *Tales* have been coupled with disparagement of earlier editorial inventions which reflect very different ideological concerns and assumptions about what constitutes evidence of authorship. On closer consideration, however, the inclusion of the *Plowman's Tale*, coupled with its placement (c.1550) between the Manciple's and Parson's tales works remarkably well in establishing a cohesive and artistically compelling ending for the *Tales*. First of all, there is some logic to the pairing of the tales of the Parson and the Plowman even in the edition of 1542, in which the Plowman's tale follows the Parson's, since the two men are described together in the *General Prologue*, where they are represented as brothers (I.529). Moreover, this arrangement might indicate an awareness of the importance for Chaucer's artistic purpose of the traditional division of society into three estates. The *General Prologue* had included an idealised portrait of one member of each estate: the

---

15 Thomas Heffernan, 'Aspects of the Chaucerian Apocrypha: Animadversions on William Thynne's Edition of the *Plowman's Tale*', in *Chaucer Traditions: Studies in Honour of Derek Brewer*, ed. Ruth Morse and Barry Windeatt (Cambridge: Cambridge University Press, 1990), 155–67 (especially 164–5).
16 In *Writing Under Tyranny: English Literature and the Henrician Reformation* (Oxford: Oxford University Press, 2005), Greg Walker argues (29–99) that William Thynne may have deliberately excluded the *Plowman's Tale* from his 1532 edition as part of an attempt to construct a moderate and orthodox vision of Chaucer. His son, Francis, however, sought to emphasise the reformist credentials of both father and poet in his *Animadversions vppon the Annotacions and Corrections of Some Imperfections of Impressiones of Chaucers Workes* (1598); for an insightful critique, see Megan Cook, 'How Francis Thynne Read His Chaucer', *Journal of the Early Book Society*, 15 (2012), 215–49.
17 Griffith draws attention in particular to manuscripts such as Longleat MS 257, in which the *Knight's Tale* and the *Clerk's Tale* are sandwiched between Lydgate's *Siege of Thebes* and *Ipomedon* C. The effect of reading the *Knight's Tale* in such company must surely have been very different from reading it paired with the *Miller's Tale* in a manuscript of *The Canterbury Tales*.

Knight, the Plowman and Parson. The *Tales* began with one ideal, the Knight, and ended with another, the Parson; by pairing the *Plowman's Tale* with the *Parson's Tale*, the editor reinforced this emphasis on the ideal embodiment of each estate, but also, by insisting on the significance of the third estate, diminishes the effect of giving the final word to the Parson and the Church.[18]

With the movement of the *Plowman's Tale* before the Parson's, the 'beast group' acquired a level of cohesion that belies the fact that even the ordering of the authentic tales is spurious, not to mention that one of the works is apocryphal. Taken together, the tales of the Nun's Priest, the Manciple and the Plowman represent contrasting sub-categories of beast literature (the beast fable/beast epic; an Ovidian metamorphosis, and a bird-debate).[19] Moreover, while I would be reluctant to suggest that the attribution of the *Plowman's Tale* to Chaucer reflected an awareness that all of his authentic examples of beast literature focus on talking birds, an undeniable coherence is lent to the 'beast group' by the fact that even this apocryphal latecomer centres on garrulous avian creatures. Indeed, this coherence becomes even more striking when we recall that the c.1550 edition also includes the falcon's lament in the genuine *Squire's Tale*, the *Parliament of Fowls* and the apocryphal *Cuckoo and the Nightingale*.

It is not unreasonable to suggest, therefore, that the editors of the c.1550 edition may have been conscious of the generic coherence of the beast group as they arranged these tales together, and that such an arrangement would have been evident to readers of this and subsequent editions in which this order is preserved. Moreover, the ending of the *Plowman's Tale* contains a reference to its status as a beast fable that, when read in the context of the surrounding tales, forms part of a larger debate about fable and the wider purpose of fiction. In the relevant passage, the Plowman defends himself from accusations that he is attacking the Church by insisting that he is only telling a fable, and calling on the reader (in remarkably Chaucerian fashion) to direct blame away from the honest reporter:

> Wyteth the Pellican, and not me,
> For herof I nyl not avowe,
> In hye ne in lowe, ne in no degre,
> But as a fable take it ye mowe;
> To Holy Churche I wyll me bowe. (1373–7)[20]

---

18 For the most part, the popularity of the Plowman figure in the late medieval and early modern period (as witnessed by texts such as the *Plowman's Tale* and *Pierce the Ploughman's Crede*) reflects Lollard and reformist critiques of the Church, in which the Plowman, as the idealised representative of the third estate, often appears as the ideal Christian. See, for example, Helen Barr, 'Wycliffite Representations of the Third Estate', in *Lollards and Their Influence in Late Medieval England*, ed. Fiona Somerset, Jill C. Havens and Derrick G. Pitard (Woodbridge: Boydell, 2003), 197–216.
19 For a useful overview of the varieties of beast literature available in the medieval period, see Jill Mann, *From Aesop to Reynard: Beast Literature in Medieval Britain* (Oxford: Oxford University Press, 2009).
20 All quotations from *The Plowman's Tale* are from Dean's edition of the poem in *Six Ecclesiastical Satires*.

With its allusion to beast fable and its (ironic) deference to ecclesiastical authority, these (apocryphal) lines dovetail perfectly with the (authentic) Prologue to the *Parson's Tale*, a fact which may help explain the movement of the *Plowman's Tale* to the earlier position in the c.1550 edition. The Parson's Prologue culminates with the band of pilgrims deferring to the Parson's authority as a priest (X.61-6), and while modern readers may read this as either a deeply ironic or suitably orthodox moment of deference to the spiritual purpose of the pilgrimage, it looks rather different in the context of the Plowman's words. In such a context, the early modern reader would find ample evidence for a Chaucer who found it politic to hide his criticism of the Church under a veil, and would specifically have identified a special opposition between church authority and beast fable.[21] This becomes clear when we consider the famous passage in which the Host asks the Parson to tell a fable, a request which is brusquely rejected:

> 'Telle us a fable anon, for cokkes bones!'
> This Persoun answerde, al atones,
> 'Thou getest fable noon ytoold for me,
> For Paul, that writeth unto Thymothee,
> Repreveth hem that weyven soothfastnesse
> And tellen fables and swich wrecchednesse'. (X.29-34)[22]

Whereas in modern editions these lines read like a general critique of fiction and story-telling, for the reader of Thynne c.1550 and Stow 1561 they would read more naturally and specifically as a comment upon and rejection of the type of poetry represented by the 'beast group'. 'Fables' such as the *Plowman's Tale* are not repugnant to the Church because of their fiction, but because they are potentially seditious, and can be used to expose the greed and corruption of the medieval Church. Such a reading, I suggest, is pivotal to the success of the 'beast group' in the editorial tradition of the *Canterbury Tales*. It is a reading which may well have appealed to Spenser, but his concerns were rather broader, as he sought in 'Mother Hubberds Tale' to capitalise on Chaucer's use of the beast fable as an instrument of estates satire.

'Cloathed like a gentleman': animal fable and estates satire

'Mother Hubberds Tale' is pervasively influenced by the medieval estates satire genre that had been so central to Chaucer's work.[23] The broad influence is evident

---

21 The anonymous editor of the 1606 edition of the *Plowman's Tale* comments in relation to the lines quoted above, that 'Chaucer declineth the enuie, and auoydeth the rage of the popish Cleargie, for his writing thus plainly and boldly'. See Geoffrey Chaucer, *The Plough-Mans Tale Shewing by the Doctrine and Liues of the Romish Clergie, That the Pope Is Antichrist and They His Ministers* (London, 1606), cited in Ellison (85).
22 All quotations from Chaucer are from *The Riverside Chaucer*, ed. Larry D. Benson (Boston: Houghton Mifflin, 1987).
23 The classic study of the genre and its influence on Chaucer is Jill Mann, *Chaucer and Medieval Estates Satire: The Literature of Social Classes and the 'General Prologue' to the 'Canterbury Tales'* (Cambridge: Cambridge University Press, 1973).

in the very structure of Spenser's tale, in which the ape and the fox first infiltrate the lowest, labouring, estate (281–342), then spend a stint as churchmen (552–74) before they are embraced by the court (655–942) and ultimately usurp the Lion-king (949–1384). But while Spenser's satire is in part aimed at the corruption evident in each estate (as we find in medieval estates satires), the defining object of his satire is unquestionably the social climbing practised by the ape and fox: Spenser savagely criticises a society in which the outward imitation of diligence, piety or nobility is accepted at face-value, allowing those lacking such qualities to achieve the heights of power and influence. Indeed, the most startling thing about the adventure of the fox and ape is their remarkable success, as they are, at least initially, almost universally accepted in their fraudulently acquired roles: for a time, they are wildly popular at court (689ff.), and even gain broad acceptance when they usurp the place of the sleeping Lion (1064ff.).[24] In this, Spenser reveals himself to be rather different from Chaucer; whereas Chaucer also mocks pretension and social climbing, Spenser sharpens Chaucer's satirical weapons and writes a savage and unmistakeable satire of contemporary figures.

Chaucer and Spenser use estates satire in profoundly different ways. Estates satire is important for Spenser in 'Mother Hubberds Tale' because he has embraced the role of satirist; for Chaucer, however, the main attraction of estates satire is that, together with the pilgrimage framework, it provides a structure that facilitates the core generic and narrative principles behind the *Canterbury Tales*, namely the narration of stories from an extraordinary range of genres, each assigned to a teller broadly appropriate to a particular tale. The defining feature of the collection is its pointed variety, as romances rub shoulders with fabliaux, and pious tales and exempla compete with histories and fables. Indeed, by considering Spenser's response to one of Chaucer's most famous defences of the generic variety of the *Tales*, we can gain a better sense of how different from Chaucer's is his sense of the purpose of satire and, indeed, beast fable.

In an oft-quoted passage, the narrator of the *General Prologue* insists that he is only the reporter of the tales, and so if some are less worthy or more crude than others, it is up to the reader to take the necessary action to avoid offence:

> [...] I moot reherce
> Hir tales alle, be they bettre or werse
> Or elles falsen som of my mateere.
> And therfore, whoso list it nat yheere,
> Turne over the leef and chese another tale. (I.3173–7)

Chaucer's work is deliberately plurivocal: no single voice is ever allowed to dominate for long, as each subsequent teller responds to what has gone before. Furthermore, the tales are a sort of literary cornucopia: each reader is welcome to choose the tales that appeal to them and pass over those that do not. In Spenser's

---

24 Brown notes the *Tale*'s clear debt to estates satire, and discusses the ape and the fox as 'self-fashioning' individualists, who are remarkably successful at infiltrating different estates (176–7).

allusion to this passage (if it may be termed an allusion) the significance is changed entirely. As he expresses his dissatisfaction with his current estate, the fox suggests that finding a new position in life is as simple as turning the page of a book:

> Now therefore that no lenger hope I see,
> But froward fortune still to follow mee,
> And losels lifted vp on high, where I did looke,
> I meane to turne the next leafe of the booke. (65–8)

Chaucer's formulation had been a defence, even celebration, of the poet's freedom to imitate base styles, and of a reader's freedom to choose the styles and genres he prefers. The fox, however, twists Chaucer's image into an assertion of radical individualism and social mobility. Just as a poet is free to imitate high or low styles in his work, and as the reader is free to focus on romance, hagiography or fabliaux as he chooses, so, the fox claims, changing one's fortunes and social estate is as simple as turning a page. One need only outwardly perform the role of farmer, parson, courtier or king to accrue the benefits of one's new estate:

> Such will we fashion both our selues to bee,
> Lords of the world, and so will wander free
> Where so vs listeth, vncontol'd of anie. (167–9)

In his representation of the fox and ape as imitators of various estates, Spenser, I suggest, responds directly to Chaucer's defining literary achievement in the *Tales* (his imitation of a dizzying variety of narrative voices and *personae*) and, more importantly, demonstrates his conviction that this stylistic feature is not an end in itself (as modern critics might have it), but rather an essential aspect of Chaucer's role as a satirist. Chaucer's extraordinary talent for mimicking different styles serves to satirise social pretensions, as he describes members of a given social estate in the language appropriate to another, often effusively praising a character for qualities that would be admirable in a representative of a different estate, but which are wildly inappropriate in the given context.[25] Thus, for example, he describes the Monk in the *General Prologue* with the most elaborate praise for his skill as a hunter (I.165), for his fine horses and greyhounds (I.167, 190), and his elegant trimmings of fur and of gold (I.193–7), all of which details, of course, serve to damn the Monk for his attempt to emulate the aristocracy and perform the role of a great lord. This method is then amplified by his tale, which, far from being appropriate to his position, is a secular *de casibus* narrative about dignitaries who fell from great estate, and which is mercilessly lampooned in the Nun's Priest's account of the 'fall' of Chauntecleer.[26]

---

25 As Cooper puts it, 'Chaucer is the master of irony by way of the superlative' (29).
26 The generic relationship of these tales has often been discussed. For a particularly useful account, see Larry Scanlon, *Narrative, Authority, and Power: The Medieval Exemplum and the Chaucerian Tradition* (Cambridge: Cambridge University Press, 1994), 206–44.

The poetic technique outlined above, in which a dramatic interplay of genres and styles shines a light on the stratification of medieval society and the possibility of social mobility, is brilliantly exemplified in Chaucer's most famous beast poem, and the one that most extensively influences Spenser. The *Nun's Priest's Tale* has been described as a sort of *Canterbury Tales* in miniature, in which Chaucer grafts onto the central stem of the beast fable every imaginable literary and rhetorical form. As Rita Copeland says, the *Tale*

> is an almost impossible experiment in amplification, a beast fable dressed up in virtually every literary and rhetorical genre: epic, romance, love lyric, *de casibus* narrative, epideictic, mythography, hagiography, satire, advice to princes, exemplum and proverb, history, contemporary chronicle, tragedy, prophetic dream, and philosophical discourse.[27]

The tale's brilliance, as I am sure Spenser recognised, comes from its interplay of lower and higher registers, and its deft subversions of social hierarchies. The relationship between social class and rhetorical register is indicated from the opening of Chaucer's tale, which describes the widow as the perfect embodiment of a poor, industrious peasant who lives scrupulously within her means:

> A povre wydwe, somdeel stape in age,
> Was whilom dwellyng in a narwe cotage,
> Biside a grove, stondynge in a dale.
> This wydwe, of which I telle yow my tale,
> Syn thilke day that she was last a wyf
> In pacience ladde a ful symple lyf,
> For litel was her catel and hir rente.
> By housbondrie of swich as God hire sente
> She foond hirself and eek hir doghtren two. [...]
> No wyn ne drank she, neither whit ne reed;
> Hir bord was served moost with whit and blak –
> Milk and broun breed, in which she foond no lak,
> Seynd bacoun, and somtyme an ey or tweye [...] (VII.2821–9; 2842–5)

In this familiar passage, there is an implicit parallel between what we might call 'social decorum' (the widow lives in a style appropriate to her station) and 'rhetorical decorum' (the narrator describes the poor widow using simple language, not a lofty style that would be inappropriate to his subject matter). Of course, as Copeland notes, Chaucer's goal in the *Nun's Priest's Tale* is, in part, to wreak havoc with such notions of decorum.[28] He moves on briskly to the description of Chauntecleer, in which the black-and-white colour palette and sparse rhetorical

---

27 Rita Copeland, 'Chaucer and Rhetoric', in *The Yale Companion to Chaucer*, ed. Seth Lerer (New Haven: Yale University Press, 2006), 122–46 (138).
28 Ibid., 139.

style of the previous description is replaced by a riotously colourful and wildly inappropriate vocabulary:

> A yeerd she hadde, enclosed al aboute
> With stikkes, and a drye dych withoute,
> In which she hadde a cok, hight Chauntecleer.
> In al the land, of crowing nas his peer.
> His voys was murier than the murie orgon
> On messe-dayes that in the chirche gon.
> Wel sikerer was his crowyng in his logge
> Than is a clokke or an abbey orlogge.
> By nature he knew ech ascencioun
> Of the equynoxial in thilke toun;
> For whan degrees fiftene weren ascended,
> Thanne crew he that it myghte nat been amended.
> His coomb was redder than the fyn coral,
> And batailled as it were a castel wal;
> His byle was blak, and as the jeet it shoon;
> Lyk asure were his legges and his toon;
> His nayles whitter than the lylye flour,
> And lyk the burned gold was his colour. (VII.2848–64)

The passage joyfully undermines any notion of rhetorical decorum: its style contrasts wildly with the previous description, borrowing extensively from courtly and learned discourses, and the passage is replete with romance superlatives, as well as religious, courtly and scientific terminology that is comically inappropriate to the subject. The startling opposition of these two descriptions sets the tone for the splendid tale which follows, which runs roughshod over traditional expectations of literary decorum and delivers a kaleidoscope of riotously clashing styles that seems to defy attempts to pin down its meaning.[29] Chaucer is clearly at play here, and yet it may be that he has some serious social concerns. In her powerful explication of the tale, Helen Barr has noted that socio-political concerns are evident from the start of the tale, with its description of a poor but virtuous widow, and in the seeming parody of aristocratic affectations in the outrageous comparisons of Chauntecleer to a great lord.[30] In such a context, as she notes, there must be some significance in the fact that this is the only text in which Chaucer alludes to one of the defining historical events of his day, the Peasants' Revolt of 1381. As the fox runs off with Chauntecleer, the narrator compares the hullaballoo to the rebellion:

> So hydous was the noyse – a, benedicitee! –
> Certes, he Jakke Straw and his meynee

---

[29] Copeland argues that the *Tale* suggests that 'mimetic form may well be its own truth value: here the beast fable can be meaningful, not because it contains moral truths, but because even its meager structure can support a nearly infinite elaboration of formal possibilities' (139).

[30] Helen Barr, *Socioliterary Practice in Late Medieval England* (Oxford: Oxford University Press, 2001), 106–27.

> Ne made nevere shoutes half so shrille
> Whan that they wolden any Flemyng kille,
> As thilke day was maad upon the fox. (VII.3393-7)

In a brilliant exposition of the function of this passage, which relates rhetorical style to issues of social class, Barr writes:

> Rhetorical construction is socially freighted in a manner which erodes hierarchy and distance [...] A barnyard animal belonging to a peasant is here described in terms of aristocratic property, wealth and values [...] The tale is not just *about* the uprisings in 1381; it participates in the contest for representation which was such a key feature of the revolts. The tale is both a dazzling foray into the arts of fiction-making and an example of the social struggle for empowerment.[31]

Barr here argues that the extraordinary variety of discourses that collide in the *Nun's Priest's Tale*, which lend it such a carnivalesque tone, is more than merely playful. The tale, she suggests, is charged with social resonance, and its transgression of literary and rhetorical boundaries is determinedly political; indeed, the text has the potential to be seen as radically disruptive of traditional social structures. If Spenser detected such an agenda in Chaucer's work, I suspect he didn't much care for it. 'Mother Hubberds Tale' recoils in horror at the erosion of social hierarchies that allows the ape and fox so effectively to infiltrate successively higher social strata, and the tale's stylistic range serves to support, rather than undermine, the traditional distinctions between social estates.[32]

Nonetheless, Spenser recognised the parallel Chaucer draws between social mobility and the violation of poetic decorum by slipping between incompatible rhetorical modes. Whereas Chaucer creates a raucously comic effect by describing Chaunticleer as a great lord, Spenser serves more directly satirical ends, by having the ape and fox successfully imitate and perform the roles of great lords, and even kings. Thus, the ape carries off his new role with aplomb as he arrives at the court:

> So well they shifted, that the Ape anon
> Himselfe had cloathed like a Gentleman,
> And the slie Foxe, as like to be his groome,
> That to the Court in seemly sort they come.
> Where the fond Ape himselfe vprearing hy
> Vpon his tiptoes, stalketh stately by,
> As if he were some great *Magnifico*,
> And boldlie doth amongst the boldest go. (659-67)

---

31 Ibid., 116; 126-7.
32 It might be considered that there is some irony in Spenser's savage opposition to social climbing, since he himself was keen to climb the ladder. As Hadfield notes (19) 'Mother Hubberds Tale' is preceded by a letter that advertises Spenser's familiarity with Lady Compton and Mountegle and hints at a shared ancestry; while the dedication of 'The Teares of the Muses' to Lady Strange seeks to advertise Spenser's connection (the 'private bands of affinitie' [8]) to the Spencers of Althorp.

This passage is in some ways reminiscent of a woodcut and narrative from Geoffrey Whitney's *A Choice of Emblems and Other Devices* (1586), in which, as Erica Fudge has shown, an ape's failed imitation of a craftsman acts as a lesson not to overstep one's natural status.[33] In Spenser's beast fable, however, the irony is not that the animals are described as though they were great lords, but that they go virtually undetected once they disguise themselves and begin to act in the manner expected. The tale is fascinated with the power of clothing to transform a person's outward appearance and to make them appear to have a dignity that does not correspond to their moral or social status. It is not necessary, of course, to trace this particular insight back to Chaucer: Spenser could have found it in any number of models. And yet, I think it is worth noting that the discussion of clothing in 'Mother Hubberds Tale' is not confined to issues of aristocratic pretensions, but is in fact closely related to the problem of clerical ostentation in the wearing of vestments, and in this Spenser's work bears a striking similarity to a discussion in an anticlerical work he would have read as one of the *Canterbury Tales*, specifically the tale ascribed to the Plowman.

When the ape and the fox have fled the farmer's land, after butchering the sheep they had been employed to keep, they encounter an Anglican priest, who quickly reveals himself to be either a fool or a knave. The beasts solicit advice about how to make a living in the Church, and the priest responds with an account of the Anglican Church that suggests that the reforms have done little to provide the people with more noble spiritual shepherds. Specifically, the priest launches a stout defence of the use of fine vestments:

> Ne ar we tyde to fast, but when we list,
> Ne to weare garments base of wollen twist,
> But with the finest silkes vs to aray [...]
> For farre vnfit it is, that person bace
> Should with vile cloaths approach Gods maiestie,
> Whome no vncleannes may approachen nie [...]
> But he that serues the Lord of hoasts most high,
> And that in highest place, t'approach him nigh,
> And all the peoples prayers to present
> Before his throne, as on ambassage sent
> Both too and fro, should not deserue to weare
> A garment better, than of wooll or heare. (459–61; 464–6; 469–74)

As McCabe observes in his notes to these lines, the priest here 'exploits genuine Anglican arguments for the use of clerical vestments as a pretext for ostentation',

---

33 See the discussion of the emblem and the accompanying verse in Erica Fudge, *Perceiving Animals: Humans and Beasts in Early Modern English Culture* (Basingstoke: Macmillan, 2000), 29–30. While the field of animal studies has only an indirect bearing on the topic of the present chapter, it has of course been the focus of extensive discussion within early modern studies. See, for example, the essays collected in *At the Borders of the Human: Beasts, Bodies and Natural Philosophy in the Early Modern Period*, ed. Erica Fudge, Ruth Gilbert and Susan Wiseman (Basingstoke: Palgrave, 1999), and Laurie Shannon, *The Accommodated Animal: Cosmopolity in Shakespearean Locales* (Chicago: University of Chicago Press, 2013).

and 'need not indicate Spenser's sympathy with the Puritans in the vestiarian controversy'.[34] The lines in fact are similar to what one finds in Lollard critiques of the ostentatious vestments of Roman Catholic clergy, and notably in the *Plowman's Tale*. In this tale, the Pelican, representing the Lollard viewpoint, encounters a Gryphon, representing Papal authority, who dismisses the Pelican's assertion that churchmen should only wear humble clothing:

> Therfore, men of Holy Churche
> Shulde ben honest in all thynge:
> Worshypfully Goddes workes werche,
> So semeth it to serve Christ her kynge.
> In honest and in clene clothynge,
> Wyth vessels of golde and clothes ryche,
> To God honestly to make offrynge:
> To His lordshyppe none is lyche. (1101-8)

These lines represent only a part of tale's concern with fine vestments. There are broad similarities in thought and expression, and while Spenser may of course have found similar ideas elsewhere, it is beyond question that he was familiar with the *Plowman's Tale*. Andrew Wawn, in the *Spenser Encyclopedia*, cites six lines from *The Shepheardes Calender* that are directly influenced by the Lollard work, while also identifying a broader influence, and noting that 'of all the poems in the Chaucer canon, the *Plowman's Tale* is closest in form and spirit to the moral eclogues'.[35] Spenser's Anglican priest, it seems, is here made to parrot arguments from the Roman Catholic Gryphon. The Gryphon, of course, seeks to counter the Pelican's argument that the 'lords' of the Church are appropriating for themselves the trappings of secular lordship, when in fact they should remain subject to their true lord, and exercise their role as shepherds of the people. Indeed, the idea that the clergy should be good shepherds of their flock, and not attempt to live like lords, is one of the recurring motifs of the *Plowman's Tale*, a feature that it shares with Spenser's beast fable.

As has often been noted, the various roles into which Spenser's ape and fox step can each be imagined as a variation on the motif of the shepherd. They begin by gaining employment as literal shepherds, when the unsuspecting farmer allows them to look after his 'fleecie sheepe' (289) which they proceed to devour (318). When the priest explains the role of the clergy, he returns to this image: 'He [Christ] is the Shepheard, and the Priest is hee; / We but his shepheard swaines ordain'd to bee' (443-4). Again, the crafty beasts abuse their role as shepherds when they usurp the role of king: acting as tyrants rather than caring for their subjects, their neglect is epitomised in their failure to provide justice for the sheep whose lamb is killed by a wolf (1205-22). I would like to suggest that it is not improbable that Spenser was influenced here by the deployment of the same

---

34 McCabe, ed., 614.
35 'The Plowman's Tale', in *The Spenser Encyclopaedia*, ed. A.C. Hamilton (Toronto: University of Toronto Press, 1990), 549-50 (549).

imagery in the *Plowman's Tale*, in which the image of the shepherd and his sheep is a recurring motif, appearing first in line 282, where corrupt churchmen are compared to incompetent shepherds. It is most extensively developed in a central passage in which Peter's role as the first Pope is recast as the role of the shepherd:

> Christ badde Peter kepe His shepe,
> And with his swerde forbade hym smyte.
> Swerde is no tole with shepe to kepe,
> But to sheperdes that shepe woll byte.
> Me thynketh suche sheperdes ben to wyte
> Ayen her shepe with swerde that contende.
> They drive her shepe with great dispyte,
> But all thys God may well amende.
>
> So successours to Peter be they nought,
> Whom Christ made chefe pastoure:
> A swerde no sheperde usen ought,
> But he wold flee, as a bochoure.
> For who so were Peters successour
> Shulde bere hys shepe tyll hys backe bende,
> And shadowe hem from every shoure,
> And all thys God may wel amende. (573–88)

The metaphor is developed throughout the poem, as the Plowman continues to lambast false shepherds in lines 589–96, 675–6; 707–8; 1280–3. While such imagery is conventional, and available to Spenser from many sources, the fact that the poem is so extensively influenced by Chaucer, coupled with the fact that the *Plowman's Tale* has a demonstrable influence on *The Shepheardes Calender*, makes it plausible that the Lollard poem influenced 'Mother Hubberds Tale'. Such an interpretation is all the more attractive given that Chaucer is represented as a shepherd, Tityrus, in the *Shepheardes Calendar*, the epilogue of which contains an allusion to Chaucer and, apparently, the *Plowman's Tale*.[36]

With these associations in mind, it is possible to infer a broad pattern in Spenser's response to the tales of the 'beast group'. As we have seen, he seems to be aware that the stylistic and rhetorical variety of the *Nun's Priest's Tale*, and indeed of the *Canterbury Tales* as a whole, is charged with a social resonance. But, whereas, for Chaucer, the social diversity of his tellers enabled the generic diversity of his tales, Spenser is more troubled by the social mobility hinted at in Chaucer's work. Spenser, perhaps ironically, was drawn more naturally to the 'Chaucer' of the *Plowman's Tale*, who used the peasant narrator to offer a powerful corrective to the *Nun's Priest's Tale*: a satire that is bold and direct, not broad and evasive, aimed squarely at social issues, rather than literary ones. Underlying

---

36 Chaucer's role as Tityrus is discussed elsewhere in this volume, including the studies by Harriet Archer, Helen Barr and Megan Cook. While it is possible that Spenser is alluding to Langland in the reference to 'the Pilgrim that the Ploughman played a whyle' (line 10 of the epilogue to *The Shepheardes Calendar*), I agree with McCabe, who notes that an allusion to the *Plowman's Tale* is more likely.

the differences between their beast fables, then, we find profoundly different conceptions of what it means to be a poet.

Playing the poet: animal mimics in Chaucer and Spenser

In a radical departure from a tradition of scholarship characterised by attempts to identify and analyse its specific historical context, Richard Danson Brown has focused on 'Mother Hubberds Tale' as a poem about poetry, identifying the fox and ape as examples of the amoral poet, talented mimics who use their skills for personal rather than public gain.[37] The poem is certainly pervasively interested in mimicry and imitation, but rather than responding generally to the issue of the morality of the poet, Spenser, I suggest, is responding specifically to Chaucer's representation of himself as a mimic, and his use of mimicry as a core device in his satire. From the start of the poem, as he singles out Mother Hubberd's story as particularly worth retelling, Spenser casts himself as a strikingly Chaucerian mimic, imitating the 'mean' style of an uneducated woman:

> Ile write in termes, as she the same did say,
> So well as I her words remember may.
> No Muses aide me needes heretoo to call;
> Base is the style and matter meane withall. (41–4)

At one level, these lines, and the performance that follows, place Spenser within a long tradition of male poets mimicking female voices, which appears to have had a resurgence in the sixteenth century.[38] But what sets Spenser apart here is his mimicry of a voice that is not only female, but lower class, and the appropriation of a genre and a style that are emphatically low-brow.[39] Any attentive reader of Chaucer would be immediately struck by the echo of his oft-cited protestation that he does no more than repeat the words of his pilgrims, and that he should therefore not be blamed for the baseness of style or subject:

> Whoso shal telle a tale after a man,
> He moot reherce as ny as evere he kan
> Everich a word, if it be in his charge,
> Al speke he never so rudeliche and large. (I.731–4)[40]

---

37 See Brown, 169–212. In a recent essay, another scholar has suggested that the poem establishes an affinity, or even complicity, between the poet and rogues like the ape and fox. See Evan Gurney, 'Going Rogue: Spenser and the Vagrants', *Studies in Philology*, 113.3 (2016), 546–76.
38 See, for example, the texts considered in *Motives of Woe: Shakespeare and 'Female Complaint'*, ed. John Kerrigan (Oxford: Clarendon Press, 1991), as well as the discussion in Elizabeth D. Harvey, *Ventriloquized Voices: Feminist Theory and English Renaissance Texts* (London: Routledge, 1992).
39 The impersonation of a low style is signalled explicitly in the dedicatory letter to Lady Compton, which notes that 'Simple is the deuice, and the composition meane, yet carrieth some delight, euen the rather because of the simplicitie and meannesse thus personated' (9–11).
40 This motif is pervasive in the *Canterbury Tales*: it is recalled at the end of the Miller's prologue by way of apology for the fabliaux of the Miller and the Reeve (I.3167–86).

From the very beginning, then, Spenser responds to Chaucer precisely as an imitator of the voices of other men and women, and recalls his willingness to write about low-brow matter and adopt a low rhetorical style for poetic effect. Thus, Spenser's recitation of Mother Hubberd's tale recalls Chaucer's imitation of figures as diverse as the Wife of Bath, the Merchant, the Miller and the Reeve; while her choice of a beast fable recalls not only the *Nun's Priest's Tale* but the other members of the 'beast group'. In the final part of this chapter, I hope to show that the ape and the fox in 'Mother Hubberds Tale' are indeed, as Brown notes, types of the amoral poet, but that they also represent Spenser's response to the sequence of talking birds in Chaucer's beast group, each of which can also be understood as a model for the poet as a fabulist and satirist.

'It can hardly be by accident', Jill Mann has noted, 'that all Chaucer's forays into the realm of beast literature have birds as their central figures'.[41] As Mann makes clear, two factors seem to have been particularly important for Chaucer. Firstly, the Boethian figure of the caged bird offered a useful way to explore the relationship between nature and nurture, between animal instincts and the curtailing effects of civilisation and morality. More significant, perhaps, is the fact that birds, through their song, and in some cases speech, raise questions about the nature of speech and language that are particularly relevant to the poet.[42] Indeed, the talking birds of Chaucer's 'beast group' may all be understood as figures of the poet or the rhetorician. The loquacious Chauntecleer, with his ready store of exempla and his quick way with words is an obvious parody of the rhetorical poet, while even his name, as is often noted, includes the name of his poetic inventor.[43] A more suggestive model for the fox and ape of 'Mother Hubberds Tale', however, is found in Chaucer's *Manciple's Tale*, a retelling of the story of Phoebus and Coronis from *Metamorphosis* Book II, which focuses on the god of eloquence, his adulterous wife and the talking crow who reveals her betrayal. The poem introduces the caged crow in a passage that appears to draw a very conscious parallel with the poet of the *Canterbury Tales*:

> Now hadde this Phebus is his hous a crowe
> Which in a cage he fostred many a day,
> And taughte it speken, as men teche a jay.
> Whit was this crowe as is a snow-whit swan
> And countrefete the speche of every man
> He koude, whan he sholde telle a tale. (IX.130–5)

As Helen Cooper has observed, 'one could scarcely find a better way of summing up Chaucer's own method in the *Tales*'.[44] I suspect that the comparison, and

---

41 Mann, 192.
42 In his Epistle to *The Shepheardes Calendar*, as Harriet Archer discusses elsewhere in this volume, E.K. develops an explicit parallel between the fledgling bird and the 'new Poete'. In McCabe's edition of *The Shorter Poems*, the relevant passage may be found on p. 29, lines 147–58.
43 Peter Travis, *Disseminal Chaucer: Rereading The Nun's Priest's Tale* (Notre Dame: University of Notre Dame Press, 2010), 192.
44 Helen Cooper, *The Structure of 'The Canterbury Tales'* (Athens, GA: University of Georgia Press, 1984), 238.

particularly the word 'countrefete', would have immediately stuck the author of 'Mother Hubberds Tale', the main title of which is 'Prosopopoia', which Puttenham defined as 'the Counterfait in Personation'.[45] McCabe suggests that 'Spenser's use of the term seems to apply to his own literary skill in "counterfeiting" the poem's personae and to the malign social impersonations of the fox and ape'.[46] As this suggests, Spenser is alert to the relationship between the social impersonation of other estates and the rhetorical imitation of higher and lower styles, an awareness we have seen in the both Chaucer's *Nun's Priest's Tale* and *Manciple's Tale*. Certainly Spenser at one point draws attention to the imitative power of the fox in a way that is decidedly reminiscent of Chaucer's imitative strategy in the *Canterbury Tales* and the Manciple's description of the counterfeiting crow:

> Besides he vsde another slipprie slight,
> In taking on himselfe in common sight,
> False personages fit for euerie sted [...]
> Now like a Merchant, Merchants to deceive [...]
> Now like a Lawyer, when he land would lett [...]
> Then would he seeme a Farmer [...] (859–61; 864; 866; 871)

Here again, as with the 'turning a new leaf' passage discussed above, we see that whereas Chaucer is interested in the rhetorical and poetic potential of imitating different sorts of men, Spenser appears to twist such ideas into an attack on selfish individualism and social climbing. And yet, for both poets, the imitative skills of the social climber run uncomfortably parallel to those of the poet. Both central protagonists in 'Mother Hubberds Tale' appear to be influenced by Chaucer's crow; certainly, the ape is informed by the familiar trope of art as the ape of nature (*ars simia naturae*), and is very much represented as a figure of the amoral poet.[47] In a scene that recalls Chaucer's parallels between poets and talking birds, Spenser describes the ape as an aspiring poet:

> Ne, them to pleasure, would he sometimes scorne
> A Pandares coate (so basely was he borne);
> Thereto he could fine louing verses frame,
> And play the Poet oft. But ah, for shame
> Let not sweete Poets praise, whose onely pride
> Is vertue to aduance, and vice deride,
> Be with the worke of losels wit defamed,
> Ne let such verse Poetrie be named:

---

45 George Puttenham, *The Arte of English Poesie*, ed. Gladys Doidge Willcock and Alice Walker (Cambridge: Cambridge University Press, 1970 [1936]), 239.
46 McCabe, ed., 608.
47 The figure of the artist as the ape of Nature is discussed in a seminal excursus, 'The Ape as Metaphor', in Ernst Robert Curtius, *European Literature and the Latin Middle Ages* (Princeton: Princeton University Press, 1953; repr. 1983), 538–40. Of course, in addition to such metaphorical significance, the ape may refer to a historical person, such as Jean de Simier, the ambassador of the Duc d'Alençon.

> Yet he the name on him would rashly take,
> Maugre the sacred Muses, and it make
> A seruant to the vile affection
> Of such, as he depended most vpon,
> And with the sugrie sweete thereof allure
> Chast Ladies eares to fantasies impure.
> To such delights the noble wits he led
> Which him relieu'd, and their vaine humours fed
> With fruitles follies, and vnsound delights. (807–23)

Chaucer is surely not far from Spenser's thoughts here, as we may surmise from the allusion to Pandarus in line 807. Like the crow who imitates every man, the ape is an image of poet as imitator, but here the poet-figure makes no claim to tell the truth, only to please his audience and gain favour. In a number of ways, the ape is an inversion of the crow: whereas the ape hides his base nature under flattery, the crow hides his under the pretence of being a plain-speaking truth-teller.

When the crow reports to Phebus that his wife has been cheating on him with a man of base degree, he chooses the most crude and cruel way to convey the information, circling around the truth until the brutal final line of his speech: 'For on thy bed thy wife I saugh hym swyve' (IX.256). On hearing this, Phebus kills his wife, before repenting his rash actions and taking vengeance on the crow:

> I wol thee quite anon thy false tale.
> Thou songe whilom lyk a nyghtyngale;
> Now shaltow, false theef, thy song forgon,
> And eek thy white fetheres everichoon,
> Ne nevere in al thy lif ne shaltou speke. (IX.293–7)

Phebus deprives the bird of his song, strips his white feathers and condemns him and his progeny to be black forever. As Michaela Paasche Grudin has noted, the tale offers an extensive reflection on the relationship between discourse and power, and the dangers of telling unpalatable truths to powerful men.[48] And yet, while the ape seems to take the safer route, neither beast escapes punishment, and perhaps the most striking parallel between the two tales is that both are revealed ultimately to be folktale *pourquois* about why certain animals are the way they are. Thus, the once-white crow is stripped of its white feathers and beautiful singing voice:

> And to the crowe he [Phebus] stirte, and that anon,
> And pulled his white fetheres everychon,
> And made hym blak, and refte hym al his song,
> And eek his speche, and out at dore hym slong
> Unto the devel, which I hym bikate;
> And for this caas been alle crowes blake. (IX.303–8)

---

48 See Michaela Paasche Grudin, *Chaucer and the Politics of Discourse* (Columbia: University of South Carolina, 1996), 149–63.

So too, the ape is stripped of qualities it had then but has no longer:

> But th'Apes long taile (which then he had) he [the Lion] quight
> Cut off, and both eares pared of their hight;
> Since which, all Apes but half their eares haue left,
> And of their tailes are vtterlie bereft. (1381-4)

This aspect of the tale appears to have made a distinct impression on some early readers. Richard S. Peterson notes that Thomas Tresham considered that the poem's readers must be 'madder then marche hares, that thus desire to be resolved howe apes did first forgoe their tayls: principallie when the discourse therof proceedeth from mother Hubber that ould fooll'.[49] The ending of the fable is certainly curious: as Brown has noted, unlike the fables of, say, Henryson, Spenser's fable offers no moral (169-72). But in fact this brings Spenser even closer to Chaucer's treatment of the form in the 'beast group', since the *Nun's Priest's Tale* ends with no discernible moral, or rather too many to isolate just one, while the *Manciple's Tale* ends not with a moral about truth telling, but a caution to remain silent and never to criticise powerful men. The tale finishes with the Manciple recalling the words of his mother, who advised him: 'My sone, be war, and be noon auctour newe / Of tidynges, wheither they be false or trewe' (359-60). In the modern order of the *Canterbury Tales*, the *Manciple's Tale* (the last of the tales told in verse) has come to be read, along with the Parson's Prologue and *Tale* and the Retraction, as part of Chaucer's abandonment of poetry.[50] Of course, this narrative would not have been available to Spenser: the positioning of the *Canterbury Tales* at the head of early modern printed editions was not likely to suggest to any reader that Chaucer was ready to abandon poetry, especially since the Retraction was never published in the sixteenth century; while the addition of the *Plowman's Tale* just after the *Manciple's Tale* would have indicated that Chaucer was not even finished with beast literature, let alone poetry itself.

The *Plowman's Tale* appealed to Spenser, I suggest, precisely because it so forcefully reclaims for Chaucer the role of poet as satirist, willing to boldly critique the abuses of his society and speak the truth without fear. After the comical Chauntecleer and the brutally honest crow, the *Plowman's Tale* offers a new bird-model for the poet in the Pelican, a figure not only of Christ, but of the truth-teller who unabashedly speaks out in the face of the powerful Gryphon and the authority of the Roman Catholic Church. Towards the end of the tale, the identity of poet and Pelican begin to merge as the Pelican expresses a wish that his debate be recorded in writing:

---

49 Richard S. Peterson, 'Laurel Crown and Ape's Tail: New Light on Spenser's Career from Sir Thomas Tresham', *Spenser Studies*, 12 (1998), 1-35 (23). Peterson is here transcribing a letter from Tresham to Lewis, Lord Mordaunt, in the ownership of L.G. Stopford Sackville Esq., Drayton House Northants, on loan at Northamptonshire Record Office, Wootton Hall Park, MS. S.S. 234.
50 For example, see Stephen D. Powell, 'Game Over: Defragmenting the End of the *Canterbury Tales*', *Chaucer Review*, 37.1 (2002), 40-58.

> God wolde that any of Christes shepe
> Had herde, and ytake kepe
> Eche a worde that here sayd was,
> And wolde it wrytte and well it kepe! (1280–4)

The narrator steps forward to volunteer his services, 'Yf for my travayle any man wolde pay' (1286). The narrator claims to be a truth-teller who will precisely mimic what he has heard, but of course the poet is suggesting a deeper and more politically engaged sort of truth-telling than that. At the end of the poem, the voice of the Pelican and the poet appear to have fully merged as the Pelican asks:

> For my wrytynge, yf I have blame,
> Who wyll for me fyght of flyght? [...]
> Therefore I praye every man
> Of my wrytynge have me excused. (1358–9; 1365–6)

In the final stanza, the narrator claims to be nothing more than an honest reporter, and that the substance of the tale is nothing but a fable, in a passage which, paradoxically, both claims the complete identity of the narrator's words and the Pelican's, while distancing the poet from responsibility for the content:

> Thys wrytynge wryteth the Pellican,
> That thus these people hath dyspysed
> Wyteth the Pellican, and not me [...] (1367–8; 1373)

The Plowman is here echoing a familiar Chaucerian motif (I.725–42; I.3167–86), which is gleefully deployed in the *Nun's Priest's Tale* when the narrator blames Chauntecleer for his own misogyny: 'Thise been the cokkes wordes, and nat myne' (VII.3265). As we saw at the beginning of this section, of course, Spenser directly alludes to this motif when he attributes the tale and its faults to Mother Hubberd (41–4; 1385–8), claiming, like Chaucer, to merely mimic what he has heard. Both writers are profoundly aware of the need to cultivate authority while seeming to eschew it; both are aware also of the satirical (or even seditious) potential of speaking the truth under a veil, though it would be misguided to expect them both to have reached the same conclusions, especially when Spenser is reading a version of Chaucer which includes texts the medieval poet never wrote. Ultimately, Spenser's beast fable is the end result of extensive reflection on what it means to be an author, while his engagement with Chaucer's beast group has served to radically underline both the continuity and discontinuity between the 'new poet' and the old.

Conclusion

Looking at them in a modern edition, from which the *Plowman's Tale* has been expunged, Chaucer's 'authentic' beast tales would not lead one to suspect that he placed much stock in the fable as a political or satirical tool. The *Nun's Priest's Tale*, while broadly satirical, takes aim at the liberal arts curriculum, at the excesses of rhetoric and intellectual pretension, and at the medieval tendency to seek a moral in every tale. The *Manciple's Tale* is arguably of even less use to the satirist, since it insists on the dangers of speaking truth to power, and ends with a counsel to silence. And yet, Spenser's reading of these tales, which he found grouped with the *Plowman's Tale* near the end of Chaucer's great work, must have been profoundly different from our own. Reading them as a group, he would have found at the end of the *Canterbury Tales* a rich discourse on the responsibilities of the poet, mediated through three texts that explore three contrasting types of beast literature as a vehicle for satire. Read as a group, the beast fables of the *Canterbury Tales* provide an extraordinary vision of a writer struggling to conceptualise the role of the poet, and invoking three very different talking birds as potential models: the loquacious Chauntecleer, who says nothing of consequence yet can always talk himself out of harm; the crow, whose ill-advised truth telling lands him in hot water; and the Christ-like Pelican, who stands his ground and commits to speak truth to power. Spenser, I suggest, was ultimately more drawn to the Pelican than the 'authentic' models provided by Chaucer, but if this seems ironic, it is nonetheless appropriate, and perhaps even oddly characteristic of Spenser's desire to imitate Chaucer without replicating his manner of imitation: to mimic the great mimic without ever becoming his ape.

11

Propagating authority: poetic tradition in *The Parliament of Fowls* and the Mutabilitie Cantos

Craig A. Berry

As in his other dream visions, Chaucer begins his *Parliament of Fowls* with an account of the occasion of the dream, an account that leads into and frames the dream itself. In the case of the *Parliament of Fowls*, the frame is a particularly bookish one in which Chaucer summarises Cicero's *Dream of Scipio*, which he has been reading, and then narrates how, after he puts down the book and falls asleep, he dreams his own dream of Scipio. In Chaucer's dream, Scipio Africanus appears to him and announces:

> Thow hast the so wel born
> In lokynge of myn olde bok totorn,
> Of which Macrobye roughte nat a lyte,
> That sumdel of thy labour wolde I quyte.[1]

Scipio Africanus has apparently kept an eye on his reputation in the centuries following his death, for what we have here is an ancient Roman authority telling a late medieval English poet that Macrobius, the late antique commentator, thought his book was something special. Africanus overreaches a bit to claim the 'olde bok totorn' as his own, since in that book his first-person narrative is introduced and framed by another first-person narrative in the voice of his adopted grandson Scipio the Younger; and in any case the *Dream of Scipio* forms the last part of Cicero's *De re publica*, so Cicero might be thought to have a better claim to the book than Africanus. Chaucer portrays unmediated access to the most ancient link in a chain of reported speech, but then, by mentioning Macrobius, steps back to call attention to the process of transmission. Chaucer's dream is thus nearly as crowded with authorities at its outset as it will later be with squabbling birds, and just as the birds gather to ensure the propagation of their kinds, the appearance of

---

1 My thanks to Judith H. Anderson, Richard Danson Brown, Claire Eager, Jeff Espie, Mark Sherman and this volume's editors for stimulating questions and comments that made this revised chapter much better than it had been. Remaining defects are of course mine.
  Geoffrey Chaucer, *The Parliament of Fowls* in *The Riverside Chaucer*, ed. Larry D. Benson (Boston: Houghton Mifflin, 1987), 109–12.

an authority who keeps track of his own literary history suggests a preoccupation with the propagation of literary authority itself.

Spenser shares this preoccupation in his sophisticated treatment of poetic tradition near the middle of the Mutabilitie Cantos. In refusing to describe the garments of Dame Nature, who arrives on Arlo Hill early in canto vii to adjudicate the dispute between Jove and Mutabilitie, Spenser sends us to Alan of Lille, whose authoritative description of the goddess's clothing appears in his *De planctu naturae*. In mentioning Alan, Spenser reminds us that Chaucer invokes Alan's authority for the same purpose in *The Parliament of Fowls*. Critics who have taken this double acknowledgement as a serious statement about Spenser's literary debts have often concerned themselves either with elucidating the differences among Alan's, Chaucer's and Spenser's versions of the goddess Natura, or have found Spenser's more significant indebtedness to Alan and Chaucer in his exploration of sexual love in Books III and IV of *The Faerie Queene*.[2] Not surprisingly, Spenser's simultaneous allusion to two predecessors has also evoked comment as a statement about poetic tradition and authority.

John Guillory has written eloquently on the continuity of authority in the Mutabilitie Cantos, but he narrowly limits the scope of that continuity in claiming that 'we can enclose the entire rhetoric of continuity within a larger structural discontinuity', a discontinuity he identifies as the rift between the secular and the sacred.[3] Guillory argues that in the absence of some transcendent but inaccessible authority,

> [...] a rhetoric of textual continuity seems a small victory. But it is the only ground of authority on this side of the impassable boundary of the sacred [...] Until or unless a voice on the other side speaks again, the human word remains its own authority, built up out of past voices that declare their continuity with the present merely by continuing to speak.[4]

But a voice on the other side is precisely what Chaucer gives us in Scipio Africanus, who not only crosses the boundary between transcendent and temporal, but also literally pushes the dreaming Chaucer across the threshold between secular and

---

2 For the former approach, see for example Alice Miskimin, *The Renaissance Chaucer* (New Haven: Yale University Press, 1975), 42–3; Thomas Bulger, 'Platonism in Spenser's *Mutabilitie Cantos*', in *Platonism and the English Imagination*, ed. Anna Baldwin and Sarah Hutton (Cambridge: Cambridge University Press, 1994), 126–38 (134–6). For the latter, see Maureen Quilligan, 'Words and Sex: The Language of Allegory in the *De planctu naturae*, the *Roman de la Rose*, and Book III of *The Faerie Queene*', *Allegorica*, 2 (1977), 195–216, where she argues, 'If, however, we examine the *De planctu* in the context of Book III rather than Book VII of *The Faerie Queene*, we can see that the source Spenser merely mentions in the *Mutabilitie Cantos* states the basic problem considered in the *Book of Chastitie*' (195). On the widespread 'refracted' influence of the *Parliament of Fowls* throughout *The Faerie Queene* but especially in the Temple of Venus episode in Book IV see Judith H. Anderson, *Reading the Allegorical Intertext: Chaucer, Spenser, Shakespeare, Milton* (New York: Fordham University Press, 2008), 135–53.
3 John Guillory, *Poetic Authority: Spenser, Milton, and Literary History* (New York: Columbia University Press, 1983), 64.
4 Ibid., 66.

sacred. Guillory may be right that the Mutabilitie Cantos record the impossibility of capturing the sacred in poetry, but we gain a deeper understanding of Spenser's interest in Chaucer by noting that Chaucer literalises and dramatises the very same difficulty in *The Parliament of Fowls*. Maureen Quilligan offers a helpful revision of Guillory's argument by pointing out that Alan of Lille is not merely the name of an authority but also an actual author, perhaps even one whom Spenser read.[5] By reminding us that Alan's elusive text is a real book by a real author, Quilligan seeks to show that the rhetoric of continuity is not such a small victory after all:

> To insist [...] on the actual continuity between Spenser and one of his named sources is not only to save the source, it is also to understand the pivotal function of the reader in the tradition of narrative allegory. What is important for Spenser about Alain's work is that it is a text within a community of readers [...] If the origin of a poem's composition is not itself sacred, the work of reading it may be.[6]

Dreamers eventually wake up and goddesses leave off visiting Arlo Hill, but a poet who can function as audience while also reaching an audience of successor poets nevertheless enacts a human connection that stretches across time. As T.S. Miller says of Chaucer's dream visions, 'Chaucer's model readers [...] are writers, and writers who must prove themselves first-class rereaders, willing to innovate as well as preserve and share the memory of the past'.[7] Spenser's representation of poetic tradition thus shares with Chaucer's *Parliament of Fowls* an interest in rhetorically linking the earth-bound poet with a community of readers who also write, a community depicted as both historically bound and transcendent.

Walled gardens, gated communities and authoritative introductions

The importance of community in *The Parliament of Fowls* appears most obviously in the congregation of birds who gather to choose their mates, but the dream vision frame offers a different – and more ascetic – view of community: Chaucer gives an accurate summary of the *Dream of Scipio*, a text in which Scipio Africanus exhorts his grandson to 'be more zealous in safeguarding the commonwealth' (3.1),[8] or, in

---

5 Quilligan, 'Words and Sex', surveys the issue of whether Spenser knew Alan's work. See 212 note 3 and the Appendix (214–16) for a discussion of the difficulties Spenser faced in locating the *Plaint* and the manuscripts he may have known (a printed edition was not available in England at the time). Quilligan offers a compressed and revised account of the manuscript situation in *Milton's Spenser: The Politics of Reading* (Ithaca, NY: Cornell University Press, 1983), 162.
6 Quilligan, *Milton's Spenser*, 161. Judith Ferster, 'Reading Nature: The Phenomenology of Reading in the *Parliament of Fowls*', *Mediaevalia*, 3 (1977), 189–213, makes a similar point about the *Parliament of Fowls* when she writes 'the poem chooses to demonstrate the possible creativity of loving discourse with the world through the part of the chain of discourse it occupies: the discourse between readers and writers' (208).
7 T.S. Miller, 'Writing Dreams to Good: Reading as Writing and Writing as Reading in Chaucer's Dream Visions', *Style*, 45.3 (2011), 528–48 (543).
8 Marcus Tullius Cicero, *Somnium Scipionis*, in *Macrobius: Commentary on the Dream of Scipio*, trans. William Harris Stahl, Records of Civilization, 48 (New York: Columbia University Press, 1952), 70.

Chaucer's words, to work for the 'commune profit' (75).⁹ But the overall purpose of Africanus's appearance in Chaucer's version is to instruct his grandson in divine mysteries that make the things of earth seem trivial:

> Thanne tolde he hym, in certeyn yeres space
> That every sterre shulde come into his place
> Ther it was first, and al shulde out of mynde
> That in this world is don of al mankynde. (67–70)

The austere sense of worldly vanity may explain the mood of the Chaucerian narrator, who is filled with weariness and dissatisfaction as he puts down his book to go to sleep (88–94), but Chaucer ultimately seems unconvinced that earthly life is inconsequential. Africanus's tour of the heavens and assurance that all the accomplishments of human history shall pass 'out of mynde' at the end of the platonic world-year (the time when the planets return to their original positions) require revision by the poet who values old books and dreams of a direct meeting with an ancient authority.

The Africanus who appears to Chaucer may traverse centuries and cosmic spheres in order to be present in Chaucer's dream, but he also, unlike his Ciceronian predecessor, speaks in a bossy, familiar tone, and the sacred space into which he leads the poet is an exuberant garden filled with talking – and thus unmistakably human – birds. Time and mortality add urgency to the various birds' search for proper mates, but the atmosphere of posturing and class rivalry roots the poem firmly in the world of courtly negotiation in which Chaucer and his writings participated. Moreover, Chaucer's Africanus explicitly tells the dreamer that the vision he witnesses is not directly applicable to him (because he is a non-participant in matters of love), but rather rewards his diligent labour in reading and gives him 'mater of to wryte' (168).[10]

To gain access to the writing material promised to him by Africanus, the dreaming Chaucer must pass through an obviously Dantean gate in a scene dense with the intersecting relationships among reading, writing and authority. As Daniel Pinti, who includes the tradition of Dantean commentary in this nexus of readers and writers, says:

> the comedic nature of the reception and representation of Dante manifests itself in the interrogation of the reading moment and the reading subject in *The Parliament of Fowls*, through a carefully structured exploration of the relationship between authorship as both a self-construction and the construction of other readers.[11]

---

9 On community in the *Parliament of Fowls*, see Paul A. Olson, 'The Parlement of Foules: Aristotle's Politics and the Foundations of Human Society', *Studies in the Age of Chaucer*, 2 (1980), 53–69.
10 On gardens as sites of poetic inspiration in Chaucer and Spenser, see Claire Eager's chapter in this volume.
11 Daniel Pinti, 'Commentary and Comedic Reception: Dante and the Subject of Reading in *The Parliament of Fowls*', *Studies in the Age of Chaucer*, 22 (2000), 311–40 (339).

The mutual construction of authors and readers is already present in the fundamental situation of Dante's entry into the underworld led by Vergil, a situation that, as Albert Ascoli explains, gives him unmediated access to authority and 'allows him to imagine a community of poets from different times and places entering directly into timeless conversation'.[12] But unlike the dark words on the gate of hell in *Inferno* canto III, the inscriptions on Chaucer's gate, puzzling though they are, offer encouragement as well as a warning, and there are illuminating differences as well as deep similarities between Chaucer's treatment and Dante's. While there are two inscriptions in the *Parliament of Fowls*, there is still only one gate, so there is no choice between 'the well of grace' (129) on the one hand and the domain of 'Disdayn and Daunger' (136) on the other; both describe the things that happen to lovers. Chaucer simply freezes in considering whether to go through the gate at all, and his difficulty, like Dante's, seems to have less to do with reading the text than it does with acting in the face of it. Dante's complaint about the words before him – 'Master, their sense is hard for me'[13] – registers a fear of proceeding through the gate at least as much as any difficulty of interpretation, and Vergil's reply provides not a literal explication ('Abandon every hope' seems clear enough already), but rather encouragement and context. Vergil advises Dante to abandon not hope but rather suspicion and cowardice (III.13), and provides ongoing commentary as he leads Dante by the hand into the mysteries of the underworld.

Significantly, Chaucer, unlike Dante, does not speak before the gate he encounters, but as retrospective narrator merely reports his fear of going through it:

> Right as betwixen adamauntes two
> Of even myght, a pece of yren set
> Ne hath no myght to meve to ne fro –
> For what that oon may hale, that other let –
> Ferde I, that nyste whether me was bet
> To entre or leve, til Affrycan, my gide,
> Me hente and shof in at the gates wide. (148–54)

The silent Chaucer is pushed, rather than led, emphasising his passivity. We may regard such an abject and utterly incapacitated narrator as typically Chaucerian, and with good reason, but this moment also recalls *Inferno* X, where Dante is 'pushed [...] among the sepulchers' by Vergil for a meeting with Farinata.[14] The banished Dante requires physical compulsion to confront such a plangent reminder of the Florentine political strife that caused his exile, and Chaucer, self-exiled from matters of love, also needs authoritative impetus to face the alarming reminders of his greatest deficiency inscribed on the gate before him.

---

12 Albert Russell Ascoli, *Dante and the Making of a Modern Author* (Cambridge: Cambridge University Press, 2008), 316.
13 'Maestro, il senso lor mè duro', Dante Alighieri, *Inferno* III.12 in *The Divine Comedy of Dante Alighieri*, ed. and trans. Robert M. Durling (Oxford: Oxford University Press, 1996–2011), 3 vols.
14 *Inferno* X.38. I am indebted to Richard Danson Brown for alerting me to the relevance of this passage.

We should remember, though, that Dante is not Chaucer's only source and that the narrator of Alan's *Plaint* suffers a breakdown similar to Chaucer's when approached by Nature herself:

> When I saw that she had drawn close to me, I fell on my face, stricken by stupor, abandoned consciousness and sank into total disorientation. My sensory powers suspended, I was neither living nor dead, but reduced to a neutral state between the two.[15]

Whereas Alan is suspended between death and life, Chaucer is pulled in equal but opposite directions by the powerful forces of two magnets ('adamauntes'), and thus each narrator is entirely incapable of even passive participation until the authority in his presence intervenes to assist him. But there the similarity ends. Alan's Nature, though she gently revives the swooning Alan, goes on to identify his 'disorientation of mind' (6.3) with the general moral torpor of humanity upon which she will lecture him at some length. Africanus, on the other hand, tells Chaucer, after pushing him through the gate, 'dred the not to come into this place, / For this writyng nys nothing ment bi the' (157–8), and assures him (via a wrestling analogy) that observation as well as participation may lead to knowledge. Chaucer's category mistake in believing that the inscriptions on the gate apply to him results from communal exclusion: he is not 'Loves servaunt' (159), but with an authoritative introduction he can join a different community of those who write about love even though they are not participants. Africanus leads Chaucer by the hand into the garden, and like Dante when Vergil takes his hand, Chaucer finds comfort in this most child-like of human interactions; an intimate connection with ancient authority provides the poet with courage to behold the marvels he will eventually write about. Reading and writing thus link the mysteries of another world to the affairs of this one, and Chaucer's resolve after awakening to read more in the hope of another dream makes the end of the *Parliament* an essentially forward-looking moment.

Old books and heavenly aspirations

For Spenser, the longing for a diachronic community begins to appear in the opening stanzas of canto 7 as he leaves behind the 'woods and pleasing forrests' of faeryland to describe a parliament, not of birds but of gods, who gather on Arlo Hill to hear Dame Nature's judgement of Jove and Mutabilitie. Spenser pleads inadequacy for such a 'high flight' and he invokes his 'greater Muse' for help:

> […] in my feeble brest
> Kindle fresh sparks of that immortall fire,
> Which learned minds inflameth with desire

---

15 Alan of Lille, *The Plaint of Nature*, in *Alan of Lille: Literary Works*, ed. and trans. Winthrop Wetherbee (Cambridge, MA: Harvard University Press, 2013), 6.1.

> Of heauenly things: for, who but thou alone,
> That art yborne of heauen and heauenly Sire,
> Can tell things doen in heauen so long ygone;
> So farre past memory of man that may be knowne.[16]

Like most such invocations, this one focuses on the limitations of the mortal poet, and suggests that with the proper divine help, he can treat elevated subjects above the reach of his own memory or skill. That the source of inspiration is an 'immortall fire' whose passage through human breasts causes a 'desire / Of heauenly things' suggests a neoplatonic emanation and return, except that the return is not complete: the things of heaven are only desired and not attained, thus keeping the poet in his mortal frame for the time being. And since the muse's help is required not merely to overcome the individual poet's inadequacy but also because her knowledge is 'farre past memory of man', Spenser is not alone in his frailty, and he thus casts his lot with other human minds who also serve as the channels through which divine inspiration flows. In other words, Spenser's conventional need for a muse's divine wisdom to see him through difficult poetic territory is supplemented in this case by a desire to have intellectual company for the journey, and seeking an 'immortal' authority – that is, an authority outside history – is paradoxically an endeavour he shares with the 'learned minds' *of* history, minds whose learning is presumably mediated to Spenser via the books they have written.

Human tradition and divine inspiration become more explicitly joined a few stanzas later when Spenser pauses over the impossibility of describing Nature's clothing: 'Her garment was so bright and wondrous sheene, / That my fraile wit cannot deuize to what / It to compare' (VII.7.7). Comparison, the essence of poetic figuration, fails, and Spenser makes the best of his predicament by pointing out that he has excellent company in his failure. He first likens his situation to that of the apostles who witnessed the Transfiguration, and then moves closer to home and identifies another English poet who, he claims, also hesitated before the description of Dame Nature:

> So hard it is for any liuing wight,
>   All her array and vestiments to tell,
>   That old *Dan Geffrey* (in whose gentle spright
>   The pure well head of Poesie did dwell)
>   In his *Foules parley* durst not with it mel,
>   But it transferd to *Alane*, who he thought
>   Had in his *Plainte of kindes* describ'd it well:
>   Which who will read set forth so as it ought,
> Go seek he out that *Alane* where he may be sought. (VII.vii.9)

There is a curious duality about the description of Chaucer here, a duality that reveals Spenser's efforts to find something transcendent in the human activity

---

16 Edmund Spenser, *The Faerie Queene*, ed. A.C. Hamilton, 2nd edn (Harlow: Pearson, 2001), VII. vii.1–2.

of making poems. Chaucer, who was once a 'liuing wight' like Spenser himself and thus equally incapable of describing Nature's dazzling clothes, is also a 'gentle spright' infused with the 'pure well head of Poesie', which implies an unmediated access to the essence of poetic invention. There are subtle differences here from Spenser's earlier invocation of 'Dan *Chaucer*, well of English vndefyled' in Book IV (IV.ii.32). There Spenser addresses Chaucer in the second person and proposes to continue the fragmentary *Squire's Tale* 'through infusion sweete / Of thine owne spirit, which doth in me surviue' (IV.ii.34).[17] As is appropriate for the Book of Friendship, this earlier moment of spiritual infusion is direct and immediate, with no need for an intermediary, but in the Mutabilitie Cantos, where the 'pure well head of Poesie' dwells *in* Chaucer's gentle spirit rather than Chaucer *being* the 'well of English vndefyled', we see Spenser calling attention to the role of an intermediary even as he reaches beyond him. Just as Chaucer dreams of a direct encounter with the remote authority Scipio Africanus while giving but slight mention to the important role of Macrobius in transmitting and interpreting the *Dream of Scipio*, Spenser represents his intermediary as a transparent vessel who simply points the way to the original – and more authoritative – source. Chaucer's authority as a flesh-and-blood precursor who shares Spenser's human frailty exists side by side with his status as a spiritual transmitter of poetic inspiration, and by suggesting that diligent readers will seek out Alan's text for themselves, Spenser takes his place alongside Chaucer as one whose individual contribution is also part of something larger.

Although invited to do so by the Chaucerian narrator's self-presentation as a mere reporter, Spenser misrepresents Chaucer by claiming that he 'durst not [...] mel' with Alan's description. There is nothing in the *Parliament of Fowls* to suggest that Chaucer's courage failed him at the prospect of describing Nature; his deferral to Alan simply notes the relevance of the earlier poet's description: 'right as Aleyn, in the Pleynt of Kynde, / Devyseth Nature of aray and face, / In swich aray men myghte hire there fynde' (316–18). It is unclear whether 'there' refers to Alan's text, where Chaucer found Nature, or the garden hilltop in his own poem where he puts her. And as Judith Ferster points out, the verb *finden* 'means not only "discover" but "invent". To choose something from a source is to render it for one's self; to interpret it is to re-invent it'.[18] A full account of Chaucer's reinvention of the *De planctu naturae* lies outside of my present scope, but suffice it to say that Alan's 'council of the creatures of the air' that produces 'the dreamlike effect of art' (2.19), a figurative description of one part of Nature's dress, becomes in the *Parliament of Fowls* a literal congregation of jostling, squawking, talking birds seen

---

17 On Spenser's intimate connection with Chaucer in his continuation of the *Squire's Tale*, see Craig A. Berry, '"Sundrie Doubts": Vulnerable Understanding and Dubious Origins in Spenser's Continuation of the Squire's Tale', in *Refiguring Chaucer in the Renaissance*, ed. Theresa M. Krier (Gainesville: University Press of Florida, 1998), 107–27; Jonathan Goldberg, *Endlesse Worke: Spenser and the Structures of Discourse* (Baltimore: Johns Hopkins University Press, 1981), 28–46; Stephen Guy-Bray, 'Chaucer and Spenser and Other Male Couples', ch. 2 of *Loving in Verse: Poetic Influence as Erotic* (Toronto: University of Toronto Press, 2006).
18 Ferster, 202.

in a dream. Far from avoiding Alan's description, Chaucer takes his source's still picture and animates it.[19] Thus 'mel' (an alternate spelling of 'meddle') is precisely what Chaucer does with Alan's text. 'Meddle' did not yet have the pejorative connotations it now does; its most significant meanings for Chaucer's treatment of Alan are 'to interpose, take part *in*' and 'to mix or join in company; to mingle, associate with'.[20] Interposing himself in poetic tradition and joining in company with his source are in fact more apt descriptions of Chaucer's role than Spenser's claim that he simply 'transferd to *Alane*' a task he found too difficult.

Spenser may exchange Chaucer's real place in literary history for another one of his own making at least partly because his goddess Nature does indeed owe more to Alan's than to Chaucer's. As Glenn Steinberg notes, 'Spenser's Nature, unlike Chaucer's, requests no human input and receives none',[21] and as Alan's Nature herself says, expressing a pointedly self-contained model of artistic making that leaves no room for human agency: '[God] is the maker, I was made. He is the artisan of my work, I am the work of the artisan' (6.14). But while Spenser's Nature removes herself from human concerns 'whither no man wist' (VII. vii.59), Spenser's model of artistic production is considerably less aloof than that of Alan's Nature. In addition to regarding Chaucer as a fellow link in a chain of mortal minds, Spenser also imagines the individual mutations of poetic tradition subordinated to a more transcendent authority that expresses itself through that tradition. Spenser's representation of Chaucer as an individual precursor who is also a transparent vessel of divine inspiration locates the poet within the mythos of Mutabilitie subsumed by Nature: ever-changing and yet still the same, eternally linked in poetic tradition even as Mutabilitie threatens the temporal artefacts of poetic production and the poet himself. As Robert Lanier Reid says, 'embracing Chaucer's more positive view of change is a key to resolving Mutabilitie's boisterous assaults', but Spenser's embrace reaches through Chaucer for something beyond even as it encompasses the most immediate author in a chain of authorities.[22] Whether acknowledging or suppressing the distinctive contribution of a predecessor, Spenser's invocation of tradition attempts to transcend the limits of

---

19 Maureen Quilligan, 'Allegory, Allegoresis, and the Deallegorization of Language: The *Roman de la rose*, the *De planctu naturae*, and the *Parlement of Foules*', in *Allegory, Myth and Symbol*, ed. Morton W. Bloomfield, Harvard English Studies, 9 (Cambridge, MA: Harvard University Press, 1981), 163–86, describes Chaucer's treatment of the *De planctu* and *Le roman de la rose* in *The Parliament of Fowls* as 'deallegorization'; 'Chaucer's process', she says, 'is essentially to transform the silent, unvoiced textuality of his allegorical sources into a dramatic, mimetic fiction of audible, voiced sound' (164). Quilligan hints that part of Spenser's task in *The Faerie Queene* was to 'turn his master's narratives back into allegory' (181). On Chaucer's treatment of his sources, see also chap. 5 of Theresa M. Krier, *Birth Passages: Maternity and Nostalgia, Antiquity to Shakespeare* (Ithaca, NY: Cornell University Press, 2001).
20 'Meddle', defs. 8 and 4 respectively, *The Oxford English Dictionary* (Oxford: Oxford University Press, 1971).
21 Glenn A. Steinberg, 'Chaucer's Mutability in Spenser's *Mutabilitie Cantos*', *Studies in English Literature 1500–1900*, 46.1 (2006), 27–42 (37).
22 Robert Lanier Reid, 'Spenser's Mutability Song: Conclusion or Transition?' in *Celebrating Mutabilitie: Essays on Edmund Spenser's 'Mutabilitie Cantos'*, ed. Jane Grogan (Manchester: Manchester University Press, 2010), 61–84 (65).

the individual poet just as Nature's power over Mutabilitie comes not from an immunity to change but from an infinite capacity for it.

Spenser is no more a participant in the events on Arlo Hill than Chaucer is of the avian parliament he describes, and both poets present themselves as ordinary mortal witnesses to heavenly goings-on. It is striking that these poets in particular should pose as mere observers. Chaucer participated directly in parleys of various kinds as a minor royal bureaucrat, and of course Spenser's view of Galtymore (the presumed original of Arlo Hill) from the window of Kilcolman Castle places him squarely in the middle of a colonial project that involved no small amount of suppressing rebellious impulses and adjudicating disputes. The parliament of birds in Geoffrey's dream and the parliament of gods and goddesses on Arlo Hill seem designed to evoke the affect and immediacy of the worlds these poets knew while removing the poets themselves from the dangers and disappointments so common there. Neither poet, moreover, can quite make up his mind whether the divine or the mortal has the greater claim on him. In the oft-quoted eighth canto of Book VII, which contains only two stanzas, Spenser summarises and responds to the debate between Nature and Mutabilitie in a fashion that suggests he is ambivalent about the numinous events he has witnessed. These enigmatic lines have been much puzzled over, and with good reason; for any premise they can be shown to affirm, they can also be shown to affirm its opposite. Harry Berger points out that in the first stanza when the poet claims that the power of Mutabilitie makes him 'loath this state of life so tickle' (VII.vii.1), that he not only loathes his mutable 'state of life', but also that he is loath to cast it away. In the final stanza, where Spenser yearns for the sight of 'that great Sabbaoth God' (VII.vii.2), it is unclear whether the sight the poet is most eager to behold is the Lord of Hosts or a host of some divine community.[23] A.C. Hamilton has suggested that the Sabbaoth God refers at least obliquely to Queen Elizabeth, a reading that potentially makes the poet's yearning for eternity into a final plea to his earthly ruler for some sort of attention or recognition.[24] Angus Fletcher discusses the inconclusiveness and nonlinearity of the *Cantos* in terms of complexity theory,[25] the science of our own day, and Sarah Powrie, invoking the scientific debates of Spenser's time, concludes that 'the eighth canto, paralyzed by ambivalence and ambiguity, subverts the allegorical orientation toward poetic ecstasy and totalizing answers'.[26] A resistance to 'totalizing answers' sounds downright Chaucerian, and the shifting line between physics and metaphysics joins the other uncertainties present in this final canto, so aptly deemed 'vnperfite' in its heading.

---

23 Harry Berger, Jr., *Revisionary Play: Studies in the Spenserian Dynamics* (Berkeley: University of California Press, 1988), 269.
24 A.C. Hamilton, 'Our New Poet: Spenser, "well of English undefyld"', in *A Theatre for Spenserians*, ed. Judith M. Kennedy and James A. Reither (Toronto: Toronto University Press, 1973), 101–23 (110). See also James Nohrnberg, *The Analogy of The Faerie Queene* (Princeton: Princeton University Press, 1976), 83.
25 Angus Fletcher, 'Complexity and the Spenserian Myth of Mutability', *Literary Imagination: The Review of the Association of Literary Scholars and Critics*, 6.1 (2004), 1–22.
26 Sarah Powrie, 'Spenser's Mutabilitie and the Indeterminate Universe', *Studies in English Literature 1500–1900*, 53.1 (2013), 73–89 (85).

In short, the renunciation of earth resonates with nostalgia, and the embrace of eternity contains overtones of more worldly aspirations. These closing stanzas repeat the symmetrical contrast of worldly vanity and platonic transcendence that Scipio Africanus uses to exhort his grandson, but such thoughts present the same problems for Spenser that they do for Chaucer. The end of earth's cyclical patterns in the 'time when no more *Change* shall be' (VII.viii.2) may be in some respects a comforting thought, but like the platonic world-year that completes all subsidiary revolutions, the demise of Mutabilitie means that poetic achievements, along with the rest of human history, will go 'out of mynde', and if a consensus emerges from the myriad interpretations of Spenser's final stanzas, it is that the poet has both feet firmly planted on the ground as he reaches for heaven.[27]

Poetic tradition provides a unique rhetorical opportunity for Chaucer and Spenser to link their heavenly aspirations with their earthly calling, though the *Parliament of Fowls* is by no means the only Chaucerian text where Spenser could have found such a link. The famous ending of *Troilus and Criseyde*, itself an imitation of the end of of Statius's *Thebaid*, shows us Chaucer exhorting his 'litel book' to 'kis the steppes' of the great poets of the past only a few lines before the slain Troilus looks down from the eighth sphere upon the vanities of this world (V.1786–92; V.1807–27). But Spenser had already imitated this ending in his career-launching *Shepheardes Calender*, and in the somewhat scattershot ending of the *Troilus* he would find no coherent model for integrating earthly and heavenly concerns.[28] Chaucer's *Retraction*, in which a full and thus efficacious confession produces as a welcome side effect a list of the author's works recorded for posterity, might have offered some potential for thinking about literary continuity, but it was not included in the editions most readily available in Spenser's lifetime, and even if Spenser knew it, its confessional mode may have been too Catholic or at least less than amenable to the neoplatonic ethos of the Mutabilitie Cantos.[29] However, for the Chaucer of the *Parliament* the yearning for heaven is at least partly satisfied by reading an old book: his reading inspires him to dream of unmediated confrontation with an ancient authority, a dream he in turn records in a book for others to read, thus propagating an authority to which he has added his own voice. Spenser simultaneously acknowledges and suppresses Chaucer's individual place in the chain of authorities, a move that is itself an imitation of Chaucer's approach to tradition, but Spenser's treatment of poetic predecessors is a more platonised one in which inspiration is presented as an 'immortal fire' or a 'pure well head' that expresses itself through mortal vessels

---

27 David Quint, *Origin and Originality in Renaissance Literature: Versions of the Source* (New Haven: Yale University Press, 1983) notes that 'In playing the Neoplatonic game of participation and withdrawal, Spenser might find himself unable to make it back: he does not share [Giordano] Bruno's enthusiastic desire to annihilate his own individuality in the contemplation of the One' (246 note 52).

28 See the prefatory poem 'To His Booke' which opens *The Shepheardes Calender* in *The Yale Edition of the Shorter Poems of Edmund Spenser*, ed. Willam A. Oram *et al.* (New Haven: Yale University Press, 1989).

29 Thomas R. Lounsbury, *Studies in Chaucer: His Life and Writings* (New York: Harper and Brothers, 1891), I, 413.

even as it transcends them. Like Spenser's deferral to a remote authority through an intermediary, Chaucer's chain of dreamers and books figures the poet's reaching for a durable source of literary connection, and for both poets, bookish mediation may be the most acceptable compromise between the demands of secular and sacred; however fragile the link to the past and however uncertain the prospects of an enduring and favourable reception, the glimmer of tradition gives the poet a sense of crossing the boundaries of his own mortality while maintaining ties to the sublunary activity of writing poems.

12

'New matter framed upon the old': Chaucer, Spenser and Luke Shepherd's 'New Poet'

Harriet Archer

In 1579, Edmund Spenser's persona or associate 'E.K.' introduced the anonymous author of *The Shepheardes Calender* simply as 'the new Poete'.[1] Use of the definite article announced the work's iconoclastic ambitions; in addition to an aesthetic and intellectual mission statement, the epithet worked well as a modesty *topos*, signalling the author's relative youth and obscurity. Scholarship has identified many of the various ways in which Spenser's writing does represent a new departure for vernacular verse. Indeed, for a long time E.K.'s appellation, at once triumphal and deeply unassuming, shaped English literary history. For C.S. Lewis, Spenser the 'new Poete' ended the so-called 'Drab Age': reading *The Shepheardes Calender*, Lewis proposed, 'we should feel as if we were passing from winter to spring'.[2] But I will suggest that, amid the interrogation of Spenser's poetic novelty, the particular hermeneutic force of the phrase itself has been overlooked. What did it mean to be a 'new Poete' in late sixteenth-century England? This chapter will bring E.K.'s formulation into dialogue with another Tudor new poet, a figure constructed by the gospeller Luke Shepherd in his anticlerical satire, *Philogamus* (1548). Shepherd's poem helps to recontextualise E.K.'s 'new Poete' in the distinct cultural queasiness around the idea of novelty which pervades early modern writing, and the complex shades of Protestant reform and Catholic-associated fantasy it evokes. Spenser's engagement with this web of signification throughout *The Shepheardes Calender* allows him to situate himself within and against an emerging early modern poetic canon, headed up by the figure of Chaucer. But it also hints at Spenser's debts to the non-canonical, for whom Chaucer also somehow stands in, as attempts to locate poetic authority are turned inside-out.

---

1 I wrote this chapter during a Leverhulme Early Career Fellowship at Newcastle University; I am grateful to the Leverhulme Trust and Newcastle's School of English for making the research possible, and to Mike Pincombe, as well as the volume's editors, for reading and commenting on various drafts.
  'E.K.', 'To the most excellent and learned both Orator and Poete, Mayster Gabriell Haruey', in Edmund Spenser, *The Shepheardes Calender: Conteyning Twelue Aeglogues Proportionable to the Twelue Monethes* (London: Hugh Singleton, 1579), ¶. ij^r. All subsequent references to *The Shepheardes Calender* will be given in parentheses after the quotation.
2 C.S. Lewis, *Studies in Medieval and Renaissance Literature* (Cambridge: Cambridge University Press, 1966), 128.

As regards the place of the 'new' within such a canon, or 'literary system', Richard Helgerson notes, 'a different kind implies other kinds. Indeed, it implies the existence of a system whose individual elements take meaning from their relationship to the whole'.[3] The new is necessarily defined against the old, and in *The Shepheardes Calender*'s paratexts this is a role fulfilled by 'the olde famous Poete Chaucer' (¶. ij), who makes his first named appearance in Spenser's original poetic debut as the mouthpiece for E.K.'s opening words. It would take more space than I have here to unpick the working of the ostensible dialectic of old and new within *The Shepheardes Calender*, let alone Spenser's oeuvre as a whole. From the outset, irony and contradiction are built into the vocabulary with which it is addressed; for example, E.K.'s use of 'obsolete' in the Epistle to describe Spenser's unfamiliar language is the *Oxford English Dictionary*'s first recorded instance of the term.[4] The paratexts' circularity is immediately apparent, and well documented.[5] Spenser is a 'new Poete' writing himself into an old tradition, 'applying an olde name to a new worke' (¶. iij^r). Where 'Immeritô' apologises for his greenness, E.K. grounds it in a reputable literary heritage. Spenser's most striking innovations often turn out to be imitative, and vice versa, while of course Immeritô's statement of his poem's unknown parentage begins with the ironic Chaucerian allusion, 'Goe little booke', providing himself with a clear heredity by echoing *Troilus and Criseyde*.[6]

Such circularity resonates with Chaucer's own poetic practice. The deployment of archaic words under the guise of neologisms has been identified as a Chaucerian trait, and it has been suggested that Chaucer himself asserted his own credentials as a new kind of poet by rejecting 'conventional standards of order and truth'.[7] For Derek Brewer, Chaucer's 'modernity' inheres in the recognition that 'he wrote what he evidently came in the end to regard as purely "literary", recreational, that is, fictional, works, which did not aim to edify'; works characterised by 'realism, occasional bawdiness, satire, irony'.[8] Brewer's identification of aspects of Chaucer's writing within his own sense of a twentieth-century modernity itself feels like an outdated critical strategy. But his association of the modern with freedom – from aesthetic and moral constraints, from convention, from context – speaks to the ways in which Spenser's 'newness' intermittently operates. 'The rejection of the "archaic" is itself "archaic"', Brewer argues, because such a rejection would be based

---

3 Richard Helgerson, *Self-Crowned Laureates: Spenser, Jonson, Milton and the Literary System* (Berkeley and London: University of California Press, 1983), 2.
4 See Judith H. Anderson, *Reading the Allegorical Intertext: Chaucer, Spenser, Shakespeare, Milton* (New York: Fordham University Press, 2008), 155.
5 See Paula Blank, *Broken English: Dialects and the Politics of Language in Renaissance Writings* (London: Routledge, 1996), 119.
6 Geoffrey Chaucer, *Troilus and Criseyde*, in *The Riverside Chaucer: Third Edition*, ed. Larry D. Benson *et al.* (Oxford: Oxford University Press, 1988), V.1786.
7 See Christopher Cannon, *The Making of Chaucer's English: A Study of Words* (Cambridge: Cambridge University Press, 1998), 5, cited in Hannah Crawforth, *Etymology and the Invention of English in Early Modern Literature* (Cambridge: Cambridge University Press, 2013), 30–1; Jaqueline Miller, 'The Writing on the Wall: Authority and Authorship in Chaucer's *House of Fame*', *Chaucer*, 17 (1982), 96–115 (101).
8 Derek Brewer, *Tradition and Innovation in Chaucer* (London and Basingstoke: Macmillan, 1982), 9; 18.

on temporally contingent value judgements, and therefore not truly 'modern', or context-free.[9] In addition, though, Chaucer engages with the challenges of poetic inheritance in the *Squire's Tale*, which reveals 'the self-conscious intersection of literary imitation and inherited authority'.[10]

While its irony is self-evident, there has been a tendency to overlook the potential humour in this back-and-forth between old and new, which we can be sure from their correspondence that Spenser and his university friend Gabriel Harvey would have enjoyed.[11] Tongue-in-cheek quibbling of this kind peppers the *Three Proper and Wittie Familiar Letters* (1580) between the two writers, as well as Harvey's manuscript correspondence: Harvey, posing as the secretary recording a fictitious committee's response to a poetic essay of Spenser's, objects, for example, 'Sir, yower newe complaynte of ye newe worlde is nye as owlde as Adam and Eve, and full as stale as ye stalist fasshion that hath bene in fasshion since Noes fludd'.[12] The lexical mischief evidenced here, which underpins many of Spenser and Harvey's exchanges, has not always been taken into account when considering a text which draws in many ways on that friendship. Judith H. Anderson, among others of course, suggests that the 'obsoleteness' of *The Shepheardes Calender* 'is purposeful and constructive [...] It is antique but not antiquated, and by virtue of its antiquity it is, according to E.K., authoritative, authentic, and enduring'.[13] If we approach E.K.'s recommendations with scepticism, though, as Spenser seems throughout *The Shepheardes Calender* and its off-kilter commentary to encourage us to do, this authoritative platform collapses. This chapter will suggest that Spenser's ironic approach to the reductive old–new dialectic is informed by a playful irreverence for new and old alike, and is designed to lead us into 'a hall of broken mirrors where origins are undecidable', and where poetic authority is constantly receding.[14] This is Chaucer's *House of Fame*: redux.

As noted above, Spenser's poetic newness is largely uncontested.[15] Andrew Hadfield describes the *Faerie Queene* as 'a unique poem, a new departure in English poetry that changed its course and nature. Everything about the poem is new'.[16] Helgerson reads in Spenser's identification as 'the new Poete' an even more radical proposal, 'to redefine the limits of poetry, making it once again (if in England it had ever been) a profession that might justifiably claim a man's life'; '*The Shepheardes Caldender* is meant to distinguish the New Poet from all other writers of English verse'.[17] In addition to the poetic innovation evident in *The Shepheardes*

---

9   Ibid., 21.
10 Craig A. Berry, 'Flying Sources: Classical Authority in Chaucer's *Squire's Tale*', *ELH*, 68 (2001), 287–313 (287; 291).
11 On Spenser's ludic interaction with Chaucer, see Helen Barr's chapter in this volume.
12 Gabriel Harvey, *Letter-Book of Gabriel Harvery, A.D. 1573–1580*, ed. Edward Scott (London: Camden Society, British Library, 1884), 82–3.
13 Anderson, 156.
14 Richard Chamberlain, *Radical Spenser: Pastoral, Politics and the New Aestheticism* (Edinburgh: Edinburgh University Press, 2005), 50.
15 See William Kuskin, *Recursive Origins: Writing at the Transition to Modernity* (Notre Dame: University of Notre Dame Press, 2013), Introduction and chap. 2.
16 Andrew Hadfield, *Edmund Spenser: A Life* (Oxford: Oxford University Press, 2012), 254.
17 Helgerson, 60; 69.

Calender, both the *Calender* itself and the later *Complaints* (1591) also contain poems about poetic invention, predicated on their own 'break with the past'.[18] However, the paradox of old versus new dogs accounts of Spenser's linguistic and stylistic innovation. Richard Danson Brown notes that 'Spenser's archaic diction is paradoxically a function of his readiness to make stylistic innovations rather than a symptom of chronic conservatism. No new poetry can emerge outside the context of traditional forms of writing'.[19] Hannah Crawforth sees as one of the central problems of criticism of *The Shepheardes Calender* 'that of how to reconcile the obvious indebtedness to Chaucer expressed in both Spenser's prefatory poem and through the imitation of his predecessor's diction in the *Calender* as a whole, with the apparent criticisms levelled by E.K. at those who have diluted the purity of the English language with excessive borrowings, of which Chaucer was the widely acknowledged champion in Spenser's day'.[20] Crawforth resolves this difficulty by positing that both E.K. and Spenser are looking back beyond Chaucer to Anglo-Saxon English. The 'estrangement from language' which the *Calender*'s diction forces on its readers, though, perpetuates the circularity of old-as-new, new-as-old, which both Chaucer's works and burgeoning Anglo-Saxon scholarship embodied.[21] Danson Brown suggests that 'the "new Poet" achieves distinction through his recovery of a pure English in his verse. His poetry is new in turn by its self-conscious desire to renovate the "heritage" of English words'.[22] The use of the term 'renovate' here encapsulates the difficulty of Spenser's approach – not merely to make new, but to make new *again*.

New poets and periodisation

To ask what it means to be a 'new Poete' in the sixteenth century demands that we interrogate sixteenth-century notions of periodisation. To be a 'new Poete' in the sense that criticism has read into E.K.'s tag, implies, as noted above, a consciously effected break with a literary mode which has gone before. Was such a thing feasible for sixteenth-century writers, and the early modern process of literary change as they perceived it?

In the *Goodly Garlande or Chapelet of Laurell* (1523), Skelton includes Horace 'with his new poetry' in his list of illustrious writers, alluding to Horace's participation in the movement of Latin poetic innovation in the first century BCE.[23] Nicknamed the Alexandrians, these poets' own 'novelty', or break with contemporary fashion, was predicated in turn on their imitation of the

---

18 Richard Danson Brown, *'The New Poet': Novelty and Tradition in Spenser's 'Complaints'* (Liverpool: Liverpool University Press, 1999), 8; see 7–9.
19 Ibid., 12.
20 Crawforth, 23.
21 Ibid., 27.
22 Danson Brown, 85–6.
23 John Skelton, *A Ryght Delectable Treatyse upon a Goodly Garlande or Chapelet of Laurell* (London: Richard Faukes, 1523), A.vii^v.

third-century Hellenistic neoterics, among them the pastoral writer Theocritus.[24] Theocritus's *Bucolics* is clearly an important text in the genealogy of Spenser's pastoral poetry. But in fact the work of his near contemporary Callimachus, and its reception, offers a more useful insight into the workings of Spenser's own neoteric project. In the *Aetia*, Callimachus voices his objections to treading familiar poetic paths; Apollo asks the shepherd-poet to 'fatten his flocks, but to keep his muse slender', expressing, it is thought, Callimachus's antipathy towards Homeric imitation in preference for a briefer, plainer style.[25] It is with an irony akin to Spenser's citation of Chaucer even as he disowns the notion of antecedents, then, that Virgil echoes Callimachus in his sixth *Eclogue*, when 'the Cynthian', Apollo, 'grasped / my ear and warned me: "Tityrus, a shepherd / should graze fat sheep, but sing a slender song"'.[26] The elision in E.K.'s Epistle of the Virgilian Tityrus with Chaucer reinforces not only Spenser's position within a vernacular poetic continuum, but specifically evokes Virgil's recollection of a neoteric antecedent of his own. From as early as the Augustan period, 'new poetry' appears to have been associated with the simultaneous rejection and assimilation of traditions, an association which evidently informed Spenser's identification as 'new' in 1579.

Despite continued critical consensus over Spenser's radical newness, recent developments in Tudor studies have done away with Lewis's notion of a Drab Age, an age which purportedly ended with the publication of *The Shepheardes Calender* and a revolution in English poetics.[27] However, William Webbe, whose *Discourse of English Poetry* (1586) is as much a paean to *The Shepheardes Calender* as it is a literary history, does indeed mark the second half of the sixteenth century as a literary turning point. Webbe praises Chaucer, Lydgate, Langland and Skelton, but his new age belongs to Surrey, Norton, Tusser, Heywood, Whetstone, Munday and Churchyard, and above all Gascoigne, 'the very cheefe of our late rymers'.[28] Even so, Webbe is not quite satisfied that the revolution has come to fruition. In his 'Preface', he argues that English has been 'purged from faultes, weeded of errours, and polished from barbarousness', yes, but asks, why has 'our English speech in some of the wisest mens judgements [...] never attained to any sufficient ripeness'? Webbe believes it is 'the cankered enmitie of curious custome' which is at fault; that only by 'breaking custome' could writers 'adorne their Countrey and advance their style with the highest and most learned toppe of true Poetry'.[29]

---

24 See, for example, N.B. Crowther, 'Horace, Catullus, and Alexandrianism', *Mnemosyne*, 31 (1978), 33–44 (33–4).
25 Callimachus, *Aetia, Iambi, Hecale and Other Fragments*, ed. C.A. Trypanis, T. Gelzer and Cedric H. Whitman (Cambridge, MA: Harvard University Press, 1973), *Aetia*, Book 1, 6–7.
26 Virgil, *Eclogues. Georgics. Aeneid: Books 1–6*, ed. H. Rushton Fairclough (Cambridge, MA: Harvard University Press, 1999), Eclogue VI, 60–1. Interestingly, John Lyly's character 'Callimachus' in *Euphues and his England* (1580), printed the year after *The Shepheardes Calender*, also becomes embroiled in an intergenerational conflict arising out of a clash between youth and old age. See Lyly, *Euphues and his England* (London: T. East for Gabriell Cawood, 1580), 2ʳ–12ᵛ.
27 See Mike Pincombe and Cathy Shrank, 'Doing Away with the Drab Age: Research Opportunities in Mid-Tudor Literature (1530–1580)', *Literature Compass*, 7 (2010), 160–76.
28 William Webbe, *A Discourse of English Poetrie, Together, with the Authors Iudgment, Touching the Reformation of our English Verse* (London: John Charlewood for Robert Walley, 1586), C.iiiᵛ.
29 Webbe, 'A Preface to the Noble Poets of England', (1586), A.iiiiᵛ.

Fashion, sometimes the medium of unwelcome modernity, is here the force which holds progress back, and a further 'break' with tradition is needed before a new poetic age may be fully inaugurated.

Webbe, who most objects to the debasing effects of rhyme on English poetry, would have been sympathetic to the efforts of Spenser and Harvey, but also Thomas Blenerhasset, another proponent of unrhymed verse and experimental quantitative metres who was explicitly opposed to the perceived Catholic associations of the 'rude Gotish rhyming', ushered in by the barbarism of late antiquity.[30] Just a year before *The Shepheardes Calender* was printed, an aside in Blenerhasset's *Second Part of the Mirror for Magistrates* (1578) frames the contemporary debate over rhyme and metre as a threshold of poetic innovation.[31] As I have noted elsewhere, this is an unappreciated moment of periodisation and poetic prophecy.[32] From a safe remove of ironic detachment, Blenerhasset's narrators, Inquisition and Memory, predict a stand-off between the champions of unrhymed verse and the critics. Inquisition bewails how great Churchyard, Sackville, Phaer, Turberville, Golding and Gascoigne could have been if they had chosen not to write in rhyme, but Memory replies,

> Truely [...] let it be as it is, you shall see good sport shortly. I smyle to see how *Zoilus* and *Momus*, will crie out O vayne glorious heade, whiche now for a singularitie dooth indeuour to erect a newe kinde of Poetrie in England.[33]

Memory's smug enjoyment of the unfolding 'sport' masks Blenerhasset's confessional and aesthetic stake in this 'newe kinde of Poetrie'. Of Inquisition's list of poets who could have achieved greater things had they eschewed rhyme, in fact many did experiment with new modes of writing and translation, and Blenerhasset demonstrates himself to be thoroughly in their debt. Spenser, then, participates in the construction of a poetics of novelty in the late 1570s and 1580s, of which he is only the most prominent exponent. John N. King suggests by contrast, for example, that the so-called 'Drab Age school' posits Philip Sidney as the writer who 'formulated a new aesthetics suitable to the changed circumstances of his time'.[34]

A survey of references to 'new poetry' in the sixteenth century demonstrates that the rhetoric of poetic innovation is also bound up with a list of key names, who recur in this context throughout the century. Along with those already associated with E.K.'s Epistle, such as Chaucer, Lydgate and, latently, Skelton, there

---

30 Thomas Blenerhasset, *The Second Part of the Mirror for Magistrates* (London: Robert Webster, 1578), 40ᵛ.
31 Ibid., 40ʳ⁻ᵛ.
32 Harriet Archer, '"Those Chronicles whiche other men had": Paralipsis and Blenerhasset's *Seconde Part of the Mirror for Magistrates* (1578)', in *'A Mirror for Magistrates' in Context: Literature, History and Politics in Early Modern England*, ed. Harriet Archer and Andrew Hadfield (Cambridge: Cambridge University Press, 2016), 147–63 (160).
33 Blenerhasset, 40ᵛ.
34 John N. King, *English Reformation Literature: The Tudor Origins of the Protestant Tradition* (Princeton: Princeton University Press, 1982), 11.

are others we should add: Horace, Langland, Wyatt and Surrey, perhaps more unexpected additions like Tusser, Sternholde and Sackville, and Phaer, Golding and, most prominently, Gascoigne. To allude to poetic innovation was to call up an evolving version of this list of antecedents.

The majority of sixteenth-century accounts of poetic novelty or change hinge on the question of vernacular language, although opinion is thoroughly divided over whether Chaucer and Gower represent the beginning or the end of a process of perfection.[35] Skelton's *Goodly Garlande* erects the scaffolding of periodisation even as it collapses the centuries into a sort of diachronic drinks party, at which all key names of literary history from Homer to Lydgate and on to his own time are simultaneously present. Skelton divides three English poets from the rest, and has them embrace as brothers: Gower, who 'first garnished' English, Chaucer, who made 'our English' 'fresh', and Lydgate, are a distinct group by virtue of their innovative approach to the vernacular.[36] Skelton's own presence as a member of this brotherhood, King argues, also allows him to attack 'the imported criteria of Continental humanism'.[37] In the prefatory verse to the 1568 edition of Skelton's *Works*, Thomas Churchyard constructs more of a separation between past and present, but essentially follows suit by aligning Chaucer and Langland with 'our rare poetes newe' on account of their use of vernacular English.[38]

By contrast, George Puttenham's *Arte of English Poesie* (1589) seems to synthesise or at least align Webbe and Churchyard's generation of 'poetes newe' with the influence of vernacular Italian poetry on early Tudor writers. Puttenham's critical tract provides a clear run-down of shifting literary cultures and the evolution of the canon predicated on moments of newness, again stemming from the perfection of vernacular writing in the time of Edward III and Richard II.[39] This is a clear epochal turning point for Puttenham, and renders Chaucer and Gower both chronologically 'the first of the age', and metaphorically the first, along with Lydgate and Harding, in Puttenham's estimation. Literary novelty, though, arrives later, when towards the end of Henry VIII's reign, there 'sprong vp a new company of courtly makers', chiefly Wyatt and Surrey, like 'nouices newly crept out of the schooles of *Dante Arioste* and *Petrarch*'. Such was the influence of their new poetry, Puttenham suggests, that they 'may iustly be sayd the first reformers of our English meetre and stile'.[40] Puttenham's emphasis on the new is striking, and he even breaks out of his customary delineation of literary culture by regnal period to isolate this novel phase. He rates Sternhold, Heywood and Ferrers most highly among the Edwardians, and Phaer and Golding under Mary I, before

---

35 See, for example, Harriet Archer, 'Holinshed and the Middle Ages', in *The Oxford Handbook of Holinshed's Chronicles*, ed. Paulina Kewes, Ian W. Archer and Felicity Heal (Oxford: Oxford University Press, 2013), 171–86 (178–9).
36 Skelton, A.viii[r].
37 King, 44.
38 John Skelton, *Pithy Pleasaunt and Profitable Workes of Maister Skelton, Poete Laureate* (London: Thomas Marshe, 1568).
39 George Puttenham, *The Arte of English Poesie* (London: Richard Field, 1589), 48.
40 Ibid., 48.

adding that, 'in her Maiesties time that now is, are sprong vp an other crew of Courtly makers, Noble men and Gentlemen of her Maiesties owne seruauntes'.[41] The repetition here of language used above ('sprong vp', 'Courtly makers') draws a direct comparison between Puttenham's contemporaries – Sidney, Raleigh, Greville, Gascoigne, Breton and Turbervile – and the 'new' Henrician court poets.[42] This suggests that in the late 1570s and early 1580s, Puttenham believes English writing has entered another era, perhaps also based on the 'stile of Italian Poesie' in Puttenham's eyes.[43] It seems that the unfolding of literary change is conceived of at a reasonably granular level, and regularly sewn into narratives of nation-forming and national difference. However, the received account of its precise workings across the sixteenth century remains unstable, and inklings of poetic change can be greeted with anything from pride, to scepticism, to derision.

E.K.'s Epistle, as well as Spenser's wider oeuvre, does at times present poetic novelty, youth and greenness in a positive light. The 'new Poete' is 'as young birdes, that be newly crept out of the nest, by little first to proue theyr tender wyngs, before they make a greater flyght', in common with the pantheon of Virgil, Mantuan, Petrarch, Boccaccio, Marot and Sannazaro, 'whose foting this Author every where followeth' (¶.iij^r). E.K. states optimistically that 'so finally flyeth this our new Poete, as a bird, whose principals be scarce grown out, but yet as that in time shall be hable to keepe wing with the best' (¶.iij^r). This simile anticipates Spenser's depiction in the *Faerie Queene* of the Redcrosse Knight,

> As Eagle fresh out of the Ocean waue,
> Where he hath left his plumes all hoary gray,
> And deckt himselfe with feathers youthly gay,
> Like Eyas hauke vp mounts vnto the skies,
> His newly budded pineons to assay,
> And marueiles at himselfe, still as he flies:
> So new this new-borne knight to battell new did rise.[44]

The self-reflexivity in this passage harks back to Spenser's meditation on his own poetic development in *The Shepheardes Calender*, and conveys above all the promise and buoyancy of Redcrosse's baptismal emergence from the Well of Life. The excitement of the new, and an evocation of invention's elevating properties, also permeates Philip Sidney's contemporary *Apology for Poetry* (1595), which famously presents invention as a fruitful poetic freedom: unlike other professions, 'onely the Poet, lifted vp with the vigor of his owne inuention, dooth growe in effect another nature, in making things either better then Nature bringeth forth, or quite newe formes'.[45] Spenser certainly felt this excitement, as his multiple uses

---

41 Ibid., 49.
42 Ibid., 49.
43 The grouping of pre- and post-1580s poets seems to belie Spenser's revolutionary status at least in this regard.
44 Edmund Spenser, *Faerie Queene* (London: Richard Field for William Ponsonby, 1596), I.xi.34.
45 Philip Sidney, *An Apologie for Poetrie* (London: James Roberts for Henry Olney, 1595), C1^v.

of the phrase 'new adventure' in the *Faerie Queene* attest, while the freshness and purity of his portrayals of new births have not staled despite their familiarity. The image of the Palmer, for example, 'at last [...] turning to his charge' to try 'his troubled pulse', and finally perceiving a flutter of life 'as chicken newly hatcht' (II. viii.9), highlights the visceral thrill of this combination of ideas.[46]

Gabriel Harvey, too, shared Spenser's enthusiasm for newness.[47] His allusions to Spenser's *Calender* in the *Proper and Wittie Familiar Letters* foreshadow E.K.'s epithet, but additionally raise some intriguing possibilities. Harvey repeatedly refers to the text as the 'new Calender' or 'new shepheardes calender', which strikes a perplexing note, given that he also calls the book 'famous' several times.[48] While this contradiction fits with Harvey's arch, wry tone in the *Letters*, and sly sidelong references to 'a certain famous book', for example, this elision of the work's title and its author's alias is suggestive. It might be that Spenser and Harvey referred in conversation to the 'new calendar', differentiating Spenser's work-in-progress from Robert Copland's 'old' *Shepardes Kalender* (1570) (or even George Turbervile's recent *Eclogs* (1567) or Abraham Fleming's *Bucolikes* (1575)). Protestant England, though, had just witnessed the instigation of another 'new calendar': the reformed Elizabethan liturgical calendar which did away with Catholic saints' days from the 1560s – giving the idea of the 'new' yet more confessional freight.

Religion, poetic invention and the 'New'

Protestant reforms did not simply replace inherited practices and institutions. As Brian Cummings and John N. King observe, 'the Reformation of 1534 engulfed the nation in literary radicalism, as evangelical printers rushed into publication not only new evangelical texts and new imprints of old Lollard tracts but also newly radicalized editions of Langland, Gower, and even Chaucer, dressed in reformed royalist national colours'.[49] Chaucer and a growing Chaucerian apocrypha began to be co-opted to augment a nascent national Protestant literature, akin to how Matthew Parker and his circle would repackage Anglo-Saxon texts for similar purposes under Elizabeth I. King identifies a bifurcation of reformed intellectual culture, as 'at the same time that native literature fell into disrepute with the humanists, many earlier writers began to acquire reputations as crypto-Protestants', while 'reformers first eluded censorship by disguising the virulently anticlerical *Plowman's Tale* (c.1535) as a gathering out of a legitimate Chaucer

---

46 See Helen Cooper, *Pastoral: Mediaeval into Renaissance* (Michigan: D.S. Brewer, 1977), 154, and Richard Mallette, 'Spenser's Portrait of the Artist in *The Shepheardes Calender* and *Colin Clouts Come Home Againe*', *SEL*, 19 (1979), 19–41 (23–7).
47 David Norbrook, *Poetry and Politics in the English Renaissance* (Oxford: Oxford University Press, 2002), 71–3.
48 See Edmund Spenser and Gabriel Harvey, *Three Proper, and Wittie, Familiar Letters* (London: Henry Bynneman, 1580), 39–38 [i.e. 38–39]. Is it too far-fetched to read this typographical error reversing the order of the page numbers as deliberate, on pages linked by catchword 'newe' (in 'newe Shepheardes Calender')?
49 Brian Cummings, *The Literary Culture of the Reformation: Grammar and Grace* (Oxford: Oxford University Press, 2002), 232.

edition'.⁵⁰ One of the many contradictions in Spenser's work is borne out by the fact that it straddles these strands, rehabilitating and reframing pre-Reformation literary traditions in the service of a new national literature, committed 'to a humanist tradition of public service', by drawing on the desire of, for example, John Leland, 'to recover a native literary tradition'.⁵¹ Old Chaucer had been made new by the renovating ardour of Protestant reform, and as his heir, the 'new Poete' represented the epitome of vernacular Protestant Englishness.

In addition to a newly created Protestant identity, or humanist educative programme, though, 'novelty' and its cognates as readily connoted an opposing set of ideas. The sixteenth-century sees the emergence of the term 'novel' used as a noun, to refer to a story or fable compiled as part of a compendium: Boccaccio's *Decameron* is the classic example, cited by William Painter in his *Palace of Pleasure* (1566). Painter's 'novels' are explicitly 'gathered out of Boccaccio, Bandello, Fiorentino' and other French and Italian authors, compounding the oxymoronic sense that a 'novel' is not something new but rather something pre-existing, imported and repackaged.⁵² More widely, throughout the century but peaking in its later decades, the term was heavily associated with religious and political threat in the form of doctrinal heresy. In the wake of the Reformation, to speak of 'new books' could easily evoke confessional conflict, while 'novelty' is explicitly allied with heretical challenges to established teaching. The new might have stood for Protestant reform, but 'novelties' more often than not denoted Catholic threats. Meanwhile, writers from Thomas More to William Webbe complained more practically that new books were a menace to a country already over-stuffed with texts. It is impossible to argue that such a ubiquitous term as 'new' can take on a specific aesthetic, political or confessional identity. But Spenser, a writer so alive to the layering of meaning and nuance, must have been aware of the tensions between the multiple connotations of his 'new' title.

The instability of the term 'uncouthe' across Spenser's oeuvre alone, shading from 'new', 'strange' and 'unfamiliar' to 'distasteful' or even 'foreign' embodies the multiple significances of this uncomfortable, slippery concept, and the deep anxiety about origins which it conveys. Mutable and alien like water itself, the river Medway's bridal garments for her marriage to the Thames, 'of vnknowen geare, / And vncouth fashion', showcase this sequence of meanings: as unnerving as they are impressive, her clothes are made of a fabric which 'was no mortall worke', 'That seem'd like siluer [...] that seem'd and yet was not' (IV.xi.45).⁵³ Such uncertainty underpins the suspicion with which many Elizabethan commentators greet the concept of new poetry, which is often associated with invention, fantasy and

---

50 King, 50–1. See also the chapters by Gareth Griffith and Brendan O'Connell in this volume.
51 Cathy Shrank, *Writing the Nation in Reformation England, 1530–1580* (Oxford: Oxford University Press, 2004), 222; 226.
52 William Painter, *The Palace of Pleasure* (London: John Kingston and Henry Denham for Richard Tottell and William Jones, 1566), 'Epistle', *.iij^r.
53 See Rachel E. Hile, 'The Limitations of Concord in the Thames-Medway Marriage Canto of *The Faerie Queene*', *Studies in Philology*, 108 (Winter 2011), 70–85.

falsehood, while new poetics are regularly dismissed as the product of foolishness and bad taste.

Although the boundary between literature and history was yet to be thoroughly theorised, poetry in general, and new poetry specifically, is held up in mid-century chronicles as the enemy of historical truth. James Harrison, in his *Exhortation to the Scots to Conform Themselves to the Union* (1547), defers to the authority of the Saxon Bede, rather than trust 'the new fonde fables of our Scottishe Poetes, framed vpon phantasie'.[54] In Edward Hall's contemporary *Union*, 'newe inuented coment and poeticall peynted fable' are framed as agents of civil discord, a far cry from Henryson's relaxed attitude to Chaucer's authority in the *Testament of Creseyde*, where the narrator wonders aloud, 'Who wot if al that Chaucer wrate was trewe / Nor I wotte nat if thee narration / Be authorysed or forged of the newe / Of some poete by his inuention'.[55] As Peter C. Herman points out, early Protestants, including William Tyndale, had attacked the Roman Catholic Church for 'creating a church whose essence is not truth, but *fiction*', and consequently 'attacked fiction as part of their attack on the corruptions of the Church'.[56] Among more predictable contributors to a pervasive contemporary antipoetic discourse, George Puttenham, who reputedly held a virulent antipathy towards Puritanism, another form of heretical 'novelty', also mounted a vigorous rejection of poetic innovation and 'new fashions': writers 'affect new words and phrases', 'coigne fine wordes out of the Latin, and [...] vse new fangled speaches' which, he says, are often 'many tymes worse then the old'.[57]

As the century wore on, reactionary comparisons between a modern 'barbarous time' and civilised 'former ages' began to reverse the humanist distinction between the cultural and religious light of the English Reformation, and preceding 'aeons of "horrible darkness"'.[58] In this way, the valence of the new begins to return from a reforming good to a disruptive violation. In the light of this background antipoetic discourse, it may be surprising that Spenser's 'efforts to defend poetry are clouded by doubts and ambiguities' in *The Shepheardes Calender*, in which instead 'many of the eclogues explore the *problematic* of poetry'.[59] Herman puts this down to 'a kind of crisis of confidence', stemming 'from the difficulty Spenser had in reconciling his poetic ambitions with the antipoetic strain within Protestantism'.[60] I would

---

54 James Harrison, *An Exhortacion to the Scottes to Conforme them selfes to the Honorable, Expedie[n]t, and Godly Vnion, Betwene the Twoo Realmes of Englande and Scotlande* (London: Richard Grafton, 1547), d.v^r.
55 Edward Hall, *The Vnion of the Two Noble and Illustre Famelies of Lancastre [and] Yorke* (London: Richard Grafton, 1548), 'The vii Yere of King Henry the VII', 32^r; Geoffrey Chaucer [i.e. Robert Henryson], 'The Testament of Creseyde', in *The Workes of Geffray Chaucer*, ed. William Thynne (London: Thomas Godfray, 1532), 219^v.
56 Peter C. Herman, '*The Shepheardes Calender* and Renaissance Antipoetic Sentiment', *Studies in English Literature 1500–1900*, 32 (1992), 15–33 (16).
57 Puttenham, 210.
58 See Cathy Shrank, 'John Bale and Reconfiguring the "Medieval" in Reformation England', in *Reading the Medieval in Early Modern England*, ed. Gordon McMullan and David Matthews (Cambridge: Cambridge University Press, 2007), 179–92 (179).
59 Herman, 17.
60 Ibid., 29. See Joseph Campana, 'On Not Defending Poetry: Spenser, Suffering, and the Energy of Affect', *PMLA*, 120 (2005), 33–48 (46).

argue, though, that reading this difficulty through the semantics of innovation and tradition in the period reveals a greater degree of irreverence and iconoclasm than a more sheepish view of Spenser admits.

The idea of the 'new Poete' clearly has the potential to carry negative force, a potential to which Spenser must have been alert. References which frame new poetry as a positive largely do so on the condition that it is still, nevertheless, founded on imitative practices: William Webbe's translation of Horace's *Epistles*, appended to his *Discourse of English Poetry*, tells us that 'Newnes is gratefull if it be learned: for certaine it is, Artes are not both begunne and perfected at once, but are increased by time and studie'.[61] And in 'An Hymne of Heavenly Love', Spenser depicts a 'waste and emptie place', 'base, vile, and *next* to nought' [my italics], creatively transformed by God to instigate a 'new vnknowen Colony therein'; a definitive, originary act of making which is nevertheless underpinned by 'an heauenly patterne wrought, / Which he had fashiond in his wise foresight'.[62] The negativity of novelty, then, is apparently mitigated by the imitation of canonical figures, 'or following the example of the best and most aunciaent Poetes' (¶.iij^r), as E.K.'s Epistle posits. So far, so predictable. The closer attention to the line-ups of the poetic great and good which feature in contemporary works of incipient literary criticism which this study has foregrounded should recalibrate our perception of that canon, and shed more light on a wider network of names and conflicting resonances into which Spenser was propelled when he was presented as the 'new Poete', but these nonetheless do no more than reinforce, albeit more inclusively, E.K.'s strictures. However, one further example suggests that Spenser's newness is yet more complicated than this process of innovation tempered by decorous adherence to tradition. I will turn now to the undeniable link to be drawn between E.K.'s 'new Poete' and the persona created some thirty years earlier by the reformist gospeller, Luke Shepherd.

Luke Shepherd's 'new poet'

John N. King suggests that 'we have tended to look with wonder at *The Shepheardes Calender*, seeing it as an example of a "new poetry" that appeared full-grown out of a dormant epoch', while in fact we should regard this work as 'built upon the advances of the preceding generation of English Protestant authors'.[63] It is within that generation that we may locate this significant but hugely complicating antecedent for Spenser's 1579 epithet. Shepherd's *Philogamus*, a reformist satire sending up antipathy towards clerical marriage, directs its scorn at a ridiculous figure he calls 'the new poet'. Shepherd, whose name seems to have been an efficient Protestant pseudonym, was one of the group of Edwardian poets who saw themselves as speaking for the people in simple, unaffected verse, writing frequently

---

61 Webbe, Kiiii^v.
62 Edmund Spenser, 'An Hymne of Heavenly Love', in *Fowre Hymnes* (London: William Ponsonby, 1596), 28.
63 King, 18.

in Skeltonics.[64] By contrast, Shepherd's new poet writes in ostentatious 'meter passing measure'. It is, Shepherd claims sarcastically, a 'treatise of hygh treasure! [...] Lapte vp in suche fyne latyn / As passeth both sylk and satyn'.[65] In an alliterative put-down which is at once damning and viciously circumspect, Shepherd calls him a 'Poet rare and Recent', opening with a series of satirically laudatory-critical puns: his writings are 'So new founde and *not able*', 'That no man vnder skye / Can prayse them worthely' (Aiii^v, my italics). Printed in the same year as Cranmer's revocation of the feast of Corpus Christi, the poem also satirises the sympathy for transubstantiation shown by the new poet: 'he fayneth no lesse / But that yf God were dead / He myght be raysed in Bread' (Aii^v); this association between feigning, poetic invention and purportedly fantastical Catholic doctrine runs throughout the work. Given the conservatism of the new poet's religious views, then, his novelty is profoundly empty and ironic. The poet, 'always inventing news', is, says Shepherd, as stable as a ship in bad weather without anchor, mast or sail (Avii^r). Such antipathy towards an unstable, groundless imaginative agency is clearly also at work in E.K.'s Epistle, and anticipates the wider antipoetic discourse of the Elizabethan period.[66] E.K. says that he scorns 'our ragged rymers [...] which without learning boste, without judgement jangle, without reason rage and fome' (¶.iij^r), and this extract's diction, governed by lack, chimes precisely with Shepherd's scorn for the bankrupt literary practice of his own new poet. Elsewhere, Spenser's oeuvre also exhibits similar anxieties surrounding the creation of fantasies *ex nihilo*, against a superstitious backdrop which often associates imagination and magic with witchcraft and Catholicism. In particular, the chamber of Phantastes in the House of Alma literally buzzes with malign and groundless imaginative manifestations, 'idle thoughts and fantasies, / Deuices, dreames, opinions vnsound, / And all that fained is' (II.ix.51). Such barren, idle and destructive imaginings exemplify the worst accusations of contemporary antipoetic discourse against literary invention. The chaos of disordered thoughts hints at a wider sixteenth-century concern regarding the capacity of printed text to give voice to an uncontrollable hubbub of discordant and damaging ideas, although engagement with this concern also reaches back beyond the invention of the printing press to Chaucer.

E.K. equates poetic claims to divine inspiration with this kind of disordered, empty invention in the Epistle. However, this is countered by the Argument of the 'October' eclogue, in which composition is described as 'rather no arte, but a divine gift and heavenly instinct not to bee gotten by laboure and learning' (39^r). The 'October' emblem also subsequently suggests that 'Poetry is a divine instinct and unnatural rage passing the reache of comen reason' (44^r). Colin Clout's comic stand-in, Cuddie, bathetically concludes that it is wine which causes 'the numbers [to] flowe as fast as spring doth ryse' (42^r), but this assertion, in combination

---

64 See Mark Rankin, 'Biblical Allusion and Argument in Luke Shepherd's Verse Satires', in *The Oxford Handbook of Tudor Literature, 1485-1603*, ed. Mike Pincombe and Cathy Shrank (Oxford: Oxford University Press, 2009), 254-72.
65 Luke Shepherd, *Philogamus* (London: W. Hill, 1548), Av^r.
66 See Kreg Segall, 'Skeltonic Anxiety and Rumination in *The Shepheardes Calender*', *Studies in English Literature 1500-1900*, 47 (2007), 29-56 (30).

with the gloss which states that this 'Aeglogue is made in imitation of Theocritus his XVI. Idilion' (42ʳ) – not, actually, the case – proffers its own disordered narrative of literary origins. In particular, Cuddie's thirst calls to mind Skelton's *Goodly Garlande*, in which a repeated refrain tells how, 'of closters engrosyd with [Bacchus's] ruddy droppes / These orators and poetes refreshed there throtis', such that Skelton, again, figures latently within a passage of *The Shepheardes Calender* which questions the basis for poetic creation.[67] The allusion also echoes Barnabe Googe's translation of *The Zodiake of Life* (1565):

> Eche one presuming of his wyt,
> inuenteth matters newe,
> But Poets specially, to whome
> most confidence is dewe:
> For they may by autority
> of any matters write:
> Wyth *Bacchus* rage they moued be,
> and wyth *Apolloes* sprite.[68]

Read through Chaucer and Spenser, this extract which assigns ultimate authority to the poetic invention of 'matters newe' feels heavy with irony, particularly when it attributes this literary production to '*Bacchus* rage' and '*Apolloes* sprite'. The episode demonstrates, though, that even when a poet aspires to such divinely inspired invention, as Cuddie does, he does so within a framework of analogues.

Shepherd's new poet, too, seeks to bypass the models of precedents and contemporaries alike, as if he had directly accessed a divine source:

> As he had sene the Muses
> Newe Poetry he vses
> And yours he cleane refuses.
> For wakyng sodenly
> He wrote ryght wortheily
> Suche kynde of Poetrye
> As neuer one of you
> Had hearde or sene tyl nowe. (Aiiʳ–iiiᵛ)

In fact, Shepherd's narrator states sarcastically, all existing literature may be dispensed with:

> Your bokes we nede no more
> They maye be rent and tore
> What though ye crye and rore
> We nede not now your lore

---

67 Skelton, from Aviiᵛ.
68 Marcello Palingenio Stellato, *The Zodiake of Life*, trans. Barnabe Googe (London: Henry Denham for Rafe Newberye, 1565), Yiᵛ–iiʳ.

> For yf thys arte were drowned
> Agayne it may be found
> Euen by the very sound
> Of these new Poetes Tooles. (Avi^r)

Additionally, though, Shepherd's poet's novelty, expressed in Skeltonics and Skeltonic pig Latin, is one of oppressive overworking, which, although new, is already stultifying – in contrast to the bright freshness of Spenser's fledgling artist. These examples serve to demonstrate that E.K.'s invocation of such a figure through his epithet for Spenser is, to say the least, problematic, in the light of his apparent reverence for tradition. If Shepherd's satirical poem was known to Spenser, how can we begin to get these two works to speak usefully to one another?

Philogamus, like *The Shepheardes Calender*, is laden with ironic contradictions. It is a reformist tract, advocating an end to traditional Catholic practices, which mocks the new poet through an ironic rejection of canonicity. We do not have the piece to which *Philogamus* is a response, but Shepherd clearly wishes to embarrass its alleged author, John Mason, with jibes about his surpassing poetic skill: addressing Homer, Horace, Virgil and Ovid, the narrator says that such is the talent of the new poet, 'Yf he your bokes had sene / He wolde haue shamed them clene' (Av^r). Mason had been a close acquaintance of Wyatt (one of Puttenham's new poets, as we saw above); while Shepherd's satire therefore shames Mason in comparison with his more skilled poetic associate, Wyatt may himself have been open to similar accusations from detractors.[69] Shepherd also plays on Mason's name to suggest that he is a craftsman like a smith or painter who creates; invents; forges. As a result, 'He sheweth Poetry / Hyghly professyng Romery' (Avi^r). While the equation of Shepherd's new poet with E.K.'s is awkward, then, Shepherd's poem sets up a vital series of contexts for Spenser's own, and usefully narrows the gap between Spenser's poetic manifesto and his updated pastoral satire.

Spenser's 'Maye' eclogue engages closely with the conventional old-new dialectic, in its dialogue between Piers and Palinode on clerical marriage – the topic of *Philogamus*.[70] As Thomas H. Cain notes, 'Elizabethans associated the name Piers with a satirical, supposedly proto-Protestant tradition stemming from Langland, *The Plowman's Tale*, and other Chaucerian apocrypha'; Piers's programme of reform represents, at least for Palinode, 'an innovative assault on the traditional "right" of clergy to an unlearned, self-serving, nearly secular lifestyle', which advocates for a return of the 'ancient church', and would allow clerical marriage without its attendant corruptions.[71] *Philogamus*'s new poet represents another kind of innovative assault; for Shepherd it is the new which is 'unlearned' – Piers and Shepherd's satire as a whole ultimately find themselves in agreement. Spenser's Piers, the voice of ecclesiastical innovation, rejects the organic signifiers of youth which Palinode would celebrate – 'greene leaves' and

---

69 See Rankin, 259–60.
70 See also Crawforth on the 'Februarie' eclogue.
71 Thomas H. Cain, 'Maye', in Oram *et al.* (eds), 85.

'bloosming Buds' – claiming 'For Younkers Palinode such follies fitte, / But we tway bene men of elder witt' ('Maye', 16ᵛ). Spenser breaks down the simplistic association between new foliage and new doctrine, instead allying the merry-England festivity of May-games with an *older* era, or a previous *youthful* phase he has outgrown. Likewise, while tradition represents learning and textual authorisation for Shepherd and E.K., for Piers it is more associated with custom and oral culture. Crawforth states that the claims which framed proposed ecclesiastical reforms regarding clerical marriage as 'the recovery of an ancient tradition, rather than an innovation', are inseparably bound up with the recovery by Matthew Parker's circle of Anglo-Saxon texts and lexical understanding, upon which Spenser draws in his *Shepheardes Calender*, and 'from which speakers of sixteenth-century English have become similarly estranged'.[72] The interpolation of Shepherd's *Philogamus* into this debate and Spenser's frame of reference makes for an even more profound interrogation of the semantics of tradition and innovation, drawing together the questions of religious reform and linguistic change more concertedly than even Crawforth suggests.

Conclusions

Perhaps Spenser's evocation of the new poet figure scorned by Shepherd plays into the late sixteenth-century rejection of, or departure from, the vernacular reformist movement. Andrew Hadfield contends that in *The Shepheardes Calender*, Spenser 'forged a new tradition of pastoral poetry that effectively sidelined that of earlier Tudor writers', who 'appeared repetitive and old-fashioned for a generation eager to experiment with new verse forms and styles and not committed to an English tradition alone'.[73] If one of the satirical objects of *Philogamus* is indeed the 'new' Italianate verse which became fashionable in the first half of the sixteenth century, the epithet may signal Spenser's antithetical debt to the vernacular poetry of continental Europe. His allusion to Shepherd's new poet could represent not an affinity but in fact a break – it is the literary legacy of Shepherd himself, rather than the concept of learning, that Spenser rejects, as Hadfield suggests. Certainly, the contortions demanded of the reader to assimilate Shepherd's portrayal of his new poet into E.K.'s presentation of his, bear out Hadfield's argument that 'for ambitious Elizabethan writers' the tradition of pastoral anticlerical writing 'had become something to be absorbed, challenged, and confronted, not simply adopted'.[74] One solution would be to propose that the 'new Poete' of *The Shepheardes Calender* is inflected by *Philogamus*'s model of ephemeral argument, topical in-jokes and satire in cheap print, but drives the discourse of English vernacular pastoral forward by acknowledging and subsuming the empty, rudderless face of poetic

---

72 Crawforth, 37.
73 Andrew Hadfield, 'Foresters, Ploughmen, and Shepheards: Versions of Tudor Pastoral', in Pincombe and Shrank (eds), 537–54 (551, 548); see Gregory Kneidal, '"Mightie Simplenesse": Protestant Pastoral Rhetoric and Spenser's *Shepheardes Calender*', *Studies in Philology*, 96 (1999), 275–312.
74 Hadfield, 553.

novelty, simultaneously proposing their opposite as a rich and grounded way forward for English writing.

I would suggest that there is no single answer, but rather that the foregoing series of contradictions must be held in suspension. Further, I would argue that this is not quite the cop-out that it at first appears – and Spenser's reception of Chaucer is central to this assertion. It has already been recognised that *The Shepheardes Calender*'s paratexts are fraught with ironic contortions, and allusions which unpick what has gone before. For example, William Kuskin effectively deconstructs the workings of E.K.'s concise allusion to *Troilus and Criseyde* – 'uncouthe, unkiste' – by rereading the quotation's context, to reveal its troubled and compromising significance, positing a form of artifice which 'appears unmediated but is by definition all the more artificial for doing so'.[75] The 'baudy brocage' which E.K. remarks was successful for Pandarus corresponds to the 'pimping' or sale of the 'new Poete' himself, on the basis of his artificial artlessness, resulting in his being 'kiste', 'embraced' and 'known' by 'most men' (¶.ij^r), reducing E.K.'s high-minded enumeration of poetic authorities to a joke about prostitution and promiscuity. The apparent reference to Shepherd's new poet arguably operates in the same way, glancingly invoking an antecedent which has the capacity to undermine the conceit if examined too closely. Their relationship may also usefully be read through Judith H. Anderson's analysis of Spenser's debt to Chaucer; Anderson observes that Spenser's Faery Queen, 'whose literary origin lies in Chaucer's *Sir Thopas*, affords an ever-elusive alternative' to Elizabeth I.[76] I want to consider this doubled Queen as a figure for Spenser's approach to poetic inheritance. Anderson goes on, 'if Spenser looked for meaning in Chaucer's *[General] Prologue* [...] the message he found was indirection, whose endlessly ironic techniques were to decenter and define his own doubled and redoubled representations within an allegorical medium'.[77] I would suggest that Spenser must have found a very similar message in *Philogamus*; if the 'new Poete' alludes to Shepherd, the workings of the allusion embody a similar process of ironic doubling and decentring.

Shepherd's poetic practice is riddling and contradictory, mocking both the reader and the object of his satire.[78] Mark Rankin observes that, 'if Protestants accused Catholic writers of distorting Scripture in defence of "unwritten verities", Shepherd parodies both accuser and accused'.[79] A staple of Edwardian reformist discourse, the 'unwritten verities' to which Rankin refers here anticipate *Beware the Cat* (1570, composed c.1552) by William Baldwin, another mid-century poet and satirist who, for King, shares with Shepherd 'an ability to stimulate laughter as well as indignation'.[80] Baldwin's apparent satire of Catholic faith in the 'unwritten verities' of their doctrine questions the very possibility of *written* verities through his own narrative's fiction, a layering up of fabulous accounts

---

75 Kuskin, 58.
76 Anderson, 28.
77 Ibid., 30–1.
78 King, 253.
79 See also Rankin, 271–2.
80 King, 252.

by variably unreliable authors.[81] King's analysis of the period sketches a line of influence from Spenser's *Shepheardes Calender* back to Luke Shepherd's works, *via* William Baldwin; while he does not make reference to the 'new poet' connection between Shepherd and Spenser, his argument provides compelling evidence in support of the phrase's emerging significance. He suggests that Baldwin, 'the first writer of fiction in English to construct an elaborate mock apparatus for his book as a comical or satirical device', anticipates *The Shepheardes Calender*, 'another Tudor example of this kind of learned hoax'. Shepherd and Baldwin's debt to Skelton, too ('ware the cat, Parot, ware the fals cat!'), and the unacknowledged presence of Skelton, Spenser's 'godfather in poetry', behind Colin Clout, adds to this network of irreverent, comic, Protestant satire which makes up a silent canon alongside the overtly stated poetic heritage of *The Shepheardes Calender*.[82] King's account suggests that Baldwin's inspiration for the 'reporter' *persona*, also adopted by Spenser and Shepherd, is none other than Chaucer's *House of Fame*.[83] Chaucer's lack of 'confidence that writing can truly transmit speech' pervades the works of these writers; for Spenser, Chaucer's interrogation of either spoken or written authority nullifies E.K.'s and Shepherd's demands for canonical backing.[84] While at times this is manifested as anxiety, there is also a gleeful, wanton iconoclasm, and even humour, to the repudiation of textual stability.

Like Apollo and Mercury, the doubled representatives of poetic practice in the *Squire's Tale*, Chaucer's presence in the Renaissance operates on two levels.[85] He is 'not only a great poet but the *sign* of a great poet', widely revered and known in the editions by Thynne (1532), or Speght (1598).[86] But he also heads up a shadowy counter-narrative, which poses an explicit challenge to the canon and even the notion of canonicity. In *The Shepheardes Calender*, 'the debts to anticlerical satires like *The Plowman's Tale* are unmentioned', and for this reason Chaucer may be seen as belonging both to E.K.'s list of literary worthies, as well as to the alternative, buried history which takes in Baldwin, Shepherd and Skelton.[87] Helfer has identified in the conflict between 'E.K.'s longing to cast Spenser [...] in Virgil's mold' and 'Spenser's reluctance to perform a Virgilian role in English culture', 'a crucial tension in the *Calender* between two competing patterns of imitation, two divergent models of authorial and cultural formation: Virgil's

---

81 William Baldwin, *Beware the Cat: The First English Novel*, ed. William A. Ringler and Michael Flachmann (San Marino: Huntington Library, 1988), 19, marginal note.
82 John Skelton, 'Speke Parott', in *The Complete English Poems*, ed. John Scattergood (Harmondsworth: Penguin Books, 1983), 230-46 (233). See Harriet Archer, *Unperfect Histories: The Mirror for Magistrates, 1559-1610* (Oxford: Oxford University Press, 2017), 19; Kreg Segall, 'Skeltonic Anxiety and Rumination in *The Shepheardes Calender*', *Studies in English Literature 1500-1900*, 47 (2007), 29-56 (29).
83 King, 389.
84 William A. Quinn, 'Chaucer's Recital Presence in the *House of Fame* and the Embodiment of Authority', *The Chaucer Review*, 43 (2008), 171-96 (171).
85 See Berry (305).
86 Anthony M. Esolen, 'The Disingenuous Poet Laureate: Spenser's Adoption of Chaucer', *Studies in Philology*, 87 (1990), 285-311 (288).
87 Norbrook, 66. For more on Spenser's relationship to Chaucer the satirist, see O'Connell's chapter in this volume.

and Cicero's'.[88] Chaucer's dual significances articulate a similar conflict between Spenser's persona and E.K., but any notional authoritative backstop recedes out of reach like the 'December' eclogue's absent motto. Using the seductive binary of the old and new, Spenser hoodwinks his readers into taking untenable stances on either side, in favour of either tradition or modernity, when in fact his work breaks down even attempts to reconcile the two. New and old are contingent, manifold values, like Protestant/Catholic, learned/unlearned. Canonical authority or status is also shown to be bifurcated by historically bound expedience: Chaucer is and isn't the author of the *Plowman's Tale*, for example. The figure of the 'new Poete' draws together both Spenser's canonical and non-canonical influences, or a conventional canon and a 'dark canon', tracing two parallel lineages back into the literary past. These lineages are held together by the poetic authority of Chaucer and Chaucer's own denial of that authority. By the end of the century, Protestant intellectual culture had arguably developed its stance to become at once both 'literature's most enthusiastic friend and its most articulate enemy'.[89] This is just one of the contemporary contradictions which the accommodation of Shepherd's new poet within *The Shepheardes Calender*, as well as Chaucer's doubled presence, allows Spenser to subsume. Spenser's 'new matter' is 'framed upon the old', as E.K. specifies, but the contours and limits of what we understand as 'old' and 'new' are radically transformed.

---

88 Rebeca Helfer, 'The Death of the "New Poete": Virgilian Ruin and Ciceronian Recollection in Spenser's *The Shepheardes Calender*', *Renaissance Quarterly*, 56 (2003), 723–56 (724).
89 Cummings, 270.

Select bibliography of books and essays on Chaucer and Spenser

Anderson, Judith H., '"Nat worth a boterflye": *Muiopotmos* and *The Nun's Priest's Tale*', *Journal of Medieval and Renaissance Studies*, 1 (1970), 89–106

Anderson, Judith H., 'What comes after Chaucer's "but": Adversative Constructions in Spenser', in *Acts of Interpretation: The Text and its Contexts, 700–1600: Essays on Medieval and Renaissance Literature in Honor of E. Talbot Donaldson*, ed. Mary J. Carruthers and Elizabeth D. Kirk (Norman: Pilgrim Books, 1982), 105–18

Anderson, Judith H., '"A Gentle Knight was pricking on the plaine": The Chaucerian Connection', *English Literary Renaissance*, 15 (1985), 166–74

Anderson, Judith H., 'The "couert vele": Chaucer, Spenser, and Venus', *English Literary Renaissance*, 24.3 (1994), 638–59

Anderson, Judith H., 'Prudence and Her Silence: Spenser's use of Chaucer's *Melibee*', *ELH: Journal of English Literary History*, 62.1 (1995), 29–46

Anderson, Judith H., 'Allegory, Irony, Despair: Chaucer's Pardoner's and Franklin's Tales and Spenser's *Faerie Queene*, Books I and III', in *Textual Conversations in the Renaissance: Ethics, Authors, Technologies*, ed. Zachary Lesser and Benedict S. Robinson (Burlington: Ashgate, 2006), 71–89

Anderson, Judith H., *Reading the Allegorical Intertext: Chaucer, Spenser, Shakespeare, Milton* (New York: Fordham University Press, 2008); collects several of her previous essays

Armstrong, Edward, *A Ciceronian Sunburn: A Tudor Dialogue on Humanistic Rhetoric and Civic Poetics* (Columbia: University of South Carolina Press, 2006)

Arthurs, Judith Gott, 'Edmund Spenser and Dan Chaucer: A Study of the Influence of *The Canterbury Tales* on *The Faerie Queene*', unpublished doctoral dissertation, University of Arkansas (1973). Abstract in *Dissertation Abstracts International*, 24 (1973), 3334A

Berlin, Normand, 'Chaucer's *The Book of the Duchess* and Spenser's *Daphnaïda*: A Contrast', *Studia Neophilologica*, 38 (1966), 282–9

Berry, Craig A., '"Former workes": The Figuration of Career in Chaucer and Spenser', unpublished doctoral dissertation, Northwestern University (1992). Abstract in *Dissertation Abstracts International*, 53 (1992), 1920A

Berry, Craig A., 'Borrowed Armour / Free Grace: The Quest for Authority in the *Faerie Queene* I and Chaucer's *Tale of Sir Thopas*', *Studies in Philology*, 91.2 (1994), 136–66

Berry, Craig A., '"Sundrie Doubts": Vulnerable Understanding and Dubious Origins in Spenser's Continuation of the *Squire's Tale*', in *Refiguring Chaucer in the Reniassance*, ed. Theresa M. Krier (Gainesville: University Press of Florida, 1998), 106–27

Bice, Deborah Marie, 'Preceptive Portraiture: Chaucerian and Spenserian *effictio*', unpublished doctoral dissertation, Case Western Reserve University (1995). Abstract in *Dissertation Abstracts International*, 56 (1995), 2230A

Boitani, Piero, and Anna Torti, eds, *The Body and the Soul in Medieval Literature: The J.A.W. Bennett Memorial Lectures, Tenth Series, Perugia, 1998* (Woodbridge: Brewer, 1999), 123–44

Boswell, Jackson Campbell, 'Chaucer and Spenser Allusions not in Spurgeon and Wells', *Analytical and Enumerative Bibliography*, 1 (1977), 30–2

Bulger, Thomas, 'Platonism in Spenser's *Mutabilitie Cantos*', in *Platonism and the English Imagination*, ed. Anna Baldwin and Sarah Hutton (Cambridge: Cambridge University Press, 1994), 126–38

Burrow, John A., '*Sir Thopas* in the Sixteenth Century', in *Middle English Studies Presented to Norman Davis*, ed. Douglas Gray and E.G. Stanley (Oxford: Oxford University Press, 1983), 69–91

Burrow, John A., 'Chaucer, Geoffrey', in *The Spenser Encyclopedia*, ed. A.C. Hamilton (Toronto: University of Toronto Press, 1990), 144–8

Cawley, Robert R., 'A Chaucerian Echo in Spenser', *MLN: Modern Language Notes*, 41 (May 1926), 313–14

Cheney, Donald, 'Narrative, Romance, and Epic', in *The Cambridge Companion to English Literature, 1500–1600*, ed. Arthur F. Kinney (Cambridge: Cambridge University Press 2007), 200–19

Cheney, Patrick, '"Novells of his devise": Chaucerian and Virgilian Career Paths in Spenser's "Februarie" Eclogue', in *European Literary Careers: The Author from Antiquity to the Renaissance*, ed. Patrick Cheney and Frederick A. de Armas (Toronto: Guernica, 2002), 231–67

Collins, Robert Arnold, 'The Christian Significance of the Astrological Tradition: A Study in the Literary use of Astral Symbolism in English Literature from Chaucer to Spenser', unpublished doctoral dissertation, University of Kentucky (1968). Abstract in *Dissertation Abstracts International*, 31 (1968), 353A

Cook, Megan L., 'Making and Managing the Past: Lexical Commentary in Spenser's *Shepheardes Calender* (1579) and Chaucer's *Works* (1598/1602)', *Spenser Studies*, 26 (2011), 179–222

Cooper, Helen, 'The Shape-Shiftings of the Wife of Bath, 1395–1670', in *Chaucer Traditions: Studies in Honour of Derek Brewer*, ed. Ruth Morse and Barry Windeatt (Cambridge: Cambridge University Press, 1990), 168–84

Cooper, Helen, *The English Romance in Time: Transforming Motifs from Geoffrey of Monmouth to the Death of Shakespeare* (Oxford: Oxford University Press, 2004)

Cooper, Helen, *Shakespeare and the Medieval World* (London: Arden Shakespeare, 2012)

Craik, Katharine A., 'Spenser's *Complaints* and the New Poet', *Huntington Library Quarterly*, 64.1/2 (2001), 63–79

Crampton, Georgia Ronan, *The Condition of Creatures: Suffering and Action in Chaucer and Spenser* (New Haven: Yale University Press, 1974)

Dillard, Nancy Frey, 'The English Fabular Tradition: Chaucer, Spenser, Dryden', unpublished doctoral dissertation, University of Tennessee (1973). Abstract in *Dissertation Abstracts International*, 34 (1973), 7186A

Dodds, M.H., 'Chaucer: Spenser: Milton in Drama and Fiction', *Notes and Queries*, 176.1 (1939), 69

Emerson, Francis Willard, 'The Spenser in John Lane's Chaucer', *Studies in Philology*, 29 (1932), 406–8

Emerson, Francis Willard, 'The Spenser-Followers in Leigh Hunt's Chaucer', *Notes and Queries*, 203 (1958), 284–6

Emerson, Francis Willard, 'The Bible in Spenser's Chaucer', *Notes and Queries*, 203 (1958), 422–3

Esolen, Anthony M., 'The Disingenous Poet Laureate: Spenser's Adoption of Chaucer', *Studies in Philology*, 87 (1990), 285–311

Fairweather, Colin, '"I suppose he meane Chaucer": The Comedy of Errors in Spenser's *Shepheardes Calender*', *Notes and Queries*, 46 (1999), 193–5

Fumo, Jamie C., *Making Chaucer's 'Book of the Duchess'* (Cardiff: University of Wales Press, 2015)

Gillespie, Alexandra, 'Unknowe, unkow, Vncovthe, uncouth: From Chaucer and Gower to Spenser and Milton', in *Medieval into Rensaissance: Essays for Helen Cooper* (Rochester: Boydell & Brewer, 2016), 15–34

Goldberg, Jonathan, *Endlesse Worke: Spenser and the Structures of Discourse* (Baltimore: Johns Hopkins University Press, 1981)

Guy-Bray, Stephen, *Loving in Verse: Poetic Influence as Erotic* (Toronto: University of Toronto Press, 2006)

Hadbawnik, David, 'The Chaucer-Function: Spenser's Language Lessons in *The Shepheardes Calender*', *Upstart: A Journal of English Renaissance Studies* (2014), https://upstart.sites.clemson.edu/Essays/hadbawnik_spenser/hadbawnik_spenser.xhtml [accessed 20 November 2018]

Hadfield, Andrew, 'Spenser and Chaucer: *The Knight's Tale* and Artegall's Response to the Giant with the Scales (*Faerie Queene*, V.ii.41–42)', *Spenser Studies*, 15 (2001), 245–9

Hamilton, A.C., ed., *The Spenser Encyclopedia* (Toronto: University of Toronto Press, 1990)

Harris, Duncan, and Nancy L. Steffen, 'The Other Side of the Garden: An Interpretive Comparison of Chaucer's *Book of the Duchess* and Spenser's *Daphnaida*', *Journal of Medieval and Renaissance Studies*, 8 (1978), 17–36

Harrison, Thomas P., *They Tell of Birds* (Austin: University of Texas Press, 1956)

Hawkins, Harriet, *Poetic Freedom and Poetic Truth: Chaucer, Shakespeare, Marlowe, Milton* (Oxford: Clarendon Press, 1976)

Helfer, Rebeca, *Spenser's Ruins and the Art of Recollection* (Toronto: University of Toronto Press, 2012)

Hieatt, A. Kent, *Chaucer, Spenser, Milton: Mythopoeic Continuities and Transformations* (Montreal: McGill-Queen's University Press, 1975)

Hieatt, A. Kent, '*The Canterbury Tales* in *The Faerie Queene*', in *Spenser and the Middle Ages: Proceedings from a Special Session at the Eleventh Conference on Medieval Studies, Kalamazoo, Michigan, 2–5 May 1976*, ed. David A. Richardson (Cleveland: Department of English, Cleveland State University, 1976), 217–29

Higgins, Anne, 'Spenser Reading Chaucer: Another Look at the "Faerie Queene" Allusions', *Journal of English and Germanic Philology*, 89 (1990), 17–36

Holahan, Michael, 'A Commentary on "*The Canterbury Tales* in *The Faerie Queene*"', in *Spenser and the Middle Ages: Proceedings from a Special Session at the Eleventh Conference on Medieval Studies, Kalamazoo, Michigan, 2–5 May 1976*, ed. David A. Richardson (Cleveland: Department of English, Cleveland State University, 1976), 230–6

Jack, A.A., *A Commentary on the Poetry of Chaucer and Spenser* (Glasgow: Maclehose and Jackson, 1920)

King, Andrew, *'The Faerie Queene' and Middle English Romance: The Matter of Just Memory* (Oxford: Oxford University Press, 2000)

King, Andrew, '"Well Grounded, Finely Framed, and Strongly Trussed up Together": The "Medieval" Structure of *The Faerie Queene*', *The Review of English Studies*, 52 (2001), 22–58

King, Andrew, 'Spenser, Chaucer, and Medieval Romance', in *The Oxford Handbook of Edmund Spenser*, ed. Richard McCabe (Oxford: Oxford University Press, 2010), 553–72

Kinney, Clare Regan, *Strategies of Poetic Narrative: Chaucer, Spenser, Milton, Eliot* (Cambridge: Cambridge University Press, 1992)

Kinney, Clare, 'Marginal Presence, Lyric Resonance, Epic Absence: *Troilus and Criseyde* and/in the *Shepheardes Calender*', *Spenser Studies*, 18 (2003), 25–39

Krier, Theresa M., ed., *Refiguring Chaucer in the Renaissance* (Gainesville: University Press of Florida, 1998)

Kuskin, William, '"The loadstarre of the English language": Spenser's *Shepheardes Calender* and the Construction of Modernity', *Textual Cultures*, 2.2 (2007), 9–33

Kuskin, William, *Recursive Origins: Writing at the Transition to Modernity* (Notre Dame: University of Notre Dame Press, 2013)

Lasater, Alice E., 'The Chaucerian Narrator in Spenser's *Shepheardes Calender*', *Southern Quarterly*, 12 (1974), 189–201

Leonard, Frances McNeely, *Laughter in the Courts of Love: Comedy in Allegory from Chaucer to Spenser* (Norman: Pilgrim Books, 1981)

Magoun, F.P., 'The Chaucer of Spenser and Milton', *Modern Philology*, 25 (1927), 129–36

Maley, Willy, 'Spenser's Languages: Writing in the Ruins of English', in *The Cambridge Companion to Spenser*, ed. Andrew Hadfield (Cambridge: Cambridge University Press 2001), 162–79

Marchand, Yvette Marie, 'Towards a Psychosomatic View of Human Nature: Chaucer, Spenser, Burton', in *The Body and the Soul in Medieval Literature: The J.A.W. Bennett Memorial Lectures, Tenth Series, Perugia, 1998*, ed. Piero Boitani and Anna Torti (Woodbridge: Brewer, 1999), 123–44

Maresca, Thomas E., *Three English Epics: Studies in Chaucer, Spenser and Milton* (Lincoln: University of Nebraska Press, 1979)

Maynard, Theodore, *The Connection Between the Ballade, Chaucer's Modification of It, Rime Royal, and the Spenserian Stanza* (Washington, DC: Catholic University of America, 1934; repr. Folcroft: Folcroft Library Editions, 1973)

McCabe, Richard, ed., *The Oxford Handbook of Edmund Spenser* (Oxford: Oxford University Press, 2010)

McElderry Jr., B.R., 'Archaism and Innovation in Spenser's Poetic Diction', *PMLA*, 27 (1932), 144–70

Miller, David Lee, 'Authorship, Anonymity, and the *Shepheardes Calender*', *Modern Language Quarterly*, 40 (1979), 219–36

Miskimin, Alice S., *The Renaissance Chaucer* (London: Yale University Press, 1975)

Mounts, Charles E., 'The Place of Chaucer and Spenser in the Genesis of "Peter Bell"', *Philological Quarterly*, 23 (1944), 108–15

Munro, Lucy, *Archaic Style in English Literature 1590-1674* (Cambridge: Cambridge University Press, 2013)

Nadal, Thomas William, 'Spenser's *Daphnaïda* and Chaucer's *Book of the Duchess*', *PMLA*, 23 (1908), 646–61

Nadal, Thomas William, 'Spenser's "Muiopotmos" in Relation to Chaucer's *Sir Thopas* and *The Nun's Priest's Tale*', *PMLA*, 25 (1910), 640–56

Oram, William A., '*Daphnaïda* and Spenser's Later Poetry', *Spenser Studies*, 2 (1981), 141–58

Parry, Joseph Douglas, 'Narrative Mobility in Layamon, Malory, Chaucer, and Spenser', unpublished doctoral dissertation, University of Utah (1995). Abstract in *Dissertation Abstracts International*, 56 (1995), 945A

Pearsall, Derek, *Chaucer to Spenser: An Anthology of Writing in English 1375-1575* (Oxford: Blackwell, 1998)

Pearsall, Derek, *Chaucer to Spenser: A Critical Reader* (Oxford: Blackwell, 1999)

Pyles, Thomas, 'Dan Chaucer', *Modern Language Notes*, 57 (1942), 437-9

Quilligan, Maureen, 'Words and Sex: The Language of Allegory in the *De planctu naturae*, the *Roman de la Rose*, and Book III of *The Faerie Queene*', *Allegorica*, 2 (1977), 195-216

Quilligan, Maureen, 'Allegory, Allegoresis, and the Deallegorization of Language: The *Roman de la rose*, the *De planctu naturae*, and the *Parlement of Foules*', in *Allegory, Myth and Symbol*, ed. Morton W. Bloomfield, Harvard English Studies, 9 (Cambridge, MA: Harvard University Press, 1981), 163-86

Rasmussen, Mark David, 'Complaint and the Poetic Career: Catullus, Virgil, Chaucer, Spenser', unpublished doctoral dissertation, Johns Hopkins University (1993). Abstract in *Dissertation Abstracts International*, 54 (1993), 171A

Reid, Robert Lanier, 'Spenser's Mutability Song: Conclusion or Transition?' in *Celebrating Mutabilitie: Essays on Edmund Spenser's 'Mutabilitie Cantos'*, ed. Jane Grogan (Manchester: Manchester University Press, 2010), 61-84

Remien, Peter, 'Silvan Matters: Error and Instrumentality in Book I of *The Faerie Queene*', *Spenser Studies*, 28 (2013), 119-43

Richardson, David A., ed., *Spenser and the Middle Ages: Proceedings from a Special Session at the Eleventh Conference on Medieval Studies, Kalamazoo, Michigan, 2-5 May 1976* (Cleveland: Department of English, Cleveland State University, 1976)

Rubel, Veré L., *Poetic Diction in the English Renaissance: From Skelton through Spenser* (New York: Modern Language Association of America, 1941)

Sanders, Arnold A., 'Ruddymane and Canace, Lost and Found: Spenser's Reception of Gower's *Confessio Amantis* 3 and Chaucer's *Squire's Tale*', in *The Work of Dissimilitude: Essays from the Sixth Citadel Conference on Medieval and Renaissance Literature*, ed. David G. Allen and Robert A. White (London: Associated University Presses, 1992), 196-215

Schofield, William Henry, *Chivalry in English Literature: Chaucer, Malory, Spenser, Shakespeare* (Cambridge, MA: Harvard University, 1912)

Silberman, Lauren, 'Making Faces and Playing Chicken in "Mother Hubberds Tale"', The Hugh Maclean Memorial Lecture, *The Spenser Review*, 37.1 (2006), 9-20

Spearing, A.C., *Medieval to Renaissance in English Poetry* (Cambridge: Cambridge University Press, 1995)

Spearing, A.C., 'The Poetic Subject from Chaucer to Spenser', in *Subjects on the World's Stage: Essays on British Literature of the Middle Ages and the Renaissance*, ed. David G. Allen and Robert A. White (London: Delaware University Press, 1995), 13-37

Staines, John D., 'Pity and the Authority of Feminine Passions in Books V and VI of *The Faerie Queene*', *Spenser Studies*, 25 (2010), 129-61

Steinberg, Glenn A., 'Toward an Aesthetic of Literary Influence: Dante, Chaucer, Spenser', unpublished doctoral dissertation, Indiana University (1994). Abstract in *Dissertation Abstracts International*, 55 (1995), 2383A

Steinberg, Glenn A., 'Spenser's *Shepheardes Calender* and the Elizabethan Reception of Chaucer', *English Literary Renaissance*, 35.1 (2005), 31-51

Steinberg, Glenn A., 'Chaucer's Mutability in Spenser's "Mutabilitie Cantos"', *Studies in English Literature*, 46 (2006), 27-42

Stewart, Vaughn, 'Friends, Rivals, and Revisions: Chaucer's *Squire's Tale* and *Amis and Amiloun* in *The Faerie Queene*, Book IV', *Spenser Studies*, 26 (2011), 75–109

Stubblefield, Jay, 'A Note on Spenser's *Faerie Queene* IV and Chaucer's *Squire's Tale*', *English Language Notes*, 36.1 (1998), 9–10

Taylor, Eric F., 'The *Knight's Tale*: A New Source for Spenser's "Muiopotmos"', *Renaissance Papers* (1966), 57–63

Watkins, John, '"Neither of idle shewes, nor of false charmes aghast": Transformations of Virgilian Ekphrasis in Chaucer and Spenser', *Journal of Medieval and Renaissance Studies*, 23.3 (1993), 345–63

Winkler, G., 'Das Relativum bei Caxton und seine Entwicklung von Chaucer bis Spenser', unpublished doctoral dissertation, Berlin (1933)

Vance, Eugene, 'Chaucer, Spenser, and the Ideology of Translation', *Canadian Review of Comparative Literature / Revue canadienne de littérature comparée*, 8 (1981), 217–38

Yuasa, Nobuyuki, 'The Art of Naming: A Study of Fictional Names as an Element of Style in Chaucer, Spenser and Shakespeare', *Poetica* (Japan), 41 (1994), 59–83

Index

Note: literary works by Geoffrey Chaucer and Edmund Spenser can be found under the authors' names. 'n.' after a page reference indicates the number of a note on that page.

Aesop 43
Alan of Lille 64, 66, 213–14, 217–20
Anglo-Saxon 104–9, 104n.18, 108n.35, 154, 154nn.11–13, 227, 232, 239
animals 8, 17, 42, 42n.15, 67, 125, 126n.62, 189–90, 201–2, 202n.33, 206, 208
anticlericalism 138, 142–3, 190, 202, 224, 232, 235, 238–9, 241
archaism 5, 16, 98–112, 127–8, 152, 157, 160, 162, 166, 174, 177, 225–7
Ariosto, Ludovico 28, 61, 130, 230
Aristotle 135, 138

Baldwin, William 44, 58, 240–1
Beaumont, Francis 150, 152, 163–4, 167, 168–70, 173–5, 181–4
biography 184
birds 10, 42–4, 50–1, 57–8, 58n.54, 63, 66–7, 77, 90–3, 109, 190, 195, 206–11, 212, 214–21, 231
Blenerhasset, Thomas 229
Boccaccio 63n.12, 192, 231, 233
Boethius 6n.18, 20, 21, 21nn.7–8, 64, 65n.13, 67, 73, 206
Braham, Robert 153–4
Burrow, J.A. 9, 12, 20n.6, 38n.5, 137, 151n.3

Callimachus 228
Camden, William 165, 178n.26
Caxton, William 6, 193

Cecil, Sir Robert 164–5, 168, 170, 173, 177
Cecil, Sir William 164
Cecilia, Saint 67–70, 193
Chaucer, Geoffrey (works)
  Anelida and Arcite 38n.3, 137, 146
  Book of the Duchess 3–5, 7–8, 12n.42, 45
  Canterbury Tales 7, 14–15, 17, 25, 41–3, 42n.15, 45, 51n.40, 67–73, 137, 139–44, 146, 161, 173, 187, 189–211
  Clerk's Tale 42n.15, 147–8
  Cook's Tale 139–40
  Franklin's Tale 16, 31, 33n.43, 62, 67–72, 75–9, 81–8, 93–6, 137, 143
  General Prologue 191, 194, 197–8, 240
  Knight's Tale 14–15, 20, 51n.40, 67–8, 72, 127, 137, 143, 145–7, 194–5
  Manciple's Tale 58, 193–5, 206–7, 209, 211
  Man of Law's Tale 43n.23, 45n.30, 69, 137
  Miller's Tale 13, 42, 43n.20, 51n.40, 65, 205n.40
  Nun's Priest's Tale 42, 50, 192–5, 198–201, 204, 206–7, 209–10
  Pardoner's Tale 145, 193
  Parson's Tale 70, 193–6, 209
  Squire's Tale 15, 61, 68, 73n.30, 98, 106–12, 116, 119, 125–7, 137–8, 144, 186–7, 195, 219, 226, 241
  Summoner's Tale 59
  Tale of Melibee 42n.15, 146

Chaucer, Geoffrey (*cont.*)
   Tale of Sir Thopas 11, 14–15, 29–31,
      43, 72, 98, 101–2, 137–8, 143, 240
   Wife of Bath's Tale 15, 25, 29, 42, 137
   House of Fame 4, 16, 22, 37–59, 84–5, 88,
      94, 226, 241
   Lack of Steadfastness 147
   Legend of Good Women 38, 55–6,
      70n.24, 146
   Parliament of Fowls 9n.26, 17, 22, 42,
      66–7, 73, 146, 195, 212–23
   Retractions 74, 209, 222
   Troilus and Criseyde 1, 5, 13–14, 16,
      19–36, 39, 41, 45, 61, 63–7, 73,
      113–37, 161–2, 166–7, 222,
      225, 240
Churchyard, Thomas 228–30
Cicero 22, 67, 127, 159n.23, 161, 164, 167,
   212, 214, 242
Cobler of Caunterburie, The 174
codicology 139, 143–4, 146–9
complaint 7, 9, 20–1, 25, 27, 31–5, 33n.43,
   37, 43, 55–6, 59, 146–7
Copland, Robert 232
Cuckoo and the Nightingale 195

Dante 40, 50, 58, 137, 215–17, 230
decorum 5, 49, 56, 159, 199–201
dreams and dream visions 1–4, 8–9, 14, 58,
   72–3, 125, 212–23, 236
du Bellay, Joachim 61n.7, 91–2

Ellesmere manuscript 193
eloquence 21, 100, 155, 159, 162, 167,
   180, 206
epic 8, 10, 21, 35, 46–7, 52, 56n.49, 57, 115,
   124–30, 126n.60, 195, 199

fable 7, 9, 17, 43, 61, 110, 161, 189–211
Fleming, Abraham 232
Floure and the Leaf, The 121–2, 121n.39,
   123n.43
font 178n.26
friendship 15–17, 62, 64, 67–8, 72, 109,
   111, 169–70, 185–7, 219, 226

gardens 8, 42, 53n.42, 63, 75–97, 214–19
Gascoigne, George 44–5, 59, 129n.77,
   131, 228–31

glossary 151, 153, 163, 166, 168, 170–1,
   173, 177
Googe, Barnabe 237
Gower, John 146, 153, 165n.35, 170n.6,
   230, 232
Greene, Robert 151, 174, 175n.20

Hall, Edward 234
Harrison, James 234
Harvey, Gabriel 75, 95, 120, 120nn.32–3,
   156–7, 160, 163–4, 192n.9, 226,
   229, 232
Henryson, Robert 146, 209, 234
Hoccleve, Thomas 79, 146, 155–6,
   168, 175
Homer 1–2, 228
Horace 27, 175, 227, 230, 235, 238
Howard, Henry (Earl of Surrey) 32,
   228, 230
humour 141–3, 141n.18, 226, 241

imitatio and imitation 2, 3, 11, 20, 58n.58,
   61, 138, 164, 190, 198, 202, 205–7,
   211, 222, 226–8, 235, 241
intertextuality 11, 16, 20–4, 28–9, 36
Ireland 4, 16, 66, 98–112, 126

Kilcolman Castle 221

'La Compleynt' 37–9, 54–9
Langland, William 14, 69, 153, 204n.36,
   228, 230, 232, 238
law 98–112, 145
Leland, John 233
Lodge, Thomas 140–1
Lollards 65, 193, 195n.18, 203–4, 232
Lybeaus Disconus 148
Lydgate, John 6–7, 13, 38, 38n.3, 39n.6,
   39n.8, 40, 40n.12, 43, 55, 59n.60,
   79, 129–30, 147, 153, 155, 160–2,
   164, 174n.16, 182, 228–30

Macrobius 212, 219
Marsh, Thomas 153
Mason, John 238
materiality 2–4, 13, 17, 22–3, 72, 96, 98,
   101–4, 111–12, 117, 123
Meres, Francis 2
Milton, John 10–11, 61, 82–3, 97

Mirror for Magistrates, The 129, 129n.81, 229
Mulcaster, Richard 166
muses 14, 21, 52, 79, 85, 87–97, 179, 205, 208, 217–18, 228, 237

Nashe, Thomas 151
neoplatonism 28, 64, 66, 66n.14, 68, 218, 222n.27
New Historicism 16, 66

Ovid 5, 14, 22, 40, 50n.39, 58, 61, 64, 70n.24, 103n.15, 162, 190, 195, 206, 238

Painter, William 233
paratexts 95, 140, 151, 163, 167, 168–9, 171, 173, 179, 182, 225, 240
Parnassus Plays, The 1–2
Parker, Matthew 154, 232, 239
pastoral 4, 27, 40–2, 45–8, 45n.31, 46n.33, 47n.34, 48n.35, 50–2, 50n.39, 56–8, 58n.57, 59n.59, 80, 83, 83n.25, 85, 228, 238–9
periodisation 3, 5–6, 6n.17, 10–11, 74, 102–9, 152, 227–30
Petrarch and Petrarchism 19, 21–2, 25, 27, 31–2, 69, 91–3, 95–6, 103n.15, 156, 178, 230–1
Plato 23, 64, 215, 222
Plowman's Tale 7, 43n.22, 65, 142–3, 146, 193–6, 202–4, 209–11, 232, 238, 241–2
polyphony 57
Ponsonby, William 189
Puttenham, George 106, 115, 124n.47, 129–30, 130n.84, 131, 207, 230–1, 234, 238

resonance 4, 16, 23, 29, 33n.43, 36, 39, 53–4, 56–9, 62, 75–6, 201, 204, 235
Robert of Sicily 147
romance 7–9, 17, 20–1, 68–71, 73n.30, 104, 134, 137–49, 197–200
Romance of the Rose 45, 64, 82n.23, 137

Saint Alex of Rome 148
satire 7, 17, 44, 190–211, 224–5, 235–42
Shakespeare, William 1–2, 6n.17, 11, 71, 86, 130, 140, 151, 153
Shepherd, Luke 17, 224, 235–42

Sidney, Sir Philip 13, 44, 87, 95–6, 130n.84, 155, 171n.9, 229, 231
Sir Bevys of Hampton 148
Sir Degrevant 146
Sir Gawain and the Green Knight 144–5
Sir Isumbras 148
Sir Perceval of Galles 145
Skelton, John 50, 80n.17, 227–30, 237, 241
Skeltonics 236, 238
space 7–8, 16, 22, 75–97, 98–112, 215
Speght, Thomas 17, 123, 151–2, 162–7, 168–88, 193, 241
Spenser, Edmund
    Colin Clout 13–14, 19, 29, 40–59, 46n.34, 47n.35, 50n.39, 52n.42, 56n.49, 57n.53, 59n.59, 75–97, 161–2, 236, 241
    E.K. 7, 13–14, 16–17, 19, 37–59, 61, 75–97, 128, 151–3, 156–67, 174, 182, 224–42
    Immeritô 13–14, 19, 44, 45n.31, 46n.34, 58, 59n.59, 161, 182, 225
    works
        Amoretti 16, 19–36, 76
        Colin Clouts Come Home Againe 12, 14, 48n.35, 141
        Complaints 95, 189–90, 227
            'Muiopotmos' 11–12, 131n.90, 132, 189–90
            'Prosopopoia, or Mother Hubberds Tale' 7, 17, 189–211
            'Ruines of Time, The' 130–1, 130n.87
            'Teares of the Muses, The' 93n.53, 129, 133n.98, 201n.32
            'Virgil's Gnat' 189–90, 131n.90
        Daphnaïda 5, 11–12, 130n.87
        Faerie Queene, The 1, 4–5, 8–9, 12, 14–16, 18–36, 52, 60–74, 76, 113–37, 140, 143, 147–8, 151, 164, 185, 192, 226, 232
            Book I 9n.26, 21, 35, 231
            Book II 8, 22, 117–18, 123n.44, 232, 236
            Book III 20, 31–5, 62–4, 66, 133–5, 213
            Book IV 9, 15, 20, 35, 60–1, 66–72, 79, 98, 109–12, 114–17, 119,

Spenser, Edmund (*cont.*)
    123–7, 134, 138, 144, 185–7, 213, 219, 233
  Book V 26, 66, 70
  Book VI 15, 102–3
  Mutabilitie Cantos 12, 15, 17, 20, 21n.8, 29, 29n.30, 67, 73–4, 117n.24, 118n.26, 212–14, 217–23
  Fowre Hymnes 130n.87
  'An Hymne of Heavenly Love' 74, 235
  Shepheardes Calender, The 4–6, 11–16, 19, 29, 37–60, 75–97, 108, 127, 129, 143, 150–67, 174, 182, 185, 203–4, 222, 224–9, 231–2, 234–42
  'February' 7, 13–14, 37–59, 61, 80–1, 156, 161
  'June' 13–14, 41–2, 47, 55, 59n.60, 75–97, 135, 156, 161
  'December' 14, 41, 51–3, 56–8, 80–1, 156, 161, 242
  Theatre for Worldlings, A 91–6
  View of the Present State of Ireland, A 4, 12, 15–16, 98–112
Statius 5, 14, 40, 61, 162, 222
Stow, John 42n.17, 55, 168, 173, 175, 177–8, 193, 196

Tale of Beryn 17, 143–7
Tale of Gamelyn 17, 139–44, 146
Tasso, Torquato 28, 61, 121, 130

temporality 3, 5–7, 39, 40n.12, 96, 99, 100–3, 102n.11, 105–6, 110–11, 152, 213, 220, 226
Theocritus 228, 237
Thynne, Francis 9, 19n.1, 170n.5, 177–80, 194
Thynne, William 19n.1, 79, 115–16, 121, 142–3, 168–9, 173, 175, 177–8, 193, 194n.16, 196, 241
Tilney, Edmund 67n.16
Tityrus 13–14, 40–3, 46, 50–2, 58, 60, 75–6, 78–81, 83, 87–8, 94–7, 156–7, 161–2, 165, 185, 204, 228
Tottel's Miscellany 129, 129n.81, 131n.90
tragedy 20–1, 30
Tresham, Thomas 209
Tuke, Brian 178, 180–1, 188
Turbervile, George 231–2
Tyndale, William 234
type 154, 157n.22, 163, 169, 178n.26
Tyrwhit, Thomas 193

Urry, John 139, 193

Van der Noot, Jan 91–2, 96
Virgil 2, 5, 13–14, 40, 46, 49–56, 60–1, 79–80, 97, 150, 156–7, 156n.19, 161–2, 164–5, 167, 186, 189–90, 228, 231, 238, 241

Webbe, William 129n.77, 228–30, 233, 235
Whitney, Geoffrey 202
Wyatt, Thomas 32, 132, 230, 238

EU authorised representative for GPSR:
Easy Access System Europe, Mustamäe tee 50,
10621 Tallinn, Estonia
gpsr.requests@easproject.com

www.ingramcontent.com/pod-product-compliance
Lightning Source LLC
Chambersburg PA
CBHW070322240426
43671CB00013BA/2341